Communications in Computer and Information Science 1691

More information about this series at https://link.springer.com/bookseries/7899

A. Augusto de Sousa · Vlastimil Havran ·
Alexis Paljic · Tabitha Peck · Christophe Hurter ·
Helen Purchase · Giovanni Maria Farinella ·
Petia Radeva · Kadi Bouatouch (Eds.)

Computer Vision, Imaging and Computer Graphics Theory and Applications

16th International Joint Conference, VISIGRAPP 2021
Virtual Event, February 8–10, 2021
Revised Selected Papers

 Springer

Editors
A. Augusto de Sousa
University of Porto
Porto, Portugal

Alexis Paljic
Mines ParisTech
Paris, France

Christophe Hurter
French Civil Aviation University (ENAC)
Toulouse, France

Giovanni Maria Farinella ⓘ
University of Catania
Catania, Italy

Kadi Bouatouch
IRISA, University of Rennes 1
Rennes, France

Vlastimil Havran
Czech Technical University in Prague
Prague, Czech Republic

Tabitha Peck
Davidson College
Davidson, NC, USA

Helen Purchase
Monash University
Melbourne, Australia

University of Glasgow
Glasgow, UK

Petia Radeva
University of Barcelona
Barcelona, Spain

ISSN 1865-0929   ISSN 1865-0937 (electronic)
Communications in Computer and Information Science
ISBN 978-3-031-25476-5   ISBN 978-3-031-25477-2 (eBook)
https://doi.org/10.1007/978-3-031-25477-2

This Springer imprint is published by the registered company Springer Nature Switzerland AG
The registered company address is: Gewerbestrasse 11, 6330 Cham, Switzerland

Preface

This book includes extended and revised versions of a set of selected papers from the 16th International Joint Conference on Computer Vision, Imaging and Computer Graphics Theory and Applications (VISIGRAPP 2021), that was exceptionally held as an online event, due to COVID-19, on February 8–10, 2021.

The purpose of VISIGRAPP is to bring together researchers and practitioners interested in both theoretical advances and applications of computer vision, computer graphics and information visualization. VISIGRAPP is composed of four co-located conferences, each specialized in at least one of the aforementioned main knowledge areas, namely GRAPP, IVAPP, HUCAPP and VISAPP.

VISIGRAPP 2021 received 371 paper submissions from 53 countries, of which 4% were included in this book.

The papers were selected by the event chairs and their selection is based on a number of criteria, including the classifications and comments provided by the program committee members, the session chairs' assessment and also the program chairs' global view of all papers included in the technical program. The authors of selected papers were then invited to submit a revised and extended version of their papers having at least 30% innovative material.

The papers selected to be included in this book contribute to the understanding of relevant trends of current research on Computer Vision, Imaging and Computer Graphics Theory and Applications, including: Deep Learning for Visual Understanding, High-Dimensional Data and Dimensionality Reduction, Information Visualization, Interactive Systems for Education and Training, Machine Learning Technologies for Vision, Software Visualization, Visualization Applications, Evaluation Paradigms and Frameworks, Early and Biologically-Inspired Vision, Deep Learning for Tracking, Impact of Avatar Representation in Virtual Reality-Based Simulations, and Techniques for Automatic 3D Cities Modeling.

We would like to thank all the authors for their contributions and also the reviewers who helped ensuring the quality of this publication.

February 2021

A. Augusto de Sousa
Vlastimil Havran
Alexis Paljic
Tabitha Peck
Christophe Hurter
Helen Purchase
Giovanni Maria Farinella
Petia Radeva
Kadi Bouatouch

Organization

Conference Co-chairs

Jose Braz · Escola Superior de Tecnologia de Setúbal, Portugal

Kadi Bouatouch · IRISA, University of Rennes 1, France

Program Co-chairs

GRAPP

A. Augusto de Sousa · FEUP/INESC TEC, Portugal
Vlastimil Havran · Czech Technical University in Prague, Czech Republic

HUCAPP

Alexis Paljic · Mines ParisTech, France
Tabitha Peck · Davidson College, USA

IVAPP

Christophe Hurter · French Civil Aviation University (ENAC), France
Helen Purchase · Monash University, Australia and University of Glasgow, UK

VISAPP

Giovanni Maria Farinella · Università di Catania, Italy
Petia Radeva · Universitat de Barcelona, Spain

GRAPP Program Committee

Francisco Abad · Universidad Politécnica de Valencia, Spain
Marco Agus · Hamad Bin Khalifa University, Qatar
Benjamin Bringier · Université de Poitiers, France
Dimitri Bulatov · Fraunhofer IOSB, Ettlingen - Fraunhofer Institute of Optronics, System Technologies and Image Exploitation, Germany
Maria Beatriz Carmo · LASIGE, Faculdade de Ciências, Universidade de Lisboa, Portugal

Xiaogang Jin	Zhejiang University, China
Cláudio Jung	Universidade Federal do Rio Grande do Sul, Brazil
Josef Kohout	University of West Bohemia, Czech Republic
Maciej Kot	Dfinity, Japan
Alejandro León	University of Granada, Spain
Marco Livesu	Italian National Research Council (CNR), Italy
Helio Lopes	PUC-Rio, Brazil
Claus Madsen	Aalborg University, Denmark
Luis Magalhães	Universidade do Minho, Portugal
Stephen Mann	University of Waterloo, Canada
Adérito Marcos	University of Saint Joseph, Macao, China
Maxime Maria	Université de Limoges - XLIM, France
Ricardo Marroquim	Delft University of Technology, The Netherlands
Miguel Melo	INESC TEC, Portugal
Daniel Mendes	INESC-ID Lisboa, Portugal
Daniel Meneveaux	University of Poitiers, France
Paulo Menezes	Universidade de Coimbra, Portugal
Stéphane Mérillou	University of Limoges, France
João Moura	Universidade de Trás-os-Montes e Alto Douro, Portugal
Adolfo Muñoz	Universidad de Zaragoza, Spain
Rui Nóbrega	DEI-FEUP, INESC TEC, Universidade do Porto, Portugal
Deussen Oliver	University of Konstanz, Germany
Lidia M. Ortega	University of Jaén, Spain
Georgios Papaioannou	Athens University of Economics and Business, Greece
Félix Paulano-Godino	University of Jaén, Spain
Aruquia Peixoto	CEFET/RJ, Brazil
João Pereira	Instituto Superior de Engenharia do Porto, Portugal
Christoph Peters	KIT, Germany
Adrien Peytavie	Claude Bernard University Lyon 1, France
Paulo Pombinho	Universidade de Lisboa, Portugal
Tomislav Pribanic	University of Zagreb, Croatia
Anna Puig	University of Barcelona, Spain
Inmaculada Remolar	Universitat Jaume I, Spain
Mickael Ribardière	University of Poitiers, XLIM, France
María Rivara	Universidad de Chile, Chile
Juan Roberto Jiménez	University of Jaén, Spain
Nuno Rodrigues	Polytechnic Institute of Leiria, Portugal

Inmaculada Rodríguez	University of Barcelona, Spain
Przemyslaw Rokita	Warsaw University of Technology, Poland
Teresa Romão	Universidade de Nova Lisboa, Portugal
Luís Romero	Instituto Politecnico de Viana do Castelo, Portugal
Holly Rushmeier	Yale University, USA
Beatriz Santos	University of Aveiro, Portugal
Luis Santos	Universidade do Minho, Portugal
Basile Sauvage	University of Strasbourg, France
Vladimir Savchenko	Hosei University, Japan
Rafael J. Segura	Universidad de Jaen, Spain
Ricardo Sepulveda Marques	Universitat de Barcelona, Spain
Ana Serrano	Max Planck Institute for Informatics, Germany
Frutuoso Silva	University of Beira Interior, Portugal
Matthias Teschner	University of Freiburg, Germany
Daniel Thalmann	Ecole Polytechnique Federale de Lausanne, Switzerland
Torsten Ullrich	Fraunhofer Austria Research GmbH, Austria
Kuwait University	Kuwait University, Kuwait
Carlos Urbano	Instituto Politécnico de Leiria, Portugal
Anna Ursyn	University of Northern Colorado, USA
Ling Xu	University of Houston-Downtown, USA
Rita Zrour	XLIM, France

GRAPP Additional Reviewers

Xavier Chermain	University of Strasbourg, France
Sandra Malpica	Universidad de Zaragoza, Spain
Gustavo Patow	Universitat de Girona, Spain

HUCAPP Program Committee

Andrea Abate	University of Salerno, Italy
Cigdem Beyan	Istituto Italiano di Tecnologia, Italy
Federico Botella	Miguel Hernandez University of Elche, Spain
Eva Cerezo	University of Zaragoza, Spain
Mathieu Chollet	University of Glasgow, UK
Yang-Wai Chow	University of Wollongong, Australia
Cesar Collazos	Universidad del Cauca, Colombia
Damon Daylamani-Zad	Brunel University London, UK
Juan Enrique Garrido Navarro	University of Lleida, Spain
Toni Granollers	University of Lleida, Spain
Michael Hobbs	Deakin University, Australia

Francisco Iniesto	The Open University (UK) Centre for Research in Education and Educational Technology, UK
Alvaro Joffre Uribe Quevedo	University of Ontario Institute of Technology, Canada
Ahmed Kamel	Concordia College, USA
Chee Weng Khong	Multimedia University, Malaysia
Suzanne Kieffer	Université catholique de Louvain, Belgium
Uttam Kokil	Kennesaw State University, USA
Fabrizio Lamberti	Politecnico di Torino, Italy
Chien-Sing Lee	Sunway University, Malaysia
Tsai-Yen Li	National Chengchi University, Taiwan, Republic of China
Flamina Luccio	Università Ca' Foscari Venezia, Italy
Sergio Lujan Mora	Universidad de Alicante, Spain
José Macías Iglesias	Universidad Autónoma de Madrid, Spain
Guido Maiello	Justus-Liebig University Gießen, Germany
Malik Mallem	Université Paris Saclay, France
Troy McDaniel	Arizona State University, USA
Vincenzo Moscato	Università degli Studi di Napoli Federico II, Italy
Evangelos Papadopoulos	NTUA, Greece
Florian Pecune	Glasgow University, UK
Otniel Portillo-Rodriguez	Universidad Autonóma del Estado de México, Mexico
Brian Ravenet	Université Paris-Saclay - LIMSI-CNRS, France
Juha Röning	University of Oulu, Finland
Andrea Sanna	Politecnico di Torino, Italy
Trenton Schulz	Norwegian Computing Center, Norway
Alessandra Sciutti	Istituto Italiano di Tecnologia, Italy
Fabio Solari	University of Genoa, Italy
Daniel Thalmann	Ecole Polytechnique Federale de Lausanne, Switzerland
Gouranton Valérie	Univ. Rennes, INSA Rennes, Inria, CNRS, IRISA, France
Gualtiero Volpe	Università degli Studi di Genova, Italy

HUCAPP Additional Reviewers

Mattia Barbieri	Istituto Italiano di Tecnologia, Italy
Antoine Costes	Inria, France
Louise Devigne	INSA Rennes/Inria/IRISA, France
Jérémy Lacoche	Orange, France
Maria Elena Lechuga Redondo	Istituto Italiano di Tecnologia, Italy

IVAPP Program Committee

Daniel Archambault	Swansea University, UK
Ayan Biswas	Los Alamos National Laboratory, USA
David Borland	University of North Carolina at Chapel Hill, USA
Alexander Bornik	Ludwig Boltzmann Institute for Archaeological Prospection and Virtual Archaeology, Austria
Romain Bourqui	University of Bordeaux, France
Michael Burch	University of Applied Sciences, Switzerland
Guoning Chen	University of Houston, USA
Yongwan Chun	University of Texas at Dallas, USA
António Coelho	Faculdade de Engenharia da Universidade do Porto, Portugal
Danilo B. Coimbra	Federal University of Bahia, Brazil
Celmar da Silva	University of Campinas, Brazil
Georgios Dounias	University of the Aegean, Greece
Achim Ebert	University of Kaiserslautern, Germany
Mennatallah El-Assady	University of Konstanz, Germany
Danilo Eler	São Paulo State University, Brazil
Sara Fabrikant	University of Zurich - Irchel, Switzerland
Maria Cristina Ferreira de Oliveira	University of São Paulo, ICMC, Brazil
Johannes Fuchs	University of Konstanz, Germany
Enrico Gobbetti	CRS4, Italy
Randy Goebel	University of Alberta, Canada
Martin Graham	Edinburgh Napier University, UK
Lynda Hardman	Centrum Wiskunde & Informatica; Utrecht University, The Netherlands
Christian Heine	Leipzig University, Germany
Seokhee Hong	University of Sydney, Australia
Torsten Hopp	Karlsruhe Institute of Technology, Germany
Jie Hua	University of Technology Sydney, Australia
Jimmy Johansson	Linköping University, Sweden
Mark Jones	Swansea University, UK
Daniel Jönsson	Linköping University, Sweden
Ilir Jusufi	Blekinge Institute of Technology, Sweden
Bijaya Karki	Louisiana State University, USA
Sehwan Kim	WorldViz LLC, USA
Steffen Koch	Universität Stuttgart, Germany
Martin Kraus	Aalborg University, Denmark
Haim Levkowitz	University of Massachusetts, Lowell, USA
Giuseppe Liotta	University of Perugia, Italy
Rafael Martins	Linnaeus University, Sweden
Brescia Massimo	INAF, Italy

Eva Mayr	Danube University Krems, Austria
Kazuo Misue	University of Tsukuba, Japan
Ingela Nystrom	Uppsala University, Sweden
Benoît Otjacques	Luxembourg Institute of Science and Technology (LIST), Luxembourg
Jinah Park	KAIST, Korea, Republic of
Fernando Paulovich	Eindhoven University of Technology, The Netherlands
Luc Pauwels	University of Antwerp, Belgium
Jürgen Pfeffer	Technische Universität München, Germany
Renata Raidou	University of Groningen, The Netherlands
Philip Rhodes	University of Mississippi, USA
Maria Riveiro	University of Skövde, Sweden
Beatriz Santos	University of Aveiro, Portugal
Angel Sappa	ESPOL Polytechnic University (Ecuador) and Computer Vision Center (Spain), Spain
Gerik Scheuermann	Universität Leipzig, Germany
Falk Schreiber	University of Konstanz, Germany and Monash University, Melbourne, Australia
Juergen Symanzik	Utah State University, USA
Roberto Theron	Universidad de Salamanca, Spain
Christian Tominski	University of Rostock, Germany
Tea Tušar	Jožef Stefan Institute, Slovenia
Thomas van Dijk	Ruhr-Universität Bochum, Germany
Gilles Venturini	University of Tours, France
Gunther Weber	Lawrence Berkeley National Laboratrory/UC Davis, USA
Marcel Worring	University of Amsterdam, The Netherlands
Hsian-Yun Wu	TU Wien, Austria
Hsu-Chun Yen	National Taiwan University, Taiwan, Republic of China
Jianping Zeng	Microsoft, USA
Yue Zhang	Oregon State University, USA

IVAPP Additional Reviewers

Tiago Araújo	Federal University of Pará, Brazil
Arindam Bhattacharya	Independent Researcher, USA
Romain Giot	Université de Bordeaux, France
Jan-Henrik Haunert	University of Bonn, Germany
Stefan Jänicke	University of Southern Denmark, Denmark
Romain Vuillemot	LIRIS, France

VISAPP Program Committee

Amr Abdel-Dayem	Laurentian University, Canada
Zahid Akhtar	University of Memphis, USA
Vicente Alarcon-Aquino	Universidad de las Americas Puebla, Mexico
Enrique Alegre	Universidad de Leon, Spain
Dario Allegra	University of Catania, Italy
Hugo Alvarez	Vicomtech, Spain
Danilo Avola	Sapienza University, Italy
Ariel Bayá	CONICET, Argentina
Annà Belardinelli	Honda Research Institute, Germany
Fabio Bellavia	Università degli Studi di Firenze, Italy
Robert Benavente	Universitat Autònoma de Barcelona, Spain
Yannick Benezeth	Université de Bourgogne, France
Stefano Berretti	University of Florence, Italy
Simone Bianco	University of Milano Bicocca, Italy
Ioan Marius Bilasco	Lille University, France
Giuseppe Boccignone	Università degli Studi di Milano, Italy
Adrian Bors	University of York, UK
Larbi Boubchir	University of Paris 8, France
Thierry Bouwmans	Université de La Rochelle, France
Marius Brezovan	University of Craiova, Romania
Alfred Bruckstein	Technion, Israel
Arcangelo Bruna	STMicroelectronics, Italy
Vittoria Bruni	University of Rome La Sapienza, Italy
Giedrius Burachas	SRI International, USA
Adrian Burlacu	Gheorghe Asachi Technical University of Iasi, Romania
Alice Caplier	GIPSA-lab, France
Bruno Carvalho	Federal University of Rio Grande do Norte, Brazil
Dario Cazzato	Université du Luxembourg, Luxembourg
Oya Celiktutan	King's College London, UK
Luigi Celona	University of Milan-Bicocca, Italy
Krishna Chandramouli	Queen Mary University of London, UK
Ming-ching Chang	State University of New York, at Albany, USA
Mulin Chen	Xidian University, China
Samuel Cheng	University of Oklahoma, USA
Manuela Chessa	University of Genoa, Italy
Chia Chong	Sunway University, Malaysia
Kazimierz Choros	Wroclaw University of Science and Technology, Poland
Laurent Cohen	Université Paris Dauphine, France
Sara Colantonio	ISTI-CNR, Italy

Bart Goossens	imec - Ghent University, Belgium
Håkan Grahn	Blekinge Institute of Technology, Sweden
Nikos Grammalidis	Centre of Research and Technology Hellas, Greece
Michael Greenspan	Queen's University, Canada
Christiaan Gribble	Advanced Micro Devices, Inc., USA
Levente Hajder	Eötvös Loránd University, Hungary
Walid Hariri	Badji Mokhtar Annaba University, Algeria
Aymeric Histace	ETIS UMR CNRS 8051, France
Wladyslaw Homenda	Warsaw University of Technology, Poland
Binh-Son Hua	VinAI, Vietnam
Hui-Yu Huang	National Formosa University, Taiwan, Republic of China
Laura Igual	Universitat de Barcelona, Spain
Francisco Imai	Apple Inc., USA
Jiri Jan	University of Technology Brno, Czech Republic
Tatiana Jaworska	Polish Academy of Sciences, Poland
Xiaoyi Jiang	University of Münster, Germany
Lucio Andre Jorge	EMBRAPA, Brazil
Martin Kampel	Vienna University of Technology, Austria
Kenichi Kanatani	Okayama University, Japan
Etienne Kerre	Ghent University, Belgium
Anastasios Kesidis	University of West Attica, Greece
Nahum Kiryati	Tel Aviv University, Israel
Nobuyuki Kita	AIST (National Institute of Advanced Industrial Science and Technology), Japan
Itaru Kitahara	University of Tsukuba, Japan
Andrey Kopylov	Tula State University, Russian Federation
Adam Kortylewski	Johns Hopkins University, USA
Camille Kurtz	Université de Paris, LIPADE, France
Demetrio Labate	University of Houston, USA
Martin Lambers	University of Siegen, Germany
Mónica Larese	CIFASIS-CONICET, National University of Rosario, Argentina
Denis Laurendeau	Laval University, Canada
Isah A. Lawal	Noroff University College, Norway
Dah-jye Lee	Brigham Young University, USA
Marco Leo	CNR, Italy
Xiuwen Liu	Florida State University, USA
Giosue Lo Bosco	Università di Palermo, Italy
Angeles López	Universitat Jaume I, Spain
Cristina Losada-Gutiérrez	University of Alcalá, Spain

Ilias Maglogiannis   University of Piraeus, Greece
Baptiste Magnier   LGI2P de l'Ecole des Mines d'ALES, France
Emmanuel Marilly   NOKIA - Bell Labs France, France
Jean Martinet   University Cote d'Azur/CNRS, France
José Martínez Sotoca   Universitat Jaume I, Spain
Mitsuharu Matsumoto   University of Electro-Communications, Japan
Mohamed Arezki Mellal   M'Hamed Bougara University, Algeria
Leonid Mestetskiy   Lomonosov Moscow State University, Russian
                                      Federation
Cyrille Migniot   Université de Bourgogne - ImViA, France
Dan Mikami   NTT, Japan
Steven Mills   University of Otago, New Zealand
Filippo Milotta   University of Catania, Italy
Pradit Mittrapiyanuruk   Autodesk, Singapore
Birgit Moeller   Martin Luther University Halle-Wittenberg,
                                      Germany
Davide Moltisanti   Nanyang Technological University, Singapore
Bartolomeo Montrucchio   Politecnico di Torino, Italy
Kostantinos Moustakas   University of Patras, Greece
Dmitry Murashov   Federal Research Center "Computer Science and
                                      Control" of Russian Academy of Sciences,
                                      Russian Federation
Yuta Nakashima   Osaka University, Japan
Mikael Nilsson   Lund University, Sweden
Shohei Nobuhara   Kyoto University, Japan
Yoshihiro Okada   Kyushu University, Japan
Félix Paulano-Godino   University of Jaén, Spain
Helio Pedrini   University of Campinas, Brazil
Francisco José Perales   UIB, Spain
Roland Perko   Joanneum Research, Austria
Stephen Pollard   HP Labs, UK
Vijayakumar Ponnusamy   SRM IST, Kattankulathur Campus, India
Charalambos Poullis   Concordia University, Canada
Antonis Protopsaltis   University of Western Macedonia, Greece
Giovanni Puglisi   University of Cagliari, Italy
Kumaradevan Punithakumar   University of Alberta, Canada
Naoufal Raissouni   University Abdelmalek Essaadi (ENSA Tetuan),
                                      Morocco
V. Rajinikanth   St. Josephs College Engineering, India
Giuliana Ramella   CNR - Istituto per le Applicazioni del Calcolo
                                      "M. Picone", Italy
Francesco Rea   Istituto Italiano di Tecnologia, Italy

Joao Rodrigues	University of the Algarve, Portugal
Peter Rogelj	University of Primorska, Slovenia
Juha Röning	University of Oulu, Finland
Pedro Rosa	Universidade Lusófona de Humanidades e Tecnologias de Lisboa, Portugal
Silvio Sabatini	University of Genoa, Italy
Ovidio Salvetti	National Research Council of Italy - CNR, Italy
Andreja Samcovic	University of Belgrade, Serbia
K. C. Santosh	University of South Dakota, USA
Nickolas Sapidis	University of Western Macedonia, Greece
Yann Savoye	Liverpool John Moores University, UK
Marco Seeland	Ilmenau University of Technology, Germany
Siniša Šegvic	University of Zagreb, Croatia
Oleg Seredin	Tula State University, Russian Federation
Fiorella Sgallari	University of Bologna, Italy
Shishir Shah	University of Houston, USA
Seppo Sirkemaa	University of Turku, Finland
Robert Sitnik	Warsaw University of Technology, Poland
Andrzej Skalski	AGH University of Science and Technology, Poland
Kenneth Sloan	University of Alabama at Birmingham, USA
Ömer Soysal	Southeastern Louisiana University, USA
Amelia Carolina Sparavigna	Polytechnic University of Turin, Italy
Mu-Chun Su	National Central University, Taiwan, Republic of China
Ryszard Tadeusiewicz	AGH University Science Technology, Poland
Norio Tagawa	Tokyo Metropolitan University, Japan
Ricardo Torres	Norwegian University of Science and Technology (NTNU), Norway
Bruno Travençolo	Federal University of Uberlândia, Brazil
Carlos Travieso-González	Universidad de Las Palmas de Gran Canaria, Spain
Du-Ming Tsai	Yuan-Ze University, Taiwan, Republic of China
Javier Vazquez-Corral	University Pompeu Fabra, Spain
Luisa Verdoliva	University Federico II of Naples, Italy
Nicole Vincent	Université de Paris, France
Panayiotis Vlamos	Ionian University, Greece
Frank Wallhoff	Jade University of Applied Science, Germany
Tao Wang	BAE Systems, USA
Wen-June Wang	National Central University, Taiwan, Republic of China
Laurent Wendling	Paris Descartes University, France

Christian Wöhler	TU Dortmund University, Germany
Pengcheng Xi	National Research Council Canada, Canada
Jiangjian Xiao	Ningbo Institute Material Technology & Engineering, CAS, China
Alper Yilmaz	Ohio State University, USA
Jang-Hee Yoo	ETRI, Korea, Republic of
Sebastian Zambanini	TU Wien, Austria
Pietro Zanuttigh	University of Padova, Italy
Jie Zhang	Newcastle University, UK
Zhigang Zhu	City College of New York, USA
Ju Zou	University of Western Sydney, Australia

VISAPP Additional Reviewers

George Azzopardi	University of Groningen, The Netherlands and University of Malta, Malta
Yuwei Chen	SUNY Albany, USA
Gianluigi Ciocca	University of Milano-Bicocca, Italy
Mariella Dimiccoli	Institut de Robòtica i Informàtica Industrial (CSIC-UPC), Spain
Fabio Galasso	Sapienza University of Rome, Italy
Luca Garello	Istituto Italiano di Tecnologia, Italy
Andreas Kloukiniotis	University of Patras, Greece
Riccardo La Grassa	University of Insubria, Italy
Nicola Landro	University of Insubria, Italy
Xiao Lin	Vicomtech, Spain
Fatima Saiz Álvaro	Vicomtech, Spain
Nikos Stagakis	University of Patras, Greece
Filippo Stanco	Università di Catania, Italy
Rameez Ur Rahman	University of Rome, Sapienza, Italy

Invited Speakers

Federico Tombari	Google and Technical University of Munich (TUM), Germany
Dieter Schmalstieg	Graz University of Technology, Austria
Nathalie Henry Riche	Microsoft Research, USA

Contents

Computer Vision Theory and Applications

Computer Graphics Theory
and Applications

Impact of Avatar Representation in a Virtual Reality-Based Multi-user Tunnel Fire Simulator for Training Purposes

Davide Calandra$^{(\boxtimes)}$ ⓘ, Filippo Gabriele Pratticò ⓘ, Gianmario Lupini, and Fabrizio Lamberti ⓘ

Politecnico di Torino, 10129 Turin, Italy
{davide.calandra,filippogabriele.prattico,
fabrizio.lamberti}@polito.it,
gianmario.lupini@studenti.polito.it

Abstract. Virtual Reality (VR) technology is playing an increasingly important role in the field of training. The emergency domain, in particular, can benefit from various advantages of VR with respect to traditional training approaches. One of the most promising features of VR-based training is the possibility to share the virtual experience with other users. In multi-user training scenarios, the trainees have to be provided with a proper representation of both the other peers and themselves, with the aim of fostering mutual awareness, communication and cooperation. Various techniques for representing avatars in VR have been proposed in the scientific literature and employed in commercial applications. However, the impact of these techniques when deployed to multi-user scenarios for emergency training has not been extensively explored yet. In this work, two techniques for avatar representation in VR, i.e., no avatar (VR Kit only) and Full-Body reconstruction (blending of inverse kinematics and animations), are compared in the context of emergency training. Experiments were carried out in a training scenario simulating a road tunnel fire. The participants were requested to collaborate with a partner (controlled by an experimenter) to cope with the emergency, and aspects concerning perceived embodiment, immersion, and social presence were investigated.

Keywords: Virtual Reality (VR) · Multi-user simulation · Emergency training · Road tunnel fire · Avatar representation

1 Introduction

Virtual Reality (VR) technology allows the creation of arbitrarily wide and sophisticated Virtual Environments (VEs), enabling the possibility to develop training scenarios that are very complex, or very expensive, to be deployed in real-life [12]. One of the most prominent fields which has taken large advantage of VR is that of emergency training, as indicated by the huge number of literature works which investigated the role of this technology in the creation of effective scenarios for managing emergencies [2,14,21,24,29]). Among the various use cases investigated so far,

ⓒ Springer Nature Switzerland AG 2023
A. A. de Sousa et al. (Eds.): VISIGRAPP 2021, CCIS 1691, pp. 3–20, 2023.
https://doi.org/10.1007/978-3-031-25477-2_1

fire emergency is indeed among the most representative and widely studied ones [1,11,13,27].

As stated in [12], for near-future developments one of the most promising challenges posed by VR technology for firefighting training is represented by the transfer of findings from other domains regarding VR experiences involving multiple users. In multi-user scenarios, two or more users can engage from different locations and at the same time in a shared virtual experience [8]. Differently than in single-user experiences, in multi-user scenarios the avatar realism is critical for the development of collaborative VEs [3].

VR kits typically include an Head-Mounted Display (HMD) and two hand controllers, providing a synchronized visuomotor feedback to the user [25]. Hence, the only available sensory information is related to the position and orientation of the user's head and hands, which is not sufficient for full-body motion capture [28]. By relying on this information, most of the single-user commercial VR experiences usually show only a virtual representation of the hand controllers (e.g., SteamVR Home[1]) or, in some cases, two floating hands/gloves aligned with the real hands (e.g., Oculus First Steps[2]) A previous work explored different visibility levels for the user's own avatar in single-user experiences, and found no significant differences in terms of perceived embodiment between fully showing, partially hiding or not showing, along with the hand controllers, a virtual body for the VR user [25], confirming the above choices.

Although these reduced avatar representations appeared be sufficient from a first-person perspective, they may not be suitable for representing the other users' avatars in shared experiences. In particular, for emergency training scenarios, these techniques may have a negative impact on the perceived realism of the simulated scenario and, consequently, on the training efficacy.

An alternative technique to represent the avatar of a VR user consists in applying Inverse Kinematics (IK) to operate a body reconstruction targeted from head and hand sensors only [28]. From a first-person point of view, these techniques may increase the user's embodiment thanks to the visuomotor correlation [20], but may also worsen it when the estimated pose is characterized by a low accuracy [33]. When seen from outside in multi-user scenarios, IK techniques also require to correctly manage the users' legs, taking into account the user's motion in the VE. This can be done by procedurally generating the gait (like, e.g., in Dead and Buried[3]) or by blending the IK outcome with animations (like, e.g., in VRChat[4]) Thanks to the possibility to show and manage a full representation of the user's body, these techniques may be effective in guaranteeing an appropriate level of immersion and embodiment, especially in case of realism-oriented, multi-user emergency simulations for training purposes.

The aim of this work is to study the impact of two avatar representation techniques, namely, the VR Kit only (no avatar, hereafter referred to as VK) and the Full-Body reconstruction obtained by blending IK and animations (hereafter referred to as FB), when used to represent VR users in a multi-user, emergency training experience. The

---

[1] SteamVR Home: https://store.steampowered.com/app/250820/SteamVR/.

[2] Oculus First Steps: https://www.oculus.com/experiences/quest/1863547050392688.

[3] Dead and Buried: https://www.oculus.com/experiences/rift/1198491230176054/.

[4] VRChat: https://hello.vrchat.com/.

scenario, named *FréjusVR* and presented in [8], consists of a VR road tunnel fire simulator provided with multi-user, multi-role and multi-technology capabilities. The scenario embeds a serious game that can be used as a training tool for firefighters and as a means for communicating correct procedures to civilians. This serious game, developed in the context of the PITEM RISK FOR[5] project, provides a good test-bench for the considered avatar representation techniques.

A user study involving 15 users was conducted, by requesting each of them to collaborate with another user (an experimenter) to respond to a fire emergency happening in the VE. All the study participants experienced both the avatar representation techniques, as they were asked to face two slightly different situations in the same simulation. Subjective measures were gathered through standard questionnaires to investigate the level of embodiment [15], social presence [5], as well as immersion and presence [17].

Results show that, even though the FB representation did not significantly increase the embodiment with respect to VK, it was judged as significantly better than the other technique in terms of ability to foster mutual awareness, mutual attention, mutual understanding, and immersion. Moreover, almost all the participants preferred the FB for representing the other user's avatar in terms of aesthetics and multi-player interaction. No clear winner emerged regarding the representation of the user's own avatar, neither in terms of usability and aesthetics, nor regarding the overall experience.

2 Background

Nowadays, the use of VR technology to simulate emergency situations has been widely studied [19,22,23,30]. Studies largely considered also the field of fire simulation. As reported in [23], tunnel fires are among the simulated scenarios that have been most commonly explored in the past, even though most of them were not exploited in multi-user experiences. To cope with this lack, a multi-user road tunnel fire simulator for training purposes was recently presented in [8], supporting multiple roles (civilian or emergency operators), various VR technologies (consumer VR kits, locomotion treadmills, and motion capture suits) that can be arranged in different configurations, as well as a real-time fire spreading logic, with the possibility to integrate Computational Fluid Dynamics (CFD) data for the smoke visualization.

As mentioned before, a critical aspect of multi-user collaborative VEs is represented by the level of realism of employed avatars, as testified by a relevant number of works on the effects of the specific avatar visualization technique being adopted [3]. The authors of [31], for instance, presented an experimental method to investigate the effects of reduced social information and behavioral channels in immersive VEs with non-realistic FB avatars (mannequins). To this purpose, both physical and verbal interactions were executed in both VR and real-life, and then compared in terms of social presence, presence, attentional focus, and task performance. Results showed that the lack of realism of the humanoid avatars hindered the social interactions and possibly reduced the performance, although the authors stated that the lack of behavioral cues such as gaze and facial expressions could be partially compensated.

---

[5] https://www.pitem-risk.eu/progetti/risk-for.

In [18], the main focus was to find out how useful was the implementation of high-fidelity avatars in a multi-user VR-based learning environment. In particular, both educators and students were endowed with the possibility to access a shared VE by means of avatars. The educator's avatar consisted of a high-fidelity representation (including facial cues and eye motion) and was motion-controlled in real-time by the educator. The student's avatars was implemented as not anthropomorphic in order not to draw attention from the educator. The results of the study suggested that representing with high-fidelity avatars the subjects with important roles in the simulation can enhance the overall user experience for everyone participating in it.

A similar approach was pursued in [4] regarding the use of avatars in rehabilitation scenarios, though with a different set of technologies. By using a Microsoft Kinect sensor coupled with virtual scenarios, the authors concentrated their efforts on reproducing human posture failures by monitoring avatars, with the aim to improve the posture of people in different rehabilitation stages. Results confirmed that the framework created had enough flexibility and precision, thus confirming that avatar representation can play a key role in a wide variety of scenarios.

As reported in [32], several studies underlined that FB and Head and Hands avatar representations are the most widely used in the current body of literature. More broadly, the authors of [26] investigated the realism that an avatar should have to sufficiently appease the user's tastes. Work in the field led to the definition of a standardized Embodiment Questionnaire [15] and to a branch of studies regarding avatar use in multi-user environments, focusing on factors such as social presence and social interactions [5].

Regarding the visualization of the avatar from a first-person point of view in VR, the authors of [25] studied the effect of the visual feedback of various body parts on the user experience and performance in an action-based game. The work considered as visual feedback a completely hidden body (except for the VK), a low visibility body (hands and forearms), and a medium visibility body (head, neck, trunk, forearms, hands, and tail for the lower limbs). Differently than some previous works, no significant differences between the three alternatives were observed in terms of perceived embodiment.

Finally, regarding the research topic about avatar movements, works such as [10,28] showed the promising capabilities of IK techniques for estimating the pose of humanoid avatars, whereas studies like [16] managed to achieve accurate results by using such IK methods on different body parts, in particular on head and hands, leaving the lower body movement to several animations cleverly blended together.

Despite the wide number of works regarding the topic of avatar representation techniques for single and multi-user VR experiences, to the best of the authors' knowledge, investigations about the impact of these techniques in the field of VR simulations for emergency training are still scarce.

3   FrèjusVR

In this section, the fire training scenario used for the experimental activity is described, along with its configuration and the customization introduced for the purpose of the evaluation.

3.1   Devices and Technologies

The application was developed with Unity 2018.4.36f and the SteamVR Software Development Kit (SDK), allowing the deployment to any OpenVR compatible VR system. Due to the wide extension of the depicted scenario (a road tunnel), additional stationary locomotion techniques [9] were included to overcome the limitations of room scale movements. Among them, the arm-swinging technique was selected for the considered experimental activity, since it did not require additional hardware and showed to outperform the other techniques in some previous investigations [6, 7].

3.2   Multi-user

Regarding the multi-user capabilities, the Unity legacy high-level network API (U-NET) was used to support a client-server architecture. The host can be either one of the user or a dedicated non-VR machine to lower the computational load of the two VR clients. To complement body-to body communication, a VOIP channel is established between the users though the Dissonance VOIP asset for Unity[6], adding two additional UNET channels (one reliable and one unreliable). Position and rotation updating of network objects is performed 60 Hz, and interpolation is employed to smooth the transition between consecutive updates. The scenario can support different roles, i.e., civilians, firefighters, and truck driver(s), which can be either played by real users, Non-Player Characters (NPCs), or be deactivated.

3.3   Avatar Representation Techniques

The training scenario provided two different avatars (male or female) to be chosen as civilian or truck driver, and a generic firefighter avatar for users playing as firefighting operators. Independent of the avatar selection in the main menu, the VR application was modified in order to allow the configuration of one of the avatar representation techniques considered in this study (Fig. 1), which are described below.

VR Kit (VK).   This technique did not require particular modifications to the application. For the own avatar, the SteamVR CameraRig Unity prefab automatically manages the visualization of the VR hand controllers and their real-time synchronization with the real ones. For the remote users, 3D meshes representing a generic VR HMD and the two hand controllers (VIVE wand[7]) were displayed in correspondence of the synchronized position and orientation of the other user's head and hands (Fig. 1a).

Full-Body (FB).   To support the FB representation, the Unity asset named FinalIK by RootMotion[8] was acquired and integrated in the scenario. The asset provides a VR-oriented FB IK (VRIK) solution, which supports both procedural locomotion steps,

---

[6] Dissonance Voice Chat: https://assetstore.unity.com/packages/tools/audio/dissonance-voice-chat-70078.

[7] Vive wand controller: https://www.vive.com/eu/accessory/controller/.

[8] https://assetstore.unity.com/packages/tools/animation/final-ik-14290.

recommended for micro-movements on the spot, as well as an animated locomotion, and was designed for room-scale movements or faster techniques. Since the navigation of the tunnel scenario requires relatively fast virtual movements, the procedural locomotion of VRIK was discarded in favour of the animated one (Fig. 1b).

For the local user, VRIK was configured to always apply the IK algorithm to the upper limbs, spine and head, whereas animated locomotion was automatically triggered when the HMD is moved on the horizontal (X, Z) plane, and the blending was adjusted on the basis of the movement speed. By default, the blended animation are managed with the Unity Mecanim animation system, through a 2D free-form directional blend-tree integrating a set of standing animations (including idle, directional walking and running). Animations for movements in crouch position were not provided by the assets. For this reason, a second blend-tree implementing crouched movements was added, and the blending between the two trees was obtained on the basis of the user's HMD position, normalized with respect to his or her height. Since the mentioned asset does not apply IK to fingers, hands were managed with an overriding layer in the Unity animator, in order to support hand gestures (i.e., open hand, fist, and pointing) which were activated based on the context. As a matter of example, if the user is pressing a button, the pointing animation will be temporarily showed. Similarly, if the user is walking around with the arm-swinging technique, the relative avatar will be displayed with his or her hands balled in tight fists.

To manage the representation of the other user, the standard VRIK behaviour had to be modified to maintain a sufficient level of naturalness. In particular, to hide out the unnatural arm-swinging gesture while walking, the upper body IK was temporarily disabled by blending it with the full movement animation. Hence, when the additional locomotion technique is triggered by a user, his or her avatar on the other user's machine will perform a FB walking animation. As soon as the user stops triggering the arm-swinging, the upper body IK is restored, and the animation is again applied to the lower limbs only.

To avoid misalignments between grabbed objects and FB animations, the grabbing position is always adjusted to either coincide with the actual controllers (when the IK is enabled) or with the hands of the other avatar's rig (when the arm-swinging is triggered and the FB animation is displayed).

VRIK allows to manage the synchronization over the network of the FB IK by synchronizing the position and orientation of the user's CameraRig (head and controller). To synchronize the additional functionalities mentioned before, a custom UNET network component was used.

3.4   Selected Procedure

As said, the considered training scenario provides different roles (civilian, firefighter, truck driver), each characterized by its own procedure and interactions (some of them depicted in Fig. 2). For the purpose of the current evaluation, it was decided to focus on the role of the civilian for both the users. The reasons behind this choice are manifold. The civilian role does not require previous knowledge (differently than for firefighters and, to some extent, the truck driver), it maximizes the percentage of time in which the two users can see each other and interact together (the two civilians can start the

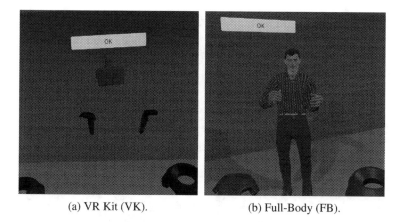

(a) VR Kit (VK).   (b) Full-Body (FB).

Fig. 1. The two avatar representation techniques considered in the evaluation, as displayed to the participant in the form of mirrored avatar before starting the simulation.

experience inside the same car), and provides the highest level of flexibility for the execution of the procedure.

In order to guarantee a good level of visibility, the CFD-based smoke simulation was disabled. Moreover, to avoid possibly confounding factors related to the visualization of the other peer, some NPC roles were disabled (the firefighters) or reduced to aesthetic features visible just at the end of the experience (the truck driver in the security shelter). Considering these modifications with respect to the complete experience detailed in [8], the considered procedure can be summarized as follows:

1. Both the civilians start on the same car, travelling from Italy to France, while the car radio is broadcasting the usual messages for tunnel users.
2. After some travel time during which the car occupants can communicate, and the passenger has access to the security brochure of the tunnel, a truck on fire is spotted in the opposite lane. In this situation, the driver can operate the brakes and stop the car at an arbitrary distance from the vehicle on fire.
3. As soon as the car stops, the two users can interact with the car interior, e.g. turning off the engine (Fig. 2a), enabling the hazard lights, or getting out of it using the doors' handles.
4. Once outside the car, the two collaborating users may press one of the many SOS buttons (Fig. 2b) placed inside the tunnel to signal the accident, and then decide whether to head to the closer SOS shelter, which is beyond the truck, or turn back and reach a farther shelter. It should be noted that after getting out of the vehicle, a second car accident involving two civilian cars occurs behind the users' vehicle, starting a second, more contained and less threatening fire. Hence, both ways will be partially occluded by damaged vehicles on fire.
5. If the two users opt for the first choice, they can take advantage of two SOS niches (Fig. 2c) on both sides of the tunnel right before the truck, provided with SOS telephones and extinguishers which can be freely used. The users can either try to extinguish the main fire (Fig. 2d), or directly run towards the selected shelter. Behind the

(a) Driver turning (b) User pressing a (c) Both users (d) Users collabo-
off the car engine.   SOS button.   interacting with a rating in the extin-
                                     SOS niche.   guishing of the fire.

(e) Users crawling (f) Users crawling (g) Users interact- (h) Users entering
under the wooden under the metal rod ing with the shelter a SOS shelter.
board to get to the heading to the far- door.
closer shelter.   ther shelter.

Fig. 2. Pictures of the the FrèjusVR scenario taken during the experimental phase.

truck on fire, the users will have to walk crouched to walk under a wooden plank
(Fig. 2e) which fell, with others, from the truck load over a civilian car blocking the
way to the shelter.
6. If the users head back to the other shelter, they will be again forced to crouch to
   pass under a metal rod (Fig. 2f) placed nearby the second accident. In this case, the
   closest extinguisher and SOS telephone will be inside the shelter. The users will be
   allowed to get back to the tunnel to try to extinguish the smaller fire. In this shelter,
   the users will meet an NPC character sitting on a bench near a locker containing a
   first aid kit and some water bottles.
7. In both cases, after opening the door one of the shelter (Fig. 2g), getting inside
   (Fig. 2h) and asking for help with the SOS telephone, the simulation ends (if the
   call was already done from a SOS niche in the tunnel, this step is not needed and the
   simulation is quickly terminated).

The possibility to extinguish both fires was disabled; however, the users were not
made aware of this aspect, and were left free to choose whether to try using the extinguishers, fail, and thus continue with the evacuation. The layout of the described version
of the tunnel scenario is reported in Fig. 3.

4   Experimental Setup

In this section, the setup used for the experimental activity and the adopted evaluation
criteria are thoroughly explained.

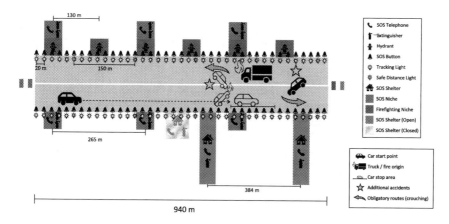

Fig. 3. Layout of the modified version of the tunnel scenario with respect to the original one detailed in [8].

4.1 Participants

The 15 participants (14 males, 1 female) were aged between 24 and 67. Most of them reported medium to high experience with video-games, VR and multi-player applications, but almost all of them had little to no experience with serious games for emergency training.

4.2 Hardware

For the experiment, two HTC Vive Pro[9] kit were employed, one worn by the participant, one by the experimenter playing the part of the second user. The VR scenario was run on two Intel i9-9820X machines, each equipped with 32GB of RAM and a NVIDIA GeForce RTX 2080 Ti video card.

4.3 Methodology

The experiment was designed as a within-subjects study, with the avatar representation technique as independent variable. The participants were initially asked to fill in a demographic questionnaire aimed to assess their previous experience with the involved technologies. Then, they were introduced to the experiment, and told what they were supposed to do in the simulation. A sample footage of the experiments with both modalities is available to download[10]:

Each participant experienced the two representation techniques in a random order. Before starting each simulation run, they were asked to select, inside the VR application, one of the two available avatars for the civilians. After that, a mirrored version of the avatar with the currently used technique was displayed to the user to show how he

---

[9] HTC Vive Pro: https://www.vive.com/eu/product/vive-pro/.
[10] http://tiny.cc/zmnnuz.

or she was going to be seen from the other user's point of view. With the VK, the choice of the avatar was not relevant, since it was not going to be displayed as a virtual body, but only as 3D meshes representing the VR equipment.

Then, for both the techniques, the participant was requested to choose the role of the driver. At this point, a second user, controlled by one of the experimenters, connected to the multi-user session and spawned as a second civilian sitting beside the driver, automatically starting the experience.

During the simulation, the experimenter tried to follow a predefined set of actions, in order to force the other peer to perform all the intended actions and interactions, as well as to uniform the experience among the various participants. To limit learning effects, the experimenter followed two distinct scripts for the first and the second experience, whose main difference concerned the selection of the evacuation route. In particular, in the first run, the experimenter:

1. Performed interactions while observed by the participant.
2. Suggested to head to the closer shelter beyond the truck.
3. Ensured that the participant notices the SOS niches and interacts with them.
4. Showed the participant how to surpass the main fire and the obstacles requiring to crouch.
5. Should the participant try to extinguish the fire, he or she encouraged him or her to give up after a while and reach the shelter.

During the second run, the experimenter:

1. Suggested to turn back and head to the farther shelter beyond the car accident.
2. Showed the participant how to surpass the main fire and the obstacles requiring to crouch.
3. After reaching the shelter, he or she suggested to equip the extinguisher and try to deal with the smaller fire encountered on the way.
4. After a brief try, he or she suggested to head back to the shelter and wait there for the rescue team to arrive.

It should be noted that these guidelines were not considered in a very strict way, as some interactions may be repeated, omitted or executed in a different order, depending of the participant's collaborativeness during the simulation. After each run, the participant was asked to fill in the evaluation questionnaire detailed in the following.

4.4 Evaluation Criteria

As mentioned before, the participants were evaluated from a subjective perspective by means of a post-test questionnaire[11].

The questionnaire was organized in four sections. In the first section, the participant was asked to fill in the Embodiment Questionnaire [15], in order to evaluate his or her level of embodiment in terms of body ownership, agency and motor control, tactile sensations, location of the body, external appearance and response to external stimuli (as in [25]). The second section corresponded to the Networked Minds Social Presence

---

[11] http://tiny.cc/1nnnuz.

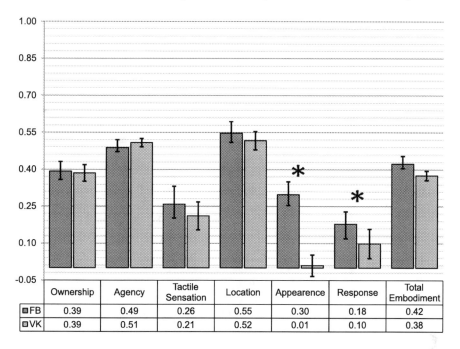

Fig. 4. Average results for the Embodiment Questionnaire [15] sub-scales (values normalized between 0 and 1). Statistically significant differences (*p*-value < 0.05) marked with a star (*) symbol.

Questionnaire [5], and it was aimed to assess the virtual representation of the other user's avatar in terms of mutual awareness, attentional allocation, mutual understanding, behavioural interdependence, mutual assistance, and dependent actions (similarly to [31]); the only exception was the empathy category, which was not included, being the relative items not suitable for the considered use case. The third section included the immersion and presence section of the VRUSE [17] questionnaire. Finally, the last section, filled in after having completed both the runs, asked the participant to express his or her preference between the two representation techniques in terms of usability, aesthetics, multi-player interactions, and overall.

5   Results and Discussion

The results obtained for the subjective metrics presented in the previous section were used to compare the VK and FB techniques.

The Shapiro-Wilk test was used to analyze the normality of data. Since data were found to be non-normally distributed, the non-parametric Wilcoxon signed-rank test with 5% significance ($p < 0.05$) was used for studying statistical differences.

5.1   Embodiment

For what it concerns the perceived embodiment, reported in Fig. 4, no significant differences were observed in most of the sub-scales, as well as for the total embodiment. For the sake of readability, the sub-scales and the total embodiment, calculated as suggested in [15], have been normalized in a range between 0 and 1, being each of them originally characterized by different minimum and maximum values. The only exceptions are represented by the appearance (0.3 vs 0, p-value < 0.001) and response to external stimuli (0.18 vs 0.1, p-value $= 0.003$) sub scales, for which the FB was perceived as better than the VK. This result is in line with some previous literature works mentioned before, which did not find significant differences between showing or not showing the user's avatar body [25].

Going into the details of scores assigned to the individual items, expressed on a 7-point Likert scale from -3 to 3 (from strongly disagree to strongly agree), the participants felt the FB as a representation of their body more than the VK (1.4 vs 0.27, p-value $= 0.042$); however, they also perceived a higher sense of having more than one body (0.73 vs -0.6, $p = 0.01$), confirming that the FB could have either positive or negative effects in terms of embodiment based on its accuracy [20,33]. This is in agreement with the results got from the item, according to which, with the FB, the participants felt as if movements of the virtual representation were influencing their real movements more than with the VK (-0.13 vs -1.13, $p = 0.0488$). Moreover, concerning the initial part of the experience in which a mirrored version of the user's avatar is displayed to the participant, FB appeared to be felt as the own body more than VK (0.73 vs -0.6, $p = 0.0412$). Regarding external appearance, with the FB the participants felt as if their real body was becoming an "avatar" body more than with the VK (0.8 vs -0.6, $p = 0.003$), that their real body was starting to take the posture of the avatar body (0.2 vs -1.13, $p = 0.009$), that at some point the virtual representation started to resembled more their real body in terms of shape and other visual features (0.13 vs -2.0, $p = 0.003$), and that they felt more like they were wearing different clothes than when they came to the laboratory (0 vs -2.26, $p = 0.005$) than with VK. For what it concerns the response to external stimuli, with the FB the participants felt as if virtual elements (fire, objects) could affect them more than with the VK (1.2 vs 0.33, $p = 0.015$), and had an higher feeling of being harmed by the fire (-0.07 vs -0.53, $p = 0.015$).

5.2   Social Presence

As for social presence, whose metrics are depicted in Fig. 5, the difference between the two techniques was more marked. Responses were given on a 7-point Likert scale in a range between 1 and 7 (from strongly disagree to strongly agree). Considering the various sub-scales, the participants perceived the VK as better than the FB in terms of mutual awareness (6.4 vs 5.43, $p = 0.003$), mutual attention (6.34 vs 5.81, $p = 0.003$), and mutual understanding (5.91 vs 5.44, $p = 0.047$). These results indicate that the use of a body to represent the other user's avatar significantly improves multi-user cooperation. In particular, with the FB, the participants noticed more the presence of the other peer (1.33 vs 3.0, $p = 0.001$), they were more aware of themselves inside the VE (6.4 vs 4.93, $p = 0.002$), and they perceived the other peer as more aware of them (6.33 vs 5.4, $p = 0.023$) than with the VK. Moreover, with the FB, the participants felt less alone (1.2 vs 1.93, $p = 0.046$), and perceived the other peer as less lonely (1.4 vs 2.2, $p = 0.039$). The FB also helped the participants to pay higher attention to the other

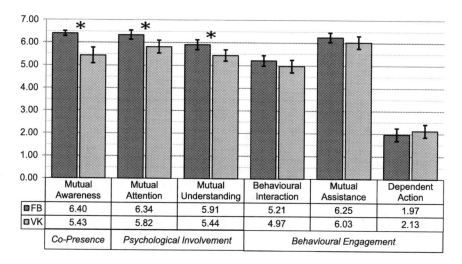

Fig. 5. Average results for the Networked Minds Social Presence Questionnaire [5] sub-scales (7-point Likert scale from strong disagreement to strong agreement). Statistically significant differences ($p < 0.05$) marked with a star (*) symbol.

peer with respect to the VK (6.33 vs 5.47, $p = 0.0312$). Furthermore, with the VK, the participants tended to ignore the other individual more than with the FB (1.67 vs 2.73, $p = 0.0117$). Finally, FB allowed participants to express their opinions (6.00 vs 5.27, $p = 0.0027$), as well as to understand the other peers' ones (5.93 vs 5.13, $p = 0.04888$) more than VK.

5.3 Immersion and Presence

The results for the immersion and presence section, derived from [17], are reported in Fig. 6. According to the scores, expressed on a 5-point Likert scale between 1 and 5 (from strongly agree to strongly disagree), the FB was judged as better than the VK only in terms of immersion (4.86 vs 4.26, $p = 0.031$), but nothing can be said in terms of presence. This outcome can be related to the fact that the training experience, being oriented towards realism, benefited of a more realistic-looking avatar representation, which was provided by the FB.

5.4 Direct Comparison

In the final section of the questionnaire, whose results are provided in Fig. 7, the participants were asked to express their preference between the VK and the FB for various aspects.

Interestingly, the FB was judged as significantly better than the VK for the other user representation for the aesthetics (93.33% vs 6.66%, $p = 0.001$), regarding multi-player interactions (86.66% vs 13.33%, $p = 0.010$) and also overall (86.66% vs 13.33%, $p = 0.010$). However, none of the two techniques prevailed for what it concerned the

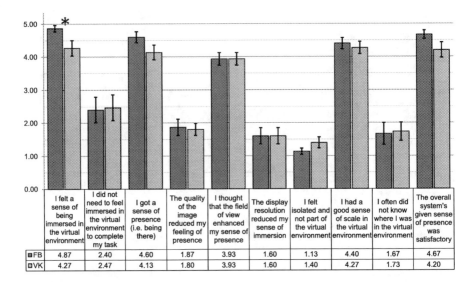

	I felt a sense of being immersed in the virtual environment	I did not need to feel immersed in the virtual environment to complete my task	I got a sense of presence (i.e. being there)	The quality of the image reduced my feeling of presence	I thought that the field of view enhanced my sense of presence	The display resolution reduced my sense of immersion	I felt isolated and not part of the virtual environment	I had a good sense of scale in the virtual environment	I often did not know where I was in the virtual environment	The overall system's given sense of presence was satisfactory
▨FB	4.87	2.40	4.60	1.87	3.93	1.60	1.13	4.40	1.67	4.67
▨VK	4.27	2.47	4.13	1.80	3.93	1.60	1.40	4.27	1.73	4.20

Fig. 6. Average results for the immersion and presence section of the VRUSE [17] questionnaire (5-point Likert scale from strong disagreement to strong agreement). Statistically significant differences (p-value < 0.05) marked with a star (*) symbol.

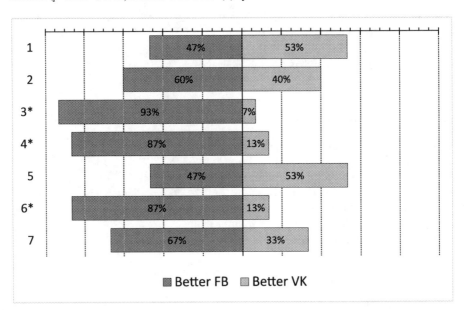

Fig. 7. Average results for the direct comparison section of the questionnaire. Statistically significant differences ($p < 0.05$) marked with a star (*) symbol. Indicate for each of the following aspect which version you preferred: #01. Regarding the usability (own avatar); #02. Regarding the aesthetics (own avatar); #03. Regarding the aesthetics (other avatar); #04. Regarding the multiplayer interactions; #05. Regarding own avatar; #06. Regarding the other avatar; #07. Regarding the overall user experience

own avatar representation. These mixed results for the own avatar are anyway in line with those regarding the embodiment, suggesting that the two representations of the own avatar may have a similar impact in multi-user experiences too.

6   Conclusions and Future Work

In this work, two different techniques to represent users' avatars in multi-user VR experiences were evaluated in the context of an emergency training simulation. In particular, a road tunnel fire simulation, presented in [8], was used as a test-bench for the considered evaluation. The first considered technique, widely used for the user's representation in commercial, single-user VR applications, consists in not providing an avatar body, but only displaying the VR Kit (VK) equipment, i.e., the hand controllers and, in case of the other user, the HMD. The second technique, referred to as Full-Body (FB), makes use of a combination of IK algorithms and animation blending to operate a full humanoid reconstruction for the user's avatar, targeted to the position and orientation of the user's head and hands. A within-subject user study, involving 15 participants, showed different outcomes regarding how the own avatar and the other user's avatar are considered. For what it concerns the own representation, no clear winners emerged in terms of embodiment or preference, although the FB was perceived significantly better than the VK in terms of appearance, response to external stimuli, and immersion. Regarding the other user's avatar, the FB appeared to improve various social presence aspects, such as mutual awareness, mutual attention and mutual understanding. Furthermore, it was also preferred over the VK for the other user's representation (in general, but also for the aesthetics and multi-player interactions).

These findings suggest that multi-user training simulations would greatly benefit of the employment of a FB approach to represent the avatar of the other user inside the shared experience, as long as the outcome of the combined use of IK and animations produces a sufficiently believable and realistic result. The situation is different for what it concerns the own representation of the user, as the investigation produced mixed results. Comments provided by some participants at the end of the experience offer possible interpretations. In particular, some participants reported of being distracted by the FB avatar whenever the estimated pose of the body differed too much from the real one. In those cases, they would have preferred not to see the avatar at all, like with the VK. For this reason some users may still perceive VK as better than FB in these particular situations.

Future developments will be devoted to widen the investigation, considering other avatar representation techniques, as well as including the other technologies (e.g., motion capture suits and leg sensors) and locomotion modalities (e.g., locomotion treadmills, walk-in-place, etc.) already supported by the considered training tool. Moreover, more complex situations could be developed, for example requiring the users to fulfill more collaboration-oriented tasks (e.g., interaction with objects that have to be handled by two users at the same time, tasks which can be only completed by working together, presence of more than two users in the simulation, etc.). To support the above scenarios, the set of animations used by the FB implementation may need to be extended, e.g., by introducing also prone crawling, jumping, climbing, and any other movement which may have to be displayed in a collaborative emergency scenario. Furthermore, machine learning-based avatar representation techniques may be added to the comparison, also estimating their impact in terms of computational load with respect to the IK algorithms. Finally, the FB implementation may be integrated with facial and eye tracking capabilities, to further improve communication and expressiveness of the other user's avatar, and to increase the perceived realism of the simulation.

Acknowledgements. This work has been carried out in the frame of the VR@POLITO initiative.

References

1. Çakiroğlu, Ü., Gökoğlu, S.: Development of fire safety behavioral skills via virtual reality. Comput. Educ. **133**, 56–68 (2019). https://doi.org/10.1016/j.compedu.2019.01.014
2. Andrade, M., Souto Maior, C., Silva, E., Moura, M., Lins, I.: Serious games & human reliability. The use of game-engine-based simulator data for studies of evacuation under toxic cloud scenario. In: Proceedings of Probabilistic Safety Assessment and Management (PSAM 14), pp. 1–12 (2018)
3. Bailenson, J.N., Yee, N., Merget, D., Schroeder, R.: The effect of behavioral realism and form realism of real-time avatar faces on verbal disclosure, nonverbal disclosure, emotion recognition, and copresence in dyadic interaction. Presence **15**(4), 359–372 (2006). https://doi.org/10.1162/pres.15.4.359
4. Benrachou, D.E., Masmoudi, M., Djekoune, O., Zenati, N., Ousmer, M.: Avatar-facilitated therapy and virtual reality: next-generation of functional rehabilitation methods. In: 2020 1st International Conference on Communications, Control Systems and Signal Processing (CCSSP), pp. 298–304 (2020). https://doi.org/10.1109/CCSSP49278.2020.9151528
5. Biocca, F., Harms, C., L. Gregg, J.: The networked minds measure of social presence: pilot test of the factor structure and concurrent validity. In: International Workshop on Presence, Philadelphia (2001)
6. Calandra, D., Billi, M., Lamberti, F., Sanna, A., Borchiellini, R.: Arm swinging vs treadmill: a comparison between two techniques for locomotion in virtual reality. In: Diamanti, O., Vaxman, A. (eds.) EG 2018 - Short Papers, pp. 53–56. The Eurographics Association (2018). https://doi.org/10.2312/egs.20181043
7. Calandra, D., Lamberti, F., Migliorini, M.: On the usability of consumer locomotion techniques in serious games: comparing arm swinging, treadmills and walk-in-place. In: Proceedings of 2019 IEEE 9th International Conference on Consumer Electronics (ICCE-Berlin), pp. 348–352 (2019). https://doi.org/10.1109/ICCE-Berlin47944.2019.8966165
8. Calandra, D., Prattico, F.G., Migliorini, M., Verda, V., Lamberti, F.: A multi-role, multi-user, multi-technology virtual reality-based road tunnel fire simulator for training purposes. In: Proceedings of 16th International Conference on Computer Graphics Theory and Applications (GRAPP 2021), pp. 96–105 (2021). https://doi.org/10.5220/0010319400960105
9. Cannavò, A., Calandra, D., Prattico, F.G., Gatteschi, V., Lamberti, F.: An evaluation testbed for locomotion in virtual reality. IEEE Trans. Visual Comput. Graphics **27**(3), 1871–1889 (2021). https://doi.org/10.1109/TVCG.2020.3032440
10. Caserman, P., Achenbach, P., Göbel, S.: Analysis of inverse kinematics solutions for full-body reconstruction in virtual reality. In: 2019 IEEE 7th International Conference on Serious Games and Applications for Health (SeGAH), pp. 1–8 (2019). https://doi.org/10.1109/SeGAH.2019.8882429

11. Corelli, F., Battegazzorre, E., Strada, F., Bottino, A., Cimellaro, G.P.: Assessing the usability of different virtual reality systems for firefighter training. In: Proceedings of 15th International Joint Conference on Computer Vision, Imaging and Computer Graphics Theory and Applications (HUCAPP 2020), pp. 146–153 (2020). https://doi.org/10.5220/0008962401460153

12. Engelbrecht, H., Lindeman, R.W., Hoermann, S.: A SWOT analysis of the field of virtual reality for firefighter training. Front. Rob. AI **6**, 101 (2019). https://doi.org/10.3389/frobt.2019.00101

13. Syed Ali Fathima, S.J., Aroma, J.: Simulation of fire safety training environment using immersive virtual reality. Int. J. Recent Technol. Eng. (IJRTE) **7**(4S), 347–350 (2019)

14. Feng, Z., González, V.A., Amor, R., Lovreglio, R., Cabrera-Guerrero, G.: Immersive virtual reality serious games for evacuation training and research: a systematic literature review. Comput. Educ. **127**, 252–266 (2018). https://doi.org/10.1016/j.compedu.2018.09.002

15. Gonzalez-Franco, M., Peck, T.C.: Avatar embodiment. Towards a standardized questionnaire. Front. Rob. AI **5** (2018). https://doi.org/10.3389/frobt.2018.00074

16. Gu, L., Yin, L., Li, J., Wu, D.: A real-time full-body motion capture and reconstruction system for VR basic set. In: 2021 IEEE 5th Advanced Information Technology, Electronic and Automation Control Conference (IAEAC), vol. 5, pp. 2087–2091 (2021). https://doi.org/10.1109/IAEAC50856.2021.9390617

17. Kalawsky, R.S.: VRUSE - a computerised diagnostic tool: for usability evaluation of virtual/synthetic environment systems. Appl. Ergon. **30**(1), 11–25 (1999). https://doi.org/10.1016/S0003-6870(98)00047-7

18. Kasapakis, V., Dzardanova, E.: Using high fidelity avatars to enhance learning experience in virtual learning environments. In: 2021 IEEE Conference on Virtual Reality and 3D User Interfaces Abstracts and Workshops (VRW), pp. 645–646 (2021). https://doi.org/10.1109/VRW52623.2021.00205

19. Kinateder, M., et al.: Virtual reality for fire evacuation research. In: Proceedings of Federated Conference on Computer Science and Information Systems, pp. 313–321 (2014). https://doi.org/10.13140/2.1.3380.9284

20. Kokkinara, E., Slater, M.: Measuring the effects through time of the influence of visuomotor and visuotactile synchronous stimulation on a virtual body ownership illusion. Perception **43**(1), 43–58 (2014). https://doi.org/10.1068/p7545, pMID: 24689131

21. Lamberti, F., De Lorenzis, F., Pratticò, F.G., Migliorini, M.: An immersive virtual reality platform for training CBRN operators. In: Proceedings of 2021 IEEE 45th Annual Computers, Software, and Applications Conference (COMPSAC), pp. 133–137 (2021). https://doi.org/10.1109/COMPSAC51774.2021.00030

22. Louka, M.N., Balducelli, C.: Virtual reality tools for emergency operation support and training. In: Proceedings International Conference on Emergency Management Towards Co-operation and Global Harmonization (TIEMS 2001), pp. 1–10 (06 2001)

23. Lovreglio, R.: Virtual and augmented reality for human behaviour in disasters: a review. In: Proceedings of Fire and Evacuation Modeling Technical Conference (FEMTC 2020), pp. 1–14 (2020)

24. Lu, X., Yang, Z., Xu, Z., Xiong, C.: Scenario simulation of indoor post-earthquake fire rescue based on building information model and virtual reality. Adv. Eng. Softw. **143**, 102792 (2020). https://doi.org/10.1016/j.advengsoft.2020.102792

25. Lugrin, J.L., et al.: Any "body" there? Avatar visibility effects in a virtual reality game. In: 2018 IEEE Conference on Virtual Reality and 3D User Interfaces (VR), pp. 17–24 (2018). https://doi.org/10.1109/VR.2018.8446229

26. Molina, E., Jerez, A.R., Gómez, N.P.: Avatars rendering and its effect on perceived realism in virtual reality. In: 2020 IEEE International Conference on Artificial Intelligence and Virtual Reality (AIVR), pp. 222–225 (2020). https://doi.org/10.1109/AIVR50618.2020.00046

27. Morélot, S., Garrigou, A., Dedieu, J., N'Kaoua, B.: Virtual reality for fire safety training: influence of immersion and sense of presence on conceptual and procedural acquisition. Comput. Educ. **166**, 104145 (2021). https://doi.org/10.1016/j.compedu.2021.104145

28. Parger, M., Mueller, J.H., Schmalstieg, D., Steinberger, M.: Human upper-body inverse kinematics for increased embodiment in consumer-grade virtual reality. In: Proceedings of the 24th ACM Symposium on Virtual Reality Software and Technology, VRST 2018. Association for Computing Machinery, New York (2018). https://doi.org/10.1145/3281505.3281529

29. Pedram, S., Palmisano, S., Skarbez, R., Perez, P., Farrelly, M.: Investigating the process of mine rescuers' safety training with immersive virtual reality: a structural equation modelling approach. Comput. Educ. **153**, 103891 (2020). https://doi.org/10.1016/j.compedu.2020.103891

30. Pratticò, F.G., De Lorenzis, F., Calandra, D., Cannavò, A., Lamberti, F.: Exploring simulation-based virtual reality as a mock-up tool to support the design of first responders training. Appl. Sci. **11**(16), 1–13 (2021). https://doi.org/10.3390/app11167527

31. Roth, D., et al.: Avatar realism and social interaction quality in virtual reality. In: 2016 IEEE Virtual Reality (VR), pp. 277–278 (2016). https://doi.org/10.1109/VR.2016.7504761

32. Schäfer, A., Reis, G., Stricker, D.: A survey on synchronous augmented, virtual and mixed reality remote collaboration systems (2021)

33. Steed, A., Frlston, S., Lopez, M.M., Drummond, J., Pan, Y., Swapp, D.: An 'in the wild' experiment on presence and embodiment using consumer virtual reality equipment. IEEE Trans. Visual Comput. Graphics **22**(4), 1406–1414 (2016). https://doi.org/10.1109/TVCG.2016.2518135

Facade Layout Completion with Long Short-Term Memory Networks

Simon Hensel[1($\boxtimes$)], Steffen Goebbels[1], and Martin Kada[2]

[1] Institute for Pattern Recognition, Niederrhein University of Applied Sciences,
Reinarzstrasse 49, Krefeld, Germany
{simon.hensel,steffen.goebbels}@hs-niederrhein.de
[2] Institute of Geodesy and Geoinformation Science, Technische Universität Berlin,
Kaiserin-Augusta-Allee 104-106, Berlin, Germany
martin.kada@tu-berlin.de

Abstract. In a workflow creating 3D city models, facades of buildings can be reconstructed from oblique aerial images for which the extrinsic and intrinsic parameters are known. If the wall planes have already been determined, e.g., based on airborne laser scanning point clouds, facade textures can be computed by applying a perspective transform. These images given, doors and windows can be detected and then added to the 3D model. In this study, the "Scaled YOLOv4" neural network is applied to detect facade objects. However, due to occlusions and artifacts from perspective correction, in general not all windows and doors are detected. This leads to the necessity of automatically continuing the pattern of facade objects into occluded or distorted areas. To this end, we propose a new approach based on recurrent neural networks. In addition to applying the Multi-Dimensional Long Short-term Memory network and the Quasi Recurrent Neural Network, we also use a novel architecture, the Rotated Multi-Dimensional Long Short-term Memory network. This architecture combines four two-dimensional Multi-Dimensional Long Short-term Memory networks on rotated images. Independent of the 3D city model workflow, the three networks were additionally tested on the Graz50 dataset for which the Rotated Multi-Dimensional Long Short-term Memory network delivered better results than the other two networks. The facade texture regions, in which windows and doors are added to the set of initially detected facade objects, are likely to be occluded or distorted. Before equipping 3D models with these textures, inpainting should be applied to these regions which then serve as automatically obtained inpainting masks.

Keywords: Deep learning · LSTM · Facade reconstruction · Structure completion · Image inpainting

1 Introduction

Most current 3D city models were created based on airborne laser scanning point clouds. Whereas roofs are clearly visible, the point density of vertical walls is much lower, and walls might be occluded by roofs. Thus, facades are often represented as planar polygons without any details. The position and size of facade objects like windows and doors can be better obtained from oblique aerial images. By utilizing camera

© Springer Nature Switzerland AG 2023
A. A. de Sousa et al. (Eds.): VISIGRAPP 2021, CCIS 1691, pp. 21–40, 2023.
https://doi.org/10.1007/978-3-031-25477-2_2

parameters, segments from these images can be mapped to become textures of facade polygons. These are low resolution images that might be distorted by occlusions and shadows. Since real facades are not exactly planar (e.g., due to balconies), artifacts from the perspective correction occur as well. However, windows and doors have to be detected on these distorted images in order to obtain semantic 3D facade models. For example, neural networks for object detection and instance segmentation, see Sect. 2, search for individual object instances but do not consider higher-level layout patterns. This also holds true for the state-of-the-art object detection network "Scaled YOLOv4" [31] that is applied in this study. Thus, relationships between windows are not taken into account to also find occluded object instances. But model knowledge can be used to add missing instances in a post-processing step. One way to do this is by applying split grammars that were introduced in [32] for building reconstruction. Such grammars consist of rules that describe the placement and orientation of objects. They allow filling in missing facade objects and also generating facades procedurally from scratch. However, the grammar rules must be appropriate for a particular building style. Individual facade layouts may require individual, manually created rules. Since it is difficult to find a suitable collection of rules, machine learning is an appropriate tool.

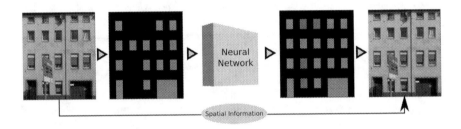

Fig. 1. Workflow for facade structure completion: Due to a flag, a satellite dish and a signpost, four windows could not be detected. They were inserted using an LSTM [14].

We propose the use of Recurrent Neural Networks (RNNs) with Long Short-term Memory (LSTM) to recover positions and sizes of missing windows and doors within a workflow shown in Fig. 1. These networks are commonly applied to time-dependent, one-dimensional input data, e.g., in the context of speech recognition. This leads to an input consisting of incomplete detection results, e.g., from the Scaled YOLOv4 network. These results are represented by (two-dimensional) bounding boxes. We obtain an irregular rectangular lattice (IRL) by extending the edges of the bounding boxes to straight lines. Thus, an IRL is a collection of horizontal and vertical lines. It is called "irregular" because the distances between the lines may vary. Bounding boxes of detected objects are not perfectly aligned, so we simplify the IRL depending on the image resolution. Lines are merged if they are closer than a resolution-specific threshold distance (see Sect. 3.3). The cells of the IRL are the rectangles that are bounded but not intersected by lines. In the beginning, cells are labeled with the initial detection results. They are either classified as background or as part of a facade object (window/door). The task of the LSTM is to correct the initial labels of the cells so that missing objects are added. To this end, we compare results of the proposed Rotated Multi-Dimensional Long Short-term Memory network (RMD LSTM [14], see Sect. 4) with results of the Multi-Dimensional Long Short-term Memory (MD LSTM) [9] and the Quasi Recurrent Neural Network (QRNN), see [3], in Sect. 6.

We are not only interested in the positions and sizes of windows and doors to create semantic 3D building models but also want to texture the models with the given oblique aerial images. Initially, undetected objects that could be added by the RNN approach help to identify occluded or distorted image regions. If a window or door is not detected in the distorted image, we assume that the object and its surrounding is occluded. Thus, an occlusion mask can be computed automatically as the union of all corresponding surroundings. Then, an inpainting algorithm can be applied to fill these regions. Inpainting is a standard computer vision technique that interpolates or extrapolates visual information to fill image regions that are typically defined by a binary masks such that edges and texture patterns should somehow fit with the given information, see, e.g., the overview paper [20]. Our approach to computing occlusion masks based on added objects differs from a more common technique based on segmenting objects that may occlude facades, see e.g. [5]. However, it is difficult to segment all objects that cause occlusions because a facade can be occluded by many different objects belonging to many object classes. This difficulty does not occur with our proposed method.

This work builds on the foundation established in [14]. We have rewritten and extended individual sections. We also introduce a new use case in Sect. 6.2 where the proposed workflow is inserted into a facade inpainting process.

2   Related Work

We are concerned with a workflow that generates semantic 3D building models. Such models are represented and exchanged with the open data model format CityGML see [10] or more recently with CityJSON[1].

In the presented workflow, windows and doors have to be recognized in facade images. Convolutional Neural Networks (CNNs) have become a standard tool for image-based object detection and segmentation. ResNET [12] was a milestone in Deep Learning. It eliminated the well-known vanishing gradient problem that can occur when training very deep neural networks. Mask R-CNN [11] is an important network architecture for segmenting individual object instances. To this end, it applies an attention mechanism that consists of detecting object instances first. Then it performs segmentation within the bounding boxes of the detection results. In the RetinaNet [19], the concept of focal loss is implemented to distinguish between foreground and background. Not only when computational resources are limited, YOLO [23] is a commonly used network. The Scaled YOLOv4 network [31] provides differently scaled deep learning models, which are chosen according to a balance of image size, channels and layers. On the MC COCO dataset, the network reached an average precision of 64.8% and outperformed the EfficientDet neural network [27] with the former best average precision of 53.0%.

---

[1] https://cityjson.org/specs/ (accessed: January 21, 2023).

We use bounding boxes of detected objects to generate an IRL. Unfortunately, the boxes may not be properly aligned. However, they often can be aligned by slightly shifting their position and changing their size. This can be done by solving a combinatorial optimization problem. Such a mixed integer linear program with integer and float variables is presented in [13]. By using predefined bounding box positions, the float variables can be eliminated so that a faster integer linear program can be applied, see [15].

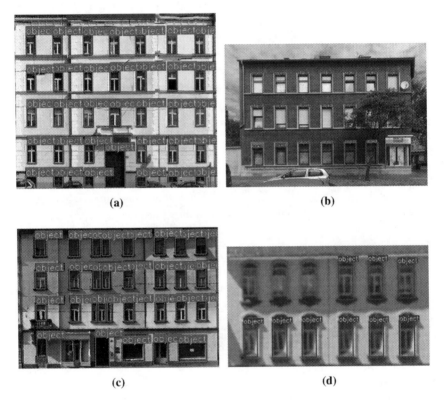

(a)   (b)

(c)   (d)

Fig. 2. Examples of object detection using Scaled YOLOv4. (a) and (c) are images from the Graz50 dataset [24], (b) has a high resolution whereas the resolution of image (d) is low.

If occluded facade regions are known (e.g., by applying semantic segmentation of trees), image inpainting techniques can be applied to fill these regions prior to object detection. Vice versa, we use image inpainting with masks obtained from analyzing object detection results.

Diffusion based inpainting methods fill regions by propagating information from the boundary to the interior. Typically, they are applied to deal with small regions. If larger regions have to be filled, texture synthesis methods like example-based inpainting are used.

General inpainting algorithms have been adopted to the completion of facade images. In [6], a Random Forest-based method is used to obtain a semantic segmentation of facade elements. The edges of the segment boundaries are used to create an IRL. The corresponding cells are initially labeled based on the semantic segmentation, similarly to our approach based on bounding boxes, see Sect. 3.3. The algorithm performs example-based inpainting by copying cell content to cells that have to be filled. To this end, the IRL is interpreted as an undirected graph and a graph labeling problem is solved to ensure structural consistency.

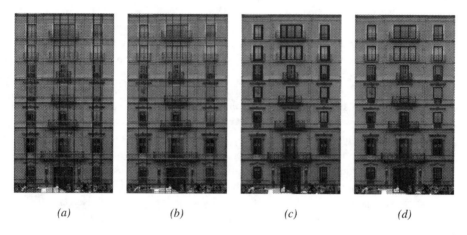

(a)   *(b)*   *(c)*   *(d)*

Fig. 3. Images *(a)* and *(b)* show an IRL representation of an example facade from the CMP dataset. Images *(c)* and *(d)* show the corresponding bounding boxes. IRL in *(b)* was computed by merging lines of the IRL in *(a)*. [14]

The article [16] deals with another inpainting algorithm that is applied in the context of facade reconstruction. The algorithm detects line segments in an image showing edges. It then clusters line segments according to vanishing points of the corresponding lines. Image regions that are covered by line segments belonging to two different vanishing points are interpreted as 2D representations of a 3D plane. This information is then used to continue textures in connection with various cost functions that measure appearance, guidance, orthogonal direction, and proximity.

With the advance of Generative Adversarial Networks (GANs), see [8], deep learning based inpainting techniques like the application of the Wasserstein GAN [2] in [33] have been developed. The EdgeConnect network [22] applies a GAN to edge images. Instead of using partial convolutions that are restricted to non-occluded pixels,

DeepFillv2 [34] learns how to apply a convolution mask that is also learned. This mechanism is called gated convolution.

Batch normalization is a standard technique in neural network training. With regard to inpainting, features of occluded regions can lead to mean and variance shifts. Instead of batch normalization, a region normalization method to overcome this problem is proposed in [35]. Given an inpainting mask, the image is divided into multiple regions. Instead of performing normalization with the images in a batch, now features are normalized with respect to the image regions.

For the application of general purpose inpainting algorithms, it is necessary to specify the regions that have to be filled. However, an automated 3D building reconstruction workflow requires automatically derived masks for facade textures. In [4], the mask is derived from a 3D-to-2D conversion of a facade point cloud. Regions without points define components of the mask. Subsequent to the definition of the mask, inpainting is performed with a GAN.

Model knowledge is applied in [18] where object detection results are used to refine a mask obtained from a segmentation network. Based on object detection, patches are marked that have to be preserved by the inpainting algorithm. The patches define important facade structures.

Our proposed workflow inter- and extrapolates a pattern of windows and doors. Thus, it has to know about typical facade layouts. Such layouts can be either learned (as proposed here) or explicitly given in terms of formal grammars like split grammars introduced in [32].

In [28], shape grammars are used to improve facade object segmentation. The terminal symbols of a grammar correspond with facade object classes. An initial probability map for terminal symbols is gained from a discriminatively trained classifier. In an iterative process, segmentation labels are optimized by applying grammar-based constrains. During this process an immediate and cumulative reward system is used for segmentations of windows, doors, and other facade objects which should better represent reality.

Formal grammars can be also applied to other data than 2D images. For example, in [7] point cloud data is analyzed by counting the number of points along horizontal and vertical lines with a kernel density estimation. Openings like windows and doors are characterized by lower point counts. Thus, these data can be interpreted with a weighted attributed context-free grammar to refine a facade model. The attributes define semantic rules which are additionally weighted with probabilities.

Since it is difficult to cover all architectural styles with explicitly defined grammars, we apply deep learning with recurrent neural networks. The concept of RNN and LSTM architectures is to equip a neural network with memory and access to previous predictions, cf. [26]. Such networks are often applied to time-dependent, one-dimensional data. For example, they are used for speech recognition and text understanding, cf. [21,25]. With regard to such applications, they can outperform other network architectures, see [36]. Extensions of LSTMs are the MD LSTM [9] and the QRNN [3]. The proposed RMD LSTM is built upon the MD LSTM, cf. [14]. To our knowledge, LSTMs have not been applied to the problem of facade reconstruction by other research groups so far. Due to memory being passed through multiple neurons and a serialized input of two-dimensional data, RNN and LSTM architectures have a high demand for hardware resources. Thus, the size of the input data has to be reduced, see Sect. 3.3.

3 Object Detection and Data Preparation

This section explains how we prepared data from different data sources and used it for training and testing. While training data was generated randomly, testing data also contained facade layouts based on object detections computed with Scaled YOLOv4.

3.1 Random Data Generation

Both the CMP dataset [30] and the Graz50 dataset [24] contain facade images and annotations for facade object classes. We restrict ourselves to windows and doors that are represented by rectangular regions taken from the datasets. To train and test the networks, window and door rectangles were removed randomly so that the networks had to add them again in their predictions. Hence, the networks did not see RGB images but only facade layouts consisting of window and door rectangles. This information was coded within an IRL, see Sect. 1.

The CMP dataset consists of 606 facades whereas the Graz50 dataset provides 50 images with corresponding annotations for segmentation. The architectural style of CMP facades differs from the style of Graz50 facades. We utilized this to avoid overfitting as we trained only with the larger CMP dataset but tested with the Graz50 facade layouts. This also showed that the networks are able to complete facade layouts of arbitrary facade types. One could either generate static test and training data prior to applying the networks or one could generate input dynamically during training and testing by randomly removing facade objects. We apply both methods. To avoid storing huge numbers of facade layouts, we applied the latter technique to dynamically remove 20% of windows and doors within the training iterations. This can additionally help to avoid overfitting, cf. [29]. Since it is easier to compare results on static data, we tested on fixed data that was also generated by removing 20% of facade objects.

3.2 Object Detection

In addition to training and testing with data generated from the CMP and Graz50 datasets by randomly removing facade objects, we also performed tests with results of real object detection. For this purpose, we used the Scaled YOLOv4 network [31], which we already mentioned in Sect. 1. For our purposes, we trained the Scaled YOLOv4 network on the CMP facade dataset to detect windows and doors. We only distinguished between objects and non-objects (binary detection). Subsequently, this trained network was used to generate additional test data. Figure 2 shows results for two Graz50 images, a manually taken photo and a facade derived from oblique aerial imaging.

3.3   Data Preparation

Instead of directly using rectangles representing doors and windows as input for the
LSTM networks, a matrix is generated based on an IRL. An initial IRL is obtained
from the straight lines which are defined by extending the edges of the rectangles, cf.
Sect. 1. The cells of this lattice are labeled to represent background (label value 0) or
windows and doors (label value 1), and the label values become entries of a matrix M.
For example, the facade in Fig. 1 is represented by the matrix in Formula (1).

$$M = \begin{bmatrix} 0 & 0 & 0 & 0 & 0 & 0 & 0 & 0 & 0 & 0 & 0 \\ 0 & 1 & 0 & 0 & 0 & 0 & 0 & 1 & 0 & 1 & 0 \\ 0 & 0 & 0 & 0 & 0 & 0 & 0 & 0 & 0 & 0 & 0 \\ 0 & 1 & 0 & 1 & 0 & 1 & 0 & 1 & 0 & 1 & 0 \\ 0 & 0 & 0 & 0 & 0 & 0 & 0 & 0 & 0 & 0 & 0 \\ 0 & 1 & 0 & 0 & 0 & 1 & 0 & 1 & 0 & 1 & 0 \\ 0 & 0 & 0 & 0 & 0 & 0 & 0 & 0 & 0 & 0 & 0 \\ 0 & 1 & 0 & 0 & 0 & 1 & 0 & 1 & 1 & 1 & 0 \\ 0 & 1 & 0 & 0 & 0 & 0 & 0 & 1 & 1 & 1 & 0 \end{bmatrix}. \tag{1}$$

Since detected facade objects are often not properly aligned, the number of cells
and thus the size of the matrix is significantly greater than necessary and might exceed
an acceptable input size of the RNN networks. Therefore, we reduce the number of
lattice lines of the initial IRL and the size of the matrix by merging neighboring lines.
To this end, we iteratively determine neighboring lines of the same orientation within a
threshold distance of eight pixels. These lines are replaced with a single line by computing a mean position. Figure 3 (b) shows how an IRL and its matrix change by merging
close lines in comparison to Fig. 3 (a). Figures 3 (c) and 3 (d) show the corresponding
bounding boxes whereas Fig. 4 visualizes the corresponding matrix representations. It
can be seen that the facade layout does not change significantly but also that merging
lines can lead to patterns and symmetry. Alternatively to the chosen merging approach,
a pre-processing step could be applied that aligns rectangles by solving an optimization
problem, see [13] or [15], cf. Sect. 2.

Whereas the RNN networks work on matrix representations, the spatial coordinates
of rectangles representing windows and doors are required to generate 3D models based
on the network output. Therefore, the simplified IRL is stored in addition to the matrix
representation.

For the considered datasets, matrices had sizes between 10 and 100 rows and
columns. Due to hardware restrictions, we choose a maximum network input size of
25×25 labels. Smaller matrices were fitted using zero padding. We experimented with
scaling to also fit larger matrices, but that did not lead to acceptable results. Therefore,
we only worked with facades that result in matrices with at most 25 rows and columns.
This leaves 359 facades of the CMP and 46 facades of the Graz50 data for training and
testing. Whereas the MD LSTM and the RMD LSTM networks are able to process 2D
matrix input, matrices have to be serialized to be processed by the QRNN.

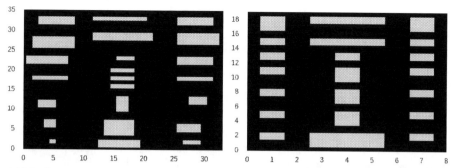

(a) Matrix representation of IRL before merging of lines within threshold distance.

(b) Resulting Matrix with merged horizontal and vertical lines.

Fig. 4. Impact of merging vertical and horizontal lattice lines in the IRL of Fig. 3(a). Note that axes are of a different scale, such that the resulting matrix of the simplified IRL is much smaller [14].

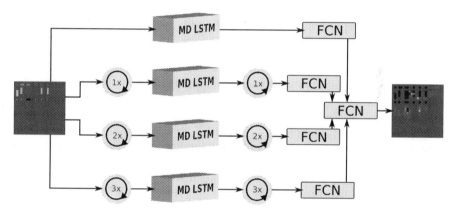

Fig. 5. Rotated Multi-Dimensional Long Short-term Memory Network [14].

4 Recurrent Neural Networks for Pattern Completion and Inpainting Mask Generation

We consider the ability of RNNs to utilize predictions from the past (previously processed spatial regions) to learn the patterns and symmetries of facade layouts. To this end, we introduce the RMD LSTM for facade completion and object recommendation, and present a comparison of outcomes from QRNN, RMD LSTM (and MD LSTM). In addition, we show how the network output can also be used to create inpainting masks for facade images.

4.1 Multi-Dimensional Long Short-Term Memory Network

MD LSTM [9] is an RNN architecture that allows for multi-dimensional input by utilizing separate memory connections for each dimension. In a two-dimensional setting, the MD LSTM network computes a value for a spatial cell (x, y) based on values of preceding cells $(x - 1, y)$ and $(x, y - 1)$. Thus, a directed spatial context is established in the network. The proposed RMD LSTM is composed of four MD LSTM networks.

4.2   Quasi Recurrent Neural Network

The QRNN is not an RNN but a CNN that emulates memory connections with an embedded pooling layer. For time-dependent inputs x_1 to x_T, the convolutional layers compute an output for time step t that consist of three vectors: a candidate vector z_t, a forget vector f_t and an output vector o_t:

$$z_t = \tanh(conv_{W_z}(x_t, \dots, x_{t-k+1}))$$
$$f_t = \sigma(conv_{W_f}(x_t, \dots, x_{t-k+1}))$$
$$o_t = \sigma(conv_{W_o}(x_t, \dots, x_{t-k+1})) \, .$$

In the convolution $conv$, a filter kernel size of k is used and the weight vectors are represented by W_z, W_f and W_o. The immediate outputs z_t, f_t, and o_t are then used to compute the hidden states c_t in the pooling layers. Let $c_0 := h_0 := 0$. Then the network output h_t for time step t is computed via

$$c_t = f_t \odot c_{t-1} + (1 - f_t) \odot z_t$$
$$h_t = o_t \odot c_t \, ,$$

where h_t is the network output for time step t.

The operator $\odot$ denotes element-wise multiplication of the vectors. With the exception of the pooling layer, the QRNN can be easily parallelized, while regular recurrent networks compute intermediate outputs sequentially. Due to efficient convolution and pooling operations, the QRNN is fast and memory efficient.

4.3   Rotated Multi-Dimensional Long Short-Term Memory Network

RNNs were developed to solve one-dimensional, time-dependent problems in which information of previous network outputs have to be taken into account for subsequent computations. When dealing with two- or three-dimensional spatial problems, often data of a spatial surrounding has to be considered. But when MD LSTM for two-dimensional input deals with cell (x, y), information of "future" cells $(x + 1, y)$ and $(x, y + 1)$ have not been computed yet. Especially when MD LSTM is applied to facade completion, missing facade objects in the upper left image region are impossible to add. To overcome this problem, we combine four MD LSTM networks. Each network operates on the input matrix rotated by $k \times 90°$, $k \in \{0, 1, 2, 3\}$, respectively. Thus, each single MD LSTM starts its iterative processing at a different corner of the facade layout. The outputs of the four networks are rotated back to the original orientation. Then they are combined by fully connected layers with sigmoid activation, see Fig. 5. We also experimented with maximum pooling layers instead of fully connected layers to combine results. This led to final results which were not significantly different.

Based on the previously described neural networks, we set up a reconstruction workflow. In principle, the networks are applied on matrices obtained from IRL simplification, see Sect. 3.3. Their output is a matrix that contains probability values for cells being labeled as windows or doors, cf. Fig. 1. If a probability exceeds a threshold value of 0.5, the cell is interpreted as a recommended object. The object is equipped with a bounding box by using the cell coordinates of the IRL. However, this could lead to multiple boxes that cover a single object. Such boxes are merged in a post-processing step.

It turned out that the results could be significantly improved by helping the networks with additional layout information, see Sect. 6. To this end, we did not use the binary matrices as inputs but replaced label values 1 that indicate facade objects with cluster numbers representing similar facade objects belonging to the same floor. To this end, we first group neighboring entries of 1 labels. If some groups are positioned in exactly the same rows and possess the same number of columns, then they belong to the same cluster. We enumerate all clusters and use the numbers as new matrix entries. Clustering is only applied to input data, ground truth and network output still consist of probability values.

With minor adjustments, this workflow is also able to automatically generate inpainting masks. By subtracting the binary version of the input matrix, we filter out the added windows and doors. The regions covered by these objects are likely to be occluded in the given facade image. Thus, a mask is generated by drawing filled circles at the positions of these objects. Positions and diameters of circles are obtained from the IRL coordinates. The radius r of each circle is calculated by

$$r = 1.5 \cdot \frac{d}{2},$$

where d is the diagonal of the IRL cell. The factor 1.5 is necessary because occlusions typically do not end at cell boundaries.

5   Network Training and Testing

To implement, train and test the networks, we used Tensorflow [1]. Our source code is freely available[2].

We trained the networks with a batch size of 16 and over 20,000 batches. Training was performed with randomly removed window and door rectangles from facade layouts of the CMP dataset whereas the original layouts served as the ground truth. This led to 320,000 distorted input matrices. To avoid overfitting, we added low-amplitude noise to background entries of the input, i.e., to the zeros. Training on an NVIDIA P6000 GPU lasted about a full day for MD LSTM and RMD LSTM whereas the QRNN could be trained within 3 h.

The networks were trained with an equal number of iterations by using the Adam optimizer and a Mean Squared Error loss function.

We tested the trained networks on matrices derived from the Graz50 dataset [24], see Sect. 3.1.

---

[2] https://github.com/SimonHensel/LSTM-Facade-Completion.

Table 1. Testing scores.

(a) Comparison of network results on binary input matrices (without cluster labels).

	Acc.	Prec.	Rec.	IoU
START	0.938	1.000	0.682	0.682
MD LSTM	0.980	0.913	0.787	0.732
QRNN	0.973	0.888	0.720	0.664
RMD LSTM	0.979	0.907	0.785	0.726

(b) Comparison of QRNN and RMD LSTM on input data labeled by clustering.

	Acc.	Prec.	Rec.	IoU
START	0.938	1.000	0.682	0.682
QRNN	0.969	0.901	0.641	0.604
RMD LSTM	**0.984**	**0.925**	**0.832**	**0.779**

6   Results

In this Section, we describe results qualitatively and quantitatively. In addition, we show inpainting examples based on masks that were generated with the RMD LSTM

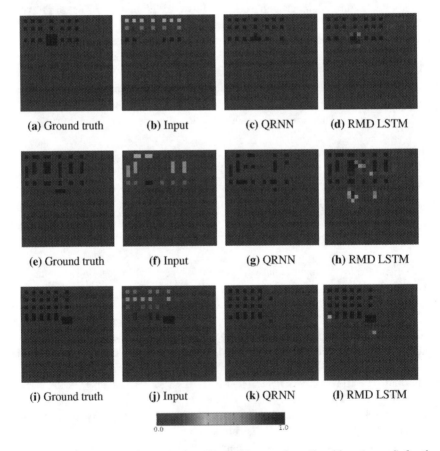

(a) Ground truth   (b) Input   (c) QRNN   (d) RMD LSTM

(e) Ground truth   (f) Input   (g) QRNN   (h) RMD LSTM

(i) Ground truth   (j) Input   (k) QRNN   (l) RMD LSTM

Fig. 6. Network output consisting of 25×25 confidence values (0 = blue, 1 = red) for three facades of the Graz50 dataset: images (a) to (c) represent the ground truth, images (d) to (f) show the input, images (g) to (i) present the QRNN output, and images (j) to (l) show the RMD LSTM results [14] (Color figure online).

as described in Sect. 4. We also describe the limitations of our approach with some examples.

Fig. 7. Detection results of the Scaled YOLOv4 network are shown in red. Objects added by the RMD LSTM are annotated with green boxes. (Color figure online)

6.1 Layout Completion

All experiments were performed on the Graz50 dataset. To be able to compare results, we computed a fixed test dataset with 10,000 facade layouts by removing 20% of facade objects, see Sect. 3.1.

We begin with a description of quantitative results and discuss qualitative results later. Tables 1a and 1b compare results with and without pre-clustering, cf. Sect. 4. The output of the neural networks consists of a probability map of confidence values. Object probabilities below a threshold of 0.5 were considered as background. For calculating evaluation scores, we counted every matrix entry in one of four sums: true positive (tp), false positive (fp), true negative (tn) or false negative (fn). Tables 1a and 1b show the average values of

$$\text{Accuracy (Acc.)} = \frac{tp + tn}{tp + tn + fp + fn}$$

$$\text{Precision (Prec.)} = \frac{tp}{tp + fp}$$

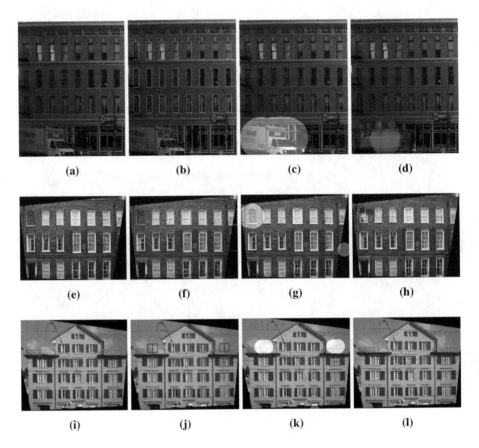

Fig. 8. Examples of generated inpainting masks and inpainting results.

$$\text{Recall (Rec.)} = \frac{tp}{tp + fn}$$

$$\text{IoU} = \frac{tp}{tp + fp + fn}.$$

The Intersection over Union (IoU) does not consider the correct classifications of the large background class and thus is especially meaningful. All scores were computed separately for each input and output pair. Afterwards, the arithmetic mean was computed.

To determine whether the networks were able to improve the facade layouts, we also calculated the scores directly on the network input without applying the networks. The outcomes are listed in the rows in Table 1 denoted by "START". The precision is equal to 1 because no false positives are present in the randomly generated input data.

As it can be seen in Table 1a, the RMD LSTM produces better results than the QRNN in terms of accuracy, recall and IoU. Figure 6 illustrates how probability values of recommendations look like. Although we trained the networks on the segregated CMP dataset, RMD LSTM was able to also complete Graz50 layouts. QRNN was not able to achieve similar results.

Figure 7 shows examples of RMD LSTM network results on the Scaled YOLOv4 data. Whereas the examples (a), (b), (h), and (i) in Fig. 10 were completed within a small margin of error, there were some difficulties with objects that are composed of more than one IRL cell. The network also adds door-shaped objects at wrong positions.

Besides testing on Graz50 data, we also tested on training data. Here, QRNN outperformed the RMD LSTM network. Compared with test data, the IoU of QRNN increased by 0.18. If this is not an effect of overfitting and if the style of facades is known and if the size of training data for this given style is sufficient, then QRNN might be superior to RMD LSTM.

Furthermore, experiments were also conducted with the GridLSTM network [17]. This network showed better results for language and text translation tasks than certain LSTM networks due to a grid of multi-way interactions. However, this grid increases memory requirements such that we were not able to apply the network with the same hyperparameters as the other networks. We had to reduce both the batch size and the number of hidden units. But under these restrictions, the network wrongly classified everything as background.

6.2   Inpainting

Besides improving facade object detection, the presented network architecture can also be used to automatically generate inpainting masks, see Sect. 4. We used these masks to replace occluded or distorted image regions with fitting textures.

We detected windows and doors with the Scaled YOLOv4 network. Then detection results were completed with the RMD LSTM network such that inpainting masks could be generated based on the added objects. The regions defined by the masks were filled with the DeepFillv2 network [34]. Figure 8 shows two examples. There is no occlusion in the second example image so that no correction is required. Additional information is required to exclude such images from automatic procession.

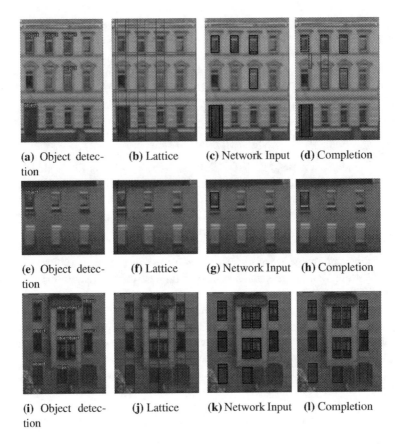

(a) Object detec-   **(b)** Lattice   **(c)** Network Input   **(d)** Completion
tion

(e) Object detec-   **(f)** Lattice   **(g)** Network Input   **(h)** Completion
tion

(i) Object detec-   **(j)** Lattice   **(k)** Network Input   **(l)** Completion
tion

Fig. 9. Examples that showcase the limitations of our workflow presented in Fig. 1. Figures (a)–(h) show the effects of an insufficient object detection. Figures (i)–(l) show the effects of separating facade structure knowledge and image information.

6.3 Limitations

Large regions without detected windows and doors make it difficult to find an IRL that represents the entire facade structure. Two examples of this problem are shown in Fig. 9 (a)–(d) and (e)–(h). Another consequence of the sole reliance on object detection is that the LSTM networks do not take pixel information into account. For example, the missing window in Fig. 9 (i)-(l) has a different size and shape than the other windows.

Results shown in Figs. 9 and 10 indicate that improvements are still possible. The main cause for detection errors are objects that are represented by more than one matrix entry. This occurs in some rare cases and is therefore troublesome for learning. Most often, doors are incomplete or mistaken for a window, see examples in Fig. 10 (a), (d) and (j).

A major limitation in the application of LSTMs is their high memory usage. MD LSTM and RMD LSTM allocate up to 23 GB of GPU memory, depending on the number of hidden units used.

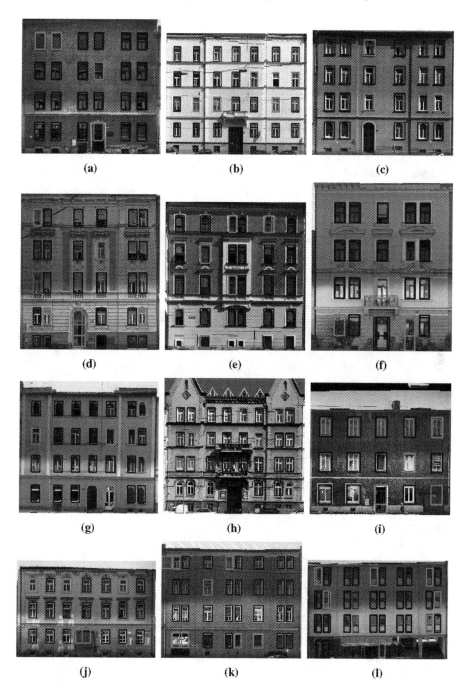

Fig. 10. Objects were randomly removed from the ground truth of the Graz50 dataset, see also Sect. 3.1. Remaining objects are annotated with red boxes. The RMD LSTM network added the missing objects within a small margin of error. Added objects are marked with green boxes [14]. (Color figure online)

7 Conclusion and Future Work

Experiments with the RMD LSTM showed that LSTMs are a suitable means to fill gaps in facade layouts. RMD LSTM outperformed the original MD LSTM and QRNN. It increases the IoU by 14%. An advantage of such deep learning methods over grammar-based algorithms is that no rules have to be defined explicitly.

So far, the training of neural networks was limited to windows and doors. However, other facade objects could be treated in a similar way. Future improvements should also target the reduction of memory consumption and the other problems listed in Sect. 6.3.

The current workflow works best if the detected objects are distributed over the entire image. An incomplete IRL resulting from insufficient detection results could be improved by detecting patterns present in the IRL.

References

1. Abadi, M., et al.: TensorFlow: a system for large-scale machine learning. In: 12th USENIX Symposium on Operating Systems Design and Implementation (OSDI 16), pp. 265–283. USENIX Association, Savannah (2016)
2. Arjovsky, M., Chintala, S., Bottou, L.: Wasserstein generative adversarial networks. In: Precup, D., Teh, Y.W. (eds.) Proceedings of the 34th International Conference on Machine Learning. Proceedings of Machine Learning Research, vol. 70, pp. 214–223. PMLR (2017)
3. Bradbury, J., Merity, S., Xiong, C., Socher, R.: Quasi-recurrent neural networks. arXiv arXiv:1611.01576 (2016)
4. Chen, J., Yi, J.S.K., Kahoush, M., Cho, E.S., Cho, Y.K.: Point cloud scene completion of obstructed building facades with generative adversarial inpainting. Sensors **20**(18), 5029 (2020)
5. Chen, L.-C., Zhu, Y., Papandreou, G., Schroff, F., Adam, H.: Encoder-decoder with atrous separable convolution for semantic image segmentation. In: Ferrari, V., Hebert, M., Sminchisescu, C., Weiss, Y. (eds.) ECCV 2018. LNCS, vol. 11211, pp. 833–851. Springer, Cham (2018). https://doi.org/10.1007/978-3-030-01234-2_49
6. Dai, D., Riemenschneider, H., Schmitt, G., Van Gool, L.: Example-based facade texture synthesis. In: Proceedings of the IEEE International Conference on Computer Vision (ICCV), pp. 1065–1072 (2013)
7. Dehbi, Y., Staat, C., Mandtler, L., Pl, L., et al.: Incremental refinement of facade models with attribute grammar from 3D point clouds. ISPRS Ann. Photogrammetry Remote Sens. Spat. Inf. Sci. **3**, 311 (2016)
8. Goodfellow, I., et al.: Generative adversarial nets. In: Ghahramani, Z., Welling, M., Cortes, C., Lawrence, N.D., Weinberger, K.Q. (eds.) Advances in Neural Information Processing Systems 27, pp. 2672–2680. Curran Associates, Inc. (2014)
9. Graves, A., Fernández, S., Schmidhuber, J.: Multi-dimensional recurrent neural networks. CoRR (2007)
10. Gröger, G., Kolbe, T.H., Czerwinski, A.: OpenGIS CityGML Implementation Specification (City Geography Markup Language). Open Geospatial Consortium Inc., OGC (2007)
11. He, K., Gkioxari, G., Dollar, P., Girshick, R.: Mask R-CNN. In: Proceedings of the IEEE International Conference on Computer Vision (ICCV), pp. 2961–2969 (2017)
12. He, K., Zhang, X., Ren, S., Sun, J.: Deep residual learning for image recognition. In: Proceedings of the IEEE Conference on Computer Vision and Pattern Recognition (CVPR), pp. 770–778 (2016)

13. Hensel, S., Goebbels, S., Kada, M.: Facade reconstruction for textured LoD2 CityGML models based on deep learning and mixed integer linear programming. ISPRS Ann. Photogrammetry Remote Sens. Spat. Inf. Sci., **IV-2/W5**, 37–44 (2019). https://doi.org/10.5194/isprs-annals-IV-2-W5-37-2019

14. Hensel, S., Goebbels, S., Kada, M.: LSTM architectures for facade structure completion. In: Proceedings of the 16th International Joint Conference on Computer Vision, Imaging and Computer Graphics Theory and Applications - Volume 1: GRAPP, pp. 15–24. INSTICC, SciTePress (2021). https://doi.org/10.5220/0010194400150024

15. Hu, H., Wang, L., Zhang, M., Ding, Y., Zhu, Q.: Fast and regularized reconstruction of building facades from street-view images using binary integer programming. ISPRS Ann. Photogrammetry Remote Sens. Spat. Inf. Sci. **V-2-2020**, 365–371 (2020). https://doi.org/10.5194/isprs-annals-V-2-2020-365-2020

16. Huang, J.B., Kang, S.B., Ahuja, N., Kopf, J.: Image completion using planar structure guidance. ACM Trans. Graph. (TOG) **33**(4), 1–10 (2014)

17. Kalchbrenner, N., Danihelka, I., Graves, A.: Grid long short-term memory. arXiv:1507.01526 (2015)

18. Kottler, B., Bulatov, D., Zhang, X.: Context-aware patch-based method for façade inpainting. In: Proceedings of the 15th International Joint Conference on Computer Vision, Imaging and Computer Graphics Theory and Applications - Volume 1: GRAPP, pp. 210–218 (2020)

19. Lin, T.Y., Goyal, P., Girshick, R., He, K., Dollar, P.: Focal loss for dense object detection. In: Proceedings of the IEEE International Conference on Computer Vision (ICCV), pp. 2980–2988 (2017)

20. Mehra, S., Dogra, A., Goyal, B., Sharma, A.M., Chandra, R.: From textural inpainting to deep generative models: an extensive survey of image inpainting techniques. J. Comput. Sci. **16**(1), 35–49 (2020)

21. Mtibaa, F., Nguyen, K.K., Azam, M., Papachristou, A., Venne, J.S., Cheriet, M.: LSTM-based indoor air temperature prediction framework for HVAC systems in smart buildings. Neural Comput. Appl. **32**, 1–17 (2020)

22. Nazeri, K., Ng, E., Joseph, T., Qureshi, F.Z., Ebrahimi, M.: EdgeConnect: generative image inpainting with adversarial edge learning. arXiv:1901.00212 (2019)

23. Redmon, J., Divvala, S., Girshick, R., Farhadi, A.: You only look once: Unified, real-time object detection. In: Proceedings of the IEEE Conference on Computer Vision and Pattern Recognition (CVPR) (2016)

24. Riemenschneider, H., et al.: Irregular lattices for complex shape grammar facade parsing. In: Proceedings of the 2012 IEEE Conference on Computer Vision and Pattern Recognition, pp. 1640–1647 (2012)

25. Salehinejad, H., Sankar, S., Barfett, J., Colak, E., Valaee, S.: Recent advances in recurrent neural networks. arXiv:1801.01078 (2017)

26. Sherstinsky, A.: Fundamentals of recurrent neural network (RNN) and long short-term memory (LSTM) network. Physica D **404**, 132306 (2020)

27. Tan, M., Pang, R., Le, Q.V.: EfficientDet: scalable and efficient object detection. In: Proceedings of the IEEE/CVF Conference on Computer Vision and Pattern Recognition, pp. 10781–10790 (2020)

28. Teboul, O., Kokkinos, I., Simon, L., Koutsourakis, P., Paragios, N.: Shape grammar parsing via reinforcement learning. In: Proceedings of the IEEE Conference on Computer Vision and Pattern Recognition (CVPR), pp. 2273–2280. IEEE (2011)

29. Tobin, J., Fong, R., Ray, A., Schneider, J., Zaremba, W., Abbeel, P.: Domain randomization for transferring deep neural networks from simulation to the real world. In: Proceedings of the 2017 IEEE/RSJ International Conference on Intelligent Robots and Systems (IROS), pp. 23–30 (2017)

30. Tyleček, R., Šára, R.: Spatial pattern templates for recognition of objects with regular structure. In: Weickert, J., Hein, M., Schiele, B. (eds.) GCPR 2013. LNCS, vol. 8142, pp. 364–374. Springer, Heidelberg (2013). https://doi.org/10.1007/978-3-642-40602-7_39
31. Wang, C.Y., Bochkovskiy, A., Liao, H.Y.M.: Scaled-YOLOv4: scaling cross stage partial network. In: Proceedings of the IEEE/CVF Conference on Computer Vision and Pattern Recognition (CVPR), pp. 13029–13038 (2021)
32. Wonka, P., Wimmer, M., Sillion, F., Ribarsky, W.: Instant architecture. ACM Trans. Graph. (TOG) 22(3), 669–677 (2003)
33. Yu, J., Lin, Z., Yang, J., Shen, X., Lu, X., Huang, T.S.: Generative image inpainting with contextual attention. In: Proceedings of the IEEE Conference on Computer Vision and Pattern Recognition (CVPR), pp. 5505–5514 (2018)
34. Yu, J., Lin, Z., Yang, J., Shen, X., Lu, X., Huang, T.S.: Free-form image inpainting with gated convolution. In: Proceedings of the IEEE/CVF International Conference on Computer Vision (ICCV) (2019)
35. Yu, T., et al.: Region normalization for image inpainting. Proc. AAAI Conf. Artif. Intell. **34**(07), 12733–12740 (2020). https://doi.org/10.1609/aaai.v34i07.6967
36. Zhang, D., Wang, D.: Relation classification: CNN or RNN? In: Lin, C.-Y., Xue, N., Zhao, D., Huang, X., Feng, Y. (eds.) ICCPOL/NLPCC -2016. LNCS (LNAI), vol. 10102, pp. 665–675. Springer, Cham (2016). https://doi.org/10.1007/978-3-319-50496-4_60

Human Computer Interaction Theory and Applications

Generating Haptic Sensations over Spherical Surface

Patrick Coe[1,2(✉)] ⬤, Grigori Evreinov[1,2] ⬤, Mounia Ziat[1,2] ⬤, and Roope Raisamo[1,2] ⬤

[1] The Faculty of Information Technology and Communication Sciences, Tampere University, Tampere, Finland
{patrick.coe,grigori.evreinov,roope.raisamo}@tuni.fi

[2] Department of Information Design and Corporate Communication, Bentley University, Waltham, MA, USA
mziat@bentley.edu

Abstract. Haptic imagery, the imagining of haptic sensations in the mind, makes use of and extends human vision. Thus, enabling a better understanding of multi-dimensional sensorimotor information by strengthening space exploration with "seeing by touch." Testing this concept was performed on a spherical surface to optimize the way of generating localized haptic signals and their propagation across the curved surface to generate dynamic movements of perceivable peak vibrations. Through testing of several spherical structure prototypes, it was found that offset actuations can dynamically amplify vibrations at specific locations. A pilot study was followed to understand the impact of haptic stimulation on viewers of video content in a passive VR environment. Results showed a correlation between heart rate and the presented content; complimenting the technical data recorded.

Keywords: High-definition haptics · Tangible mental images · Virtual tactile actuation · Interference maximum · Actuation plate

1 Introduction

Human intellectual and creative potential, as well as the development of perceptual and motor abilities, are all influenced by our visual-based culture [68]. As technology progresses, more advanced features become available for computer users. Great achievements have been made in processing visual information and communication technology. Different types and formats of digital video are becoming more common; emotional components and precise patterns in video, pictures, and audio messages may readily enhance the perceiver's experience. When emotionally rich information is unavailable, blind and visually impaired children often experience severe emotional distress, which can lead to depression and an inhibition in cognitive development. [3,7].

Immersion, interactivity, and imagination have been the focus of Virtual Reality (VR) since 1965, when Ivan Sutherland first proposed the technology [73]. Progress

This work was supported by project Adaptive Multimodal In-Car Interaction (AMICI), funded by Business Finland (grant 1316/31/2021).

A. A. de Sousa et al. (Eds.): VISIGRAPP 2021, CCIS 1691, pp. 43–68, 2023.
https://doi.org/10.1007/978-3-031-25477-2_3

in computer graphics and sound synthesis over the last 50 years has enabled VR systems to achieve fairly realistic rendering and stimulation of the human imagination. That said, the natural empathic ties of humans to other humans and to the world also contributed to their imaginative powers [70]. Moreover, sighted people are eager to live richer interactive experiences through other senses; visual exploration being the easiest way to achieve "theoretical imagination" (for example, Neo learning Kung Fu (haptic imagery) in the Matrix (through vision) [76,77]). Despite these advances in the visual realm, haptic imagery falls far short of what users expect. Most VR systems' haptic sensations pale in comparison to the vast array of haptic qualities that humans can truly detect in the real world [15,19]. From desktop haptics, surface haptics, and wearable haptics to more powerful haptic devices, haptic technology will continue to advance to the point that they are able to simulate physical properties in a natural way and in more details allowing the integration of spatially and temporally discrete sensory inputs [82].

Despite the apparent relevance of haptics in human perception development, spatial visual representations of distance, size, shape, and motion often prevail over haptic perception [62]. As a result, there is a great challenge to propose new ways to induce tactile sensations of spatial objects through dynamical haptic stimulation or modify the visual experience of the user through the use of new haptic technology and materials. Multiple tech companies such as Apple [59] focused on improving of the haptic feedback in their products attesting in an increasing demand for improved tactile feedback.

From curved edges to flexible displays, more innovative and interesting device shape factors are continuously explored [34]. As interfaces and screens become more sophisticated and nonstandard in design, adaptive tactile output will be required for further haptics improvements in consumer products. Tactile click buttons, which could formerly be felt, were quickly phased out in favor of capacitive touchscreen displays, which were also featured in the prototypes detailed in this paper. Our present study focuses on localized haptics on a spherical surface, with the goal of developing haptics with various geometries. Understanding how enhanced haptic signals may be used to introduce high quality haptics is equally important as form factors develop and we move away from standard flat displays.

We utilized a simpler method over previous studies to produce localized points of actuation in our study. Although the employment of a large number of actuators is useful, it is impractical due to the added complexity and cost. Furthermore, any system that requires constant surface monitoring may be challenging to execute outside of a laboratory context. We want to address the aforementioned concerns by lowering the number of actuators necessary to generate a localized point of vibration while determining the offsets required for a specific material.

When engaging with graphical objects via physical actions, humans mix the visual information prompted by the tangible interface, such as keystrokes on a keyboard, mouse buttons, or another haptic device. Force feedback in a personal space, in direct contact with the surface [14], is often used to verify and predict visual inputs, to prevent a collision, or present more specific physical information about the external object subject to the interaction. Nonetheless, force feedback parameters can only change within a restricted range of magnitude gradient and duration (length of tactile stimuli). Furthermore, force feedback is referred to as shared forces in most haptic interfaces that are based on direct finger contact (those tangential to the skin). When skin travels laterally across a sensitive surface, the pressure generated (65–100g) provides a contact force that causes orthogonal skin deformation (normal to the surface). The human sense of touch, on the other hand, is a more complex analyser of processing dynamic arrays of force vectors (e.g., when distinguishing the concave and convex components of surfaces). This is evident when haptic textures and objects are reproduced using 3D haptic instruments [13], but it is not yet commonly applicable to surface haptics on touchscreens [41], when ordinary haptic exciters are employed. As a result, dynamically actuated virtual vibration, sources of vector force traveling across the display surface, can be used to convey a higher bandwidth of information to the user in order to display more complex vector graphic haptic images than primitive down sampling based reliefs [21,22,40,44,47,48,56,69].

Actively explored touch surfaces provide a rich haptic experience to users by giving kinesthetic, proprioceptive, and cutaneous information. To control each "tactile pixel" (or taxel) spread out in a two-dimensional array, the approach often employed for tactile modeling of objects and their surfaces was adopted [75]. Taxels have been utilized for sparse low-resolution approximation of interactive surfaces and virtual stages rather than high-definition haptic simulation of items [13,44,48]. However, using visual perception concepts [69,71] to replicate the most sophisticated tactile display technology [79] may not work for haptic visualization since a surface can be defined by multiple physical qualities. These must be perceived, identified, and understood as a static, dynamic, or virtual (cross-section) array of identical pieces using haptic imagination. When investigating and engaging directly or indirectly with virtual surfaces, a range of technical techniques have been investigated for surface modeling and control of attributes (mechanical and acoustic) [20,22], simulating shapes [20,21,27], texture [69] properties such as stiffness, curvedness [27,35], friction [55], and compliance/elasticity [51].

It has already been shown that without curvature, the properties of vibrotactile interference can be achieved on a flat surface [42]. Taking advantage of the properties of wave interference it may be possible to create feelable precise high definition tactile points traveling across a surface with variable curvature leading to an apparent tactile motion [6,60]. This indicates that a high definition vibrotactile display would require fewer actuators (Fig. 2). This might be accomplished by accurately offsetting any number of provided actuations in sync from exciters attached to the actuation surface of contact, of which can also be curved. At the exact point of contact, the ensuing point of constructive wave interference would considerably magnify the amount of vibration signal over the ambient noise (Fig. 4). If the actuation offsets required to dynamically produce a point of maximum constructive wave interference at every point traveling over the surface are known, a matrix of values may be recorded and utilized to stimulate apparent tactile motion through inducing haptic imagination.

A music instructor encouraging a student to play the piano on their desk is an example of haptic imagination. Without manipulating the piano keys, the learner may picture and feel the music composition to be played. "The hands-on tactile exploration is the gateway to haptic imagination," as said by R. Schwaen. [66].

We may augment this notion, for example, by enabling virtual moveable haptic vibrations that can be felt traveling over the surface by consecutively activating the appropriate offsets that produce a feelable moving point of maximum interference. This vibration interference position might be dynamically positioned in order to show information to a user in an unusual manner. Tactile data may be moved around a user's hand, or the user could be told to focus on or follow a moving virtual actuator.

Previous work in this area of haptic research has demonstrated a similar strategy of induce locations of virtual actuation across a given surface by utilizing wave characteristics. Enferad and others [17], for example, who worked on establishing a controlled localized point of stimulation utilizing voltage modulated signals to activate piezoelectric patches over an aluminum beam. They accomplished superposition mostly through voltage phase modulation. Charles Hudin and his colleagues used time-reversal wave focusing to solve a similar challenge [33]. During the focusing step, a vibrometer calibrated the time-reversal wave, which was then followed by an actuation signal from an array of 32 actuators glued to the bottom perimeter of a glass plate. This worked well in terms of producing a precise, localized point of haptic stimulation. However, the usage of a closed loop control system creates substantial issues since it limits its practical application when a touch point in a consumer product is masked or repressed by a finger.

2   Concept and Design of the Spherical Haptic Display

To put the previously described design concept to the test (Fig. 1 [11]), we created a mockup of a spherical haptic display (Figs. 2–6 [11]). This preliminary design is designed to investigate the viability of virtual force actuation, as well as various methods of optimizing the configuration of actuator assembly in relation to these forces. The architecture and quantity of actuators, the characteristics of the virtual sources of vector force, and the arrangement of elementary haptic signals may all be changed to optimize the system. The prototype will also be used to assess the propagation of constructive wave interference across the curved display surface. Measurements from similar research have shown that by controlling the offset of several signals, it is feasible to obtain precise localization of enhanced vibration at a chosen point of contact [9, 12].

We employed a special combination of strong unidirectional voice coil actuators to produce a virtual vibration source at a spot on the curved touch display surface (Tectonics and Lofelt). Figure 1 [11] depicts a concept known as the Volumetric Tactile Display (VTD). It is made up of constructive wave interference that propagates sequentially to the places of contact with the skin. By combining geographically and temporally distinct sensory inputs, the resultant point of localized vibration is capable of correctly mediating haptic signals.

We created two dome-shaped prototypes to collect preliminary data. The goal of each prototype was to study several ways of localisation that all aimed at the same goal. The first sphere was concerned with wave interference, while the second was concerned with vector force concepts. Before attempting to merge both approaches, each prototype was successfully tested independently. Both prototypes were made within a 116 mm diameter polycarbonate dome. Wires were routed from the inside of both domes to an external motor controller (L298). The motor controller uses an Arduino DUE, which was chosen for its high speed of 84 Mhz, allowing for high accuracy outputs and data collecting at 5.3 μm intervals. A copper strip was utilized for exact calibration of vector forces propagating over the Spherical Haptic Surface (SHS) from the configuration of

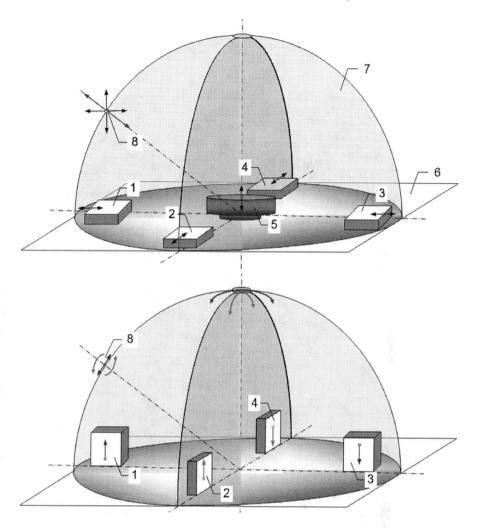

Fig. 1. The variants of haptic actuators assembly affixed to the actuation plane. 1-5 - Lofelt L5 (1-4) actuators and Tectonic exciter TEAX25C10-8HS (5). Red arrows indicate linear motion, while green arrows indicate angular motion. Black arrows indicate actuator movement. 8 - Represents a targeted point of increased magnitude or vibration; 6 - an actuation plate; 7 - a spherical haptic surface [11]. (Color figure online)

unidirectional actuators (where micro-displacements over touch surface are sensed with the MicroSense sensor).

The first dome was used to investigate the possibility of wave interference between seismic signals generated by actuators directly attached to a spherical haptic surface. It was made up of four Tectonic actuators (TEAX1402-8) that were joined from the inside and put at the vertices of the tetrahedron (Figs. 3 and 2 [11]). The controlled offset of several actuation impulses was to be used to localize the vector force at the appropriate

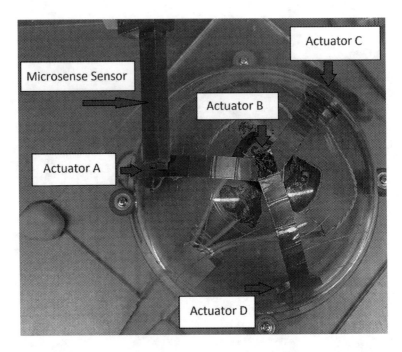

Fig. 2. Top view of the first spherical prototype, with centimeter lines on copper tape for sensor placement [11].

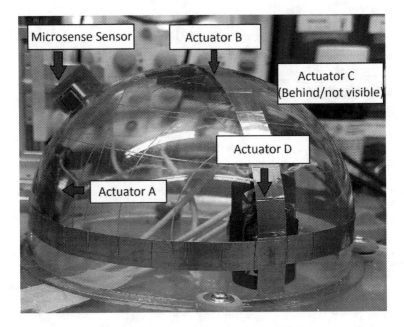

Fig. 3. A side view of the first spherical prototype with centimeter lines on copper tape for sensor placement [11].

point of contact over SHS. The controlled offset actuation intended to move the point at which constructive wave interference occurred over the hemisphere's surface.

Fig. 4. Top view of the second spherical prototype, showing centimeter markings for sensor location. This structure is made up of four Lofelt L5 actuators and a single Tectonic exciter TEAX25C10-8HS attached to a Haptic Actuation Plate (HAP) that transfers seismic waves over a spherical surface [11]. (Color figure online)

In the second dome (Figs. 5 and 4 [11]), we concentrated on putting the ideas of a shifting magnitude to the test. These effects were achieved by altering the magnitudes of lateral and vertical motions. The installed more powerful next-generation Lofelt technology L5 actuators were attached to the actuation plate along the X and Y axes, while a strong Tectonic exciter was utilized to actuate vertically in the Z-axis direction. We intended to use this design to increase the resultant force of seismic signals that initially interfered in orthogonal directions across from an actuation plate by applying various

Fig. 5. View of the second spherical prototype from the side, with red markings every two cm for measurement placement [11].

magnitudes of actuation in the vertical and horizontal axes. Nonetheless, as shown in Fig. 1 [11], unidirectional haptic actuators may be combined in a variety of ways to provide both linear (red) and angular (green) force momentum (torques).

It was discovered during the creation of the actuation plate that hydrophobic materials (such as Gorilla-glass, Teflon, and silicone) might impact the perception of convexity vs. concavity at the point of finger contact. The thickness of a material, such as glass, has an effect on the vibration that is perceived [80]. The outcome is promising for further validation via a user study. This paves the way for new methods of modeling volumetric forms in virtual and augmented reality. As a result of the combination of novel material characteristics and actuation technologies, we can produce complex haptic sensations that are required for developing haptic imagination in both healthy persons and those with perceptual difficulties.

Aside from physical dimensions, personal exploratory behavioral characteristics will have an influence on interpreting numerous tactile information obtained while interacting with SHS during the perception of mental representations of the items shown. As a result, a user-centered approach will be employed to illustrate the issues and limits of the suggested interaction strategies (Fig. 6 [11]). The spherical surface, as depicted, compliments the hand's form. Tactile feedback may now spread over the palm and fingers.

We concentrated on the impact of varied magnitudes of lateral and vertical motions while designing the second dome. Wave interference existed and happened moving across the surface due to its form, however the entire structure was moved by the vertical and horizontal movement created by connected actuators. As a result, distinct magnitudes of actuation in the vertical and horizontal axes might be used to amplify a point of maximal vibration. These magnitude maxima might potentially be used with wave interference maximum to enhance tactile signals and focus given vibration received on the surface.

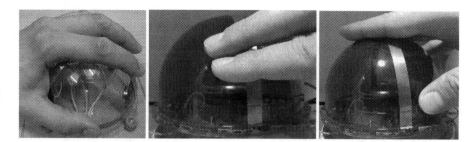

Fig. 6. Top: A relaxed hand is put over a spherical prototype to demonstrate a comfortable position. Middle: Exploratory behavior displayed by just touching the finger pads. Bottom: Four fingers extended straight ahead, as if attempting to feel the smooth edge of a surface [11].

3   Methods

We investigated two ways for determining the ideal offset in establishing a point of peak magnitude vibration approximately five centimeters from the hemisphere's base. This was determined by going vertically over the sphere's surface from the first actuator (A, Figs. 2 and 3 [11]). The first approach involved evaluating a variety of offset vibrations on the sphere between a starting pair of actuators (AB). After determining the offset necessary to achieve maximum vibration interference between these two actuators, we tested a third actuator by offsetting it against the existing offset pulse of the first two actuators (ABC). This procedure was repeated for the fourth actuator, offsetting it against the prior three actuators' offset pulses (ABCD).

MicroSense sensors were used to collect data (Model 5622-LR Probe, with 0.5 mm x 2.5 mm sensor). Because it is a capacitive sensor, a copper strip was needed to be put across the surface of the sphere in order for measurements to be taken. The sensor has an accuracy of 0–200 μm and noise of 3.44 μm-rms at 5 kHz, and it has been amplified using Gauging Electronics up to 10 V and attenuated to a range of 0 to 5 V to be compatible with the Arduino's analogue input. The sensor was positioned to track the curvature of the sphere.

4   Results

4.1   Constructive Wave Interference

Figure 7 indicates that the addition of the third actuator (C) greatly increased displacement while the addition of the fourth actuator (D) introduced just a little rise. A probable constructive wave interference occurred between the first two actuators A and B, with actuator A triggering 2 ms before actuator B, resulting in a displacement of 183 μm. The vibration was raised to 257 μm by triggering the third actuator 3 ms after actuator

B. However, activating the fourth actuator resulted in a very little increase in peak vibration. Before actuator A raised the vibration to 276 μm, the fourth actuator (D) engaged for 24 ms. Nonetheless, actuator (D) can have a good effect on the total vibration. The vibration was decreased to 203 μm by delivering a deconstructive pulse 19 ms before actuator A.

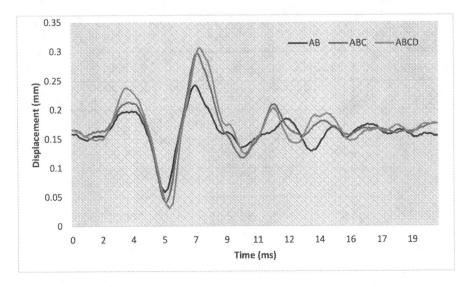

Fig. 7. Measured maximum displacement using offsets for two (AB), three (ABC) and four (ABCD) actuators.

We conducted more extensive testing because we were unsure whether the actuators in a spherical setup would interact with each other in the same way as those in a flat actuation plane. We tried out every possible combination of offsets between each of the four actuators for 15 ms before and after each other. This process's optimum offset resulted in a maximum displacement of 276 μm, which is equal to the prior result when all four actuators were triggered.

Figure 8 displays the maximum displacement when the full range offset sweep test is used to determine the offsets needed to achieve a maximum displacement. The discovered offsets varied, showing that there are numerous ways to obtain a peak vibration maximum. We also discovered that the offset is the consequence of actuators (B) and (C) being triggered 5 ms after actuator (A), and actuator (D) being triggered 9 ms after actuator (C). Although we consider the data gained by cycling through every conceivable combination offers highly precise offsets, the approach is hampered by the length of time necessary to measure all combinations as well as the volume of data that must be collected.

Based on this information, we predict that, while some waves will most likely pass over the surface, the semi-flexible connection to the base implies that actuators would most likely pull the entire object. We must consider not just the delay of wave propagation, but also the movement of the entire dome. We must test the optimal magnitudes

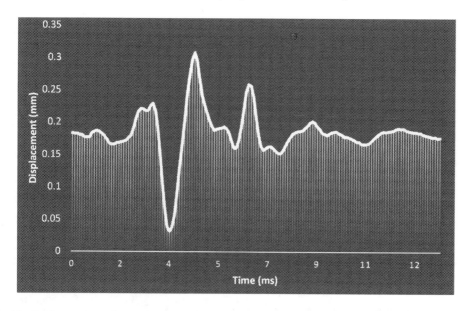

Fig. 8. Measured maximum displacement using offsets when scanning through all four actuators simultaneously.

and phases of each signal applied to each actuator in addition to determining the needed offset delays.

4.2   Combination of Peak Displacement Magnitudes

To remedy the earlier issue with wave propagation, we conducted additional testing by mixing different actuation magnitudes with offset triggering. We utilized the second prototype for this test (Figs. 4 and 5) featuring Lofelt L5 actuators for X and Y vibrations and a central Tectonic actuator for Z axis movement. In particular, we activated the Lofelt L5 actuators across the X-axis for 10 ms and the center actuator for 1 ms. This arrangement should minimize the magnitude of the central actuator's actuation in comparison to the Lofelt L5 actuators. We experimented with various offsets to calculate the optimal vibration offset (Fig. 10). The data displayed in Fig. 9 exhibits a pattern until roughly the third point, when the sphere's angle begins to become more horizontal. The practical effect of this tendency is that we are not only feeling forces attributable to wave interference from vertically positioned actuators, but also vertical displacement of the whole hemisphere caused by horizontally placed actuators. We would need to measure distinct magnitudes for a fixed offset rather than a changing offset in the future. Magnitude may be changed by modifying the size of the pulse or the voltage applied to a certain actuator. Additional testing should be performed to determine the range of these modifications and their impact on the resultant vibration.

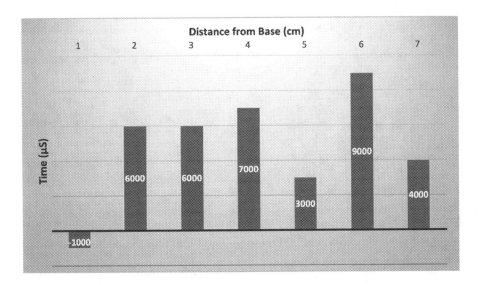

Fig. 9. Offset required for maximum peak vibrations for Lofelt L5 actuators with and without Tectonic actuator (center coil).

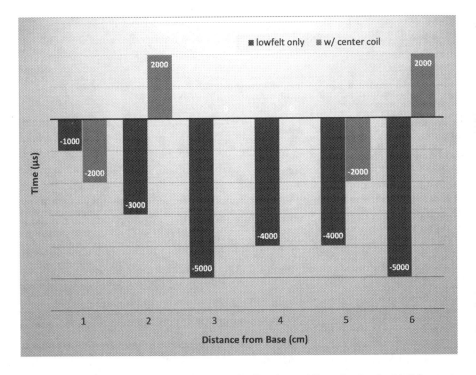

Fig. 10. Time offset required for maximum peak vibrations while activating Lofelt L5 actuator (1) for 10 ms and tectonic actuator (5) for 1 ms.

5   Providing Enhanced Immersion to Video Content Application Pilot Study

An initial pilot study has been implemented to understand the initial effectiveness of the spherical display. Haptic sequences were induced over a tactile spherical surface which supported the hands. Participants watched a 1-minute video tested under two conditions: with and in the absence of accompanying haptic signals. Their heart rate was measured during the experiment. Results revealed a significant difference in heart rate data between the two conditions. Moreover, a heart rate response has allowed to reveal significant difference between viewers with respect to visual content and haptification ($t(119) = 31.4$ vs $t(119) = 11.7$ ($p < .0001$)). This leads us to believe that an enhanced immersion and affective experience can be achieved through the addition of a haptic channel to audio-visual content that already are shared over video streaming platforms and social media.

5.1   Pilot Study Background

Haptic theater enhancements, such as D-Box Motion Effect chairs [49] are already in use in multiple locations worldwide to enhance the viewing experience by adding haptic signals to 3D visuals. Being synchronized by the action depicted in the film, the chair's effects range from soft vibration to a hard jolt backwards if, for example, a character is hit. But what about home viewers that stream videos online through platforms such as YouTube or Vimeo? People share their life experience through these tools; yet rich emotional personal experiences cannot be shared in full as other senses such as smell, taste, and touch are missing. Our focus is on the haptic channel, which has been in use already for nearly 200 years [24,57] to share, communicate, and enhance human sensations.

Haptic signals directly connected with kinesthetic sense and motor imagination are strong enough to provoke premotor or ideomotor actions (the cognitive representation of an action) [32]. Additionally, to induce or initiate haptic apprehension in observed visual actions, haptic information has to be personally and emotionally significant and linked to previous human experience.

Human vision is not only limited to visual feedback but also helps with navigation and locomotion, contributing to human proprioception. As in hunter-gatherers, human vision has been developed to predict behavior of any items, including motion, through the total control of the personal space [28]. Proprioception is the main component of the afferent flow that integrate information from different modalities to support adequate human response and behavior. Cross-modal information transfer help to more efficiently perceive and interact with an external space surrounding the body [23].

In this work, we would like to explore haptification of visual content supposed to enhance emotional effects in relation to the activity of an actor in the dramatic situation of an activity that is able to elicit fear, anxiety, or general sympathetic activation [50]. More specifically, we asked participants to watch a video clip of down-hill biking as the dramatic competition scenario while interacting with a spherical haptic surface (SHS) [11].

There are different systems for haptic effects based on haptification model [63], plethora of video clips have not been yet investigated sufficiently with respect to such a way of affective visualization. In particular, haptics does not yet integrate with dynamic visualization in multimedia, even though both are naturally and tightly connected in the ontogenesis of perception [39] and development of intermodal perception and imagination [74].

The scenario that we are interested in is users watching video clips, movies, and other dynamic art media. The viewer is a relatively passive observer and cannot directly impact to the digital content. The viewer's state of mind and video content, which are closely intertwined in human imagination, contribute to the immersion and transition of the passive observer into active participant of the visual scene, while the sensory motor activity manifests in the form of emotions and physiological reactions. To induce human imagination, video content is often accompanying with background audio (soundtrack).

5.2   Experimental Design

The experiment combined visual content presented through VR headset enhanced with a new haptic concept that combine spherical and planar sensations [10–12]. We also expect that the haptification [63] of visual content is a natural way to support affective visualization [82].

Participants. Six people participated in this study. None of the participants reported skin or cardiovascular issues.

Apparatus. The experiment is designed around a Microsoft Surface Go tablet (Fig. 11) that was used as a Haptic Actuation Plate (HAP) and was chosen for its ease of software and hardware implementation. The Spherical Haptic Surface (SHS) consists of a 116 mm diameter polycarbonate dome (Fig. 11) attached to the surface of the tablet. Parameters for local interference maximum (LIM) of seismic signals over the touchscreen tablet and propagating across SHS were determined in previous studies [10, 11].

The TEAX1402-8 actuators attached to the top of the tablet display, as well as TEAX25C10-8/HS affixed to the base of the SHS [11], are designed to strike the surface at a predetermined offset from each other. The offset creates a point of increased vibration where the seismic shear waves interfere. This allows us to create discernable, feelable, and dynamic haptic LIM signals moving over either touchscreen or other surfaces properly affixed to and being in mechanical contact with HAP. The method described can be explored in further detail in previous works. [12].

An Arduino Due was used to store the predetermined offset locations as well as the output sequence created for this experiment. Output signals were sent to an external MX1508 motor drive module driven at 7.5 V. Silicone molded legs were attached to the bottom of the tablet to provide vibration isolation. A Huawei Band 6 watch was used to track heart rate data with ECG comparable accuracy [67] that are logged in 5-second intervals.

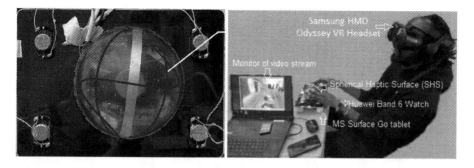

Fig. 11. Left: An arrangement of Tectonic actuators and SHS over tablet touchscreen. Blue arrows indicate virtual haptic scanpaths Right: A participant interacting with Spherical haptic surface affixed to MS Surface Go tablet during the experiment. (Color figure online)

Video Content and Haptic Actuation. A Samsung head-mounted display (HMD) Odyssey VR headset [64] was used to display the visual content that consisted of one-minute video, created from publicly available online footage and was converted to match the requirements of the display. The output signals of the actuators that generate the haptic cues were synchronized with the actions in the video footage resulting in haptic motion sequences matching the motion presented in the visual scenes. The haptification (vibration sequences) has been manually designed using video footage timings where each second of footage was visually analyzed to associate tactile sense with objects that are in proximity or visual periphery.

6 Experimental Procedure

Participants were instructed to first put the Huawei Band 6 watch on their left wrist. They were then asked to put the VR headset on, wear the headphones, and adjust the volume to a comfortable level. To start exploring the video, they were asked to rest both hands on the SHS.

A one-minute clip of down-hill biking was used (Fig. 12). This clip was played 20 times. Ten of these playbacks were with the haptic (WH) signals synchronized with the video content, while the remaining ten playbacks were with no haptification (NH), resulting in two experimental conditions.

After the experiment, participants were asked to complete the NASA-Task Load Index (TLX) questionnaire [31] along with additional questions to help us understand the effectiveness of device. These questions are shown in Table 1.

7 Results

Objective Results. We can assume participants likely had different experiences biking, ways of thinking, temperaments and possibly even moods during the test. Therefore, we cannot expect the same response from viewers to specific visual content and haptic stimulation. Nevertheless, heart rate scores have been measured 12 times and grouped

Fig. 12. Key dramatic footage at seconds 5, 24, 36, 40, 41, 43, 45, 50, 52.

Table 1. Questionnaire questions.

Did you perceive a local and/or moving vibration?
On a scale from 1–5 how well did you perceive the Localized vibration?
Are you prone to motion Sickness in VR?
If yes, did the vibration Worsen or alleviate your symptoms?
In general, which did you Prefer. The experience with or without the vibration?
In what devices do you think This would be best suited? Why?
What benefit could Localized haptification provide to an existing device?

based on the Pearson correlation coefficient $r > 0.83$ ($p < 0.001$) and $r < 0.8$ ($p < 0.001$) over all (12) presented footage.

The heart rate response has revealed significant difference between viewers with respect to visual content and haptification. In all situations observed over footage, with all participants, we see a significant consistent difference between instances when the haptic signals were enabled (WH) vs. when the haptic signals were disabled (NH) (Fig. 13). Paired Samples 2-tailed t-test revealed significant difference within the group $r = .9023$, $t(59) = -2.98$, $p = .02$, 95% CI(WH/NH) = [82/84, 75/77]. When haptic signals were enabled, we have observed a marked decrease in heart rate for the entire video sequence.

When looking at heartrate data with haptic signals enabled, we see a gradual increase from the start of the sequence up until a peak at the 30 s mark. If we compare this with the data, we have collected when haptics was disabled (NH), we see a far less pronounced synchronization $r = 0.688$ ($p < .05$) in average with the events on screen. That is to say that the data shows an increased correlation when the haptic display is in use (WH) $r = 0.90$ ($p < .0001$) in average.

Subjective Results

The NASA-TLX Questionnaire. The NASA-TLX questionnaire allows the evaluation of six sub-scales: the mental demand, physical demand, temporal demand, own performance, effort, and frustration the results of the TLX are summarized in Fig. 14.

Participants responded that the workload demand was of concern, with an average response of 50 on the NASA-TLX scale. For several of our participants this was their

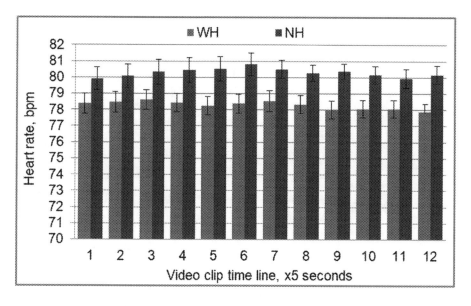

Fig. 13. A cardiovascular response in participants.

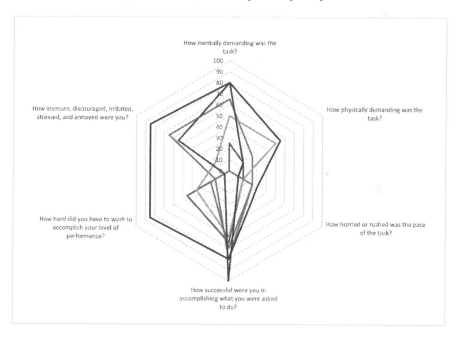

Fig. 14. Radar chart of all TLX responses.

first experience wearing a VR headset. Otherwise, with an average score of 76, participants felt that they were able to successfully complete the task they were given.

Post-experiment Questionnaire. When asked if they could feel the presence of localized moving vibrations, all participants confirmed that they could. Their ability to perceive localized vibrations obtained an average score of 3.125 out of 5 (5 being the best). 62.5% of the participants reported that they preferred watching the VR video using the SHS.

Half of our participants answered that they had felt motion sickness during the experiment. Of those who felt motion sickness, half claimed that the use of the SHS alleviated their symptoms.

Open-ended questions revealed that participants think that the SHS can be used for Gamepads to improved games interactivity, for professional training for drivers and pilots, and in-car displays to eliminate distractions.

7.1   Pilot Study Discussion

Artists have been developing the expression of motion in drawings for thousands of years. To illustrate motion, we can refer to the artists of the Lascaux caves who portrayed animals upon the walls with multiple heads, legs, and tails. The superimposition and matching successive images (e.g., juxtaposition of colors) have been used by many artists in a different ways to achieve a similar result. The visualization of dynamic motion is followed by a long tradition of motion visualization throughout the history of visual art [53,57]. The impression of movement in a still image can bring about an emotional experience. As mentioned by Barry Ackroyd "It can bring you to tears, and take you to places unimaginable" [1]. In modern cinema, it might be thought that we can only assess the meaning of audio in movies when a soundtrack has been interrupted. On the contrary, thanks to imagination, the soundtrack is often able to fully compensate the lack of visual peripheral immersion in scenes.

The collected data showed to us a significant difference between two conditions of the presence or absence the haptic information concerning signals accompanying in sync with visual content viewing with the VR headset. Furthermore, the relative accuracy at which heart rates increased to match the viewed activity on the screen was prominent with the haptic enhancement relying on SHS. This falls in-line with existing research on heart rate variability in virtual reality immersion [50]. The assumption would be that the participants are greater immersed when receiving physical sense of contact in connection with the audio-visual content.

Seeing that the use of the haptic signals subjectively may have reduced symptoms of motion sickness, we can assume that the experience may have been more immersive. Giving participants accurate haptic enhancement may have decreased the cognitive load of what would be an audio-visual only experience. Similarly Liu et al. have also found that the introduction of haptics can be used to reduce virtual reality sickness [46].

A SHS with localized dynamic haptic signals moving in sync with visual events of scenes may be the key to better immersion. While our current study was focused on the use of the SHS to improve the VR experience, the technology involved could be implemented in a wide variety of devices to enhance the user contact experience.

7.2   Pilot Study Conclusion

The hypothesis that we set to explore was shown to be valid. Yes, localized dynamic haptic signals can support affective visualization. Participants were eager and excited to try out the Spherical Haptic Surface. Even better, they were able to see and understand possible use cases for this technology in modern devices. The data we collected contained other captured sensor information, including SPO2 levels and stress levels. In the future we would like to further parse this data out so that we can get a better understanding of how this data might support our results.

The next step would be to see how a SHS might aid in the creation of visual experiences without visual data, by inducing imagination by haptic signals. How would the dynamic haptic signals affect our audio only experiences, or haptic symbolic patterns (tactons) only experiences? The use of emerging haptic technologies needs to be studied in depth to understand how they should be implemented to improve our daily interaction through computing devices.

Our contributions are as follows: We investigated the subjective perception of the video content enhanced with haptic signals dynamically presented in motion over spherical haptic surface to the palms; We found that haptic signals moving in sync with video content had a significant effect on the participant's heart rate.

8   Discussion and Future Work

A wide spectrum of users would be able to engage with the high-fidelity spherical display. The sphere has a natural shape on which a user may rest their hands for lengthy periods of time. As we continue to have access to a wider range of interactive technology, we will need to investigate new intuitive techniques of feedback and engagement.

Our visual culture has a significant influence on human intellectual and creative capacity, as well as the development of perceptual and motor skills [38]. Despite the significance of haptics in the evolution of human perception, visual information tends to prevail over haptic perception after spatial visual representations of distance, size, shape, and motion have been formed [6,43]. Much of the visual content currently available is often inaccessible to blind and visually impaired people [37]. Learning is frequently found to increase with the help of visual feedback, leaving persons with visual impairment suffering in courses. Fortunately, it has been demonstrated that the use of haptic feedback can help to bridge the gap between visual and tactile learning.

The use of haptics in education may be broadened to help all students who are compelled and linked to a subject, for example, by constructing a bridge between the sciences and physical reality. David Grow's work on educational robots has yielded successful outcomes in this area [29] as well as by Michael Pantelios [58] with input gloves and force-feedback devices. Much research available [8,25,30,54] would imply that incorporating haptics into the educational environment at all levels can boost student learning. A spherical surface, such as the one we're testing, can give a long-lasting polycarbonate surface that can sustain heavy, frequent use. It also gives kids with a unique surface to explore. It is feasible to combine it with a spherical projection [26,81,83] over the surface, displaying an interactive picture or video that may be explored via tactile feedback.

Because we do not limit our notion to any size and hope to be able to repeat our findings in larger and smaller spherical shapes, we open up the concept of spherical haptics to a wide range of applications. In place of an analog control stick on a gaming controller, we propose a haptic hemisphere. Feedback, in addition to giving accurate input, may be modified to produce a number of effects. For example, the texture of a game may vary as you go through uneven terrain, or the localization of feedback could reveal the location of an adversary. We may picture a bigger sphere being used to precisely manage heavy machinery in 3D space, such as a crane lifting a concrete slab. A spherical display in the center of a round table might be utilized as an interactive map to assist a team in collaborating with localized feedback offering extra information to prevent visual overload. Localized input might alert a taskforce to the presence of subsurface structures or other areas of interest.

Manufacturing technology are always evolving. We are moving away from the strict constraints of consumer electronics design, as the continued trend of miniaturization, as well as the development of flexible displays and innovative molded integrated circuits, means that products may now assume any imagined shape or form. Many user interfaces, such as a mouse, gamepad, or even a car steering wheel, already include significant portions with substantial curvature. We should be able to enhance the bandwidth accessible to the user by providing vibration that can be localized at any point across these surfaces, allowing us to offer new, more natural engagement cues.

To go further, we are aware that existing virtual reality headsets provide credible visual input but have yet to provide high-fidelity haptic feedback to a large number of consumers. Incorporating this improved realism into present controllers might provide a new degree of immersion to current technology [2].

There is also the possibility of using such a spherical gadget in public places. The extra benefit of accurate tactile feedback might not only make an information kiosk more generally accessible, but also assist users in navigating the device in a loud setting such as a mall [18].

Surprisingly, our recent research discovers that the offsets required to produce localized vibration locations occur within milliseconds of each other. This means that it may be feasible to swiftly and progressively trigger various offsets to generate several focus points that appear to be synchronous. This would open up a new channel for the development of haptic patterns, as well as the development of haptic imagination.

The ultimate objective of this study is to create a perceivable moveable actuation that can be mediated to any position on the spherical surface. What we'd call a virtual haptic actuator. We would need to look into this more to find the best combinations that provide the most effective (and immediately recognizable) numerous afferent flows, increasing in intensity to a specific spot or along edges around the sphere's surface. We would also need to investigate how wave interference can be combined with different magnitude combinations to increase the precision and force of a given vibration across the surface of the sphere, as well as how perceptual interference of other receptive fields can affect fingertip tactile sensation. [45].

Intermediate materials have been shown to improve an object's sensation of touch. Auto body shops, for example, have utilized cellophane film to evaluate polishing on cars [65]. Additionally, the Touch Enhancing Pad [61], a patented instrument consisting of lubricant placed between two thin plastic sheets can help identify malignancies in breast tissue. As a consequence, it would be worthwhile to experiment with various materials in order to improve the perceptible localized input in our haptic environments.

As this study progresses, we will have a greater knowledge of the use cases that this developing approach may bring to users.

9   Future Applications

Spherical interfaces do exist [4,5,16,72,78], nonetheless, they are not widely used. The suggested technology for high-fidelity haptic feedback offers up several options for future touch interaction. Because the sphere's shape adapts to the hand in its natural resting posture [36,52] it may be utilized as a generic computing interface with rich tangible information that can be used for long periods of time.

Hidden or veiled entities and deeper structures of a palpated substance, whether biological (tumor) or physical (defect inspection), can be increased with localized haptic input while investigating medical images. Similarly, the basic user interface might be improved, such as allowing a user to feel and pick icons on a desktop that are beneath a document they are working on without having to minimize or switch windows.

The spherical surface needs a significantly reduced range of motion to engage with, which might be advantageous for anyone suffering from a movement-impairing injury or sickness. High-fidelity feedback can also assist persons with little or no eyesight in navigating an operating system by employing detailed haptic images.

We don't consider the spherical interface as being restricted in size. A bigger child-sized spherical interface might enable children to study instructional content in a more engaging manner. An adult-sized spherical display may serve as a kiosk at a mall, presenting information that, on a visual-only flat display, can be confounding, such as orientation or direction. A big sphere might serve as an interface in the center of a circular meeting table, allowing people to collaborate. Meetings are frequently stopped to address minor matters, such as informing a coworker that a file has been sent or that they need to slip out. This information might be transmitted utilizing high-definition haptics, which would eliminate unwanted interruptions.

A haptic spherical interface also opens up intriguing new possibilities for enabling secure entrance into a gadget. A passcode, for example, predicated on recognizing localized light-pressure patterns, may be actively moved around the surface while still being identified by localization. Although the input pattern would stay constant, the constant change of the physical location would make capturing the passcode by a third party challenging. From the outside, each physical entry of the passcode would appear to be unique.

Overall, we envision a broad range of applications that can benefit from the usage of a high-fidelity spherical haptic interface. Unlike many consumer interfaces already on the market, we see the spherical haptic interface as extremely customizable and open to a wide range of design use cases.

10   Conclusions

We discovered that offset actuations may be employed to enhance vibrations at specified spots on a spherical surface based on objective measurements of constructive interference of spherical structure prototypes. These magnifications can be achieved through a combination of two methods: first, through wave interference, in which we can use the properties of constructive wave interference to create an amplified point on the surface, and second, through the combination of peak displacement magnitudes, in which different forces are applied to an object's X, Y, and Z axes to increase forces felt at a specific point across the surface. The current study shows that a localized vibration effect may be reproduced over a curved surface. Second, using magnitude combinations, we acquired preliminary data indicating that increased amplitude has an impact at a given position over the surface.

In this study, we discovered that once offsets are located and set, the subsequent output is very constant. Localization offsets should only need to be collected once for a particular actuator setup, which is critical for sustainability. It has also been established that the usage of numerous installed actuators compensates for observed losses owing to attenuation of individual actuators.

When compared to existing global non-localized vibrations that generate a muddled sensation, the amount of localization exhibited has the potential to boost consumers' immersion in XR settings. This field of dispersed haptic resolution can be likened to the fields of optical and auditory propagation. Improvements in haptic fidelity, like improvements in other sensory modalities, aim to improve the user experience.

The utilization of a virtual vibration point over three-dimensional curved constructions is demonstrated in this paper. When producing high-fidelity haptics, this may enable the use of fewer actuators in a variety of feedback interfaces.

References

1. Ackroyd, B.: But, is it art? (June 2021). www.britishcinematographer.co.uk/but-is-it-art/
2. Al-Sada, M., Jiang, K., Ranade, S., Piao, X., Höglund, T., Nakajima, T.: Hapticserpent: A wearable haptic feedback robot for VR, pp. 1–6 (April 2018). https://doi.org/10.1145/3170427.3188518
3. Barresi, J., Moore, C.: Intentional relations and social understanding. Behav. Brain Sci. **19**, 107–122 (1996). https://doi.org/10.1017/S0140525X00041790
4. Benko, H., Wilson, A., Balakrishnan, R.: Sphere: Multi-touch interactions on a spherical display, pp. 77–86 (January 2008). https://doi.org/10.1145/1449715.1449729
5. Bolton, J., Kim, K., Vertegaal, R.: Snowglobe: A spherical fish-tank VR display, pp. 1159–1164 (January 2011). https://doi.org/10.1145/1979742.1979719
6. Burtt, H.E.: Tactual illusions of movement. J. Exp. Psychol. **2**(5), 371–385 (1917). https://doi.org/10.1037/h0074614
7. Chartrand, T.L., Bargh, J.A.: The chameleon effect: the perception-behavior link and social interaction. J. Pers. Soc. Psychol. **76**(6), 893 (1999)
8. Christodoulou, S., Garyfallidou, D., Gavala, M., Ioannidis, G., Papatheodorou, T., Stathi, E.: Haptic devices in virtual reality used for education: Designing and educational testing of an innovative system (September 2005)

9. Coe, P., Evreinov, G., Raisamo, R.: Gel-Based Haptic Mediator For High-definition Tactile Communication, pp. 7–9 (October 2019) https://doi.org/10.1145/3332167.3357097
10. Coe, P., Evreinov, G., Sinivaara, H., Hippula, A., Raisamo, R.: Haptic actuation plate for multi-layered in-vehicle control panel. Multimodal Technol. Interact. **5**, 25 (2021). https://doi.org/10.3390/mti5050025
11. Coe, P., Evreinov, G., Ziat, M., Raisamo, R.: Generating Localized Haptic Feedback over a Spherical Surface, pp. 15–24 (Janury 2021). https://doi.org/10.5220/0010189800150024
12. Coe, P., Farooq, A., Evreinov, G., Raisamo, R.: Generating Virtual Tactile Exciter For Hd Haptics : A Tectonic Actuators' Case Study, pp. 1–4 (October 2019). https://doi.org/10.1109/SENSORS43011.2019.8956569
13. Culbertson, H., Schorr, S., Okamura, A.: Haptics: The present and future of artificial touch sensation. Annu. Rev. Control Robot. Autonom. Syst. **1** (2018). https://doi.org/10.1146/annurev-control-060117-105043
14. Cutting, J., Vishton, P.: Perceiving Layout and Knowing Distances: The Interaction, Relative Potency, And Contextual Use Of Different Information About Depth, vol. 5, pp. 69–177 (January 1995)
15. Dangxiao, W., Yuan, G., Shiyi, L., Zhang, Y., Weiliang, X., Jing, X.: Haptic display for virtual reality: progress and challenges. Virt. Reali. Intell. Hardware **1**(2), 136–162 (2019)
16. Daniel, S., Wright, C., Welland, S.: Spherical display and control device (13 July 2010), uS Patent 7,755,605
17. Enferad, E., giraud audine, C., Frédéric, G., Amberg, M., Semail, B.: Generating controlled localized stimulations on haptic displays by modal superimposition. J. Sound Vibr. **449** (2019). https://doi.org/10.1016/j.jsv.2019.02.039
18. Evreinov, G., Raisamo, R.: Information kiosks for all: issues of tactile access. In: Proceedings of WWDU 2002 (January 2002)
19. Evreinova, T., Evreinov, G., Raisamo, R.: From kinesthetic sense to new interaction concepts: Feasibility and constraints. Int. J. Adv. Comput. Technol. **3**(4), 1–33 (2014)
20. Evreinova, T., Evreinov, G., Raisamo, R.: Virtual sectioning and haptic exploration of volumetric shapes in the absence of visual feedback. In: Advances in Human-Computer Interaction 2013 (July 2013). https://doi.org/10.1155/2013/740324
21. Evreinova, T., Evreinov, G., Raisamo, R.: An exploration of volumetric data in auditory space. J. Audio Eng. Soc. **62**, 172–187 (2014). https://doi.org/10.17743/jaes.2014.0008
22. Evreinova, T., Evreinov, G., Raisamo, R.: Evaluation of effectiveness of the stickgrip device for detecting the topographic heights on digital maps. Int. J. Comput. Sci. Appli. **9**, 61–76 (2012)
23. Evrienova, T.G., Evreinov, G., Raisamo, R.: Cross-Modal Assessment of Perceptual Strength of Communication Signals Presented in Auditory and Tactile Modalities (2009)
24. Farrell, G.: Fingers for Eyes. Harvard University Press (1969)
25. Fernández, C., Esteban, G., Conde-González, M., García-Peñalvo, F.: Improving motivation in a haptic teaching/learning framework. Int. J. Eng. Educ. **32**, 553–562 (2016)
26. Ferreira, F., et al.: Spheree: A 3d perspective-corrected interactive spherical scalable display (August 2014). https://doi.org/10.1145/2614066.2614091
27. Follmer, S., Leithinger, D., Olwal, A., Hogge, A., Ishii, H.: inform: Dynamic physical Affordances and Constraints Through Shape And Object Actuation, pp. 417–426 (October 2013). https://doi.org/10.1145/2501988.2502032
28. Goldstein, E.B., Brockmole, J.R.: Sensation and perception. Cengage Learning (2017)
29. Grow, D., Verner, L., Okamura, A.: Educational Haptics, pp. 53–58 (January 2007)
30. Hamza Lup, F., Stefan, I.: The haptic paradigm in education: Challenges and case studies (November 2018)

31. Hart, S.G.: Nasa-task load index (nasa-tlx); 20 years later. In: Proceedings of The Human Factors And Ergonomics Society Annual Meeting,vol. 50, pp. 904–908. Sage publications Sage CA, Los Angeles, CA (2006)
32. Hommel, B.: Ideomotor action control: On the perceptual grounding of voluntary actions and agents. In: Action Science Foundations of an Emerging Discipline (2013). https://doi.org/10.7551/mitpress/9780262018555.003.0005
33. Hudin, C., Lozada, J., Hayward, V.: Localized tactile feedback on a transparent surface through time-reversal wave focusing. IEEE Trans. Haptics **8** (2015). https://doi.org/10.1109/TOH.2015.2411267
34. Huitema, E.: The future of displays is foldable. Inf. Display **28**, 6–10 (2012). https://doi.org/10.1002/j.2637-496X.2012.tb00470.x
35. Jang, S., Kim, L., Tanner, K., Ishii, H., Follmer, S.: Haptic Edge Display For Mobile Tactile Interaction, pp. 3706–3716 (May 2016). https://doi.org/10.1145/2858036.2858264
36. Jeannerod, M.: The timing of natural prehension movements. J. Motor Behav. **16**(3), 235–254 (1984)
37. Jones, G., Minogue, J., Oppewal, T., Cook, M., Broadwell, B.: Visualizing without vision at the microscale: Students with visual impairments explore cells with touch. J. Sci. Educ. Technol. **15**, 345–351 (2006). https://doi.org/10.1007/s10956-006-9022-6
38. Kantner, L.A., Segall, M.H., Campbell, D.T., Herskovits, M.J.: The influence of culture on visual perception. Stud. Art Educ. **10**(1), 68 (1968). https://doi.org/10.2307/1319670
39. Kellman, P.J.: Chapter 9 - ontogenesis of space and motion perception. In: Epstein, W., Rogers, S. (eds.) Perception of Space and Motion, pp. 327–364. Handbook of Perception and Cognition, Academic Press, San Diego (1995). https://doi.org/10.1016/B978-012240530-3/50011-0, www.sciencedirect.com/science/article/pii/B9780122405303500110
40. Kim, S.C., Han, B.K., Kwon, D.S.: Haptic rendering of 3d geometry on 2d touch surface based on mechanical rotation. IEEE Trans. Haptics 1 (2017). https://doi.org/10.1109/TOH.2017.2768523
41. Kim, S., Park, G., Kim, S.C., Jung, J.: Surface haptics, pp. 421–425 (November 2019). https://doi.org/10.1145/3343055.3361925
42. Klare, S., Peer, A.: The formable object: A 24-degree-of-freedom shape-rendering interface. IEEE/ASME Trans. Mechatron. **20**(3), 1360–1371 (2014)
43. Klevberg, G., Anderson, D.: Visual and haptic perception of postural affordances in children and adults. Hum. Movement Sci. **21**, 169–86 (2002). https://doi.org/10.1016/S0167-9457(02)00100-8
44. Krufka, S., Barner, K., Aysal, T.: Visual to tactile conversion of vector graphics. IEEE Trans. Neural Syst. Rehabilit. Eng. Publicat. IEEE Eng. Med. Biol. Soc. **15**, 310–21 (2007). https://doi.org/10.1109/TNSRE.2007.897029
45. Lakshminarayanan, K., Lauer, A., Ramakrishnan, V., Webster, J., Seo, N.J.: Application of vibration to wrist and hand skin affects fingertip tactile sensation. Physiol. Reports **3** (2015). https://doi.org/10.14814/phy2.12465
46. Liu, S.H., Yu, N.H., Chan, L., Peng, Y.H., Sun, W.Z., Chen, M.: Phantomlegs: Reducing Virtual Reality Sickness Using Head-worn Haptic Devices, pp. 817–826 (March 2019). https://doi.org/10.1109/VR.2019.8798158
47. Loomis, J.M.: Tactile pattern perception. Perception **10**(1), 5–27 (1981). https://doi.org/10.1068/p100005
48. Loomis, J.M., Lederman, S.J.: Handbook of Perception and Human Performance Volume 1: Sensory processes and perceptiong, 2nd. edn., vol. 1. Wiley-Interscience, New York (1986)
49. Loria, D.: A moving experience: D-box celebrates 10 years in the cinema business (July 2019). www.boxofficepro.com/d-box-immersive-seating-10-year-anniversary/

50. Malińska, M., Zużewicz, K., Bugajska, J., Grabowski, A.: Heart rate variability (hrv) during virtual reality immersion. Int. J. Occupat. Safety Ergonom. **21**, 47–54 (2015). https://doi.org/10.1080/10803548.2015.1017964

51. Mansour, N., Fath El Bab, A., Assal, S.: A Novel Sma-based Micro Tactile Display Device For Elasticity Range Of Human Soft Tissues: Design And Simulation (August 2015). https://doi.org/10.1109/AIM.2015.7222574

52. McRae, L.T., McRae, B.J.: Implements usable by persons afflicted with arthritis (19 July 1977), uS Patent 4,035,865

53. Michaud, P.A.: Aby Warburg and the image in Motion. Zone Books (2007)

54. Minogue, J., Jones, M.: Haptics in education: Exploring an untapped sensory modality. Rev. Educ. Res. - REV EDUC RES **76**, 317–348 (2006). https://doi.org/10.3102/003465430760033317

55. Müller-Rakow, A., Hemmert, F., Wintergerst, G., Jagodzinski, R.: Reflective haptics: Resistive force feedback for musical performances with stylus-controlled instruments (May 2020)

56. Oakley, I., Brewster, S., Gray, P.: Communicating with Feeling, pp. 61–68 (January 2001). https://doi.org/10.1007/3-540-44589-7_7

57. Olstrom, C.: Undaunted by Blindness, 2nd edn. Ebookit.com (2012). www.books.google.fi/books?id=k9K77s1IRgoC

58. Pantelios, M., Tsiknas, L., Christodoulou, S., Papatheodorou, T.: Haptics technology in educational applications, a case study. JDIM **2**, 171–178 (2004)

59. Parisi, D., Farman, J.: Tactile temporalities: The impossible promise of increasing efficiency and eliminating delay through haptic media. Conver. Int. J. Res. New Media Technol. 135485651881468 (2018). https://doi.org/10.1177/1354856518814681

60. Park, J., Kim, J., Oh, Y., Tan, H.Z.: Rendering moving tactile stroke on the palm using a sparse 2D array. In: Bello, F., Kajimoto, H., Visell, Y. (eds.) EuroHaptics 2016. LNCS, vol. 9774, pp. 47–56. Springer, Cham (2016). https://doi.org/10.1007/978-3-319-42321-0_5

61. Perry, D., Wright, H.: Touch enhancing pad (2009), patent No. 4,657,021, Filed April 13th., 1989, Issued Aug. 24th., 1993

62. Rock, I., Victor, J.: Vision and touch: An experimentally created conflict between the two senses. Science **143**(3606), 594–596 (1964)

63. Saboune, J., Cruz-Hernandez, J.M.: Haptic effect authoring tool based on a haptification model (3 May 2016), uS Patent 9,330,547

64. Samsung: Hmd odyssey (mixed reality) (Mar 2021). www.samsung.com/us/support/computing/hmd/hmd-odyssey/hmd-odyssey-mixed-reality/

65. Sano, A., Mochiyama, H., Takesue, N., Kikuuwe, R., Fujimoto, H.: Touchlens: Touch enhancing tool, pp. 71–72 (December 2004). https://doi.org/10.1109/TEXCRA.2004.1425003

66. Schwaen, R., Arlt, R.: Effective assignments and haptic teaching methods in architectural structure. In: Structures and Architecture, pp. 838–845. CRC Press (2016)

67. Scientist TQ: Huawei band 6 complete scientific review (Jun 2021). www.youtube.com/watch?v=QDQzzyQFYQs

68. Segall, M.H.: The influence of culture on visual perception (1966)

69. Shin, S., Choi, S.: Geometry-based haptic texture modeling and rendering using photometric stereo, pp. 262–269 (March 2018). https://doi.org/10.1109/HAPTICS.2018.8357186

70. Slote, M.: The ethics of care and empathy. Routledge (2007)

71. Sofia, K., Jones, L.: Mechanical and psychophysical studies of surface wave propagation during vibrotactile stimulation. IEEE Trans. Haptics **6**, 320–329 (2013). https://doi.org/10.1109/TOH.2013.1

72. SSI: Screen solutions international: Spherical projection displays (May 2020). www.ssidisplays.com/projection-sphere/

73. Sutherland, I.: The ultimate display. multimedia: From wagner to virutal reality (1965)
74. Turvey, M., Carello, C.: Chapter 11 - dynamic touch. In: Epstein, W., Rogers, S. (eds.) Perception of Space and Motion, pp. 401–490. Handbook of Perception and Cognition, Academic Press, San Diego (1995). https://doi.org/10.1016/B978-012240530-3/50013-4, www.sciencedirect.com/science/article/pii/B9780122405303500134
75. Vechev, V., Zarate, J., Lindlbauer, D., Hinchet, R., Shea, H., Hilliges, O.: Tactiles: Dual-mode low-power electromagnetic actuators for rendering continuous contact and spatial haptic patterns in vr, pp. 312–320 (March 2019). https://doi.org/10.1109/VR.2019.8797921
76. Wachowski, A., Wachowski, L.: The art of the matrix. Newmarket Press (2000)
77. Wachowski, L., Wachowski, L.: The matrix: The shooting script. Titan (2002)
78. Williamson, J., Sundén, D., Bradley, J.: Globalfestival: evaluating real world interaction on a spherical display. pp. 1251–1261 (September 2015). https://doi.org/10.1145/2750858.2807518
79. Xie, X., et al.: A review of smart materials in tactile actuators for information delivery, vol. 3, p. 38 (December 2017). https://doi.org/10.3390/c3040038
80. Xu, H., Peshkin, M., Colgate, J.: How the mechanical properties and thickness of glass affect tpad performance (December 2019)
81. Zhou, Q., Hagemann, G., Fafard, D., Stavness, I., Fels, S.: An evaluation of depth and size perception on a spherical fish tank virtual reality display. IEEE Trans. Visualiz. Comput. Graphics 1 (2019). https://doi.org/10.1109/TVCG.2019.2898742
82. Ziat, M., Chin, K., Raisamo, R.: Effects of visual locomotion and tactile stimuli duration on the emotional dimensions of the cutaneous rabbit illusion. pp. 117–124 (October 2020). https://doi.org/10.1145/3382507.3418835
83. Zuffo, M., et al.: Spheree: An interactive perspective-corrected spherical 3d display (July 2014). https://doi.org/10.1109/3DTV.2014.6874768

Effects of Emotion-Induction Words on Memory and Pupillary Reactions While Viewing Visual Stimuli with Audio Guide

Mashiho Murakami[1], Motoki Shino[1], Munenori Harada[2], Katsuko T. Nakahira[2(✉)] [iD],
and Muneo Kitajima[2] [iD]

[1] The University of Tokyo, Tokyo, Japan
mashiho-m@g.ecc.u-tokyo.ac.jp, motoki@k.u-tokyo.ac.jp
[2] Nagaoka University of Technology, Nagaoka, Niigata, Japan
s193369@stn.nagaokaut.ac.jp, katsuko@vos.nagaokaut.ac.jp,
mkitajima@kjs.nagaokaut.ac.jp

Abstract. This study aimed to examine the possibility of using emotion-induction words in audio guides for education via visual content. This was performed based on the findings of a previous study that focused on the provision timings of visual and auditory information [6]. Thirty emotion-induction words were extracted from the database and categorized into positive, negative, and neutral words, and three experiments were performed. The first experiment was conducted to confirm the reliability of emotional values. The results revealed a strong consistency between the values in the database and the ratings given by the participants. The second experiment assessed whether consistency was maintained if the words appeared in the sentences. The results confirmed that a certain degree of consistency was maintained, as expected, but showed larger individual differences compared with the first experiment. The third experiment was conducted to probe the effect of emotion-induction words used in the audio guide to explain the visual content of memory. Our results revealed that participants who were exposed to positive and negative emotion-induction words remembered the content better than those who were presented with neutral words. Per the three experiments, the emotion value of the neutral words was found to be sensitive to the context in which they were embedded, which was confirmed by observing the changes in pupillary reactions. Suggestions for designing audio and visual content using emotion-induction words for better memory are provided.

Keywords: Memory · Audio guide · Emotion · Omnidirectional watching · Information acquisition · Cognitive model

1 Introduction

This paper is based on the previous work originally presented in [10]. It extends the analysis of pupillary reactions in Sect. 5.2 and appendices.

The effect of an excess of information on human beings' cognitive processes has been pointed out in a variety of contexts. Simon suggested that an excess of information could result in a lack of attention [15]. Bitgood focused on how museum visitors were not able to learn because of the amount of information they were presented

A. A. de Sousa et al. (Eds.): VISIGRAPP 2021, CCIS 1691, pp. 69–89, 2023.
https://doi.org/10.1007/978-3-031-25477-2_4

with, as follows: "During museum visits, learners may fail to understand the exhibits deeply because of the abundance of exhibits and time limitations leading to information overload" [2]. With the development of Information and Communication Technology (ICT), the amount of information that can be transmitted from artifacts to human beings continues to increase. In contrast, human beings, who receive the information, are equipped with limited perceptual and cognitive capabilities for processing rich information. As described above, an excess of information may result in undesirable effects, such as lack of attention, fatigue, and ineffective learning. To balance the excess of information with human perceptual and cognitive capabilities, Pierdicca et al. suggested several methodologies that might enable the use of both novel Internet of Things (IoT) architectures and suitable algorithms to derive indicators concerning visitor attention with a significant degree of confidence in the concept of a "ubiquitous museum" [13].

Lifelong learning has become an important part of our daily lives, and visiting museums is considered a typical method supporting lifelong learning. The development of ICT has changed the style of exhibitions in that they now tend to contain an excessive amount of information. However, more information transmitted does not necessarily translate to more learning due to the challenges inherent to processing excessive amounts of information. Given excess information, learning methods should be designed considering human perceptual and cognitive capabilities.

In the context of lifelong learning, the knowledge acquired while appreciating exhibits in museum visits needs to be considered. Hirabayashi et al. [6] used omnidirectional movies as an example of an exhibition that utilizes modern advanced technologies and assessed the effect of auditory information presentation timings on memory. They suggested that if auditory information for a particular object is provided after viewing the object as projected on the surface of the dome, it would result in greater retention. To direct the viewer's attention to the object in question, they incorporated the appearance of the object into the audio guide (appearance information). The information available for explaining the object (content information), which is not directly accessible from the appearance of the object, was provided as an audio guide following the appearance information using a variety of intervals. They found experimentally that 2–3 s intervals were the most effective for creating a memory of the object. They argued that, in the best presentation interval condition, the visual and auditory processes that are carried out to comprehend the object should jointly activate part of long-term memory to generate the most richly connected network.

This study furthers Hirabayashi et al.'s study [6] by shifting the focus of research from the richness of the network connections to the contents of the richly connected network. The idea is to strengthen the constituent nodes by manipulating the words used in the audio guide while maintaining the topology of the network generated by processing visual and auditory information using the best 2–3 s interval between the timing of the appearance of information and the content information. Assuming that the generation of a richly connected memory network is assured by the best interval condition, this study investigates the possibility of making the network stronger in terms of the total amount of activation the network holds by manipulating the concrete words used in the content information.

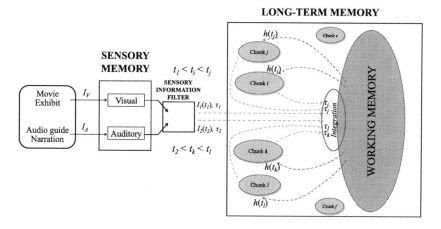

Fig. 1. A cognitive model on memory formation.

To this end, this study utilized the finding that emotion enhances episodic memory by strengthening constituent nodes. Deborah et al. [16] proposed an extension of the context maintenance and retrieval model (CMR) [14], eCMR, to explain the way people may represent and process emotional information. The eCMR model assumes that a word associated with an emotion, such as spider, is encoded with its emotional state in working memory (they called it "context layer") and that the presented emotional word establishes a stronger link than neutral words. This study operationally implements the same effect by attaching a greater weight to the emotional node in the network and assesses the effect of emotion-induction words used in audio guides on the memory of the movie viewing experience. It is likely that viewers' reactions to emotion-induction words may reflect their personal experiences or knowledge. Therefore, this study also incorporated the finding that pupil dilation reflects the time course of emotion recognition [5, 11, 12] to gather evidence that the manipulation of emotion induction has been successful.

The remainder of this paper is organized as follows. Section 2 describes the cognitive framework that shows the effect of timings and contents of the audio guide on memory. Section 3 describes three experiments that investigate the effects of emotion-induction words on memory. The first one probes participants' responses to emotion-induction words, the second one focuses on sentences with emotion-induction words, and the last one measures memory for movies with positive, negative, and neutral emotion-induction words. Sections 4 and 5 provide the results of the experiments and discuss them from the viewpoint of pupil diameter changes.

2   Integration of Visual Information and Auditory Information

Hirabayashi et al. [6] studied the importance of the timing of providing auditory information while watching movies to make the experience memorable. This study extends their findings regarding the effective provision timing of auditory information for memory formation by focusing on the effect of emotion-induction words in the context of

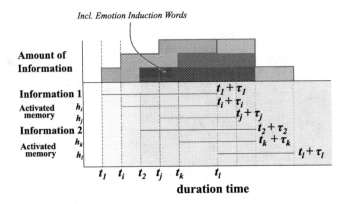

Fig. 2. Timeline of memory activation.

auditory information. This section outlines Hirabayashi et al.'s model [6] that explains the effective timing auditory information while processing visual information along with necessary modifications to deal with the effect of emotion-induction words in the context of auditory information. Starting from the introduction of the cognitive model of memory formation, this section discusses why it is essential to take timings into account.

2.1 Memory Formation by Integrating Visual and Auditory Information

Figure 1 represents the perceptual and cognitive processes involved in acquiring visual information with the support of an audio guide, incorporating the finding related to the effective timing of providing an audio guide [6]. In Fig. 1, visual and auditory information are represented as "movie exhibit" and "audio guide narration", respectively. A situation is considered whereby visual and auditory stimuli that have the amount of information of I_V and I_A are fed into sensory memory. Part of the information stored in the sensory memory, I_V and I_A, is passed to working memory (WM) via the sensory information filter as I_1 and I_2 at times t_1 and t_2, respectively. We assume that $\Delta t = t_2 - t_1 \approx 2 \sim 3$ seconds following Hirabayashi et al.'s finding [6] that their participants showed the best memory performance for the movie exhibit when auditory information was provided $2 \sim 3$ seconds after the corresponding visual information $I_1(t_1)$ and auditory information $I_2(t_2)$ are present in the WM for a duration time of τ_1 and τ_2, respectively.

The visual and auditory information in WM activate part of the long-term memory (LTM) via a resonance mechanism [9]. The activated portion of LTM is incorporated in WM, which thereafter serves as the next source of activation as long as it exists in WM. In this study , WM is considered the activated portion of LTM, which is called long-term working memory [3]. This process is expressed as follows:

Only Visual Information is Available $(t_1 \leq t < t_2)$

1. Visual information I_1 is stored in WM at t_1, which is present in WM for the duration of τ_1.
2. At $t = t_i(> t_1)$, a chunk in LTM C_i is activated by the current WM.

3. The activated chunk C_i is incorporated into WM. The information thus incorporated in WM at t_i is denoted $h(t_i)$.
4. $h(t_i)$ is present in WM for the duration of τ_i.
5. During the overlapping period of $(t_1, t_1 + \tau_1)$ and $(t_i, t_i + \tau_i)$, I_1 and $h(t_i)$ serve as the WM contents to further activate the LTM. In Fig. 1, chunk C_j is activated at t_j and incorporated into WM as $h(t_j)$ with at lifetime of τ_j.

Auditory Information is Available $(t \geq t_2)$

1. Auditory information I_2 is stored in WM at t_2, which is present in WM for the duration time of τ_2.
2. At $t = t_k (> t_2)$, a chunk in LTM C_k is activated by the current contents of WM.
3. The activated chunk C_k is incorporated into WM as $h(t_k)$ with the lifetime of τ_k.
4. During the overlapping period of $(t_2, t_1 + \tau_2)$ and $(t_k, t_k + \tau_k)$, I_2 and $h(t_k)$ serve as the WM contents to activate LTM further. The chunk C_l is activated at t_l and incorporated in WM as $h(t_l)$ with the lifetime of τ_l.

As these processes proceed, the visual information I_1 at t_1 and the auditory information I_2 at t_2 are elaborated through the cascade of activation of chunks in LTM using the dynamically updated contents of WM. The activated chunks are then integrated to make sense of the visual information and the auditory information. In text comprehension research in cognitive psychology, these processes are modeled as the Construction-Integration process [7, 8].

Figure 2 schematically shows the process how the visual information provided at t_1 collects information in LTM by activating relevant chunks at t_i and t_j. The vertical axis represents the number of chunks incorporated in WM. At $t = t_2$, where $t_1 < t_2 < t_1 + \tau_1$, auditory information is incorporated in WM, and collects information in LTM by activating relevant chunks at t_k and t_l. The information originated from the visual information and the auditory information are represented as red rectangles and blue rectangles, respectively. The number of information is the largest between the time $t_k < t < t_1 + \tau_1 = t_i + \tau_i$. It is five, three and two originated from visual and auditory information, respectively.

Assuming that the auditory information provided after the provision of visual information should be used for helping the viewers comprehend the movie better, the overlapping part of the diagram should direct to the common areas of the memory network in LTM. Hirabatashi et al. [6] examined how the intervals between the provision of visual information and auditory information should affect the number of links that could be established through these processes. Through these processes, the activated chunks establish links with the existing memory networks and as a result, it is memorized.

Figure 2 is the best timing for creating a richly connected network for better memory. If $t_2 - t_1$ gets longer or shorter, the area of overlap of the red area and the blue area becomes smaller than the case shown by Fig. 2. Therefore, not only the input information itself but also the other pieces of information that is available at the same time plays an important role in how memorable the input information is. Even if the same pieces of information are presented, if the pieces of information are perceived in different timings, it directly affects the quantity of information available for integration and organization of the acquired information.

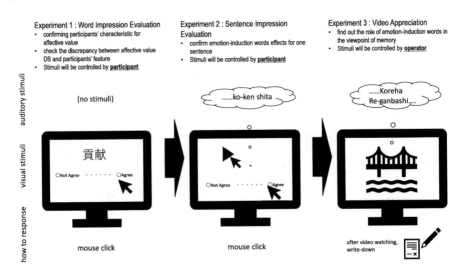

Fig. 3. The outline of three experiments flow.

2.2 Emotion-Induction Words for Better Memory

This study examines the possibility of the effect of the overlapping part of Fig. 2 by using emotion-induction words in the auditory information. In Fig. 2, the blue part that corresponds to the auditory information is represented by different color values which corresponds to the strength of the activated chunks.

According to the theory of cognition, Adaptive Control of Thought - Rational (ACT-R) [1], the stronger the chunk becomes, the more probable the chunk is retrieved. This study adopts a slightly modified version of activation level equation defined in the ACT-R theory. The activation level of the i-th chunk, A_i, is defined by the following equation:

$$A_i = B_i + \sum_{j=1}^{N} W_{ji} \times A_j.$$

In this equation, B_i, W_{ji}, and N denote the base level activation of the chunk C_i, the strength of the link between C_j and C_i (from j to i), and the number of chunks that are connected to the chunk C_i. The base level activation decays overtime. But it gets larger when the chunk is used, or activated. This study assumes that emotion-induction words should activate stronger chunks than emotionally neutral words. Figure 2 depicts the situation where the auditory information contains emotion-induction words and stronger chunks are activated and incorporated in WM. This should cause stronger memory trace than neutral words are used in the auditory information.

3 Three Experiments for Investigating Effects of Emotion-Induction Words

Three experiments were carried out to dissect the relationships between emotion-induction words and memory when watching a movie. Figure 3 outlines the relationship between the different experiments. The first experiment (Word Impression Evaluation Experiment, Exp-W) was conducted to confirm the reliability of the emotional values. The second experiment (Sentence Impression Evaluation Experiment, Exp-S) was used to examine whether consistency was maintained if the words appeared in the context of sentences. The third experiment (Video Appreciation Experiment, Exp-V) was conducted to examine the effect of emotion-induction words used in the audio guide to explain visual contents on memory. Thirty participants participated in all experiments. They first participated in Exp-S and Exp-V consecutively scheduled on a single day in the laboratory. Following an interval of approximately 10 days, they participated in Exp-W on their own computers. Different sets of induction words were used for Exp-S and Exp-V. Exp-W was conducted after Exp-S and Exp-V to probe the appropriateness of the emotion-induction words used in the sentences and audio guides presented in Exp-S and Exp-V.

3.1 Measurement Data

Impression Rating: In this study, emotion-induction words were used to assess the influence of emotion on memory. All were taken from the database [4], having been created in the following way: 618 participants were asked to rate their impressions to the presented words by using a 7-point Likert scale as follows: "very positive", "positive", "somewhat positive", "neither", "somewhat negative", "negative", and "very negative." After the rating experiment, a database of 389 words consisting of 122 negative, 146 positive, and 121 neutral valence words were constructed. In this study, impression ratings were collected for words in Exp-W, sentences in Exp-S, and videos in Exp-V. The options for rating included the ones used for constructing the above-mentioned database and a new option, "I cannot catch the meaning of this word/sentence/video." The last one was added considering the possibility of not knowing the word or not being able to get the meaning of the sentence.

Pupil Diameter: The pupil diameter dilates when emotions change [5, 11, 12]. Therefore, the participants' pupil diameters were measured in Exp-S and Exp-V. Tobii Pro Glass 2, with a sampling rate 50 Hz, was used in the experiment.

Memory: Memory was measured in the Exp-V. A questionnaire was administered to investigate the information that the participants memorized when viewing movies. Since the questionnaire was conducted soon after viewing the movie, a recall test was chosen. To quantitatively assess memory, participant responses were broken down into meaningful units using a morphological analysis technique. They were then scored from the quantitative and qualitative perspectives by providing special points to those units related to the targets and the narrative contents spoken in the audio guides (one point was given to a noun or a verb, two points to a pronoun). Those points were summed up to define "Memory Score." Table 1 represents an example of the responses from Exp-V and the calculated memory score.

3.2 Word Impression Evaluation Experiment (Exp-W)

The purpose of Exp-W was to confirm that there was no discrepancy between the emotional value of two-character words in the Japanese language in the database and participants' evaluations. Thirty participants assessed their impressions of the words

Table 1. Examples of Memory Score (n/v:noun or verb, pn: pronoun, MS: Memory Score (points)).

Response	n/v	pn	MS
Statue	1	0	1
Statue of messenger	0	1	2
Replica of statue of messenger	1	1	3
Statue of messenger was	2	1	4
Given as a proof of friendship			

displayed on their own PCs using a 7- point Likert scale. There was a total of 30 words. Considering the order effect on evaluation, multiple patterns were randomly created, and experiments were conducted on five patterns for a total of 30 words.

3.3   Sentence Impression Evaluation Experiment (Exp-S)

The purpose of Exp-S was to confirm that emotion-induction words affect emotion even when they are presented in a sentence. The procedure was carried out in the exact same method as for Exp-W, except that the stimuli consisted of sentences instead of words and were presented in audio format.

There was a total of 30 sentences randomly presented as Exp-W in the laboratory using a laptop computer with a 13-inch display. Participants operated the touch pad of a laptop computer. Ten negative words, 10 positive words, and 10 neutral words were extracted from the database. Each sentence consisted of a single sentence containing one of the extracted words. Each sentence consisted of a single sentence lasting about $3 \sim 5$ s, and was broadcast twice, read aloud by the same person in succession. The break between the two was clear. Participants listened to 30 sentences and assessed their impressions. The sentences were not visually presented on the display.

3.4   Video Appreciation Experiment (Exp-V)

Exp-V was carried out in an appreciation environment similar to the learning environment of a social education institution. Thirty participants took part in the experiments. None had visual or health problems during the experiment. They watched three movies consecutively and evaluated the impression of each movie using a 7-point Likert scale. Each movie was provided with an audio guide that contained a few positive, negative, or neutral words extracted from the database. The memory test was conducted immediately after viewing the movies by having the participants write down anything they remembered. In Exp-V, biological information was collected as a potential objective indicator that should reflect the effect of emotion-induction words on the psychological states of the participants.

Exp-V experiments were conducted in the laboratory. Participants operated the touchpad of a laptop computer. Participants evaluated their impressions of the sentences in the same way as in Exp-W after watching three movies. Three patterns were considered for the presentation order of the positive, negative, and neutral audio guides, as represented in Table 2.

Table 2. Three presentation patterns for audio guides of three movies that contain positive, negative, and neutral emotion-induction words.

Pattern	Movie 1	Movie 2	Movie 3
1	Neutral	Positive	Negative
2	Negative	Neutral	Positive
3	Positive	Negative	Neutral

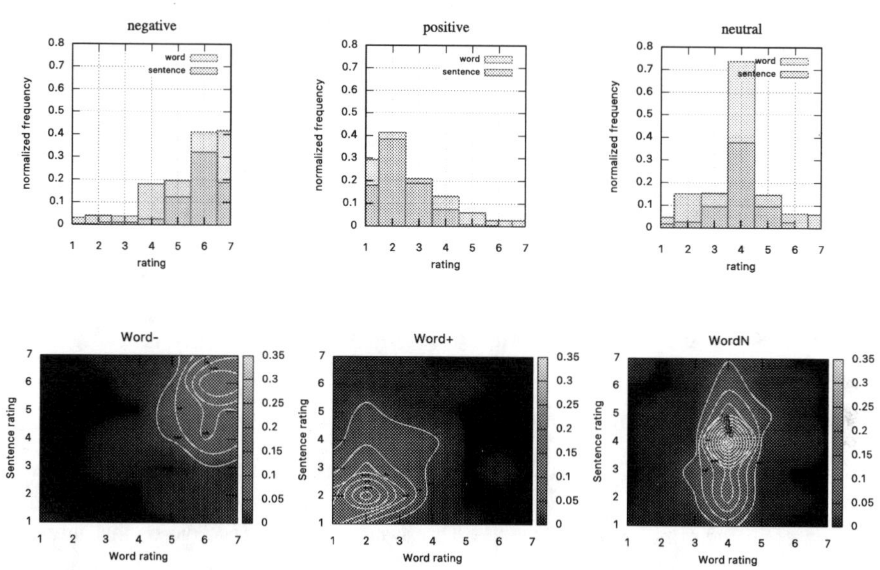

Fig. 4. Upper three graphs: frequency of ratings for "word" and "sentence." The left, middle and right sections side shows the negative, positive, and neutral modes, respectively. Lower three graphs: probability distributions for "word" versus "sentence." Word − stands for negative, Word + stands for positive, and WordN stands for neutral.

Visual and Auditory Stimuli. Three movies were created. Each movie had a respective audio guide with one of the three attributes of emotion-induction words. The movies showed the landscape taken from a slow-paced boat going down the Sumida River in Tokyo. A movie taken from a slow-paced boat was chosen as a stimulus for this experiment because it is likely to contain scenes or targets that satisfy the following conditions:

- The target in the movie should move at a slow pace. This condition was needed to make the target appear and stay in the field of view long enough for a viewer to take the required visual information of the target object.
- The target should not be easily noticed without guidance. This condition was needed to prevent viewers from paying attention to the target beforehand and to clearly see the effect of the audio guide.
- Scenes contain many objects throughout the movie. This condition was needed to simulate situations in which an audio guide is needed.

Experiment System. Viewing behavior, including pupil diameter, was recorded using a wearable eye tracker (Tobii Pro Glasses 2) at a sampling rate 50 Hz. The experiment was conducted with one participant at a time. Participants were seated on a chair and their head positions were located approximately 0.8 m from the display.

Procedure. Prior to viewing the movie, the participants were told to make themselves comfortable and to view the movie freely to simulate the actual viewing behavior. Each movie lasted approximately 1 min, and intervals were inserted between the movies. Considering the order effect, each participant was presented with a randomly chosen pattern from the three represented in Table 2. After participants finished viewing the movies, they were asked to complete the questionnaire.

4 Results

This section begins by laying forth the results of Exp-W and Exp-S concerning the impression evaluation of words that appeared in isolation and in context. This is followed by the results of Exp-V concerning memory scores for the movies that used positive, negative, and neutral emotion-induction words.

4.1 Impression of Emotion-Induction Words

The normalized frequencies in Exp-W and Exp-S are represented in the top half of Fig. 4. At a single glance, the ratings for emotion-induction words that appeared in isolation or in the context of a sentence were consistent, irrespective of the nature of the words, that is, positive, negative, or neutral. The mode of the rating for the negative words in isolation and in a sentence was 6, that for the positive words was 2, and that for the neutral words was 4.

The results represented in the histograms are further decomposed by focusing on the ratings for individual words. Each word was rated in isolation and in the context of a sentence. The bottom half of Fig. 4 shows the normalized frequency of the data points of two-dimensional space, that is, the rating of word in isolation vs. the rating of word in a sentence. There were 300 data points (10 words by 30 participants) for negative, positive, and neutral conditions. As shown in the figures, the ratings for the emotion-induction words were consistent, whether they were rated in isolation or in sentences in general. However, the neutral emotion-inducing words showed a significant difference in terms of the degree of variance in the sentence rating, as shown in the bottom-right plot in Fig. 4. This indicates that neutral emotion-induction words were rated neutral when they were presented as single words in isolation, but that the rating of the emotion value fluctuated when they were presented in a sentence. This suggests that neutral emotion-induction words cannot be emotionally neutral when they appear in a sentence.

Box plots of the ratings for the emotion-induction words, the sentences in which the emotion-induction words are embedded, and the visual content with audio that includes the emotion-induction words are represented in Fig. 5(a), (b), and (c). The ratings were significantly different across conditions, that is, positive, negative, and

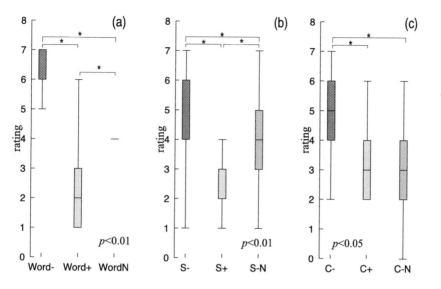

Fig. 5. Box-plots of ratings for (a) emotion-induction words in Exp-W, (b) sentences that emotion-induction words are embedded in Exp-S, and (c) visual contents with audio that includes emotion-induction words in Exp-V. The signs '+', '-', and 'N' stand for 'positive', 'negative', and 'neutral', respectively.

neutral, except for the ratings between neutral and positive emotion-induction words in Exp-V. More specifically, by comparing the results of Exp-V shown in Fig. 5(c) with the results of Exp-W and Exp-S, it is found that the impression ratings were consistent with the attributes of the emotion-induction words only in the negative condition, and that the impression ratings for the positive and neutral conditions were not consistent with the attributes of the emotion-induction words. The ratings for the positive condition in Exp-V shifted to the region of neutral impression, and those for the neutral condition shifted to the region of positive impression. This observation is consistent with the result demonstrated in the bottom-right plot in Fig. 4. It is likely that the ratings of emotion value fluctuated when emotion-induction words were presented in context.

4.2   Memory Score

A standardized summary of the memory score for each video is represented in Fig. 6. Using the t-test, a statistically significant difference was observed between C– and C+ conditions and between C– and C-N conditions. However, there was no statistically significant difference between the C+ and C-N conditions. This result is consistent with the result denoted in Fig. 5(c) for Exp-V described in Sect. 4.1. In the condition in which the emotion-induction words appeared in the audio guide for providing information about the movies, it is likely that positive and neutral words were more strongly affected by the context in which they appeared, and that they could change their context-free emotion values, which were maintained even if they appeared in sentences.

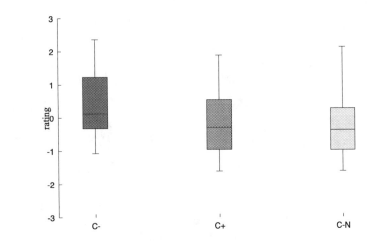

Fig. 6. Memory scores for the three movie categories; the movies in the C–, C+, and C– N categories consisted of the negative, positive, and neutral emotion-induction words, respectively.

5   Discussion

This section starts by analyzing the results of Exp-V with regard to the relationship between emotion-induction words included in movies and memory score. It follows pupil diameter dilation analysis as an objective indicator of emotional changes. Finally, this section discusses the possibility of implementing a design method based on the two aforementioned points.

5.1   Memory Score Analysis

Section 4 demonstrated that 1) the memory scores were high in the negative condition, and 2) the attributes of emotion-induction words in the impression evaluation were only maintained in the negative condition. As shown in Fig. 4, emotion-induction words should also work in sentences, regardless of whether they are positive or negative. When they were added as an audio guide to the video, it is likely that for some reason, the positive emotion-induction words did not manifest their expected effect when incorporated into the video. Therefore, it is not possible to discuss the relationship between positive emotion-induction words and memory. Further analyses are required in the future. However, these results suggest that negative emotion-induction words also influenced the evaluation of impressions and contributed to the improvement of memory in the movies.

Next, the relationship between impression evaluation and memory scores is discussed. As demonstrated in Fig. 1 and 2, the presence of emotion-induction words in a sentence should enhance memory by overlapping visual information as objects with auditory information at appropriate times. In addition, as shown in Fig. 4, the influence of neutral words on emotion varied more when they were presented in sentences than when they appeared in isolation. This suggests that this tendency is more strongly pronounced when words are presented in the context.

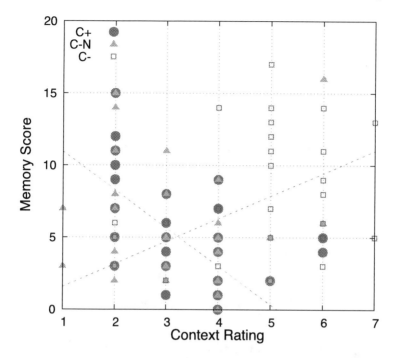

Fig. 7. Relation between context (movies) rating for emotion and memory scores. C+ represents the movies which were constructed with the positive emotive-induction words. C− represents the movies which were constructed with the negative emotive-induction words. The dotted lines represent the linear regression for each movie. The blue dotted line represents C− with an R^2 value of 0.79. The red dotted line represents C+ with an R^2 value of 0.33. (Color figure online)

The relationship between ratings and the memory scores for each of the three videos obtained from the participants is represented as a scatter plot in Fig. 7. The dotted lines represent the linear regressions for each movie. The blue dotted line represents C−, with an R^2 value of 0.79. The blue dotted line increases as the ratings increase. This indicated that the memory score increases when the movie in the C− condition was rated with the negative emotion-induction words that appeared in the audio guide. The red dotted line represents C+, with an R^2 value of 0.33. The red dotted line decreases as the ratings increase. This indicates that the memory score decreases when the movie in the C+ condition was rated with the positive emotion-induction words that appeared in the audio guide.

When emotion-induction words used to provide an explanation of the movies in the audio guide function as expected, memory scores should increase. In contrast, when they do not function as they should, memory scores should not increase.

5.2 Pupil Diameter Analysis

Figure 8 represents the pupillary reactions from the two participants, ut33 and ut19, characterized as the consistent and inconsistent participant where the degree of con-

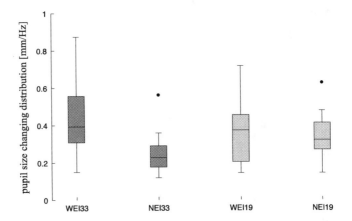

Fig. 8. Box-plots of ratings for (a) emotion-induction words in Exp-W, (b) sentences that emotion-induction words are embedded in Exp-S, and (c) visual contents with audio that includes emotion-induction words in Exp-V. The signs "+," "–," and "N" stand for "positive," "negative," and "neutral," respectively. Exp-V, Video Appreciation Experiment; Exp-W, Word Impression Evaluation Experiment; Exp-S, Sentence Impression Evaluation Experiment

sistency is defined by the degree of matching between their ratings to the emotion-induction words and the values in the database. This result indicates that ut33 has a difference in the effect of emotions between emotion-induction words and neutral words, and ut19 has a small difference between emotion-induction words and neutral words. This result corresponds to the characteristic of correlation with the database. In other words, the pupil diameter variability was greater for those who rated impressions according to the database when they heard emotion-induction words, while those who rated impressions not according to the database showed no difference in pupil diameter variability when they heard emotion-induction words compared to when they heard neutral words. The results suggest that there are individual differences in the emotional changes caused by emotion-induction words, which can be captured by the pupil diameter analysis. Further pupil diameter analysis will support this finding.

To understand the effect of emotion-induction words included in audio guide on memory, pupil diameter changes in Exp-S was analyzed as an objective evaluation index. To analyze the relationship between the attributes of emotion-induction words which each participant heard and pupil diameter changes, the participants were screened according to the following criteria.

1. There is no problem in the ratings in Exp-W and Exp-S.
2. There is no problem in the pupil diameter data.

Of those who satisfied these criteria, two participants were selected for a preliminary analysis of pupil data considering the degree of accordance with their ratings for the sentences used in Exp-S with the attributes of the sentences, i.e., S+, S-, and S-N. One participant, ut33, showed the highest correlation of 0.92 (consistent-participant) and the other, ut19, showed the lowest correlation of 0.18 (inconsistent-participant). Since the

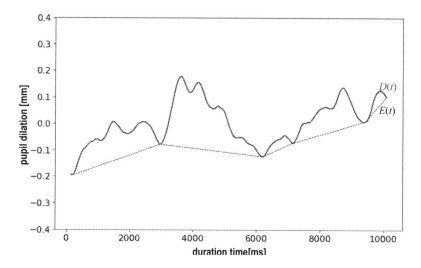

Fig. 9. A sample of $D(t)$ and $E(t)$.

pupil diameter dilation to emotional changes is smaller than the change to light changes, the dilation to emotional changes is considered to be captured by lower envelope for pupil diameter changes. Figure 9 is a graph showing the approximate lines of the lower envelopes. The difference between the value of pupil diameter curve and the value of the lower envelope was added by the time when the sentence was played, and the average was calculated by using the following procedure:

The pupil dilation at the time t represents $D(t)$, where t defines as the measurement time for pupil diameter. Here, let the pupil diameter measurement time be T_s for the starting measurement time and T_e for the ending measurement time. At this time, the measurement time is expressed by the next closed interval $[T_s, T_e]$. The local minima in this interval are obtained as follows (consult the APPENDIX 2 for the pseudo code for this procedure).

$$\{T_1, T_2, \cdots, T_N\}, \quad \text{where } T_s \le T_1 \le T_N \le T_e.$$

Here, let L_k be the line segment connecting the two points, $D(T_i)$ and $D(T_{i+j})$, which generates m line segments. If L_k does not intersect with $D(t)$ in that interval, T_j, which is the end point, is shifted by one as j. If L_k intersects with $D(t)$, L_k is determined to be the lower envelope of k, the next start point T_i is set to T_j, and the end point is set to T_{j+1} to determine again whether to draw a line segment. Here, $E(t)$ in Fig. 9 is a connection of discontinuous line segments L_k. Let S_k be the area surrounded by L_k and $D(t)$. The area surrounded by L_k and $D(t)$ is S_k, and $C(t)$ are named as cumulative pupillary reaction measure.

$$C(t) = \sum_{k=1}^{m} S_k$$

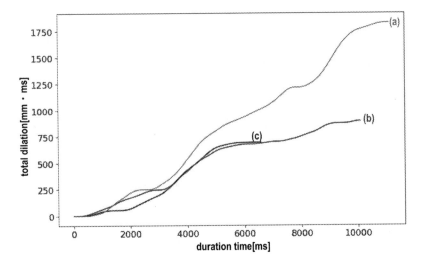

Fig. 10. An example of the cumulative pupillary reaction measure $C(t)$. The lines are drawn by using the pupillary reactions of the participant who showed (a) negative emotion, (b) positive emotion, and (c) neutral emotion to the stimuli.

Once defined $C(t)$, we can quantify the reaction characteristics between stimulus type and participants. Figure 10 represents a sample of $C(t)$. Figure 10(a) is for the negative stimulus, (b) is for the neutral stimulus, and (c) is for the positive stimulus. This participant's behavior shows a larger pupillary response to the negative stimulus, but a similar pupillary response to the positive stimulus and neutral stimulus, with no significant changes compared to the negative stimulus. These findings suggest a possibility that we could predict the audiences' emotion while viewing visual stimuli with audio guide by using their pupillary reactions.

5.3   Design Implications

This subsection discusses the design of multimodal information for better memory. First, as shown in Fig. 4, it was found that impression ratings corresponded to the attributes of emotion-induction words. Second, it is well-known that emotional changes are reflected in pupil diameter dilation. As shown in Fig. 8, for the same stimuli, the consistent participant and inconsistent participant showed significantly different reactions in terms of pupil diameter reactions. This indicates that the pupil diameter could be used to monitor how the participants might react to the stimuli. As discussed in this paper, ratings of impression, which could be subject to individual differences, as evidenced by the existence of inconsistent participants, should correlate with memory score. Monitoring participants' emotional state could represent a promising method for designing auditory information to help construct better memories. In addition, as shown in Fig. 6, memory scores should be higher when negative emotion induction words are acquired. This finding is also applicable to the design of auditory information.

6   Conclusion and Future Work

This study probed the effect of emotion-induction words in an audio guide on memory. Based on integration of visual information and auditory information, we designed three experiments which included the following probes: responses to emotion-induction words, sentences with emotion-induction words, and movies with emotion-induction words. Our findings revealed that auditory information with negative emotion-induction words was easy to remember. It was also suggested that emotional changes during appreciation behavior might be reflected in changes in pupil diameter. We proposed a method for analyzing the relation between pupil dilation and emotion. It used the cumulative pupillary reaction measure $C(t)$, which was obtained by summing S_k. This measure corresponded to the area of closed curves between envelope and a convex line of pupillary dilation profile. We showed that the plot of $C(t)$ on the plane with the duration time for the horizontal axis and the total dilation for the vertical axis was useful for grasping the relationship between the multiple categories of emotion-induction words. We further suggested that the shape of $C(t)$ might represent the characteristics of the participant's reaction to the presented words, and could be used to construct effective indices for categorizing his/her emotional reaction types, i.e., positive, neutral, or negative, for the particular words.

For now, this study only focused on two-dimensional movie viewing behaviors to simulate a real environment. However, to facilitate its application to everyday life, such as in the context of museums, galleries, and guided tours, among others, it is important to apply and examine what this study found in omnidirectional situations, such as in the context of a dome theater. In addition, a pupil diameter analysis was performed for only two participants to examine the feasibility of the research direction. These results are promising. We plan to continue this approach and try to find a way to objectively estimate the viewer's cognitive state that would enhance the learning of visual content accompanied by auditory information.

Appendix 1: Emotion-Induction Words and Sentences

The emotion induction words and the sentences used for the experiment.

No.	Word	Score	Sentence including the word
Positive			
1	[murder]	6.51	Murder is one of the worst sins a person commit
2	[tragedy]	6.38	A tragedy happened in the baseball tournament final
3	[assassinate]	6.36	Ryoma Sakamoto was assassinated on his birthday
4	[banish]	6.33	Unable to understand the situation, he was banished from the dinner party
5	[prejudice]	6.15	It is difficult to be aware of unconscious prejudice
6	[transfer school]	6.14	The first day of transfer school is full of anxiety
7	[worst]	6.13	Enter the site assuming the worst situation
8	[dismiss]	6.13	One of the college students working part-time must be dismissed
9	[penalty]	6.10	Nothing is as boring as paying a penalty
10	[fall]	6.06	I have fallen since I became a college student
Neutral			
1	[free]	1.93	Rice is often included free of charge at Iekei ramen shops
2	[contribute]	1.93	How much do I contribute to the sales of the nearest convenience store?
3	[love]	1.90	I cook curry with plenty of love
4	[experienced]	1.87	Rookie is good, but experienced veteran is also good
5	[courage]	1.80	I gave up my seat with courage
6	[holiday]	1.77	When I was in elementary school, I loved holidays
7	[plenty]	1.53	There are plenty of drink bars here, so I'll follow you
8	[fortunate]	1.50	I was fortunate to meet you
9	[achieve]	1.47	I am good at achieving goals one by one
10	[clear day]	1.47	Laundry progresses on a clear day.
Negative			
1	[field]	4.0	I think I know more about this field than most people
2	[loading platform]	4.00	I'm watching the cardboard boxes pile up on the loading platform
3	[railway route]	4.00	There are so many railway routes in Tokyo that you can't compare to the countryside
4	[job seeker]	4.07	Job seekers were in line
5	[address]	3.97	When I write my address, I'm wondering whether to write it from the prefecture
6	[jacket]	3.93	It is difficult to choose a jacket because the temperature difference between day and night is large
7	[seal]	4.11	I always carry my seal
8	[budget]	4.07	You can't decide anything else unless you decide on a budget
9	[next time]	4.1	Next time I will try to order a different menu
10	[clerk]	3.98	Turn right at the end and a clerk is standing.

Appendix 2: Algorithm for Pupil Analysis

Algorithm 1. Envelope.

1: **function** ENVLOPE_LINE(T,t,D)
2:     $delta \leftarrow t[1] - t[0]$
3:     $sp, j\_old, slope\_old, itr\_old \leftarrow 0$
4:     $ep \leftarrow 1$
5:     $slopes, itrs, LP \leftarrow []$
6:     **while** True **do**
7:         $i \leftarrow T[sp]$, $j \leftarrow T[ep]$
8:         **if** $i > j$ **then**
9:             $ep \leftarrow ep + 1$
10:             **continue**
11:         **end if**
12:         $slp \leftarrow (D[j] - D[i])/(t[j] - t[i])$
13:         $itr \leftarrow D[i] - slp * t[i]$
14:         $D\_temp \leftarrow D[i : j + 1]$
15:         $L \leftarrow t[i : j + 1] * slp + itr$
16:         $diff \leftarrow D\_temp - L$
17:         **if** $\min(diff) >= -1.5 * delta * |slp|)$ **then**
18:             $flag \leftarrow$ True
19:             **if** $j >= t.\text{length} - 1$ **then**
20:                 $LP.\text{append}(j)$
21:                 $slopes.\text{append}(slp)$
22:                 $itrs.\text{append}(itr)$
23:                 **break**
24:             **end if**
25:             $slp\_old \leftarrow slp, itr\_old \leftarrow itr, j\_old \leftarrow j$
26:         **else**
27:             **if** $flag$ is True **then**
28:                 $ep \leftarrow ep - 1$
29:                 $LP.\text{append}(j)$
30:                 $slopes.\text{append}(slp)$
31:                 $itrs.\text{append}(itr)$
32:                 $sp \leftarrow ep$
33:                 $i \leftarrow T[sp]$
34:             **end if**
35:             $flag \leftarrow$ False
36:         **end if**
37:         $ep \leftarrow ep + 1$
38:         **if** $ep >= T.\text{length} - 1$ **then**
39:             $env\_point \leftarrow SEARCH\_ENVLOPE\_POINT(j\_old, t, D, delta)$
40:             $T.\text{insert}(sp + 1, env\_point)$
41:             $ep \leftarrow sp + 1$
42:         **end if**
43:     **end while**
44:     **return** $LP, slopes, itrs$
45: **end function**

Algorithm 2. Search Envelope.

1: **function** SEARCH_ENVLOPE_POINT($sp,t,D,delta$)
2:     $ep, env\_point \leftarrow sp + 1$
3:     $env\_point \leftarrow sp$
4:     **while** $ep < t$.length **do**
5:         $slp \leftarrow (D[j] - D[i])/(t[j] - t[i])$
6:         $itr \leftarrow D[i] - slp * t[i]$
7:         $D\_temp \leftarrow D[i : j + 1]$
8:         $L \leftarrow t[i : j + 1] * slp + itr$
9:         $diff \leftarrow D\_temp - L$
10:         **if** $\min(diff) >= -1.5 * delta * |slp|)$ **then**
11:             $env\_point \leftarrow ep$
12:         **end if**
13:         $ep \leftarrow ep + 1$
14:     **end while**
15:     **return** env_point
16: **end function**

References

1. Anderson, J.R., Lebiere, C.: The Atomic Components of Thought. Lawrence Erlbaum Associates, Mahwah (1998)
2. Bitgood, S.: Environmental psychology in museums, zoos, and other exhibition centers. In: In Handbook of Environmental, pp. 461–480 (2002)
3. Ericsson, A.K., Kintsch, W.: Long-term working memory. Psychol. Rev. **102**, 221–245 (1995)
4. Gotoh, F., Ohta, N.: Affective valence of two-compound kanji words. Tsukuba Psychol. Res. **23**(23), 45–52 (2001). http://ci.nii.ac.jp/naid/110000258875/en/, in Japanese
5. Henderson, R.R., Bradley, M.M., Lang, P.J.: Emotional imagery and pupil diameter. Psychophysiology **55**(6), e13050 (2018). https://doi.org/10.1111/psyp.13050
6. Hirabayashi, R., Shino, M., Nakahira, K.T., Kitajima, M.: How auditory information presentation timings affect memory when watching omnidirectional movie with audio guide. In: Proceedings of the 15th International Joint Conference on Computer Vision, Imaging and Computer Graphics Theory and Applications, vol. 2: HUCAPP, pp. 162–169. INSTICC, SciTePress (2020). https://doi.org/10.5220/0008966201620169
7. Kintsch, W.: The use of knowledge in discourse processing: a construction-integration model. Psychol. Rev. **95**, 163–182 (1988)
8. Kintsch, W.: Comprehension: A Paradigm for Cognition. Cambridge University Press, Cambridge (1998)
9. Kitajima, M., Toyota, M.: Decision-making and action selection in Two minds: an analysis based on model human processor with realtime constraints (MHP/RT). Biol. Insp. Cogn. Arch. **5**, 82–93 (2013). https://doi.org/10.1016/j.bica.2013.05.003
10. Murakami, M., Shino, M., Nakahira, K., Kitajima, M.: Effects of emotion-induction words on memory of viewing visual stimuli with audio guide. In: Proceedings of the 16th International Joint Conference on Computer Vision, Imaging and Computer Graphics Theory and Applications - HUCAPP, pp. 89–100. INSTICC, SciTePress (2021). https://doi.org/10.5220/0010348800890100

11. Oliva, M., A., Pupil, A.: dilation reflects the time course of emotion recognition in human vocalizations. Sci. Rep. **8**, 4871 (2018). https://doi.org/10.1038/s41598-018-23265-x
12. Partala, T., Surakka, V.: Pupil size variation as an indication of affective processing. Int. J. Human-Comput. Stud. **59**, 185–198 (2003). https://doi.org/10.1016/S1071-5819(03)00017-X
13. Pierdicca, R., Marques-Pita, M., Paolanti, M., Malinverni, E.S.: Iot and engagement in the ubiquitous museum. Sensors **19**(6), 1387 (2019). https://doi.org/10.3390/s19061387
14. Polyn, S.M., Norman, K.A., Kahana, M.J.: A context maintenance and retrieval model of organizational processes in free recall. Psychol. Rev. **116**, 129–156 (2009)
15. Simon, H.A.: Designing organizations for an information rich world. In: Greenberger, M. (ed.) Computers, Communications, and the Public Interest, pp. 37–72. Johns Hopkins University Press, Baltimore (1971). https://opacplus.bsb-muenchen.de/search?isbn=0-8018-1135-X
16. Talmi, D., Lohnas, L.J., Daw, N.D.: A retrieved context model of the emotional modulation of memory. Psychol. Rev. **126**, 455–485 (2019)

A Bimanual Flick-Based Japanese Software Keyboard Using Direct Kanji Input

Yuya Nakamura[1] and Hiroshi Hosobe[2(✉)]

[1] Graduate Shchool of Computer and Information Sciences, Hosei University, Tokyo, Japan
[2] Faculty of Computer and Information Sciences, Hosei University, Tokyo, Japan
hosobe@acm.org

Abstract. Direct kanji input is a Japanese text input method that is totally different from kana-kanji conversion commonly used in Japan. Direct kanji input is said to enable the user to efficiently input kanji characters after mastering it. In this paper, we propose a bimanual flick-based Japanese software keyboard for a tablet that uses direct kanji input. Once the user masters it, the user can efficiently input kanji characters while holding a tablet with both hands. We present three kanji layouts that we designed for this software keyboard. We show the results of the three experiments that we conducted to evaluate the performance of this keyboard. In the first experiment, we compared it with exiting software keyboards. In the second experiment, we evaluated how much the user can learn it by using its learning support functions. In the third experiment, one of the authors continuously used it for 15 months.

Keywords: Text input · Touch panel · Software keyboard

1 Introduction

Most people in Japan use "kana-kanji" conversion to input Japanese text with computers including tablets and smartphones. Kana and kanji are characters that are commonly used in Japan: while the Chinese-originated kanji characters have meanings, the Japanese own kana characters do not have meanings but are associated with speech sounds instead. A kana-kanji conversion method allows the user to first input kana characters and then to select necessary kanji characters from the candidates suggested by the conversion method.

Direct kanji input is a Japanese text input method that is totally different from kana-kanji conversion. It allows the user to directly select kanji characters, without the prior input of kana characters. Direct kanji input is said to enable the user to efficiently input kanji characters after mastering it, because the user does not need to find necessary kanji characters from the suggested candidates. For hardware keyboards, there are several direct kanji input methods such as T-Code [16]. However, there are no such methods commonly used for touch-panel devices including tablets and smartphones.

In this paper, we propose a Japanese software keyboard for a tablet that uses direct kanji input. For this purpose, we extend the bimanual flick-based tablet keyboard that

ⓒ Springer Nature Switzerland AG 2023
A. A. de Sousa et al. (Eds.): VISIGRAPP 2021, CCIS 1691, pp. 90–111, 2023.
https://doi.org/10.1007/978-3-031-25477-2_5

we previously proposed [9]. Once the user masters our new keyboard, the user can efficiently input kanji characters while holding a tablet with both hands. Also, we present three kanji layouts that we designed for this software keyboard, one based on elements of kanji called bushu, one based on other elements of kanji called on'yomi, and one that is a revision of the first bushu-based layout. Our keyboard supports the direct input of the 2136 kanji characters called joyo-kanji.

We show the results of the three experiments that we conducted to evaluate the performance of our software keyboard. In the first experiment, we compared the bushu-based layout and the on'yomi-based layout with two types of a QWERTY software keyboard and with a flick-based software keyboard. In the second experiment, we evaluated how much the user can learn our keyboard by using the learning support functions that we developed for the keyboard. In the third experiment, to evaluate whether the long-term use of the keyboard enables its mastery, one of the authors continuously used the bushu-based layout for 15 months.

This paper is a revised and extended version of the paper that we previously published as [10]. Especially, the following parts of this paper are newly added or updated:

- We propose a new layout called the revised bushu-based layout, which we describe in the last paragraph of Subsect. 4.2;
- We propose three support function for the user's learning our software keyboard, which we describe in Subsect. 4.5;
- We present the result of an experiment on the performance of the revised bushu-based layout and the learning support functions in Sect. 7 and discuss it in Subsection 9.2;
- We update the result of the long-term experiment in Sect. 8 by extending the term of the experiment from 12 months to 15 months;
- We include a discussion on direct kanji input in Subsect. 9.4.

2 Related Work

We extend our previous bimanual flick software keyboard for a tablet [9]. It improved screen space efficiency by splitting a flick keyboard into the left and the right. However, it was not suitable for kana-kanji conversion because the conversion space generally extends from the left to the right edge of the screen. In this paper, we solve this problem by introducing direct kanji input.

Many Japanese input method uses predictive conversion, which presents conversion suggestions based on previously used words. For example, Ichimura et al. proposed a predictive kana-kanji conversion system [5]. It used the current mainstream predictive conversion method that had been proposed several years before, and reduced users' keystrokes to 78 %.

Unlike predictive conversion that is used in many current Japanese input methods, direct kanji input lets the user select a kanji character. There are two types of direct kanji input: associative and non-associative. Associative direct kanji input has clear relationships between keystrokes and kanji characters. This method has the advantage of being more intuitive and easier to use [16]. On the other hand, non-associative direct kanji input does not have such clear relationships between keystrokes and kanji characters. From the user's point of view, it is a random key placement. For this reason, it is more difficult to use than the associative method. T-Code [16] is one of the most famous methods of non-associative direct kanji input. T-Code uses a combination of two keystrokes on the QWERTY keyboard to enter a kanji character. There is no regularity in such key combinations, and the user needs to first learn them. The non-associative method takes longer time to learn than the associative method, but allows faster input [16]. This is because the associative method requires the user to associate kanji characters with keystrokes, but the non-associative method does not. However, whichever method is used, direct kanji input requires the user to more practice than kana-kanji conversion-based input. In this paper, direct kanji input keyboard was not included in the comparative experiment. The reason is that we were not able to find any available software keyboards for tablets that used direct kanji input.

Research and development of input methods for Chinese characters are not limited to the Japanese language. Pinyin input is a widely used Chinese character input method that uses Chinese readings of characters [7]. Cangjie is a direct Chinese character input method used in Hong Kong. In this method, users think of a Chinese character as a combination of parts. A keystroke corresponds to such a part, and a combination of keystrokes is used to input a Chinese character. Liu and Lin [8] proposed an extension of Cangjie to classify similar Chinese characters. Niu et al. [11] proposed Stroke++, a Chinese character input method for mobile phones, in which an input is made by combining bushu elements.

Various research has been done on keyboards for tablets. Sax et al. proposed an ergonomic QWERTY tablet keyboard [14]. Bi et al. proposed a bimanual gesture keyboard to reduce display space and to shorten finger movement [1]. Hasegawa et al. studied input of a software keyboard, with a focus on aging effects and differences between dominant and non-dominant hands [4]. Odell studied feedbacks of software keyboards [12]. Takei and Hosobe proposed a Japanese kana input keyboard that input one character with two strokes by using 2×6 keys [18]. Yajima and Hosobe proposed a Japanese software keyboard for tablets that reduced user fatigue [20].

In Japan, much research on flick keyboards has been done. Sakurai and Masui proposed a QWERTY flick keyboard [13]. This keyboard enabled input of Japanese kana characters and English letters without mode changes. Fukatsu et al. proposed an eyes-free Japanese kana input method called no-look flick [2]. This method enabled flick input for vowels and consonants in two keystrokes. Hakoda et al. proposed a kana input method using two fingers for touch-panel devices [3]. This method was also an eyes-free Japanese input method, but enabled gesture input by two fingers.

3   Japanese Characters and Keyboards

3.1   Kana Characters

Japanese text is composed of Chinese-originated kanji characters and Japanese kana characters. While a kanji character typically has a meaning, a kana character is associated with a speech sound. There are two kinds of kana characters called hiragana and katakana. Although they are used for different purposes, they correspond to each other;

for each hiragana character, there is a corresponding katakana character, and vice versa. There are approximately 50 basic kana characters, which are further divided into 10 groups that are ordered, each of which typically consists of 5 characters. The first group is special because its 5 characters indicate 5 vowels that are pronounced "a," "i," "u," "e", and "o". The other 9 groups are associated with the basic consonants, "k", "s", "t", "n", "h", "m", "y", "r", and "w". A kana character in these 9 groups forms the sound that combines a consonant and a vowel. For example, the 5 characters of the "k" group are pronounced "ka", "ki", "ku", "ke", and "ko". This grouping of kana characters is basic knowledge of the Japanese language.

3.2   Elements of Kanji Characters

We explain bushu and on'yomi elements of kanji characters that we use in our software keyboard.

Bushu.   Bushu, also called a radical, indicates an element of kanji characters. Kanji characters are generally made up of dots and lines. A bushu element is a common collection of such dots and lines. For example, Fig. 1 shows kanji characters for a pine and cherry blossoms. The red boxes in the figure indicate their bushu elements. This type of bushu is called "kihen" and is typically used in kanji characters related to trees. Other kanji characters that use kihen correspond to, for example, a small forest and a bridge. The total number of bushu elements used in Japan is 214.

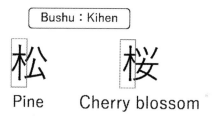

Fig. 1. Examples of bushu elements.

On'yomi.   Kanji characters typically have two kinds of readings, on'yomi and kun'yomi. The on'yomi of a kanji character indicates its old Chinese reading, while the kun'yomi indicates its Japanese reading. In general, the on'yomi of a kanji character does not make sense in Japanese while the kun'yomi does. For example, the kun'yomi of the kanji character for cherry blossoms in the Fig. 1 is "sakura", which means cherry blossoms by itself. By contrast, its on'yomi, which is "ou", has no meaning in Japanese.

3.3   Japanese Keyboards

Figure 2-a shows a typical Japanese flick keyboard. The main key layout is composed of 4×3 keys. If a user flicks a key to the left, upward, to the right, or downward with a thumb, the keyboard inputs a character corresponding to the direction (Figs. 2-b and 2-c). A conversion space is located at the top of the keyboard. When a user touches a word, kana characters are converted to kanji or other characters. If a user touches the upward arrow, it will show other kanji candidates.

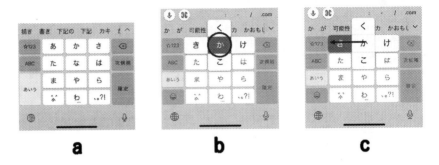

Fig. 2. Typical Japanese flick keyboard (available on iOS).

4 Proposed Method

4.1 Bimanual Flick

We propose a software keyboard for tablets that splits a flick keyboard into the left and right sides. It is based on our previous bimanual split flick keyboard [9] that uses normal kana-kanji conversion. Instead of using such normal kana-kanji conversion, our new software keyboard introduces direct kanji input. Since the user can use the keyboard while holding the tablet with both hands, the advantages of split keyboards are not lost. If the user wants to input a kana character, the user only needs to flick a key on one side as with other splits keyboards.

A primary reason for developing a new direct kanji input method is that previous methods were designed for desktop computers with hardware keyboards. Although these previous methods could be adapted to newer devices such as tablets and smartphones, there has not been much research, and their effectiveness is unclear. Also, the proposed method might be applicable to the Chinese language. This is because Cangjie is similar to our bushu-based method and Pinyin input is similar to our on'yomi-based method (although Japanese and Chinese use different sets of standard Chinese characters, which would require extra efforts.)

A typical input flow for a kanji character is shown in Fig. 3. This example inputs the kanji character meaning "cherry blossoms" previously shown in Fig. 1. Figure 3-a shows a state in which no input is made. This kanji character uses the bushu element called "kihen", which belongs to the "ki" group. The "ki" group further belongs to the "k" group. Therefore, the user first touches the "ka" key that represents the "k" group (Fig. 3-b). Then the user flicks the finger to the left to show the "ki" group (Fig. 3-c). The user looks for the kanji character for cherry blossoms, finding that it belongs to the top left key. Therefore, the user touches the top left key (Fig. 3-d). Then the user flicks the finger to the right (Fig. 3 -e), which completes the input of the kanji character.

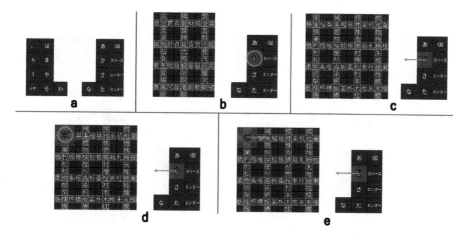

Fig. 3. Typical input flow for a kanji character.

The number of kanji characters that can be input with this method is 2136. These kanji characters, called joyo-kanji, are indicated as the standard for using kanji characters in social life in Japan. According to a survey conducted by the Japanese Agency for Cultural Affairs, more than 96 % of the total number of kanji characters regularly used in Japanese society are joyo-kanji characters [17]. It was possible to cover more kanji characters in the proposed method. However, we decided that no more kanji characters were needed. Other kanji and kana characters can be input using the conversion function of the previous bimanual flick keyboard. It also should be noted that our method covers more characters than T-Code [16], which covers 1600 characters.

4.2 Kanji Layouts

We propose three kanji layouts: the bushu-based layout, the on'yomi-based layout, and the revised bushu-based layout. We used the first two methods in the comparative experiment, and used the revised bushu-based layout in the experiment on learning.

Bushu-based Layout. The bushu-based layout uses bushu elements of kanji characters. The layout is shown in Figs. 4 and 5. Each cross in Fig. 4 indicates a key that can be flicked upward, downward, to the left, and to the right, and the positions of the crosses correspond to the shape of the keyboard. The bushu elements that appear more than once in the figure are those that have many kanji characters. On the contrary, the bushu elements shown in Fig. 5 have a few kanji characters. They are grouped together in the parts labeled with the numbers in Fig. 4. In the case of kanji characters with the same bushu element, they are arranged by on'yomi from the top left. Also, since there is a limit on the size of the keyboard, four bushu elements with large numbers of characters are divided into two keys. In this case, they are located symmetrically.

On'yomi-based Layout. The on'yomi-based layout arranges kanji characters by using their readings. Since dakuon is also present in on'yomi, the "k," "s," "t," and "h" groups

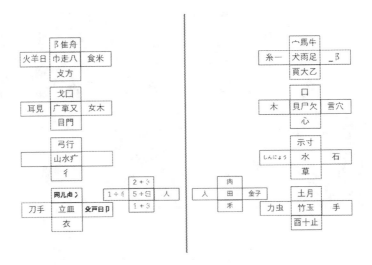

Fig. 4. Bushu-based layout.

can be replaced with the dakuon keyboard. Figure 6 shows the process of inputting the kanji characters of the "ka" group. If the user presses the top left key on the kanji keyboard, it is replaced with the dakuon keyboard. If the user presses the top left key on the dakuon keyboard, it is replaced with the original keyboard.

Revised Bushu-based Layout. The third layout is a revision of the bushu-based layout. We designed this layout, motivated by the requests that we obtained from the participants in the comparative experiment that we present in Sect. 6. This revised bushu-based layout places the bushu elements according to the numbers of their components (Fig. 7), where the key sizes are not limited even for the bushu elements with many kanji characters. Since bushu elements with many kanji characters correspond to single keys, there is perfect correspondence between bushu elements and kana characters.

4.3   Direct Kanji Input

Our keyboard is based on direct kanji input. Previous direct kanji input methods were categorized into associative input and non-associative input. We regard the bushu-based layout as being semi-associative because it is neither associative nor non-associative in the original senses. It basically arranges kanji characters by bushu elements, but there is no perfect correspondence between kana characters and bushu elements. By contrast, the on'yomi layout is associative since there is correspondence between kanji characters and kana characters.

4.4   Key Arrangement

Our software keyboard is of 240-px height and 180-px width before conversion. This layout reduces the display space by 73 % in the portrait mode and by 83 % in the

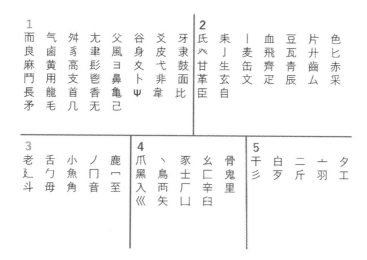

Fig. 5. Bushu elements with a few kanji characters.

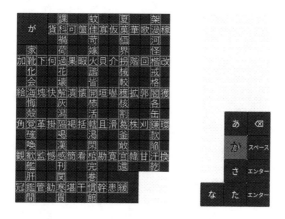

Fig. 6. On'yomi-based layout (for inputting a kanji characters in the "ka" group).

landscape mode, compared with the QWERTY keyboard with the maximum display width. The size and the position of the bushu-based layout are based on the heat map used in the design of the Windows 8 touch keyboard [6]. This limited the bushu-based layout to 4×4. By contrast, the on'yomi layout does not have this limit. Therefore, in the case of the on'yomi-based layout, there may be much more kanji characters for a kana character than in the case of the bushu-based layout. In the case of the bushu-based layout, the maximum number of kanji characters for a kana character is 80. Since there are 50 kana characters in total, the total number of kanji characters that can be placed is 4000. We adopted 2136 joyo-kanji characters. Kana keys with a few kanji characters are composed of a 2×2 kanji layout. The keyboard in the bushu-based layout is of the maximum size of 320-px height and 320-px width on one side. The keyboard in the on'yomi-based layout is of the maximum size of 480-px height and 400-px width.

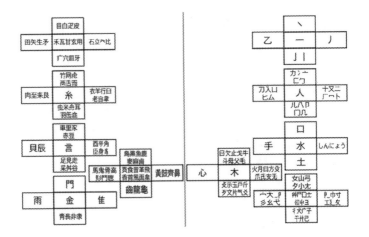

Fig. 7. Revised bushu-based layout.

4.5   Learning Support Functions

Our software keyboard provides the following three learning support functions:

1. Support function for learning the type of the bushu element of a kanji character (Fig. 8);
2. Support function for leaning the location of the bushu element of a kanji character (Fig. 9);
3. Support function for learning the location of a kanji character on the keyboard (Fig. 10).

We developed these functions, motivated by the result of the comparative experiment that we present in Sect. 6. In the development of these functions, we reflected the participants' comments that we obtained from the comparative experiment, as well as our own experience in the long-term experiment that we present in Sect. 8.

Fig. 8. Support function 1 for learning the type of the bushu element of a kanji character.

Support function 1 displays Fig. 8 while the user is pressing the hint button. Support function 2 displays the bushu element of a kanji character in the target text, which allows

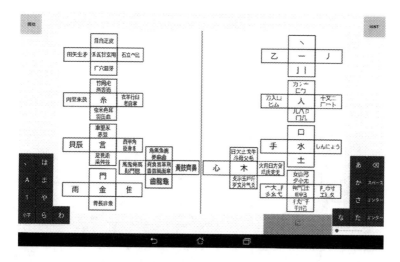

Fig. 9. Support function 2 for learning the location of the bushu of a kanji character.

the user to switch to the bushu element of the next kanji character by pressing the hint button. Support function 3 colors the kanji characters with red whose readings match with the kana characters that are being input.

5 Implementation

We implemented the proposed software keyboard on an ASUS ZenPad 10 tablet (Android OS 7.0, 1920 × 1200-px screen) as shown in Fig. 11. The keys are of 60 × 60 px, and the keyboard is placed symmetrically at the lower ends of the screen. In the proposed keyboard, its position was adjustable with a bar at the bottom of the screen. The red part in the figure indicates the conversion space that is used to enter non-joyo-kanji and katakana characters. The user can display different characters by swiping the conversion space to the left or to the right. The radio button in the center of the figure allows the user to change the key layout.

6 Comparative Experiments

To evaluate the proposed software keyboard, we conducted an experiment on its comparison with existing software keyboards. We compared the bushu-based layout, the on'yomi-based layout, two QWERTY keyboards, and a flick keyboard. There are two types of QWERTY keyboards, one with the learning of predictive conversion enabled and one with the learning disabled. The reason why the direct input method was not compared is that we were not able to find any available software keyboards for tablets that used direct kanji input. The learning of the predictive conversion is reset for each participant. The comparative experiments treated the landscape mode of each keyboard layout. In the proposed keyboard, its position was adjustable with a bar at the bottom of the screen. The position of the keyboard was set by each participant.

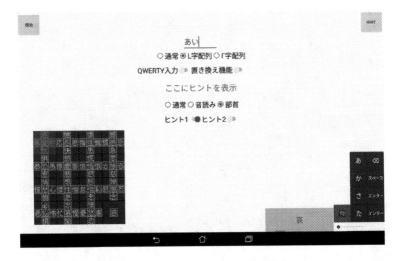

Fig. 10. Support function 3 for learning the location of a kanji character on the keyboard.

We recruited 8 participants who were Japanese university students and workers. Their ages ranged from 23 to 24, and all the participants were male. They were seated on a chair and held a tablet in the landscape mode with both hands. If participants were not able to reach the center of the keyboard in using the QWERTY, they were allowed to release their hands. The comparative experiments were composed of two input experiments and subjective evaluation. After the input experiments, we investigated subjective evaluation for each method. In addition to the UEQ, free descriptions were also collected.

We measured the input speed and the error rate. The input speed is measured by the number of characters per minute CPM, which is calculated as follows:

$$CPM = \frac{T - E}{S} \times 60 \tag{1}$$

where T is the length of the input string, S is the input time, and E is the number of characters that were wrong. This means the number of characters typed correctly per minute. On the other hand, the error rate ER is calculated as follows:

$$ER = \frac{IF}{C + IF + INF} \tag{2}$$

where C is the total number of correct words, IF is the number of incorrect but fixed (backspaced) words, and INF is the number of incorrect (but not fixed) words. These equations are based on Bi et al.'s research [1], and we adjust them to Japanese character input.

The comparative experiments treated two kinds of input: sentence input and kanji conversion-required word input. In the following, we describe the details and the results of the two experiments.

Fig. 11. Implementation of the proposed software keyboard.

6.1 Sentence Input

In the sentence input experiment, five input sentences were selected for each method from a book [19] about learning joyo-kanji with example sentences. One of the QWERTY keyboards and the flick keyboard enabled learning in predictive conversion, but the sentences were specific to each method, and therefore the learning was limited to the inside of a method. Before the experiment, participants warmed up with a few sentences for each method. They started the experiment by pushing the start button on the upper left corner of the screen, and moved to the next sentence by pushing the enter key. A target sentence was displayed on the text field at the top of the screen. The sentences included in the list were of about 20-character length and mixed kana and kanji characters.

Since the bushu-based layout generally takes long time for users to learn, and also since the short warm-up before the experiment was not sufficient for the participants' learning, a support function was provided. It consisted of two hints: a hint for the bushu element of a kanji character and a hint for the position of a kanji character. The hint for bushu was displayed by pressing the hint button in the upper right corner of the screen (Fig. 11). When the button was pressed, the bushu elements of kanji characters in the target sentence were displayed one by one. The hint for a kanji position was shown in Figs. 4 and 5. The participants were able to look at this diagram if they did not know the positions of kanji characters.

6.2 Result of the Sentence Input Experiment

The results of the input speeds and the error rates are shown in Figs. 12-a and 12-b respectively. In the charts, "QWERTY_ON" and "Flick" indicate the QWERTY keyboard and the flick keyboard with learning in predictive conversion respectively. A higher input speed is better, and a high error rate is worse. The results show large differences between the proposed methods and the existing methods (shown as the three bars on the right sides of the charts). The ANOVA on the two proposed methods also showed a significant difference in the input speeds ($p < 0.05$), but not in the error rates. Among the existing methods, the flick keyboard was the fastest, and the two QWERTY keyboards were of about the same speeds. Also, the flick keyboard was the highest in the error rates, and the two QWERTY keyboards showed about the same error rates.

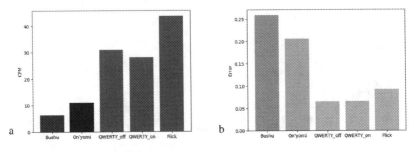

Fig. 12. Result of the sentence input experiment: (a) input speeds and (b) error rates.

6.3　Kanji Conversion-Required Word Input

The experiment on the kanji conversion-required word input treated the same layouts as the sentence input experiment. Its procedure was almost the same as that of the sentence input experiment, and the only difference was what the participants input. In this experiment, the participants input words written in kana characters at the top of the screen and converted them into kanji characters. The experiment was conducted after the sentence input experiment and there was no warm-up time. Five words were used for each method, and when a participant pressed the enter key, the next word was displayed. The target word was the word that appeared in the sentence input experiment. For this reason, the hints used in the sentence input experiment were not used in the word input.

6.4　Result of the Kanji Conversion-Required Word Input Experiment

The results of the input speeds and the error rates are shown in Figs. 13-a and 13-b respectively. The results show large differences between the proposed methods and the existing methods. The ANOVA on the two proposed methods showed a significant difference in the input speeds ($p < 0.05$), but not in the error rates. Among the existing methods, the QWERTY keyboard with learning in predictive conversion and the flick keyboard were the fastest and almost comparable. The three existing methods showed similar low error rates.

6.5　Subjective Evaluation and Participants' Comments

The subjective evaluation was performed by using the UEQ [15] to investigate the two proposed methods and the QWERTY keyboard with learning. Figures 14-a and 14-b show the results of the subjective evaluation. In the bushu-based layout, the UEQ showed an excellent rating for novelty although the ratings of the other items were low.

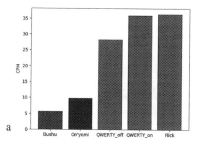
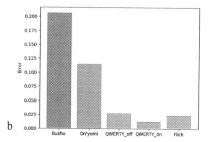

Fig. 13. Result of the kanji conversion-required word input experiment: (a) input speeds and (b) error rates.

In particular, ratings for perspicuity and efficiency were very low. The on'yomi-based layout was rated higher than the bushu-based layout except novelty. When the on'yomi-based layout and the existing methods were compared, the existing methods were better in perspicuity, efficiency, and dependability, and the on'yomi-based layout was better in novelty.

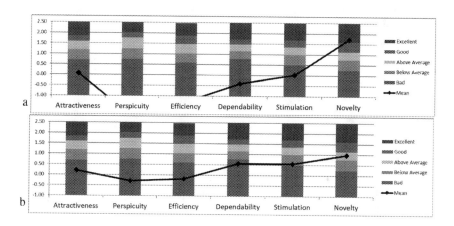

Fig. 14. Results of the UEQ on (a) the bushu-based layout and (b) the on'yomi-based layout.

The comparison of the on'yomi-based layout and the existing methods is shown in Fig. 15. Both the QWERTY and the flick keyboard obtained higher ratings in perspicuity, efficiency, and dependability. The proposed method was rated higher in novelty.

The participants' comments mainly indicated the difficulty of inputting with the proposed methods. The comments included "It is like a mental exercise", "I'm tired", and "It is not for me". The on'yomi-based layout had more positive comments than the bushu-based layout.

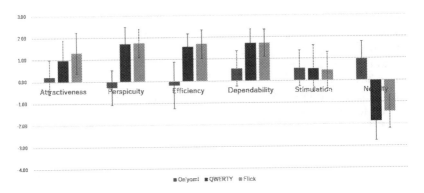

Fig. 15. Result of the comparison of the on'yomi-based layout, the QWERTY keyboard, and the flick keyboard in the UEQ.

7   Experiment on Learning

After the comparative experiment, we revised the bushu-based layout and added three learning support functions. To evaluate the revised layout and the support functions, we conducted an experiment.

7.1   Method

We recruited 8 participants who were Japanese university students and company employees, 21 to 24 years old, and all male. The experiment consisted of two sessions: the practice session in which the participants input 100 sentences, and the main session in which they input 30 sentences. Each sentence for the practice session contained one kanji character, and 5 kanji characters were selected from 20 bushu elements with many kanji characters. The sentences for the main session consisted of 10 sentences used in the practice session, 10 sentences with kanji characters whose bushu elements were the same as the ones used in the practice session, and 10 sentences with kanji characters whose bushu elements were not used in the practice session. The experiment were divided to sections, each of which consisted of 10 sentences; there were pauses of several seconds between the sections. After the main session, we conducted a subjective evaluation using the UEQ and collected comments from the participants.

7.2   Result

Figures 16-a and 16-b show the results of the input speeds and the error rates in the practice session. The horizontal axes correspond to the every 10 inputs. Figure 16-a suggests that the input speeds generally increased according to the numbers of the inputs. Around the 100th input, The input speed became nearly the double of the first 10 inputs. By contrast, according to Fig. 16-b, the error rate for the first 10 inputs were significantly high, and those after that indicated almost the average result.

Figures 17-a and 17-b show the results of the input speeds and the error rates in the main session. The horizontal axes correspond to (1) the 10 sentences used in the practice session, (2) the 10 sentences with kanji characters whose bushu elements were the same as the ones used in the practice session, and (3) the 10 sentences with kanji characters whose bushu elements were not used in the practice session. The mean input speeds were the fastest for (1), the next for (2), and the slowest for (3). The error rates were the best for (3), the next for (1), and the worst for (2).

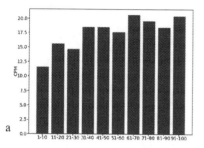
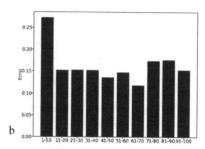

Fig. 16. Result of the practice session in the experiment on learning: (a) input speeds and (b) error rates.

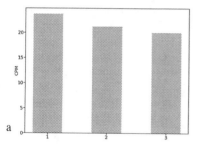
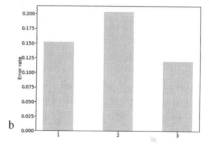

Fig. 17. Result of the main session in the experiment on learning: (a) input speeds and (b) error rates.

7.3   Subjective Evaluation and Participants' Comments

We conducted subjective evaluation by using the UEQ. Figure 18 shows the result. It obtained high ratings for stimulation and novelty, a nearly average rating for attractiveness, and low ratings for perspicuity, efficiency, and dependability. Compared with the evaluation of the bushu-based layout and the on'yomi-based layout, the evaluation of the revised bushu-based layout is similar but appears superior. However, it is still largely inferior to the existing methods especially in perspicuity, efficiency, and dependability.

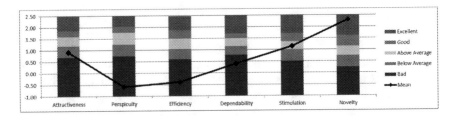

Fig. 18. Result of the UEQ on the revised bushu-based layout.

The positive comments of the participants included "Kanji flick input is rare", "Inputting kanji characters became easy after I memorized their locations". The negative comments included "The method was difficult because there were many kanji characters for single keys", "The method was confusing when similar looking kanji characters were near". Also, there was an opinion about the unclear display of the learning support functions.

8   Long-Term Experiment

Direct kanji input is a method that takes time to learn. Therefore, one of the authors by himself conducted an experiment to confirm its mastery by using the proposed method for 15 months.

8.1   Method

The experiment consisted of the input of sentences. Every day the author entered five sentences chosen at random from 602 sentences in the literature [19]. The 602 sentences contain 68 % of the joyo-kanji characters. The author is a 23-year-old male graduate student in the field of computer science. In the experiment, the author was seated on a chair and held a tablet with both hands. The experiment was conducted with the bushu-based layout, and a search function was used when the location of a kanji character was not known.

8.2   Result

Figure 19-a and 19-b show the results of the input speeds and the error rates respectively. In both charts, the main line indicates the average value for a day. The green bars represent the maximum and the minimum values for the day. For comparison, the author entered the same sentences by using the QWERTY keyboard on the ASUS ZenPad 10 (red line) and our previous bimanual flick keyboard [9] (purple line). The QWERTY keyboard on the ASUS ZenPad 10 also enabled learning in predictive conversion. According to the charts, both the input speeds and the error rates gradually improved day by day. The reason why the bimanual flick keyboard had a high error rate was because it used the backspace key to make adjustments during the conversion.

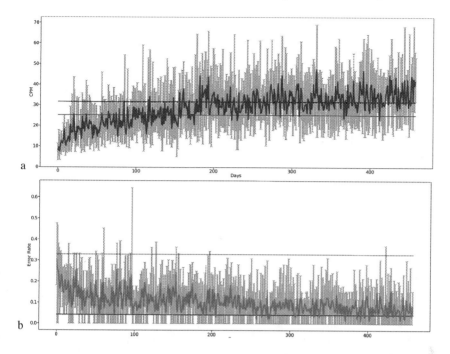

Fig. 19. Result of the long-term experiment (15 months): (a) input speeds and (b) error rates.

9   Discussion

9.1   Comparative Experiment

Sentence Input. The result of the sentence input experiment showed that the proposed methods were inferior to existing methods in terms of the input speeds. There was also a significant difference in the input speeds between the proposed methods. We think that this is because the bushu-based layout is a semi-associative direct kanji input method and the on'yomi-based layout is associative. The semi-associative method takes longer time for users to learn than the associative method, but can be expected to enable faster input. The experiment tried to compensate for the difference by providing hints, but it was not successful.

The result also showed that the proposed methods were inferior to the existing methods in terms of the error rates. However, there was no significant difference between the proposed methods in terms of the error rates. We think that the error rates of the on'yomi-based layout in the sentence input experiment were higher than its error rates in the kanji conversion-required word input experiment because the given sentences were written in kanji and kana characters. In this case, if a participant could not read kanji, he would have trouble in input.

Therefore, to compare input speeds, users who used the proposed method for a long time are needed. One solution might be to distribute the software of the proposed method. We could implement a function to measure the input speed and evaluate it. However, it would be difficult to have many users of the proposed method. Another solution might be to have a small number of participants who would use the proposed method for a long term. Either way, it would be difficult to measure the performance for one year. Therefore, we think that the immediate solution is to increase the efficiency of the learning of the proposed method. Specifically, better key layouts and learning support software are needed.

Kanji Conversion-Required Word Input. The results of the experiments showed that the input speeds of the proposed methods in the kanji conversion-required word input were not very different from those in the sentence input. However, there was a difference between the existing methods. The QWERTY keyboard and the flick keyboard with learning in predictive conversion showed high input speeds. As in the sentence input experiment, a significant difference in the input speeds was shown between the bushu-based layout and the on'yomi-based layout.

Overall, the error rates in the kanji conversion-required word input were lower than those in the sentence input. We think that this is because of the small number of characters entered. However, there was a difference in the error rates between the bushu-based layout and the on'yomi-based layout. We think that the reason is that the participants using the on'yomi-based layout were able to easily associate kanji characters with kana characters, which was not applicable to the bushu-based layout. However, there was still no significant difference between the bushu-based and the on'yomi-based layout. We think that this is because the on'yomi-based layout is not always associative. Since the bushu-based layout is semi-associative and the on'yomi-based layout is associative, the input speeds and the error rates might be reversed depending on the degree of learning. For accurate assessment, we need to find out what is the ratio of the two degrees of learnability.

There was no large difference in the error rates between the on'yomi-based layout and any existing method. According to this result, although it is difficult to compare the input speeds without the long-term use of the methods, we think that the error rates of the methods could be compared even without the long-term use. To reduce the error rate, another associative layout should be proposed and compared with the on'yomi-based layout.

Subjective Evaluation. The subjective evaluation showed that the bushu-based layout was of high novelty. However, all the other ratings were low, and in particular, those of perspicuity and efficiency were very low. We think that this is because of the complicated layout that is difficult to use without learning. We also think that this is because the user evaluated the bushu-based and the on'yomi-based layout by comparing them.

The on'yomi-based layout was higher than the bushu-based layout in all the items except novelty. Still, other than stimulation and novelty, it was rated low. One major factor is the short amount of time that the participants spent using the proposed methods. However, in order for users to use it for a long time, the proposed methods should give a good impression at the beginning. The goal is to improve each item to the point that cause no large difference between the proposed methods and the existing methods.

9.2 Experiment on Learning

The input speeds in the practice session in the experiment on learning generally increased according to the numbers of inputs although there was some variation in the increase. We think that this variation was due to the bushu elements of the kanji characters in the sentences. In fact, their order was not systematic since we did not place any priorities on the kanji characters for the practice session.

The error rates in the practice session showed significantly high for the first 10 sentences and became almost average after the first 10 sentences. We observed that many participants made significantly high error rates especially for the first 5 sentences. We think that this was because they were not used to the proposed method. After the first 10 sentences, the error rates remained almost the same and did not improve.

The input speeds in the main session were the fastest for the sentences used in the practice session, the next for the sentences with kanji characters whose bushu elements were the same, and the slowest for the sentences with kanji characters whose bushu elements were not used in the practice session. The results were expected because the speeds for the already practiced kanji characters and bushu elements were faster. We think that this shows the effectiveness of our learning support functions. However, in this experiment, we asked all the participants to use the learning support functions. Therefore, we were not able to measure the input speeds for the case that these functions were not used.

The error rates were the best for the unpracticed bushu elements, the next for the practiced kanji characters, and the worst for the practiced bushu elements. The results were unexpected because the error rate for the practiced kanji characters was not the best. We think that this was because the participants became careful in inputting the sentences with the unpracticed bushu elements but became careless otherwise. Also, we think that the error rate for the practiced kanji characters were not much worse because the participants memorized their locations, and that the error rate for the practiced bushu elements were worse because they did not know the locations of the kanji characters. We think that our learning support functions were not effective from the viewpoint of the error rates.

9.3 Long-Term Experiment

According to the result of the long-term experiment, the input speed of the bushu-based layout after 15 months was about the same as that of the QWERTY keyboard. The long-term experiment was conducted by one of the authors alone, and therefore it is not objective. However, it shows that the input speed of the bushu-based layout could improve with a long-term use.

Based on the author's experience, we think that there are three stages of growth in the input speeds. The first is to learn the placement of bushu elements. In other words, the user can remember the locations of bushu elements without referring to Fig. 4. The next stage is to identify bushu elements of kanji characters whose bushu is confusing.

For example, a kanji character is confusing if it has more than one bushu-like element. The final stage is to learn the location of a kanji character. After this, the author knows where frequently used kanji characters are located. We expect that the number of such kanji characters will increase as the author further continues it.

The error rate of the bushu-based layout after 15 months is still higher than that of the QWERTY keyboard. There are several reasons. The first is due to a mistake in the bushu element of a kanji character. Because of the specification of the input, if the user makes a mistake in the bushu, a kana character will be input. The error rate also increases if the user makes a mistake in the kanji character itself. Since some kanji characters have similar shapes, users may make inputting errors. These problems might be solved after a longer-term use.

We have not yet compared the bushu-based layout with other methods with a long-term use. Especially, it would be desirable to include the on'yomi-based layout in the experiment.

9.4   Direct Kanji Input

Direct kanji input may enable the users to efficiently input kanji characters once they master after the long time for learning it. The results of our research also show that it is true to a certain degree. However, there are currently no popular kanji direct input methods for touch-panel devices such as smartphones and tablets. We believe that direct kanji input has potential for a more efficient and more learnable kanji input method for such devices.

From the observation of our experimental results, we think that kanji direct input typically shows large variation in the input speed before it is mastered. This is because it requires learning for individual kanji characters and causes different input speeds based on the mastery of individual kanji characters. We think that such variation in the input speed should be smaller.

10   Conclusions and Future Work

We proposed a bimanual flick-based Japanese software keyboard using direct kanji input. We also presented three layouts for this keyboard, the bushu-based, the on'yomi-based, and the revised bushu-based layout. We evaluated the performance of our method by conducting a comparative experiment, an experiment on learning, and a long-term experiment.

Our future work is to allow the users to learn our software keyboard during its daily use by enabling the learning support functions to work whenever necessary. Other future directions include developing a learning support function for reducing the error rate, determining the kanji layout by comparing the changes of the input speeds in the long-term use of the on'yomi-based layout and the revised bushu-based layout, and enabling the users to add necessary non-joyo-kanji characters.

References

1. Bi, X., Chelba, C., Ouyang, T., Partridge, K., Zhai, S.: Bimanual gesture keyboard. In: Proceedings of UIST, pp. 137–146 (2012)
2. Fukatsu, Y., Shizuki, B., Tanaka, J.: No-look flick: Single-handed and eyes-free Japanese text input system on touch screens of mobile devices. In: Proceedings of MobileHCI, pp. 161–170 (2013)
3. Hakoda, H., Fukatsu, Y., Shizuki, B., Tanaka, J.: An eyes-free kana input method using two fingers for touch-panel devices. IPSJ SIG Tech. Rep. **154**(6), 1–8 (2013). In Japanese
4. Hasegawa, A., Hasegawa, S., Miyao, M.: Characteristics of the input on software keyboard of tablet devices: Aging effects and differences between the dominant and non-dominant hands for input. J. Mobile Interact. **2**(1), 23–28 (2012)
5. Ichimura, Y., Saito, Y., Kimura, K., Hirakawa, H.: Kana-kanji conversion system with input support based on prediction. In: Proceedings of COLING, vol. 1, pp. 341–347 (2000)
6. Knox, K.: Designing the Windows 8 touch keyboard (2012). https://learn.microsoft.com/en-us/archive/blogs/b8/designing-the-windows-8-touch-keyboard
7. Li, G., Li, Y.: Chinese pinyin input method in smartphone era: a literature review study. In: Yamamoto, S., Mori, H. (eds.) HCII 2019. LNCS, vol. 11569, pp. 34–43. Springer, Cham (2019). https://doi.org/10.1007/978-3-030-22660-2_3
8. Liu, C.-L., Lin, J.-H.: Using structural information for identifying similar Chinese characters. In: Proceedings of ACL HLT, pp. 93–96 (2008)
9. Nakamura, Y., Hosobe, H.: A Japanese bimanual flick keyboard for tablets that improves display space efficiency. In: Proceedings of VISIGRAPP, vol. 2, pp. 170–177 (2020)
10. Nakamura, Y., Hosobe, H.: A flick-based Japanese tablet keyboard using direct kanji input. In: Proceedings of VISIGRAPP, vol. 2, pp. 49–59 (2021)
11. Niu, J., Zhu, L., Yan, Q., Liu, Y., Wang, K.: Stroke++: a hybrid Chinese input method for touch screen mobile phones. In: Proceedings of MobileHCI, pp. 381–382 (2010)
12. Odell, D.: On-screen keyboard: Does the presence of feedback or tactile landmarks improve typing performance? In: Proceedings of MobileHCI, pp. 131–136 (2015)
13. Sakurai, Y., Masui, T.: A flick-based Japanese input system for a QWERTY software keyboard. IPSJ SIG Tech. Rep. **154**(5), 1–4 (2013). In Japanese
14. Sax, C., Lau, H., Lawrence, E.: LiquidKeyboard: an ergonomic, adaptive QWERTY keyboard for touchscreens and surfaces. In: Proceedings of ICDS, pp. 117–122 (2011)
15. Schrepp, M., Hinderks, A., Thomaschewski, J.: Construction of a benchmark for the user experience questionnaire (UEQ). Int. J. Interact. Multimedia Artif. Intell. **4**(4), 40–44 (2017)
16. T-Code Project. T-Code laboratory (2003). https://openlab.ring.gr.jp/tcode/index.html. In Japanese
17. Takeda, Y.: A survey of the occurrence of kanji characters. In: 4th Meeting of the Working Group on the Standard of Japanese Education. Japanese Agency for Cultural Affairs (2019). In Japanese
18. Takei, K., Hosobe, H.: A 2-by-6 button Japanese software keyboard for tablets. In: Proceedings of VISIGRAPP, vol. 2, pp. 147–154 (2018)
19. Waragai, H.: Learning Joyo-Kanji by Reading One Sentence. Goto Shoin (2008). In Japanese
20. Yajima, T., Hosobe, H.: A Japanese software keyboard for tablets that reduces user fatigue. In: Proceedings of COMPSAC, pp. 339–346 (2018)

Comparison of Cardiac Activity and Subjective Measures During Virtual Reality and Real Aircraft Flight

Patrice Labedan[(✉)] ⓘ, Frédéric Dehais ⓘ, and Vsevolod Peysakhovich ⓘ

ISAE-SUPAERO, Université de Toulouse, Toulouse, France
patrice.labedan@isae.fr

Abstract. Pilot training requires significant resources, both material and human. Immersive virtual reality is a good way to reduce costs and get around the lack of resources availability. However, the effectiveness of virtual flight simulation has not yet been fully assessed, in particular, using physiological measures. In this study, 10 pilots performed standard traffic patterns on both real aircraft (DR400) and its virtual simulation (in head-mounted device and motion platform). We used subjective measures through questionnaires of immersion, presence, and ability to control the aircraft, and objective measures using heart rate, and heart rate variability. The results showed that the pilots were able to fully control the aircraft. Points to improve include updating the hardware (better display resolution and hand tracking) and the simulator dynamics for modelling ground effect. During the real experience, the overall heart rate (HR) was higher (+20 bpm on average), and the heart rate variability (HRV) was lower compared to the virtual experience. The flight phases in both virtual and real flights induced similar cardiac responses with more mental efforts during take-off and landing compared to the downwind phase. Overall, our findings indicate that virtual flight reproduces real flight and can be used for pilot training. However, replacing pilot training with exclusively virtual flight hours seems utopian at this point.

Keywords: Virtual reality · Flight simulation · Heart rate · Heart rate variability · Piloting

1 Introduction

Despite a significant passenger traffic decrease in aviation due to the COVID-19 pandemic, the global air transport sector is recovering. The post-COVID-19 aviation industry will inevitably face challenges of pilot and instructors shortage. Pilot training requires significant resources, both material and human, such as flight simulators, flight instructors, and, of course, aircraft. It represents a high cost and generates constraints on the availability of these means. Safety is also a paramount aspect of pilot training, particularly, while flying on real aircraft (breakdowns, weather phenomena, etc.).

Immersive virtual reality (VR) seems to be an adequate alternative to reduce costs and get around the lack of availability of resources (aircraft, simulators, instructors) for skill acquisition [19,44]. The recent development makes the design of virtual environments such as cockpit or flight simulators more flexible [1]. The VR is already used

© Springer Nature Switzerland AG 2023
A. A. de Sousa et al. (Eds.): VISIGRAPP 2021, CCIS 1691, pp. 112–131, 2023.
https://doi.org/10.1007/978-3-031-25477-2_6

professionally or evaluated for training in various fields such as UAV piloting [36], fire fighting [6,7], maritime domain [29], first responsers training [24], evacuation training [12], or mining industry training [45].

The medical field is a forerunner in the field of VR adoption [5,20,22,28,34]. VR now allows to deliver, in some cases, cost-effective, repeatable, standardized clinical training on demands. It is a powerful educational tool and implementation is growing worldwide [33]. In surgery, the use of virtual reality has been successfully tested for many years [38]. Surgeons in training can acquire skills without threatening the lives of patients, especially in laparoscopic surgery [16], with positive results in terms of feelings of presence and the ability to transfer the training to the real operation. This is also the case in cataract surgery [40], in oral and maxillofacial surgery [3], etc. These promising results in the field of surgery and its similarities to flight, including high levels of stress, accuracy, and risk-taking [35], make VR worthy of consideration for pilot training.

However, the use of VR as an operational learning tool still presents challenges [13] in terms of immersion, sense of presence [42], fatigue, and motion sickness [26]. Indeed, it is recognized that simulators do not reproduce the level of engagement that pilots may experience in real-world conditions [14,31]. Studies comparing VR and simulator training [2,27,31] or simulator and real flight training [17], have already been conducted. A recent study [26] with pilot instructors showed that the strong feeling of immersion, combined with good controllability of the aircraft, generates high presence levels. Another study [32] showed that VR is an efficient tool for learning checklists in the early stages of pilot training. But recently it was shown that virtual reality flight simulations induce higher workload, physical demand, and effort, exceeding acceptable levels [2]. To date, to our best knowledge, no research except one has been found directly comparing VR and real flights. This study [25], with 4 participants, showed preliminary results with a higher heart rate and a lower heart rate variability in real flight compared with virtual reality. An interesting perspective for such a comparison is to measure subjective and objective indicators of the mental effort of pilots in both virtual and real flight situations. Cardiac activity, in particular, is a possible indicator for cognitive load [30], even in operational conditions [37]. A similar approach had already been carried out to compare simulators to virtual reality [27] and disclosed a slightly higher heart rate in virtual reality than in a flight simulator.

The present study focuses on the data acquisition and analysis of heart activity parameters, in real and virtual flight conditions, with student pilots in training. We also report subjective measures of pilots' experience in virtual reality, particularly the feeling of presence and the difficulty perceived by the pilots to perform different actions during the flight of the chosen scenario.

We build up upon a previous preliminary experiment with a limited participant number ($N = 4$) [25]. The present work includes 10 pilots, thus, allowing to perform a statistical analysis between different conditions and flight phases. Previous insights can be thus statistically verified. We also added other subjective questionnaires such as the Presence Questionnaire, the Immersive Tendencies Questionnaire, and the Flight Difficulty Questionnaire to evaluate the difficulties to perform the virtual reality flight.

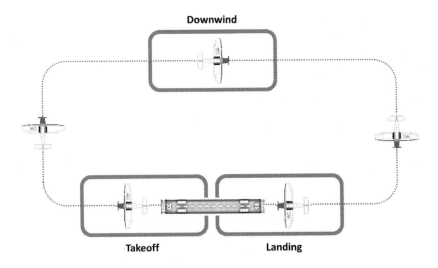

Fig. 1. The three flight phases: take-off, downwind and landing, each lasting 60 s.

2   Materials and Methods

2.1   Participants

Ten student pilots of the ISAE-SUPAERO, Toulouse, France, holding a private pilot's license (PPL) or in training to obtain it, participated in the experiment (all males, mean age 22.4 ± 4.4 years; mean flight experience 154 h). All were in good health, as evidenced by their flight medical certificates. No participant had a history of cardiac or neurological disease and, as required by aviation regulations, no participant was taking psychoactive substances or medications. Participants signed a consent form prior to the experiment. The virtual reality experience was approved by the Ethics and Research Committee of Toulouse (n2019-193). The flight experience was approved by the European Aviation Safety Agency with the permit to fly N°0147/21/NO/NAV (the flight conditions are defined in the document Monitoring Pilot's brain activity in real flights dated 26/01/2021, approved by EASA 60077217 on 24/03/2021).

2.2   Real Aircraft

The aircraft used during the experiments was the ISAE-SUPAERO experimental four-seater airplane Robin DR400 (160 HP). It is the same aircraft that is used to train our volunteers who participated in the study (Fig. 2). The experiment took place at Toulouse-Lasbordes airfield, in France (OACI code: LFCL).

2.3   Virtual Aircraft

We used the VRtigo platform (Fig. 4) [25,26], a VR flight simulator, that realistically reproduces the DR400 cockpit and Lasbordes Airfield environment to allow comparison with the real flight settings. This platform is composed of:

Fig. 2. The aircraft used for the experiment (Robin DR400).

Fig. 3. DR400 cockpit panel identically reproduced in virtual reality.

- Aerofly FS2 flight simulation software (IPACS);
- Runway 33 of Toulouse-Lasbordes airfield (OACI code: LFCL), identically reproduced, with some buildings commonly used for visual cues;
- DR400 panel, also identically reproduced to the aircraft used during real flights (Fig. 3);
- The 6-axis motion platform MotionSystems PS-6TM-150 with the following characteristics: heave −106.9 mm +117.1 mm, pitch −25° +25.6°, roll ±26°, yaw ±22.5°, surge −100 mm +121 mm, sway −99.5 mm +121 mm;
- Simple and conventional controls: stick, rudder, throttle, and flap lever;
- A cockpit, including the controls and a pilot's seat;
- A virtual reality headset (HTC Vive);
- An Alienware "VR ready" Laptop computer.

Fig. 4. VRtigo: the virtual flight simulator at ISAE-SUPAERO.

2.4 Flight Scenario

The scenario consisted of three consecutive standard traffic patterns. This exercise is highly formalized [8,37] in terms of flight procedures and flight path which makes it a relevant candidate for comparing pilot's behavior in the two experimental conditions (i.e. VR vs real flight). The scenario was identical in both virtual and real flights, and consisted of three traffic patterns, with a touch-and-go between each of them. After the last pattern, the pilots made a final landing and complete stop of the aircraft. In this study, we focused our analyses on three specific phases of the standard traffic pattern (Fig. 1):

- Take-off (from maximum power setting);
- Downwind (the center of the return path);
- Landing (before touchdown).

The separation into 60-s phases allowed to compare with the previous study performed in similar conditions [37], and to improve our previous study [25].

2.5 Measures

Cardiac Activity. The cardiac data were acquired with a Faros 360 eMotion electro-cardiogram (ECG) device. It provides the raw ECG signal at a sampling rate 500 Hz and R-R intervals data using a built-in R-detection algorithm. To improve the signal quality, we applied a conductive gel to each of the three electrodes connected to the Faros system. Physiological measures were synchronized with the flight parameters with the Lab Streaming Layer (LSL) [23].

Flight Parameters. In the VR flights, the following Aerofly FS2 simulator flight parameters were streamed, recorded, and stored via the LabRecorder:

- Altitude (feet)
- Pitch and bank angle (degrees)
- Groundspeed (knots)
- Indicated airspeed (knots)
- Longitude/Lattiude (degrees)
- Mach number (feet)
- Magnetic and true heading (degrees)
- Throttle (%)
- Vertical airspeed (feet/min)

For the real flights, an ILevil 3-10-AW acquisition unit was used to collect the trajectory (via GPS), accelerations, altitude (in feet), speed (in knots), and yaw/pitch/roll information. Similarly, these data were recorded and stored via the LabRecorder. This acquisition unit had to be mounted in the aircraft's cargo area at a specific location that guaranteed the accuracy of the attitude data (roll, pitch, and yaw). These parameters were then used to automatically identify the three flight phases of interest.

Questionnaires. Regarding the ten pilots, four participated in the experiment without filling out the questionnaires (2019). The other six (2021) participated in the experiment with three subjective questionnaires about the virtual environment. All the questionnaires used a visual analog scale from 1 to 7 for each answer, with different significations according to the question.

The Presence Questionnaire (PQ). This questionnaire measures the feeling of presence in a virtual environment. There are many versions of it and the one we used is composed of 17 questions. It is inspired by the 2002 french version from The Cyberpsychology Lab of UQO (Université du Quebec en Outaouais) [4]. The signification of the answer on the visual scale from 1 to 7 is different for each question (please refer to the 2002 Cyberpsychology Lab version for more details);

The Immersive Tendencies Questionnaire (ITQ). This questionnaire measures differences in the tendencies of individuals to experience presence. We selected the 2002 french version from The Cyberpsychology Lab of UQO (Université du Quebec en Outaouais) [4]. This version is inspired by Witmer and Singer's 1998 original version

[43]. It is composed of 18 questions that measure the level to which the individual can cut off from external distractions to concentrate on different tasks. The participant must answer each question on a 7-point scale. A score from 1 to 7 is associated with each answer and the global score is calculated. These 18 questions are also divided into 4 sub-scales, which measure different aspects of immersion propensity (Focus, Involvement, Emotion, and Game). The "Focus" subscale measures the sustained attention generated by an activity (5 items). The "Emotion" subscale deals with the individual's ease of feeling intense emotions evoked by the activity (4 items). The "Game" subscale refers to the individual's ability to project him/herself into a playful context (video game, etc.) (3 items). The "Involvement" subscale measures the tendency of an individual to identify with characters or to feel completely absorbed by an activity (4 items). A score is calculated for each subscale. The Cyberpsychology Lab has established certain norms (minimum scores for the overall and per subscale). Like the presence questionnaire, the answer on the visual scale had different signification according to the question (more details in the 2002 Cyberpsychology Lab version [4]);

A Flight Difficulty Questionnaire (FDQ). A set of 14 questions, specific to aircraft piloting in our flight scenario, was used to assess and compare the level of difficulty of the different flight segments across conditions. This questionnaire was created in 2019 in our lab and was already used for a previous study [26]. For questions 1 to 4, the answer on the visual scale could be from 1 (not at all) to 7 (completely). For questions 5 to 14, the answer could be from 1 (not similar) to 7 (very similar). See Fig. 8 for details about the 14 questions.

2.6 Experimental Protocol

Real Flight. Three people were present on the aircraft: the left seated pilot-participant, the right seated flight instructor (FI) acting as a safety pilot (right seated), and the experimenter (backseater). Before getting on the plane, the participants received a briefing about the experiment and completed their pre-flight inspection. The experiment then placed the ECG electrodes on their torso.

During the flight, an LSL's Viewer application displayed ECG data and flight parameters in real-time, which was necessary for the experimenter to ensure data consistency over time. The first data check was performed between engine start and taxi. The experimenter started the ECG and flight parameters data recordings before the aircraft's first take-off and stopped after the last landing. The meteorological conditions were compatible with the flights. In most cases, the Ceiling and Visibility were OK (CAVOK), and the wind was calm. For some subjects, the wind was stronger, with 15 knots gusting 25 knots, with a 30 angle from the runway's axis. Temperatures sometimes rose to 36 °C in the cockpit on the ground.

Virtual Flight. The virtual reality flights were conducted in a temperature-controlled room. Three people were inside the room: the participant (on the VRtigo platform), the experimenter (monitoring ECG data and aircraft configuration), and the safety technician (controls the correct functioning of the moving platform, ready to interrupt the

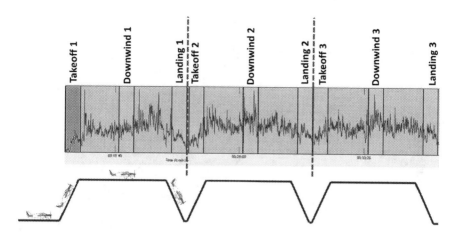

Fig. 5. The three flight phases on each of the three traffic patterns, over the R-R data for a complete flight (a 25-min. duration in this example). The green line schematically depicts the aircraft's altitude. (Color figure online)

simulation at any time by pressing an emergency stop button). The weather conditions were CAVOK, and no wind was programmed. The recordings were switched on and off at the same time as the real flights.

2.7 Data Analyses

Electrocardiogram. The R-R intervals of the raw ECG signal were detected using the built-in QRS detection algorithm of Kubios HRV software [39]. All the recordings were visually inspected to correct for potentially missed or false positive R-peak detection. We then computed the mean values of heart rate (HR; in beats per minute) and heart rate variability (HRV; assessed as Root Mean Square of the Successive Differences of the R-R intervals – RMSSD in ms, and NN50 and pNN50 – number and percentage, respectively, of R-R intervals that differ from each other by more than 50 ms) within the 60-s window of the three phases (take-off, downwind, landing) of the three traffic patterns (Fig. 5). Usually, studies report a decrease in HR and an increase in HRV (i.e. higher variability) as task demand gets lower [10,37,41].

The Kubios software also computes other metrics such as LF, HF, LF/HF in the frequency domain, but their computations on short-term signals are not recommended [18], therefore, given the 60-s window length, we only considered HR, RMSSD, NN50, and pNN50 metrics.

Statistical Analyses. The statistical analyses were carried out with JASP 0.16.1 software. Two-way (3 flight phases × 2 settings) repeated analyses of variances (ANOVAs) were computed over the HR and HRV metrics. The Greenhouse-Gessier sphericity correction was applied and the Holm correction was used for all post hoc comparisons. The significance level was set at p < .05 for all analyses.

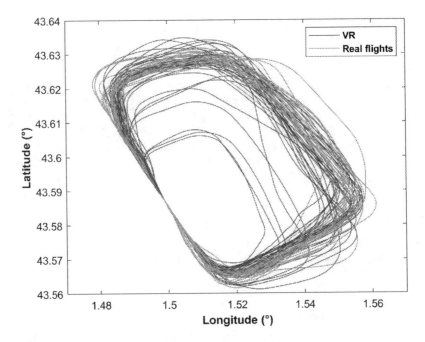

Fig. 6. Cumulative trajectories in virtual reality (blue) and real flights (orange). (Color figure online)

3   Results

3.1   Flight Parameters

The flight parameters have not been fully exploited for the moment. They were used in this study for the extraction of the three flight phases by the analysis of the following parameters: longitude, latitude, altitude, heading, and power. We then only visually checked the trajectories to verify their coherence between real and virtual reality flights (Fig. 6).

3.2   Subjective Measures

The Presence Questionnaire. Figure 7 represents the results of the Presence Questionnaire. The min score is 2.14 for question 10 ("How much of a delay did you feel between your actions and their consequences?"). The response could be from 1 ("no delay") to 7 ("long delay"). The max score is 6.57 for question 9 ("How involved were you in the experience in the virtual environment?"). The response could be from 1 ("no at all") to 7 ("completely").

The Immersive Tendencies Questionnaire. Participants showed a global mean score of 79.00 (SD = 11.98), and mean scores of 24.67 (SD = 4.37) for the Focus subscale, 21.42 (SD = 5.12) for the Involvement subscale, 15.75 (SD = 4.05) for the Emotion subscale, and 11.67 (SD = 2.94) for the Games subscale.

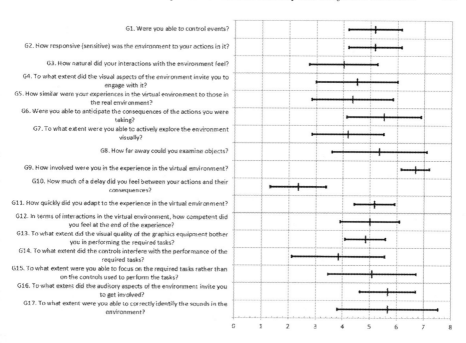

Fig. 7. Results of the presence questionnaire.

Means and standard deviations for the ITQ global score and subscales are presented in Table 1, along with norms from The Cyberpsychology Lab of UQO [4];

Table 1. ITQ results score (global and sub-items).

	Score	Norms
Global	**79.00 ± 11.98**	**64.11 ± 13.11**
Focus	24.67 ± 4.37	24.81 ± 7.54
Involvement	21.42 ± 5.12	15.33 ± 8.67
Emotion	15.75 ± 4.05	14.25 ± 6.70
Games	11.67 ± 2.94	6.56 ± 4.95

The Flight Difficulty Questionnaire. Figure 8 shows the results of the Flight Difficulty Questionnaire. The min score is 3.43 for question 14 ("How similar were your experiences during the landing phase in the virtual environment to those in the real environment?"). The response could be from 1 ("not similar") to 7 ("very similar"). The max score is 6.57 for question 4 ("How well were you able to control the thrust of the aircraft?"). The response could be from 1 ("not at all") to 7 ("completely").

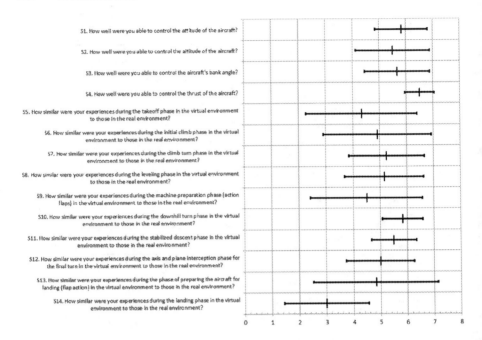

Fig. 8. Results of the flight difficulty questionnaire.

3.3 Physiological Measures

Heart Rate. A first two-way repeated ANOVA disclosed a main effect of the flight setting on HR, $F(1,9) = 14.0, p = .005, \eta_p^2 = 0.610$, and a main effect of the flight phase on HR, $F(2,18) = 19.1, p < .001, \eta_p^2 = 0.680$, as well as a significant flight setting $\times$ phase interaction, $F(2,18) = 7.6, p < .01, \eta_p^2 = 0.461$, see Fig. 9A. Post-hoc analyses revealed that all the three flight phases in real flight led to higher HR than their counterpart in VR ($p = 0.02$). In real flight setting, the take-off and the landing led to significantly higher HR than during downwind ($p < .001$). In VR setting, only the take-off induced significantly higher HR than during the downwind ($p = .02$).

Heart Rate Variability. A second two-way repeated ANOVA disclosed a main effect of the flight setting on RMSSD, $F(1,9) = 17.2, p = .002, \eta_p^2 = 0.657$, as well as a main effect of the flight phase on heart rate, $F(2,18) = 13.9, p = .001, \eta_p^2 = 0.608$, but no significant flight setting $\times$ phase interaction, see Fig. 9B. Post-hoc analyses revealed that all the RMSSD was lower during real flight than during VR flight ($p < 0.01$) and that HRV was lower during the landing than the two other phases ($p < 0.03$) and also lower during the landing compared to the take-off ($p < 0.03$).

Similar to RMSSD, a two-way repeated ANOVA on NN50 (Fig. 9C) revealed a significant main effect of flight settings, $F(1,9) = 14.0, p = .005, \eta_p^2 = 0.608$, as well as a main effect of the flight phase, $F(2,18) = 4.7, p = .042, \eta_p^2 = 0.345$. No significant interaction was found. Post-doc analyses showed lower NN50 values for the landing phase compared to the downwind ($p = .021$).

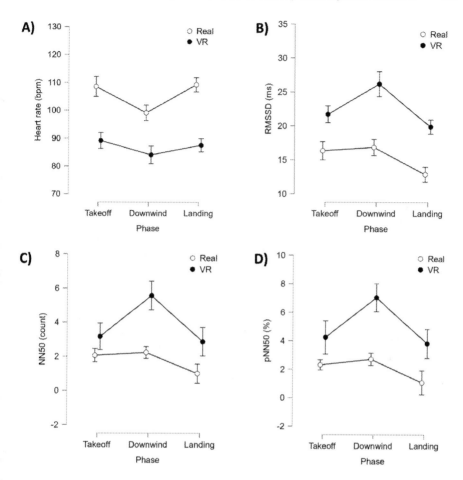

Fig. 9. A) mean HR (in bps); B) mean HRV (RMSSD in ms); C) mean NN50; D) mean pNN50 (%).

Finally, a two-way repeated ANOVA on pNN50 (Fig. 9D) revealed the same results as for the NN50 measure: a signiifcant main effect of flight settings, $F(1, 9) = 14.5, p = .004, \eta_p^2 = 0.617$, as well as a main effect of the flight phase, $F(2, 18) = 4.5, p = .049, \eta_p^2 = 0.332$. No significant interaction was found. Post-doc analyses showed lower NN50 values for the landing phase compared to the downwind ($p = .026$).

4   Discussion

In this study, we compared pilots' behavior through subjective questionnaires and cardiac activity during virtual reality and real flight. This study builds upon a previous conference paper [25] with a preliminary report of data from 4 subjects. In the present work, we analyze the data from 10 pilots who performed the same traffic pattern in a

DR400 light aircraft in a VR flight simulator and in actual flight condition. We also computed additional metrics of heart rate variability, i.e. NN50 and pNN50, as compared to only RMSSD in the previous study. Finally, using additional questionnaires allowed us to better understand what parts of virtual flight need to be considered in more detail to increase the realism of the simulation.

4.1 Subjective Measures

Sens of Presence. The analysis of the answers to the presence questionnaire revealed several positive aspects thus showing that the VR simulator was immersive. However, some negative points also appeared in these results such as a low definition of the graphics and interactions related issues.

Immersion. First of all, the feeling of immersion came out quite positively in the responses. Several factors contributed to this result: the quality of the global graphic environment, the similarity with a known real environment, and the realism of the audio environment of the simulation. The interactions with the aircraft also allowed the pilots to quickly feel in control.

The pilots, while performing this flight in an identically reproduced virtual environment, immediately felt at ease by judging themselves capable of controlling the events (question 1 = 5.17 ± 0.98). The score of question 9 shown a strong involvement of the pilots in the virtual environment experience (question 9 = 6.67 ± 0.52), this is even the highest score of the questionnaire. The other two highest scores were for questions 16 and 17 about the audio environment. Pilots were perfectly able to recognize the sounds (engine), which strongly invited them to be involved in the experiment (question 16 = 5.67 ± 1.03; question 17 = 5.67 ± 1.86).

They also felt involved because of some visual aspects of the environment (question 8 = 5.33 ± 1.75) and felt quite capable of anticipating the consequences of their actions (question 6 = 5.50 ± 1.38). In addition, the low score of question 10 represents a positive evaluation here, as this question allowed for judging the delay between actions and consequences (question 10 = 2.33 ± 1.03). Thus, the pilots did not feel any delay, which also contributed to their immersion in the experiment.

Finally, the score on the sensitivity of the environment following the pilots' actions (question 2 = 5.17 ± 0.98), and on the speed with which the pilots adapted to the virtual environment (question 1 = 5.17 ± 0.75) are also elements that suggest a good level of immersion.

All of these factors (interface quality, realism, and interactions) allowed the pilots to experience a strong sense of immersion, which fostered a high level of self-confidence, and allowed them to feel a strong sense of presence. This immersion did not generate any particular distraction since the maneuvers were perfectly performed by the pilots.

Points to Improve. Given the relatively low scores for some questions, several points of the virtual simulation can be improved. Question 3 disclosed that the interactions with the virtual environment are not necessarily well or poorly rated since the score is perfectly neutral on this scale from 1 to 7 (question 3 = 4 ± 1.26). The sensitive point was related to the absence of tracking of the hands in the virtual environment. While it was not an issue to operate the stick and the rudder since our participants could sense them with their hands and feet, it remained challenging to find and interact with the physical throttle and the flap levers. However, the technologies of motion capture and the synthesis of the virtual hands evolve quickly [21] including using own hands in mixed reality [11] for better seamless interactions, and while the current version of the VRtigo simulator did not include the hands' synthesis, the further studies will include these aspects.

Question 7 on the ability to visually explore the environment (question 7 = 4.17 ± 1.33) also highlighted a weakness noticed in a previous study [26]. The pilots also pointed out the difficulty to read accurately some critical cockpit instruments such as the anemometer due to relatively low graphics definition. This made the virtual flight more complicated than the real ones in this respect. However, todays' virtual reality headsets improved greatly since the beginning of this study, and recently released headsets such as Varjo XR-3 provide a higher resolution that could increase the readability of the instruments and parameter values.

Immersive Tendencies. Concerning the overall score of the ITQ, we know that the higher this score is, the more the participants will have a propensity to be immersed in the virtual reality experience. Here, the results show that this score is 79, which greatly exceeds the norms established by the Cyberpsychology laboratory at UQO (+15 points, i.e. +23%). Our group of participants, therefore, had a high propensity for immersion and the experiment could proceed.

The results by subscale show us first of all that the Focus subscale, even if slightly below the norm (24.67 vs. 24.81, i.e. –0.5%), corresponds well to it. Then, the Emotion subscale is slightly above the norm (15.75 vs 14.25, i.e. +10%). On the other hand, we note that the scores of the other two subscales are well above the norms (Involvement +39% and Game +77%). This could be explained by the relatively young age of the participants (22.4 ± 4.43 years), a generation more in contact with new technologies.

Flight Control in Virtual Reality. Keeping in the mind that in terms of virtual reality hardware on the VRtigo simulator, we only used the virtual reality headset and not the two classical stick controllers associated. We decided to provide the pilot with more intuitive aircraft control elements than virtual reality controllers (a rudder, a control stick, a flap lever, and a throttle). The answers to the questionnaire on the difficulties in accomplishing certain tasks or parts of the flight are therefore to be taken into consideration in relation to these control elements that are more typical of aircraft and not virtual reality controllers.

Questions 1 to 4 were related to the ability to control the aircraft (attitude, altitude, bank angle, and thrust), while questions 5 to 14 were related to the evaluation of the similarity of certain parts of the flight in real vs. virtual reality.

Control of the Aircraft. Regarding the first part of the questions about the controllability of the aircraft, our participants answered quite positively and felt comfortable with flying the virtual aircraft. Question 4, on the ease of controlling the thrust of the aircraft, done by the throttle lever, obtained the highest score on the questionnaire (score

= 6.5 ± 0.55). The other three scores, for attitude, altitude, and bank angle, were also highly rated with respective values of 5.83 ± 0.98, 5.67 ± 1.38, and 5.5 ± 1.21. These 4 scores are among the 5 highest on the questionnaire. This indicated that the pilots were comfortable with the different aircraft controls such as stick, rudder, and throttle. This observation on the controllability of the aircraft was important in our case of light aircraft piloting in virtual reality. This allowed pilots to feel involved and successful, as evidenced by the score of question 9 on involvement in the presence questionnaire (6.67 ± 0.52). These initial results corroborated from our previous 2018 study [26].

Similarity of the Virtual Experience. Responses to questions about the similarity of different parts of the traffic pattern between the virtual and real flights were more nuanced overall. Question 10, about the descending turn (score = 5.83 ± 0.75), and question 11 about the descent phase (5.50 ± 0.84) are the two best scores in this second part of the questions. The descending part of the traffic pattern is thus highly rated by the participants. However, we can also note that some phases get lower scores. Question 14 in particular, about the landing phase (score = 3 ± 1.55) as well as question 5 about the take-off phase (score = 4.33 ± 2.07). This shows us that the phases close to the ground, take-off, and landing, the most stressful and dangerous phases, in reality, were the least representative, which is also consistent with previous study [26].

One of the reasons could be related to some limitations of the virtual reality simulator already noted in the same study [26], in particular, the low resolution of the virtual reality headset, which negatively impacted the pilots' ability to correctly read the speed on the anemometer. We also found, during post-flight discussions with the pilots, that the physical sensations during the phases closed to the ground, mainly landing, were not completely realistic, even with the 6-axis mobile platform. The ground effects were not simulated realistically enough, which may have disturbed the pilots during the landing to execute flare phase. Another reason could be a lower experience level when using the VR simulator than the real aircraft.

4.2 Cardiac Activity

Heart Rate. As far as the real flights were concerned, the HR analyses showed that the closer the plane was to the ground (take-off and landing), the higher the HR was (Fig. 9A), with a maximum for landing (close to the take-off). The mean HR in real flight was 9.5% higher (take-off) and 10.2% higher (landing) than during the downwind phase. These results were consistent with previous findings reported during a traffic pattern experiment in real flight conditions [25, 37].

Regarding the virtual reality flights, it was interesting to note that the comparison of these three phases was similar to real flights with respectively an increase of 6.1% (take-off) and 4.1% (landing) compared to the downwind phase, with a maximum for takeoff.

In both environments (virtual and real), the HR of the downwind phase was, therefore, lower than that of the other two phases. We also noted, both in VR and in real flight, that the evolution of the HR following the three flight phases tended to be similar. The HR analysis also revealed a gap between virtual reality and real flights (Fig. 9A). The

HR was higher in real flight by about 22% (take-off), 18% (downwind), and 25% (landing) compared to virtual reality. This result could be interpreted as a lack of feeling of immersion experienced by participants in the VR condition. However, it is important to mention that the real flights were performed with crosswinds, especially for some pilots (16 G 26 kt at 30° from the runway axis). The crosswind induced in return higher mental demand (constant correction of trajectories). These aerological differences conditions could thus explain this difference between VR and reality findings.

Hear Rate Variability

The RMSSD Parameter. The analysis of the mean RMSSD during the real fight condition (Fig. 9B) disclosed higher values in downwind than during the take-off and landing phases, with a minimum for landing. These results for real flights were similar to previous studies [25,37]. However, the difference of the RMSSD values between take-off and downwind was more pronounced in the 2021 study [25].

The results in virtual reality (Fig. 9B), followed a similar shape than in real flight with a higher average RMSSD in downwind than during the take-off and landing phases, and a minimum for landing too. Note however that the difference between take-off and downwind was much more marked than in virtual reality (–5 ms vs. –0.5 ms).

Again, these results seem to suggest that the real flight condition induced higher mental demand and psychological stress than the simulated condition [10]. The analysis of the RMSSD also revealed a gap between real flights and virtual reality. The RMSSD values were on average 25% (take-off), 36% (downwind), and 35% (landing) lower in reality than in VR. This is also in line with the results of the HR analysis, but with reversed lag.

The NN50 and pNN50 Parameters. The same analyses from the RMSSD were obtained for these two parameters describing the HRV (Figs. 9C and 9D). We have also a higher value for the downwind phase, and lower for the landing phase, for both virtual reality and real flights. Values for the three phases are also lower in real flights than in VR. The NN50 values were on average 35% (take-off), 60% (downwind), and 65% (landing) lower in reality than in VR. The pNN50 values were on average 46% (take-off), 62% (downwind), and 72% (landing) lower in reality than in VR.

4.3 Motion Sickness

The large majority of pilots did not report motion sickness after using virtual reality during the experiments. Only one pilot was slightly bothered. It must be said that the virtual flight lasted about 25 min, which can seem relatively long in terms of immersion for this kind of activity (important mental load for the management of a flight). This pilot immediately felt better once the experiment was over. This information this time confirms our previous study [25] for which we had too few participants.

4.4 Conclusion

Virtual reality technology continues to gain terrain in simulation and training with advanced state-of-the-art headsets with improved display resolution, embedded eye and hand tracking for natural interactions, and improved comfort. Recently, the first virtual flight simulator for rotary pilot training was qualified by European Aviation Safety Agency. This first step of larger VR technology integration into the pilot training domain requires an in-depth understanding of how virtual flight differs from flying a real aircraft. While seeking the identical render of the flight instruments, as well as a motion platform for providing the pilot the vestibular cues, are paramount, neuroergonomic studies are also required [9, 15]. Such neuroergonomics evaluations allow to go beyond observable behaviors and compare different flight settings using objective neuro- and psycho-physiological measures such as electroencephalography, functional near-red spectroscopy, gaze tracking, or electrocardiography.

In this work, we compared standard flight patterns on a DR400 light aircraft in virtual reality (head-mounted device and motion platform) and real flight. We used subjective measures through different questionnaires of immersion, presence, ability to control the aircraft, but, most importantly, objective measures via cardiac activity. To the best of our knowledge, it is the first study comparing real and virtual flight (with a repeated measures analysis) using physiological measures.

The results showed that virtual flight is a decent resource for pilot training and pilots were able to fully perform the required actions for controlling the aircraft. Points to improve include updating the hardware (for better display resolution and hand tracking) but also to better model near-ground effects for the motion platform as these vestibular cues are important for the piloting experience. Heart rate and heart rate variability measures pointed out that real and virtual flights induce different stress and workload levels. The same pattern followed different flight phases in both virtual and real flights, i.e. more complicated and stressful operations during take-off and landing compared to the downwind phase yielding higher heart rates and lower HRV values. However, the overall heart rates were, generally, higher during the real experience (+20 bpm on average), and lower HRV values during the real flight compared to the virtual experience.

Overall, these results indicated that virtual flight represents real flight and can be used for pilot training. It reproduced the changes in stress/workload throughout the flight but a real flight is required to experience the level of cardiac activity associated with real operations. Further studies with simulators using more advanced hardware can further reduce these differences between the real and virtual flight experiences. However, replacing pilot training with exclusively virtual flight hours remains utopian at this point.

Acknowledgements. The authors would like to thank Stéphane Juaneda, the safety pilot, for his availability to perform flights and his precious know-how in-flight experimentation. Special thanks to Fabrice Bazelot and Benoît Momier, LFCL mechanics, for their help during the configuration of the experiments. A special thanks to Boris Jost and Alexandre Iche, ISAE-SUPAERO students, for their involvement in this project. Thanks to Guillaume Garrouste for the 3D development of the LFCL environment, and Jérôme Dartigues for building the mechanical part of the VRtigo platform.

References

1. Ahmed, S., Irshad, L., Demirel, H.O., Tumer, I.Y.: A comparison between virtual reality and digital human modeling for proactive ergonomic design. In: Duffy, V.G. (ed.) HCII 2019. LNCS, vol. 11581, pp. 3–21. Springer, Cham (2019). https://doi.org/10.1007/978-3-030-22216-1_1

2. Auer, S., Gerken, J., Reiterer, H., Jetter, H.C.: Comparison between virtual reality and physical flight simulators for cockpit familiarization. In: Mensch und Computer 2021, pp. 378–392 (2021)

3. Ayoub, A., Pulijala, Y.: The application of virtual reality and augmented reality in oral & maxillofacial surgery. BMC Oral Health **19**(1), 1–8 (2019)

4. Bouchard, S., Robillard, G., Renaud, P.: Questionnaire sur la propension à l'immersion. Lab Cyberpsychologie L'UQO (2002)

5. Bric, J.D., Lumbard, D.C., Frelich, M.J., Gould, J.C.: Current state of virtual reality simulation in robotic surgery training: a review. Surg. Endosc. **30**(6), 2169–2178 (2016)

6. Chae, J.: Study on firefighting education and training applying virtual reality. Fire Sci. Eng. **32**(1), 108–115 (2018)

7. Clifford, R.M., Jung, S., Hoermann, S., Billinghurst, M., Lindeman, R.W.: Creating a stressful decision making environment for aerial firefighter training in virtual reality. In: 2019 IEEE Conference on Virtual Reality and 3D User Interfaces (VR), pp. 181–189. IEEE (2019)

8. Dehais, F., et al.: Monitoring pilot's mental workload using erps and spectral power with a six-dry-electrode eeg system in real flight conditions. Sensors **19**(6), 1324 (2019)

9. Dehais, F., Karwowski, W., Ayaz, H.: Brain at work and in everyday life as the next frontier: grand field challenges for neuroergonomics. Front. Neuroergon. **1** (2020)

10. Durantin, G., Gagnon, J.F., Tremblay, S., Dehais, F.: Using near infrared spectroscopy and heart rate variability to detect mental overload. Behav. Brain Res. **259**, 16–23 (2014)

11. Feng, Q., Shum, H.P., Morishima, S.: Resolving occlusion for 3d object manipulation with hands in mixed reality. In: Proceedings of the 24th ACM Symposium on Virtual Reality Software and Technology, pp. 1–2 (2018)

12. Feng, Z., González, V.A., Amor, R., Lovreglio, R., Cabrera-Guerrero, G.: Immersive virtual reality serious games for evacuation training and research: a systematic literature review. Comput. Educ. **127**, 252–266 (2018)

13. Fussell, S.G., Truong, D.: Preliminary results of a study investigating aviation student's intentions to use virtual reality for flight training. Int. J. Aviat. Aeron. Aeros. **7**(3), 2 (2020)

14. Gateau, T., Ayaz, H., Dehais, F.: In silico vs. over the clouds: on-the-fly mental state estimation of aircraft pilots, using a functional near infrared spectroscopy based passive-bci. Front. Human Neurosci. **12**, 187 (2018)

15. Gramann, K., et al.: Grand field challenges for cognitive neuroergonomics in the coming decade. Front. Neuroergon. **2** (2021)

16. Grantcharov, T.P., Kristiansen, V.B., Bendix, J., Bardram, L., Rosenberg, J., Funch-Jensen, P.: Randomized clinical trial of virtual reality simulation for laparoscopic skills training. Brit. J. Surg. **91**(2), 146–150 (2004). https://doi.org/10.1002/bjs.4407

17. Hays, R.T., Jacobs, J.W., Prince, C., Salas, E.: Flight simulator training effectiveness: a meta-analysis. Milit. Psychol. **4**(2), 63–74 (1992)

18. Heathers, J.A.: Everything hertz: methodological issues in short-term frequency-domain hrv. Front. Physiol. **5**, 177 (2014)

19. Jensen, L., Konradsen, F.: A review of the use of virtual reality head-mounted displays in education and training. Educ. Inf. Technol. **23**(4), 1515–1529 (2018)

20. Joda, T., Gallucci, G., Wismeijer, D., Zitzmann, N.: Augmented and virtual reality in dental medicine: a systematic review. Comput. Biol. Med. **108**, 93–100 (2019)

21. Jörg, S., Ye, Y., Mueller, F., Neff, M., Zordan, V.: Virtual hands in vr: motion capture, synthesis, and perception. In: SIGGRAPH Asia 2020 Courses, pp. 1–32 (2020)
22. Kim, Y., Kim, H., Kim, Y.O.: Virtual reality and augmented reality in plastic surgery: a review. Arch. Plast. Surg. **44**(3), 179 (2017)
23. Kothe, C., Medine, D., Boulay, C., Grivich, M., Stenner, T.: Lab streaming layer (2014). https://github.com/sccn/labstreaminglayer
24. Koutitas, G., Smith, S., Lawrence, G.: Performance evaluation of ar/vr training technologies for ems first responders. Virt. Reality **25**(1), 83–94 (2021)
25. Labedan, P., Darodes-De-Tailly, N., Dehais, F., Peysakhovich, V.: Virtual reality for pilot training: study of cardiac activity. In: VISIGRAPP (2: HUCAPP), pp. 81–88 (2021)
26. Labedan, P., Dehais, F., Peysakhovich, V.: Evaluation de l'expérience de pilotage d'un avion léger en réalité virtuelle. In: ERGO'IA (2018)
27. Lawrynczyk, A.: Exploring Virtual Reality Flight Training as a Viable Alternative to Traditional Simulator Flight Training. Ph.D. thesis, Carleton University (2018). https://doi.org/10.22215/etd/2018-13301
28. Li, L., et al.: Application of virtual reality technology in clinical medicine. Am. J. Transl. Res. **9**(9), 3867 (2017)
29. Markopoulos, E., et al.: Neural network driven eye tracking metrics and data visualization in metaverse and virtual reality maritime safety training (2021)
30. Meshkati, N.: Heart rate variability and mental workload assessment. In: Hancock, P.A., Meshkati, N. (eds.) Human Mental Workload, Advances in Psychology, vol. 52, pp. 101–115. North-Holland (1988). https://doi.org/10.1016/S0166-4115(08)62384-5, http://www.sciencedirect.com/science/article/pii/S0166411508623845
31. Oberhauser, M., Dreyer, D., Braunstingl, R., Koglbauer, I.: What's real about virtual reality flight simulation? Aviation Psychology and Applied Human Factors (2018)
32. Peysakhovich, V., Monnier, L., Gornet, M., Juaneda, S.: Virtual reality versus real-life training to learn checklists for light aircraft. In: 1st International Workshop on Eye-Tracking in Aviation (2020)
33. Pottle, J.: Virtual reality and the transformation of medical education. Fut. Healthcare J. **6**(3), 181 (2019)
34. Pourmand, A., Davis, S., Lee, D., Barber, S., Sikka, N.: Emerging utility of virtual reality as a multidisciplinary tool in clinical medicine. Games Health J. **6**(5), 263–270 (2017)
35. Galasko, C.S.: Competencies required to be a competent surgeon. Ann. Roy. Coll. Surg. Engl. **82**, 89–90 (2000)
36. Sakib, M.N., Chaspari, T., Behzadan, A.H.: Physiological data models to understand the effectiveness of drone operation training in immersive virtual reality. J. Comput. Civil Eng. **35**(1), 04020053 (2021)
37. Scannella, S., Peysakhovich, V., Ehrig, F., Lepron, E., Dehais, F.: Assessment of ocular and physiological metrics to discriminate flight phases in real light aircraft. Hum. Fact.: J. Hum. Fact. Ergon. Soc. **60**(7), 922–935 (2018). https://doi.org/10.1177/0018720818787135
38. Silverstein, J.C., Dech, F., Edison, M., Jurek, P., Helton, W., Espat, N.: Virtual reality: immersive hepatic surgery educational environment. Surgery **132**(2), 274–277 (2002). https://doi.org/10.1067/msy.2002.125723, http://www.sciencedirect.com/science/article/pii/S0039606002000843
39. Tarvainen, M.P., Niskanen, J.P., Lipponen, J.A., Ranta-Aho, P.O., Karjalainen, P.A.: Kubios hrv-heart rate variability analysis software. Comput. Methods Progr. Biomed. **113**(1), 210–220 (2014)
40. Thomsen, A.S.S., et al.: Operating room performance improves after proficiency-based virtual reality cataract surgery training. Ophthalmology **124**(4), 524–531 (2017)
41. Togo, F., Takahashi, M.: Heart rate variability in occupational health __a systematic review. Ind. Health **47**(6), 589–602 (2009). https://doi.org/10.2486/indhealth.47.589

42. Walters, W.T., Walton, J.: Efficacy of virtual reality training for pilots: a review of links between user presence, search task performance, and collaboration within virtual reality. In: Proceedings of the Human Factors and Ergonomics Society Annual Meeting, vol. 65, pp. 919–922. SAGE Publications, Los Angeles (2021)
43. Witmer, B.G., Singer, M.J.: Measuring presence in virtual environments: a presence questionnaire. Presence **7**(3), 225–240 (1998)
44. Xie, B., et al.: A review on virtual reality skill training applications. Front. Virt. Reality **2**, 49 (2021)
45. Zhang, H.: Head-mounted display-based intuitive virtual reality training system for the mining industry. Int. J. Min. Sci. Technol. **27**(4), 717–722 (2017)

Information Visualization Theory
and Applications

Improving Self-supervised Dimensionality Reduction: Exploring Hyperparameters and Pseudo-Labeling Strategies

Artur André A. M. Oliveira[1] , Mateus Espadoto[1(✉)] , Roberto Hirata Jr.[1] ,
Nina S. T. Hirata[1] , and Alexandru C. Telea[2]

[1] Institute of Mathematics and Statistics, University of São Paulo, São Paulo, Brazil
{arturao,mespadot,hirata,nina}@ime.usp.br
[2] Department of Information and Computing Sciences, Utrecht University,
Utrecht, The Netherlands
a.c.telea@uu.nl

Abstract. Dimensionality reduction (DR) is an essential tool for the visualization of high-dimensional data. The recently proposed Self-Supervised Network Projection (SSNP) method addresses DR with a number of attractive features, such as high computational scalability, genericity, stability and out-of-sample support, computation of an inverse mapping, and the ability of data clustering. Yet, SSNP has an involved computational pipeline using self-supervision based on labels produced by clustering methods and two separate deep learning networks with multiple hyperparameters. In this paper we explore the SSNP method in detail by studying its hyperparameter space and pseudo-labeling strategies. We show how these affect SSNP's quality and how to set them to optimal values based on extensive evaluations involving multiple datasets, DR methods, and clustering algorithms.

Keywords: Dimensionality reduction · Machine learning · Deep learning · Neural networks · Autoencoders

1 Introduction

Visualization of high-dimensional data to find patterns, trends, and overall understand the data structure has become an essential ingredient of the data scientist's toolkit [24, 29]. Within the palette of such visualization methods, dimensionality reduction (DR) techniques, also called projections, have gained an established position due to their high scalability both in the number of samples and number of dimensions thereof. In the last decades, tens of DR techniques have emerged [12, 38], with PCA [22], t-SNE [33], and UMAP [36] having become particularly popular.

Neural-network-based techniques have been used to support DR, early examples of such approaches being self-organizing maps [26] and autoencoders [19]. More recently, the NNP technique [10] was proposed to mimic any DR technique. In parallel, the ReNDA method [3] was proposed to improve the projection quality offered by autoencoders.

A. A. de Sousa et al. (Eds.): VISIGRAPP 2021, CCIS 1691, pp. 135–161, 2023.
https://doi.org/10.1007/978-3-031-25477-2_7

Deep learning based DR methods are very fast, simple to implement, generically work for any type of quantitative high-dimensional data, are parametric, thus stable to small-scale data variations and offering out-of-sample capability, and – in the case of autoencoders – also provide the inverse mapping from the low-dimensional projection space to the high-dimensional data space. However, such methods also have some limitations. Such methods cannot typically offer the same projection quality, measured *e.g.* in terms of neighborhood preservation or cluster delineation, as classical methods like t-SNE and UMAP [9,10,37]. Inverse projection typically requires training a separate network [13]. NNP-class methods offer a higher quality than autoencoders, but require supervision in terms of using a classical DR method to project a subset of the data [10].

Recently, the Self-Supervised Neural Projection (SSNP [11]) method was proposed to alleviate the above limitations of deep learned projections. SSNP uses a single neural network trained with two objectives – *reconstructing* the projected data (as an autoencoder does) and *classifying* the same data (based on pseudo-labels created by a clustering algorithm). In more detail, SSNP aims to provide the following characteristics:

Quality (C1): Better cluster separation than standard autoencoders, and close to state-of-the-art DR methods, measured by well-known metrics in DR literature;

Scalability (C2): Linear complexity in the number of samples and dimensions, allowing the projection of datasets of a million samples and hundreds of dimensions in a few seconds on consumer-grade GPU platforms;

Ease of Use (C3): Minimal or no hyperparameter tuning required;

Genericity (C4): Projects any dataset whose samples are real-valued vectors;

Stability and Out-of-Sample Support (C5): The trained SSNP model can project new samples along existing ones in a parametric fashion;

Inverse Mapping (C6): Ability to infer the high-dimensional point corresponding to a low-dimensional point in the projection space;

Clustering (C7): Ability to label (cluster) unseen data. This feature of SSNP also supports requirement C1: Intuitively, clustering aggregates low-level distance information between sample points to a higher level, telling how groups of samples relate to each other. Next, this information is used by SSNP to produce projections which preserve such data clusters well in the low dimensional space.

In our original paper [11], we show how SSNP achieves the above requirements by evaluating it on four synthetic and four real-world datasets, using two clustering algorithms to produce pseudo-labels, and compare its results with four existing DR techniques. However, this leaves the 'design space' of SSNP insufficiently explored. Similarly to [9], where the authors explored in detail the design space of NNP [10], in this paper we aim to provide more insights on how SSNP's results depend on its technical components and their hyperparameter settings. For this, we extend the evaluation in [11] by considering two additional projection techniques (MDS and Isomap) and four additional clustering algorithms (affinity propagation, DBSCAN, Gaussian mixture models, and spectral clustering). Separately, we study how SSNP's performance is influenced by the setting of the hyperparameters of both the clustering algorithms and the underlying neural network. All in all, our extended evaluation proves that SSNP indeed complies well with requirements C1-C7, being a serious contender in the class of deep-learning-based DR techniques.

We structure this chapter as follows: Sect. 2 introduces notations and discusses related work. Section 3 details the SSNP method. Section 4 describes our experimental setup. Section 5 presents the results of SSNP, including the additional experiments outlined above. Section 6 discusses the obtained findings. Section 7 concludes the paper.

2 Background

Notations: Let $\mathbf{x} = (x^1, \ldots, x^n)$, $x^i \in \mathbb{R}$, $1 \leq i \leq n$ be a n-dimensional (nD) sample (also called a data point or observation). Let $D = \{\mathbf{x}_i\}$, $1 \leq i \leq N$ be a dataset of N such samples, *e.g.*, a table with N rows (samples) and n columns (dimensions). All datasets D used in this paper have class labels. Let C be the number of classes (or labels) in a dataset D. A DR, or projection, technique is a function

$$P : \mathbb{R}^n \to \mathbb{R}^q, \tag{1}$$

where $q \ll n$, and typically $q = 2$. The projection $\mathbf{p} = P(\mathbf{x})$ of a sample $\mathbf{x} \in D$ is a point $\mathbf{p} \in \mathbb{R}^q$. Projecting an entire dataset D yields a q-dimensional scatterplot, denoted next as $P(D)$. The inverse of P, denoted $\mathbf{x} = P^{-1}(\mathbf{p})$, maps a q-dimensional point $\mathbf{p}$ to the high-dimensional space $\mathbb{R}^n$, so that, ideally, $P(\mathbf{x}) = \mathbf{p}$, or in practice, $P(\mathbf{x})$ is close to $\mathbf{p}$.

Dimensionality Reduction: Many DR methods have been proposed in the last decades [5,8,12,20,29,34,38,48,56]. We next outline how a few representative ones comply with the requirements mentioned in Sect. 1, supporting our point that no DR method fully covers all those requirements. For further evidence for this statement, we refer to the above mentioned surveys.

Principal Component Analysis [22] (PCA) is very popular due to its simplicity, speed (C2), stability and out-of-sample (OOS) support (C5), and ease of use (C3) and interpretation. PCA is also used as pre-processing step for other DR techniques that require not-too-high-dimensional data [38]. Yet, due to its linear and global nature, PCA lacks on quality (C1), especially for data of high intrinsic dimensionality.

Methods of the Manifold Learning family (MDS [51], Isomap [49], and LLE [45] and its variations [7,57,58]) aim to map to 2D the high-dimensional manifold on which data lives. Such methods generally yield higher quality (C1) than PCA. Yet, such methods can be hard to tune (C3), do not have OOS capability (C5), do not work well for data that is not restricted to a 2D manifold, and generally scale poorly (C2) with dataset size.

Force-directed methods (LAMP [21] and LSP [40]) can yield reasonably high visual quality (C1), good scalability (C2), and are simple to use (C3). However, they generally cannot do OOS (C5). For LAMP, a related inverse projection (C6) technique iLAMP [1] exists. Yet, LAMP and iLAMP are two different algorithms. Clustering-based methods, such as PBC [39], share many characteristics of force-directed methods, such as good quality (C1) and lack of OOS (C5).

SNE (Stochastic Neighborhood Embedding) methods, of which t-SNE [33] is the most popular, have the key ability to visually segregate similar samples, thus being very good for cluster analysis. While having high visual quality (C1), t-SNE has a high complexity of $O(N^2)$ in sample count (C2), is very sensitive to small data changes (C5), is hard to tune (C3) [54], and has no OOS capability (C5). Tree-accelerated t-SNE [32], hierarchical SNE [42], approximated t-SNE [43], and various GPU accelerations of t-SNE [4,44] improve computation time (C2). Yet, these methods require quite complex algorithms, and still largely suffer from the aforementioned sensitivity, tuning, and OOS issues. Uniform Manifold Approximation and Projection (UMAP) [36] generates projections with comparable quality to t-SNE (C1) but is faster (C2) and has OOS (C5). Yet, UMAP shares some disadvantages with t-SNE, namely the sensitivity to small data changes (C5) and parameter tuning difficulty (C3).

Deep Learning: Autoencoders (AE) [19,25] create a low-dimensional data representation in their bottleneck layers by training a neural network to reproduce its high-dimensional inputs on its outputs. They produce results of comparable quality (C1) to PCA. However, they are easy to set up, train, and use (C3), are easily parallelizable (C2), and have OOS (C5) and inverse mapping (C6) abilities.

ReNDA [3] is a deep learning approach that uses two neural networks, improving on earlier work from the same authors. One network implements a nonlinear generalization of Fisher's Linear Discriminant Analysis [15]; the other network is an autoencoder used as a regularizer. ReNDA scores well on quality (C1) and has OOS (C5). However, it requires pre-training of each individual network and has low scalability (C2).

Neural Network Projections (NNP) [10] select a training subset $D_s \subset D$ to project by any user-chosen DR method to create a so-called training projection $P(D_s) \subset \mathbb{R}^2$. Next, a neural network is trained to approximate $P(D_s)$ having D_s as input. The trained network then projects unseen data by means of 2-dimensional non-linear regression. NNP is very fast (C2), simple to use (C3), and stable and with OOS ability (C5). However, the projection quality (C1) is lower than the learned projection. The NNInv technique [13], proposed by the same authors as NNP, adds inverse projection ability (C6). However, this requires setting up, training, and using a separate network.

Table 1 summarizes how the above DR techniques fare with respect to each characteristic of interest. The last row highlights SSNP which we describe separately in Sect. 3.

Table 1. Summary of DR techniques and their characteristics. Names in *italic* are techniques we compare with SSNP.

Technique	Characteristic						
	Quality	Scalability	Ease of use	Genericity	Out-of-sample	Inverse mapping	Clustering
PCA	Low	High	High	High	Yes	Yes	No
MDS	Mid	Low	Low	Low	No	No	No
Isomap	Mid	Low	Low	Low	No	No	No
LLE	Mid	Low	Low	Low	No	No	No
LAMP	Mid	Mid	Mid	High	No	No	No
LSP	Mid	Mid	Mid	High	No	No	No
t-SNE	High	Low	Low	High	No	No	No
UMAP	High	High	Low	High	Yes	No	No
Autoencoder	Low	High	High	Low	Yes	Yes	No
ReNDA	Mid	Low	Low	Mid	Yes	No	No
NNP	High	High	High	High	Yes	No	No
SSNP	**High**	**High**	**High**	**High**	**Yes**	**Yes**	**Yes**

Clustering: As for DR, clustering is a field that goes back decades, with many techniques proposed over the years. Despite using different approaches, all techniques use some form of similarity measure to determine whether a sample belongs to a cluster or not. *Centroid-based* techniques, such as K-means [30], compute cluster centers and assign cluster membership based on closeness to a center. *Connectivity-based* techniques, such as Agglomerative clustering [23], group samples based their relative distances rather than distances to cluster centers. *Distribution-based* techniques, such as Gaussian Mixture Models [6], fit Gaussian distributions to the dataset and then assign samples to each distribution. *Density-based* techniques, such as DBSCAN [14], define clusters as dense areas in the data space. More recent techniques use more specialized approaches, such as Affinity Propagation [16], which uses message passing between samples, and Spectral Clustering [47], which uses the eigenvalues of the data similarity matrix to reduce the dimensionality of the data to be clustered.

3   SSNP Technique

As stated in Sect. 2, autoencoders have desirable DR properties (simplicity, speed, OOS, and inverse mapping abilities), but create projections of lower quality than, *e.g.*, t-SNE and UMAP. A likely cause for this is that autoencoders do not use neighborhood information during training, while t-SNE and UMAP (obviously) do that. Hence, we propose to create an autoencoder architecture with a *dual* optimization target that explicitly uses neighborhood information. First, we have a *reconstruction* target, as in standard autoencoders; next, we use a *classification* target based on labels associated with the samples. These can be "true" ground-truth labels if available for a given dataset. If not, these are pseudo-labels created by running a clustering algorithm on the input dataset. The key idea behind this is that (pseudo)labels are a compact and high-level way to encode neighborhood information, *i.e.*, same-label data are more similar than different-label data. Since classifiers learn a representation that separates input data based on labels, adding an extra classifier target to an autoencoder learns how to project data with better cluster separation than standard autoencoders. We call our technique Self-Supervised Neural Projection (SSNP).

SSNP first takes a training set $D_{tr} \subset D$ and assigns to it pseudo-labels $Y_{tr} \in \mathbb{N}$ by using some clustering technique. We then take samples $(\mathbf{x} \in D_{tr}, y \in Y_{tr})$ to train a neural network with a reconstruction and a classification function, added to form a joint loss. This network (Fig. 1a) contains a two-unit bottleneck layer, same as an autoencoder, used to generate the 2D projection when in inference mode. After training, we 'split' the layers of the network to create three new networks for inference (Fig. 1b): a *projector* $N_P(\mathbf{x})$, an *inverse projector* $N_I(\mathbf{p})$, and a *classifier* $N_C(\mathbf{x})$, which mimics the clustering algorithm used to create Y_{tr}. The entire training-and-inference way of working of SSNP is summarized in Fig. 2.

4   Experimental Setup

In this section we detail the experimental setup we used to evaluate SSNP's performance. The obtained results are discussed next in Sect. 5.

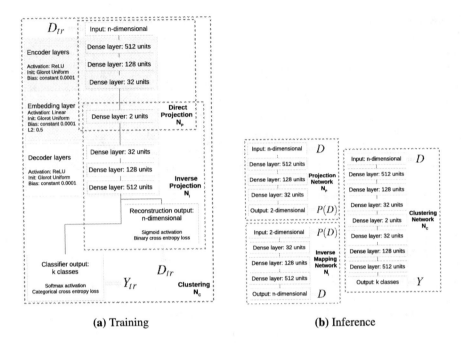

(a) Training   **(b)** Inference

Fig. 1. SSNP network architectures used during training (a) and inference (b).

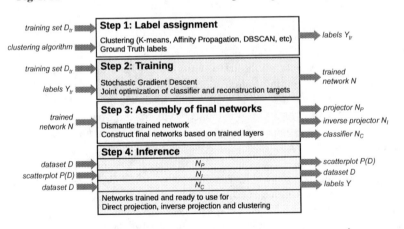

Fig. 2. SSNP training-and-inference pipeline.

4.1 Datasets

We first evaluate SSNP on synthetic datasets consisting of blobs sampled from a Gaussian distribution of different dimensionalities (100 and 700), number of clusters (5 and 10), and standard deviation σ, yielding datasets with cluster separation varying from very sharp to fuzzy clusters. All synthetic datasets have 5K samples. Next, we evaluate SSNP on four public real-world datasets that are high-dimensional, reasonably large (thousands of samples), and have a non-trivial data structure (same datasets as used in the original SSNP paper [11]):

MNIST [28]: 70K samples of handwritten digits from 0 to 9, rendered as 28x28-pixel gray scale images, flattened to 784-element vectors;

Fashion MNIST [55]: 70K samples of 10 types of pieces of clothing, rendered as 28x28-pixel gray scale images, flattened to 784-element vectors;

Human Activity Recognition (HAR) [2]: 10299 samples from 30 subjects performing activities of daily living used for human activity recognition grouped in 6 classes and described with 561 dimensions.

Reuters Newswire Dataset [50]: 8432 samples of news report documents, from which 5000 attributes are extracted using TF-IDF [46], a standard method in text processing.

All datasets had their attributes rescaled to the range $[0,1]$, to conform with the sigmoid activation function used by the reconstruction layer (see Fig. 1a).

4.2 Projection Quality Metrics

We measure projection quality by four metrics widely used in the projection literature (see Table 2 for their definitions). All metrics range in $[0,1]$ with 0 indicating poorest, and 1 indicating best, values:

Table 2. Projection quality metrics used in evaluating SSNP.

Metric	Definition
Trustworthiness (T)	$1 - \frac{2}{NK(2n-3K-1)} \sum_{i=1}^{N} \sum_{j \in U_i^{(K)}} (r(i,j) - K)$
Continuity (C)	$1 - \frac{2}{NK(2n-3K-1)} \sum_{i=1}^{N} \sum_{j \in V_i^{(K)}} (\hat{r}(i,j) - K)$
Neighborhood hit (NH)	$\frac{1}{N} \sum_{\mathbf{y} \in P(D)} \frac{y_K^l}{y_k}$
Shepard diagram correlation (R)	Spearman's ρ of $(\|\mathbf{x}_i - \mathbf{x}_j\|, \|P(\mathbf{x}_i) - P(\mathbf{x}_j)\|), 1 \le i \le N, i \ne j$

Trustworthiness T [53]: is the fraction of close points in D that are also close in $P(D)$. T tells how much one can trust that local patterns in a projection, *e.g.* clusters, represent actual data patterns. In the definition (Table 2), $U_i^{(K)}$ is the set of points that are among the K nearest neighbors of point i in the 2D space but not among the K nearest neighbors of point i in $\mathbb{R}^n$; and $r(i,j)$ is the rank of the 2D point j in the ordered-set of nearest neighbors of i in 2D. We choose $K = 7$ following [34,35];

Continuity C [53]: is the fraction of close points in $P(D)$ that are also close in D. In the definition (Table 2), $V_i^{(K)}$ is the set of points that are among the K nearest neighbors of point i in $\mathbb{R}^n$ but not among the K nearest neighbors in 2D; and $\hat{r}(i,j)$ is the rank of the $\mathbb{R}^n$ point j in the ordered set of nearest neighbors of i in $\mathbb{R}^n$. As for T, we use $K = 7$;

Neighborhood Hit NH [40]: measures how well-separable labeled data is in a projection $P(D)$, in a rotation-invariant fashion, from perfect separation ($NH = 1$) to no separation ($NH = 0$). NH is the number y_K^l of the K nearest neighbors of a point $\mathbf{y} \in P(D)$, denoted by $\mathbf{y}_K$, that have the same label as $\mathbf{y}$, averaged over $P(D)$. In this paper, we use $K = 3$;

Shepard Diagram Correlation R [21]: The Shepard diagram is a scatter plot of the pairwise distances between all points in $P(D)$ *vs* the corresponding distances in D. The closer the plot is to the main diagonal, the better overall distance preservation is. Plot areas below, respectively above, the diagonal show distance *ranges* for which false neighbors, respectively missing neighbors, occur. We measure how close a Shepard diagram is to the diagonal by computing its Spearman rank correlation R. A value of $R = 1$ indicates a perfect (positive) correlation of distances.

4.3   Dimensionality Reduction Techniques Compared Against

We compared SSNP against six DR techniques, namely t-SNE, UMAP, MDS, Isomap, autoencoders (AE), and NNP (see also Table 1). We selected these techniques based on popularity (t-SNE, UMAP, MDS, Isomap) or on similar operation (AE and NNP are also deep learning based, like SSNP) and also on having desirable properties to compare against. For instance, t-SNE and UMAP are known to produce strong visual cluster separation by evaluating local neighborhoods. MDS, on the other hand, tries to preserve global distances between samples. Isomap can be seen as an extension of MDS that uses local neighborhood information to infer geodesic distances. AE produce results similar to PCA, which preserves global distances. Finally, NNP does not have specific built-in heuristics but rather aims to mimic and accelerate other DR techniques. For all these DR techniques, we used default values for their hyperparameters.

4.4   Clustering Techniques for Pseudo-Labeling

In addition to using ground-truth labels in SSNP, we also used six clustering algorithms to generate the pseudo-labels for using during SSNP training (Sect. 3). Table 3 lists all clustering algorithms used, as well as the hyperparameters used in all experiments, except when noted otherwise. Hyperparameters not listed in Table 3 used default values. We used these algorithms since they employ quite different approaches to clustering, which could produce different results for SSNP.

We selected two of these clustering algorithms alongside two datasets — K-means and DBSCAN, HAR and MNIST — to further explore the effect of their main hyperparameters on the quality of the SSNP projection. For K-means, we studied the *n_clusters* parameter by choosing values well below and above the known number of clusters C in the data — *n_clusters* $= \{5, 10, 15, 20, 30\}$ for MNIST ($C = 10$), *n_clusters* $= \{3, 6, 9, 12, 18\}$ for HAR ($C = 6$). For DBSCAN, we explored the *eps* parameter, which determines the maximum distance between samples for them to be considered as neighbors. We used *eps* $= \{6.1, 6.3, ..., 6.9\}$ for MNIST and *eps* $= \{1.9, 2.1, ..., 2.7\}$ for HAR.

Table 3. Clustering algorithms used as for pseudo-label creation and their hyperparameters used during testing. Ground-truth is listed here as another labeling strategy.

Algorithm	Acronym	Hyperparameters
Ground truth labels	SSNP(GT)	None
Affinity propagation	SSNP(AP)	None
Agglomerative clustering	SSNP(Agg)	$n\_clusters = 2 \times C$
DBSCAN	SSNP(DB)	$eps = 5$
Gaussian mixture model	SSNP(GMM)	$n\_components = 2 \times C$
K-means	SSNP(Km)	$n\_clusters = 2 \times C$
Spectral clustering	SSNP(SC)	$n\_clusters = 2 \times C$

4.5 Neural Network Hyperparameter Settings

We further evaluated SSNP by using several hyperparameter settings for its neural network. To avoid a huge hyperparameter space, for each parameter explored, we kept the other parameters set to their defaults, similarly to the strategy used to explore NNP [9]. The explored hyperparameters are described next (see also Table 4).

L2 Regularization [27]: decreases layer weights to small but non-null values, leading to every weight only slightly contributing to the model. It works by adding a penalization term $\lambda \|\mathbf{w}\|^2$ to the cost function, where $\mathbf{w}$ are the weights of a selected network layer. The parameter $\lambda \in [0,1]$ controls the amount of regularization;

Embedding Layer Activation: The embedding (bottleneck) layer creates the 2D projection after training (Fig. 1). Changing the activation function of this layer affects the projection's overall shape. We used four activation functions for this layer (see Table 4);

Weight Initialization: A neural network has thousands of parameters whose initialization can affect the training outcome. We used three common initialization types: random uniformly distributed in the range $[-0.05, 0.05]$, Glorot uniform [17] with the range $[-b, b]$ for $b = \sqrt{6/(l_{in} + l_{out})}$, where l_{in} and l_{out} are the number of input and output units in the layer, and He uniform [18], which uses the range $[-b, b]$ with $b = \sqrt{6/l_{in}}$;

Training Epochs: We explored SSNP's performance for different numbers of epochs η ranging from 1 to 20.

Table 4. SSNP neural network parameters explored with default values in bold.

Dimension	Values
L2 regularization	$\lambda = \{\mathbf{0}, 0.1, 0.5, 1.0\}$
Embedding layer activation	$\alpha = \{$ **ReLU**, sigmoid, tanh, Leaky RELU $\}$
Weight initialization	$\phi = \{$**Glorot uniform**, He uniform, Random uniform $\}$
Training epochs	$\eta = \{1, 2, 3, 5, \mathbf{10}, 20\}$

5   Results

We next present the results for all experiments conducted to demonstrate SSNP's quality and robustness to hyperparameter selection.

5.1   Quality on Synthetic Datasets

Figure 3 shows the SSNP projection of the synthetic blob datasets with SSNP(Km) with K-means set to use the correct (ground-truth) number of clusters alongside AE, t-SNE, and UMAP. In most cases SSNP(Km) shows better visual cluster separation than autoencoders. The t-SNE and UMAP projections look almost the same regardless of the standard deviation σ of the blobs, while SSNP(Km) shows more spread clusters for larger σ, which is the desired effect. We omit the plots and measurements for NNP for space reasons and since these are very close to the ones created by the learned technique [10].

Table 5 shows the quality metrics for this experiment for datasets using 5 and 10 clusters. For all configurations, SSNP performs very similarly quality-wise to AE, t-SNE, and UMAP. Section 5.2, which studies more challenging, real-world, datasets will bring more insight in this comparison.

Table 5. Quality metrics, synthetic blobs experiment with 100 and 700 dimensions, 5 and 10 clusters, and $\sigma \in [1.3, 11.2]$.

Projection	σ	100 dimensions								σ	700 dimensions							
		5 clusters				10 clusters					5 clusters				10 clusters			
		T	C	R	NH	T	C	R	NH	σ	T	C	R	NH	T	C	R	NH
AE	1.3	0.923	0.938	0.547	1.000	0.958	0.963	0.692	1.000	1.6	0.909	0.914	0.739	1.000	0.953	0.955	0.254	1.000
T-SNE		0.937	0.955	0.818	1.000	0.967	0.977	0.192	1.000		0.917	0.951	0.362	1.000	0.960	0.976	0.346	1.000
UMAP		0.921	0.949	0.868	1.000	0.957	0.970	0.721	1.000		0.906	0.933	0.878	1.000	0.954	0.965	0.471	1.000
SSNP(Km)		0.910	0.919	0.687	1.000	0.956	0.959	0.602	1.000		0.904	0.908	0.568	1.000	0.953	0.955	0.399	1.000
AE	3.9	0.919	0.926	0.750	1.000	0.959	0.963	0.484	1.000	4.8	0.910	0.914	0.615	1.000	0.953	0.954	0.354	1.000
t-SNE		0.931	0.953	0.707	1.000	0.966	0.978	0.227	1.000		0.914	0.950	0.608	1.000	0.960	0.977	0.331	1.000
UMAP		0.911	0.940	0.741	1.000	0.956	0.969	0.537	1.000		0.906	0.931	0.697	1.000	0.954	0.965	0.390	1.000
SSNP(Km)		0.910	0.918	0.622	1.000	0.955	0.958	0.549	1.000		0.905	0.907	0.612	1.000	0.953	0.954	0.296	1.000
AE	9.1	0.905	0.901	0.569	1.000	0.938	0.945	0.328	0.999	11.2	0.911	0.906	0.600	1.000	0.955	0.954	0.382	1.000
t-SNE		0.913	0.951	0.533	1.000	0.948	0.974	0.254	1.000		0.914	0.950	0.492	1.000	0.959	0.977	0.296	1.000
UMAP		0.888	0.939	0.535	1.000	0.929	0.966	0.342	1.000		0.905	0.931	0.557	1.000	0.953	0.965	0.336	1.000
SSNP(Km)		0.888	0.917	0.595	0.998	0.927	0.952	0.437	0.995		0.904	0.906	0.557	1.000	0.950	0.945	0.314	0.998

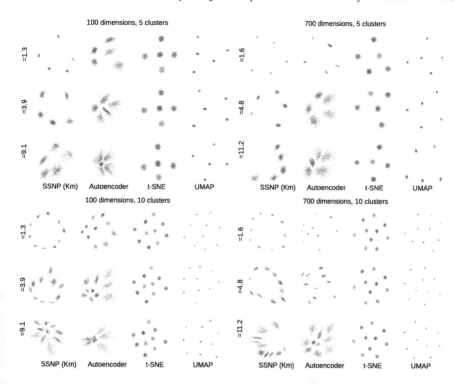

Fig. 3. Projection of synthetic blobs datasets with SSNP(Km) and other techniques, with different number of dimensions and clusters. In each quadrant, rows show datasets having increasing standard deviation σ.

5.2 Quality on Real-World Datasets

Figure 4 shows the projections of real-world datasets by SSNP with ground-truth labels (SSNP(GT)), SSNP with pseudo-labels created by the six clustering algorithms in Table 3, and projections created by AE, t-SNE, UMAP, MDS, and Isomap. We omit again the results for NNP since they are very close to the ones created by t-SNE and UMAP. SSNP and AE were trained for 10 epochs in all cases. SSNP used twice the number of classes as the target number of clusters for the clustering algorithms used for pseudo-labeling.

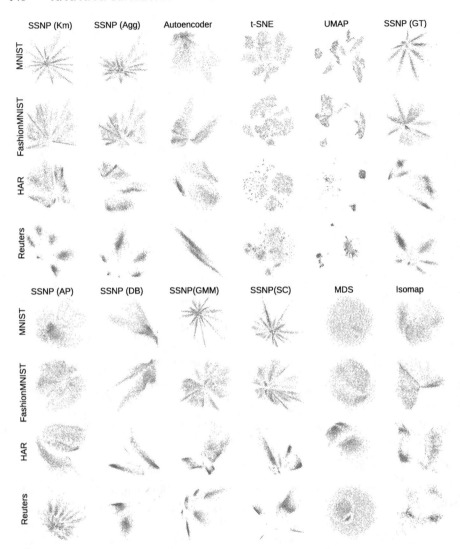

Fig. 4. Projection of real-world datasets with SSNP (ground-truth labels and pseudo-labels computed by six clustering methods) compared to Autoencoders, t-SNE, UMAP, MDS, and Isomap.

SSNP with pseudo-labels shows better cluster separation than AE but slightly worse than SSNP(GT). For the more challenging HAR and Reuters datasets, SSNP(GT) looks better than t-SNE and UMAP. In almost all cases, SSNP yields a better visual cluster separation than MDS and Isomap. We see also that, for almost all clustering algorithm-dataset combinations, SSNP creates elongated clusters in a star-like pattern. We believe this is so since one of the network's targets is a *classifier* (Sect. 3) which is trained to partition the space based on the data. This results in placing samples that are near a decision boundary between classes closer to the center of the star; samples that are far away from a decision boundary are placed near the tips of the star, according to its class. Table 6 shows the four quality metrics (Sect. 4.2) for this experiment. SSNP with pseudo-labels consistently shows better cluster separation (higher NH) than AE as well as better distance preservation (higher R). For the harder HAR and Reuters datasets, SSNP(GT) shows NH results that are similar to and even higher than those for t-SNE and UMAP. Also, SSNP(GT) scores consistently higher than MDS and Isomap on all quality metrics, which correlates with these two projection techniques having been found as of moderate quality in earlier studies [12]. For the T and C metrics, SSNP(GT) outperforms again AE in most cases; for FashionMNIST and HAR, SSNP yields T and C values close to the ones for NNP, t-SNE, and UMAP. Separately, we see that the clustering algorithm choice influences the four quality metrics in several ways. DBSCAN (DB) yields in nearly all cases the lowest quality values while K-means (Km) and Agglomerative (AG) yield overall the best quality values. Spectral clustering (SC) is also a quite good option if one is mainly interested in cluster separation (high NH values). Finally, Affinity Propagation (AP) and Gaussian Mixture Models (GMM)

Table 6. Quality measurements for the real-world datasets (Sect. 5.2).

Dataset	Method	T	C	R	NH	Method	T	C	R	NH
MNIST	SSNP(Km)	0.882	0.903	0.264	0.767	SSNP(AP)	0.827	0.940	0.094	0.729
	SSNP(AG)	0.859	0.925	0.262	0.800	SSNP(DB)	0.689	0.802	0.032	0.588
	AE	0.887	0.920	0.009	0.726	SSNP(GMM)	0.880	0.895	0.257	0.755
	SSNP(GT)	0.774	0.920	0.398	0.986	SSNP(SC)	0.849	0.925	0.164	0.831
	NNP	0.948	0.969	0.397	0.891	MDS	0.754	0.862	0.618	0.580
	TSNE	0.985	0.972	0.412	0.944	Isomap	0.759	0.958	0.528	0.618
	UMAP	0.958	0.974	0.389	0.913					
FashionMNIST	SSNP(Km)	0.958	0.982	0.757	0.739	SSNP(AP)	0.947	0.986	0.750	0.728
	SSNP(AG)	0.950	0.978	0.707	0.753	SSNP(DB)	0.890	0.921	0.431	0.665
	AE	0.961	0.977	0.538	0.725	SSNP(GMM)	0.952	0.982	0.689	0.737
	SSNP(GT)	0.863	0.944	0.466	0.884	SSNP(SC)	0.957	0.981	0.706	0.756
	NNP	0.963	0.986	0.679	0.765	MDS	0.923	0.957	0.903	0.652
	TSNE	0.990	0.987	0.664	0.843	Isomap	0.920	0.976	0.749	0.685
	UMAP	0.982	0.988	0.633	0.805					
HAR	SSNP(Km)	0.932	0.969	0.761	0.811	SSNP(AP)	0.929	0.972	0.736	0.787
	SSNP(AG)	0.926	0.964	0.724	0.846	SSNP(DB)	0.852	0.909	0.759	0.690
	AE	0.937	0.970	0.805	0.786	SSNP(GMM)	0.924	0.966	0.768	0.796
	SSNP(GT)	0.876	0.946	0.746	0.985	SSNP(SC)	0.893	0.952	0.811	0.805
	NNP	0.961	0.984	0.592	0.903	MDS	0.911	0.890	0.941	0.765
	TSNE	0.992	0.985	0.578	0.969	Isomap	0.925	0.971	0.896	0.861
	UMAP	0.980	0.989	0.737	0.933					
Reuters	SSNP(Km)	0.794	0.859	0.605	0.738	SSNP(AP)	0.631	0.768	0.039	0.742
	SSNP(AG)	0.771	0.824	0.507	0.736	SSNP(DB)	0.574	0.650	0.360	0.705
	AE	0.747	0.731	0.420	0.685	SSNP(GMM)	0.622	0.788	0.460	0.793
	SSNP(GT)	0.720	0.810	0.426	0.977	SSNP(SC)	0.607	0.758	0.027	0.730
	NNP	0.904	0.957	0.594	0.860	MDS	0.575	0.757	0.551	0.699
	TSNE	0.955	0.959	0.588	0.887	Isomap	0.634	0.785	0.150	0.765
	UMAP	0.930	0.963	0.674	0.884					

score in between Km and AG (best overall) and DB (worst overall). From the above, we conclude that Km and AG are good default clustering methods that SSNP can use in practice.

5.3   Quality *vs* Clustering Hyperparameters

Figure 5 shows projections of the HAR and MNIST datasets created by SSNP with pseudo-labels assigned by DBSCAN and K-means and using the various clustering hyperparameter settings described in Sect. 4.4.

For DBSCAN, we see that as the value of *eps* increases, the SSNP projection seems to vary between global- and local-distance preservation. This effect is more pronounced for the HAR dataset, where we see the number of clusters in the data varying from two (*eps* = 1.9) and three (*eps* = 2.7). For the MNIST dataset, the increase in *eps* only makes the entire projection take a sharper shape, with no improvement in cluster separation. Overall, SSNP with DBSCAN having low *eps* values produces results similar to an autoencoder, which defeats the purpose of using SSNP. This correlates to the earlier findings in Sect. 5.2 that showed that DBSCAN is not a good clustering companion for SSNP. The quality metrics in Table 7 strengthen this hypothesis – we do not see any clear trend of these metrics being improved by varying *eps* in a specific direction.

Table 7. Quality measurements for the cluster hyperparameter experiment (Sect. 5.3).

Dataset	Technique	Parameter	T	C	R	NH
MNIST	DBSCAN	eps=6.1	0.685	0.821	0.097	0.555
		eps=6.3	0.679	0.798	0.012	0.570
		eps=6.5	0.722	0.812	0.044	0.614
		eps=6.7	0.698	0.801	0.022	0.576
		eps=6.9	0.729	0.825	0.011	0.605
	K-means	n_clusters=5	0.782	0.905	0.408	0.641
		n_clusters=10	0.834	0.916	0.379	0.697
		n_clusters=15	0.867	0.927	0.410	0.760
		n_clusters=20	0.880	0.909	0.047	0.755
		n_clusters=30	0.899	0.932	0.358	0.790
HAR	DBSCAN	eps=1.9	0.854	0.928	0.917	0.696
		eps=2.1	0.848	0.920	0.841	0.650
		eps=2.3	0.875	0.914	0.717	0.685
		eps=2.5	0.896	0.924	0.844	0.725
		eps=2.7	0.898	0.933	0.887	0.749
	K-means	n_clusters=3	0.887	0.939	0.932	0.693
		n_clusters=6	0.921	0.959	0.749	0.767
		n_clusters=9	0.920	0.965	0.877	0.812
		n_clusters=12	0.930	0.968	0.854	0.815
		n_clusters=18	0.937	0.972	0.840	0.812

For K-means, we see that the value of *n_clusters* has a great effect on the overall shape of the SSNP projection. Particularly, when *n_clusters* is higher than the true number of classes in the data (10 for MNIST, 6 for HAR), we see that the cluster separation gets sharper. This suggests that, when the true number of clusters is not known, starting with a reasonably high number of clusters will produce better results for SSNP with K-means. This is confirmed by the quality metrics in Table 7 which show higher values for higher *n_clusters* settings.

5.4   Quality *vs* Neural Network Settings

We next show how the different neural network hyperparameter settings affect the SSNP results following the sampling of these parameters discussed in Sect. 4.5. We also use this analysis to derive good default values for these parameters.

L2 Regularization: Figure 6 shows projections created with different amounts of L2 regularization during SSNP's training. We see that regularization has a detrimental effect to the visual quality of the projection. For values of $\lambda \geq 0.5$, the projection points collapse to a single point, marked by the red circles in the figure. Table 8 shows the metric values for this experiment confirming that all quality values decrease with λ. We conclude that SSNP obtains optimal results without regularization.

Activation Functions: Figure 7 shows the effect of using different activation functions α in the embedding layer. We see that the ReLU and LeakyReLU activations produce

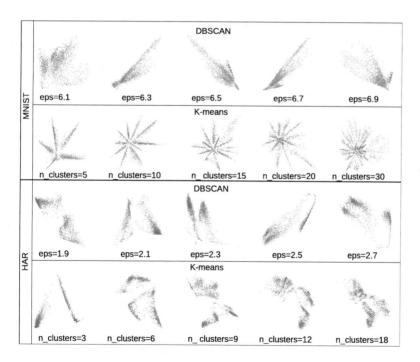

Fig. 5. Projections of MNIST and HAR datasets using different hyperparameters for the DBSCAN and K-means clustering methods (see Sect. 5.3 and Table 7).

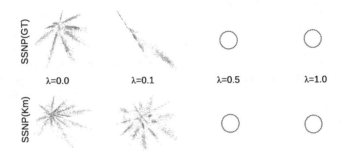

Fig. 6. Projections created with SSNP(GT) and SSNP(Km) for the MNIST dataset varying the amount of L2 regularization λ (Sect. 5.4).

similarly good results. Both produce visual cluster separation comparable to t-SNE and UMAP (see Fig. 4), albeit with a distinct star or radial shape. The sigmoid activation collapses all data points into a single diagonal, making it a poor choice for the embedding layer. Finally, the tanh activation produced the best cluster separation of all, with results that look very close to the ones by t-SNE and UMAP for this dataset (see again Fig. 4). We conclude that the tanh activation function is the best option for SSNP.

Initialization: Figure 8 shows how weight initialization affects projection quality. We see that both Glorot and He uniform initializations produce good and comparable

Table 8. Quality measurements for SSNP for different training hyperparameters. NA indicates that the measurement failed for the respective experiment (Sect. 5.4).

Method	Parameter	Value	T	C	R	NH
SSNP(GT)	α	LeakyReLU	0.780	0.930	0.429	0.971
		ReLU	0.789	0.921	0.402	0.983
		sigmoid	0.703	0.891	0.088	0.746
		tanh	0.784	0.929	0.190	0.983
	η	2	0.781	0.924	0.428	0.903
		3	0.787	0.926	0.428	0.940
		5	0.786	0.925	0.419	0.966
		10	0.789	0.921	0.402	0.983
		20	0.797	0.920	0.391	0.989
	φ	Glorot	0.789	0.921	0.402	0.983
		He	0.789	0.928	0.328	0.982
		Random	0.758	0.905	0.071	0.927
	λ	0	0.789	0.921	0.402	0.983
		0.1	0.757	0.909	0.360	0.870
		0.5	0.538	0.502	NA	0.101
		1	0.538	0.502	NA	0.101

(continued)

Table 8. (*continued*)

Method	Parameter	Value	T	C	R	NH
SSNP(Km)	α	LeakyReLU	0.863	0.919	0.177	0.748
		ReLU	0.888	0.916	0.119	0.768
		sigmoid	0.678	0.872	0.196	0.568
		tanh	0.884	0.928	0.265	0.774
	η	2	0.847	0.927	0.267	0.726
		3	0.827	0.926	0.244	0.714
		5	0.854	0.915	0.323	0.775
		10	0.881	0.908	0.188	0.770
		20	0.886	0.911	0.128	0.766
	φ	Glorot	0.884	0.915	0.333	0.784
		He	0.874	0.903	0.267	0.753
		Random	0.741	0.869	0.115	0.640
	λ	0	0.888	0.924	0.351	0.763
		0.1	0.872	0.910	0.352	0.753
		0.5	0.538	0.502	NA	0.101
		1	0.538	0.502	NA	0.101

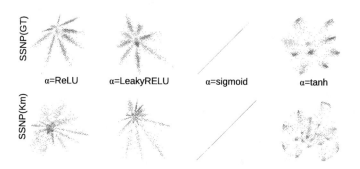

Fig. 7. Projections of the MNIST dataset using SSNP(GT) and SSNP(Km) varying the activation function α (Sect. 5.4).

results, whereas random initialization yields very poor results. We opt for using He uniform as the default initialization, which correlates with the same choice (obtained by an independent investigation) for NNP [9].

Training Epochs: Finally, Fig. 9 shows projections created with SSNP trained for different numbers η of epochs. With as little as η = 3 training epochs, SSNP already produces good cluster separation. As η increases, the created visual clusters become sharper. However, there seems to be little improvement when going from η = 10 to η = 20. As such, we conclude that a good default is η = 10 training epochs. Interestingly, this is significantly less than the 50 epochs needed by NNP to achieve good

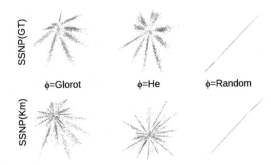

Fig. 8. Projections of the MNIST dataset using SSNP(GT) and SSNP(Km) varying the weight initialization strategy ϕ (Sect. 5.4).

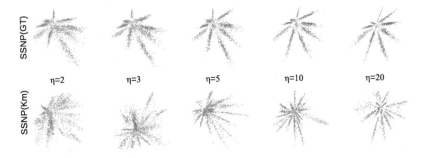

Fig. 9. Projections of MNIST dataset using SSNP(GT) and SSNP(Km) varying the number of training epochs η (Sect. 5.4).

projection quality [9], especially if we consider that SSNP has to train a more complex, dual-objective, network.

5.5 Computational Scalability

Using SSNP means (a) training the network and next (b) using the trained network in inference mode (see also Fig. 1). We analyze these two times next.

Setup Time: Table 9 shows the time needed to set up SSNP and three other projection techniques. For SSNP, NP, and AE, this is the training time of the respective neural networks using 10 training epochs. Note that we used 10K training samples, which is largely sufficient to train SSNP to obtain good results. In practice, SSNP obtains good results (quality-wise) with as few as 1K samples. For UMAP and t-SNE, this is the time needed to actually project the data since these techniques do not have a training phase. We see that the SSNP variants using clustering take about the same time as t-SNE and UMAP and less than NNP. SSNP(GT), which does not need clustering, is far faster than these competitors, with the exception of AE which is about twice faster. This is explainable since SSNP uses a dual-objective network (Sect. 3), one of these being essentially the same as AE.

Table 9. Setup time for different projection methods for 10K training samples, MNIST dataset.

Method	Setup time (s)
SSNP(GT)	6.029
SSNP(Km)	20.478
SSNP(Agg)	31.954
AE	3.734
UMAP	25.143
t-SNE	33.620
NNP(t-SNE)	51.181

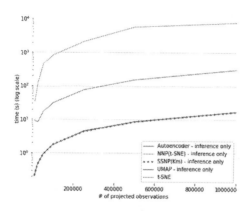

Fig. 10. Inference time for SSNP and other techniques (log scale). Techniques using training use 10K samples from the MNIST dataset. Inference is done on MNIST upsampled up to 1M samples.

Inference Time: Figure 10 shows the time needed to project up to 1M samples using SSNP and the other compared projection techniques. For SSNP, AE, and NNP, this is the inference time using the respective trained networks. For t-SNE and UMAP, this is the actual projection time, as described earlier in this section. Being GPU-accelerated neural networks, SSNP, AE, and NNP perform very fast, all being able to project up to 1M samples in a few seconds – an order of magnitude faster than UMAP, and over three orders of magnitude faster than t-SNE. We also see that SSNP, AE, and NNP have practically the same speed. This is expected since they have comparably large and similar-architecture neural networks which, after training, take the same time to execute their inference.

5.6 Inverse Projection

Recalling from Sect. 2, an *inverse* projection $P^{-1}(\mathbf{p})$ aims to create a data point $\mathbf{x}$ so that its projection $P(\mathbf{x})$ is as close as possible to $\mathbf{p}$. Hence, we can test how well a method computes P^{-1} for a given direct projection function P by evaluating how close

$P^{-1}(P(\mathbf{x}))$ is to the data point $\mathbf{x}$ itself. To test this, we consider points $\mathbf{x}$ being images in the MNIST dataset and P and P^{-1} being computed by SSNP as described in Sect. 3).

Figure 11 shows a set of digits from the MNIST dataset – both the actual images $\mathbf{x}$ and the ones obtained by $P^{-1}(P(\mathbf{x}))$. We see that SSNP(Km) yields results very similar to AE, both of these being visually quite close images to the actual images $\mathbf{x}$, modulo a limited amount of fuzziness. Hence, SSNP's dual-optimization target succeeds in learning a good inverse mapping based on the direct mapping given by the pseudo-labels (Sect. 3). Table 10 strengthens this insight by showing the values of the Mean Squared Error (MSE) between the original and inversely-projected images $\frac{1}{|D|} \sum_{\mathbf{x} \in D} \|\mathbf{x} - P^{-1}(P(\mathbf{x}))\|^2$ for SSNP(Km) and AE for both the training and test sets. These errors, again, are very similar. Furthermore, the SSNP MSE errors are of the same order of magnitude – that is, very small – as those obtained by the recent NNInv technique [13] and the older iLAMP [1] technique that also compute inverse projections – compare Table 10 with Fig. 2 in [13] (not included here for space reasons). Summarizing the above, we conclude that SSNP achieves a quality of inverse projections on par with existing state-of-the-art techniques.

Table 10. Inverse projection Mean Square Error (MSE) for SSNP(Km) and AE, trained with 5K samples and tested with 1K samples, different datasets.

Dataset	SSNP(Km)		Autoencoder	
	Train	Test	Train	Test
MNIST	0.0474	0.0480	0.0424	0.0440
FashionMNIST	0.0309	0.0326	0.0291	0.0305
HAR	0.0072	0.0074	0.0066	0.0067
Reuters	0.0002	0.0002	0.0002	0.0002

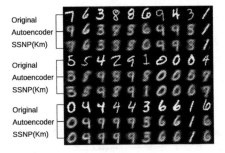

Fig. 11. Sample images from MNIST inversely projected by SSNP and AE, both trained with 10 epochs and 5K samples, MNIST dataset. Bright images show the original images that the inverse projection should be able to reproduce.

5.7 Data Clustering

Table 11 shows how SSNP performs when doing classification or clustering, which corresponds respectively to its usage of pseudo-labels or ground-truth labels. We see that

SSNP generates good results in both cases when compared to the ground-truth (GT) labels and, respectively, the underlying clustering algorithm K-means (Km), which emerged as one of the best clustering companions for SSNP (Sect. 5.2). However, we should stress that classification or clustering is only a *side* result of SSNP, needed for computing the dual-objective cost that the network uses (Sect. 3). While one gets this by-product for free, SSNP only *mimics* the underlying clustering algorithm that it learns, rather than doing data clustering from scratch. As such, we do not advocate using SSNP as a potential replacement for clustering algorithms.

Table 11. Classification/clustering accuracy of SSNP when compared to ground truth (GT) and clustering labels (Km), trained with 5K samples, tested with 1K samples.

Dataset	SSNP(GT)		SSNP(Km)	
	Train	Test	Train	Test
MNIST	0.984	0.942	0.947	0.817
FashionMNIST	0.866	0.815	0.902	0.831
HAR	0.974	0.974	0.931	0.919
Reuters	0.974	0.837	0.998	0.948

5.8   Implementation Details

All experiments discussed in this section were run on a 4-core Intel Xeon E3-1240 v6 at 3.7 GHz with 64 GB RAM and an NVidia GeForce GTX 1070 GPU with 8 GB VRAM. Table 12 lists all open-source software libraries used to build SSNP and the other tested techniques. Our neural network implementations leverages the GPU power by using the Tensorflow Keras framework. The t-SNE implementation used is a parallel version of Barnes-Hut t-SNE [31,52], run on all four available CPU cores for all tests. The UMAP reference implementation is not parallel, but is quite fast (compared to t-SNE) and well-optimized. The implementation of MDS, Isomap, and all clustering techniques comes from Scikit-Learn [41]. Our implementation, plus all code used in this experiment, are publicly available at https://github.com/mespadoto/ssnp.

Table 12. Software used for the SSNP implementation and evaluation.

Technique	Software used publicly available at
SSNP (our technique)	keras.io (TensorFlow backend)
Autoencoders	
t-SNE	github.com/DmitryUlyanov/Multicore-t-SNE
UMAP	github.com/lmcinnes/umap
Affinity propagation	scikit-learn.org
Agglomerative clustering	
DBSCAN	
Gaussian mixture model	
K-means	
Spectral clustering	

6   Discussion

We discuss next how the available hyperparameter settings influence the performance of SSNP with respect to the seven criteria laid out in Sect. 1.

Quality (C1): As shown in Figs. 3 and 4, SSNP provides better cluster separation than Autoencoders, MDS, and Isomap, and comparable quality to t-SNE and UMAP, as measured by the selected metrics (Tables 5 and 6). Interestingly, using ground-truth labels (SSNP(GT)) does not always yield the highest quality metrics as compared to using pseudo-labels produced by clustering. Related to the latter, K-means (Km) and Agglomerative clustering (AG) yield, overall, higher quality metrics for most tested datasets as compared to DBSCAN, Gaussian mixture models, Spectral clustering, and Affinity propagation. When we consider the neighborhood hit (NH) metric, which models the closest from all studied metrics the ability of a projection to segregate similar samples into visually distinct clusters, SSNP(GT) performs better than all tested methods, t-SNE and UMAP included. Importantly, note that SSNP uses labels only during training and *not* during inference, so it can be fairly compared with such other projection methods.

Scalability (C2): SSNP(GT) is roughly half the speed of Autoencoders during training which is expected given its dual-optimization target. Training SSNP with pseudo-labels is slower, roughly the speed of t-SNE or UMAP, which is explained by the time taken by the underlying clustering algorithm which dominates the actual training time. In our experiments, K-means seems to be faster than Agglomerative clustering, being thus more suitable when training SSNP with very large datasets. Inference time for SSNP practically identical to Autoencoders and NNP, and one order of magnitude faster than UMAP and three orders faster than t-SNE, being also linear in the sample and dimension counts. This shows SSNP's suitability to situations where one needs to project large amounts of data, such as streaming applications;

Ease of Use (C3): SSNP yielded good projection results with little training (10 epochs), little training data (5K samples) and a simple heuristic of setting the number of clusters for the clustering step to twice the number of expected clusters in the data. Furthermore, we examined several hyperparameters of SSNP and found good default values (in terms of obtaining high quality metrics) as follows: no L2 regularization, tanh activation function for the embedding layer, and He uniform weight initialization. The clustering algorithm default is K-means or Agglomerative, with K-means slightly preferred for speed reasons. As such, SSNP can be used with no parameter tweaking efforts needed.

Genericity (C4): We show results for SSNP with different types of high-dimensional data, namely tabular (HAR), images (MNIST, FashionMNIST), and text (Reuters). As these datasets come from quite different sources and as the SSNP method itself makes no assumption on the nature or structure of the data, we believe that SSNP is generically applicable to any high-dimensional real-valued dataset.

Stability and Out-of-Sample Support (C5): All measurements we show for SSNP are based on inference, *i.e.*, we pass the data through the trained network to compute them. This is evidence of the out-of-sample capability, which allows one to project new data without recomputing the projection, in contrast to t-SNE and other non-parametric methods.

Inverse Mapping (C6): SSNP shows inverse mapping results which are, quality-wise, very close to results from Autoencoders, NNInv and iLAMP, these being state-of-the-art methods for computing inverse projections. Additionally, SSNP computes the inverse projection at no extra cost or need for a separate implementation, in contrast to NNInv and iLAMP.

Clustering (C7): SSNP is able to mimic the behavior of the clustering algorithm used as its input, as a byproduct of its training with labeled data. We show that SSNP produces competitive results when compared to pseudo- or ground truth labels. Although SSNP is not a clustering algorithm, it provides this for free (with no additional execution cost), which can be useful in cases where one wants to do both clustering and DR. However, we stress that SSNP should not be considered as a replacement for state-of-the-art clustering algorithms, since it only learns to *mimic* the actual clustering. This is similar to the distinction between a classifier and an actual clustering technique.

In addition to the good performance shown for the aforementioned criteria, a key strength of SSNP is its ability to performing all its operations after a *single training phase*. This saves effort and time in cases where all or a subset of those results (*e.g.*, direct projection, inverse projection, clustering) are needed.

Limitations: While scoring high on several criteria, SSNP also has several limitations. Quality-wise, its operation in pseudo-labeling mode cannot reach the high quality values for all metrics that are delivered by t-SNE or UMAP for challenging datasets (Table 6). We believe that this is affected by the number of clusters used during training, which is related to the neighborhood size that t-SNE and UMAP use. More involved strategies in setting this number of clusters can be explored to further increase SSNP's quality. Visually, while we argue for the reason of the star-shaped cluster structures produced by SSNP (Sect. 5.2), such patterns can be less suitable for visual exploration than the blob-like patterns produced typically by t-SNE. Using a tanh activation function partially alleviates this issue (Sect. 5.4). However, more studies are needed to explore other activation functions that allow even better control of the visual cluster shapes. Most importantly however, SSNP is a *learning* method. As with any such method, its quality will decrease when inferring on (that is, projecting) datasets which are too far away from the ones used during training, an issue also present for NNP and autoencoders. In contrast, methods that do not use training can obtain similar quality for any input dataset. Yet, the price to pay for such methods is that they cannot guarantee stability and out-of-sample behavior, which come with SSNP by default.

7 Conclusion

We presented an in-depth analysis of a dimensionality reduction (DR) method called Self-Supervised Neural Projection (SSNP) recently proposed by us. SSNP uses a neural network with a dual objective – reconstruction of the high-dimensional input data and classification of the data – to achieve several desirable characteristics of a general-purpose DR method. SSNP is, to our knowledge, the only technique that jointly addresses *all* characteristics listed in Sect. 1 of this paper, namely producing projections that exhibit a good visual separation of similar samples, handling datasets of millions of elements in seconds, being easy to use (no complex parameters to set), handling generically any type of high-dimensional data, providing out-of-sample support, and providing an inverse projection function.

Our evaluation added two additional dimensionality reduction methods, four clustering algorithms, and also explored the hyperparameter space of both the clustering algorithms and neural network training to gauge SSNP's behavior. The evaluation results led to establishing default values for all these hyperparameters which obtain high quality values and also turn SSNP into a parameter-free method. Additionally, the obtained results show that SSNP with ground-truth labels yields higher quality in terms of visual cluster separation than all tested projections including the state-of-the-art t-SNE and UMAP methods. When pseudo-labels are used due to the lack of true labels, SSNP achieves lower but still competitive results with t-SNE and UMAP, slightly to significantly higher quality than autoencoders, and significantly higher quality than MDS and Isomap.

As future work, we consider studying better heuristics for controlling the clustering process which we believe are a low hanging fruit towards improving SSNP's quality. Another interesting direction is to explore other activation function designs that can offer control to the end users on the shape of the visual clusters that the projection creates, which would be, to our knowledge, an unique feature in the family of projection techniques. A more ambitious, but realizable, goal is to have SSNP learn its pseudo-labeling during training and therefore remove the need for using a separate clustering algorithm.

Acknowledgments. This study was financed in part by FAPESP grants 2015/22308-2, 2017/25835-9 and 2020/13275-1, and the Coordenação de Aperfeiçoamento de Pessoal de Nível Superior - Brasil (CAPES) - Finance Code 001.

References

1. Amorim, E., Brazil, E.V., Daniels, J., Joia, P., Nonato, L.G., Sousa, M.C.: iLAMP: exploring high-dimensional spacing through backward multidimensional projection. In: Proceedings of IEEE VAST, pp. 53–62 (2012)
2. Anguita, D., Ghio, A., Oneto, L., Parra, X., Reyes-Ortiz, J.L.: Human activity recognition on smartphones using a multiclass hardware-friendly support vector machine. In: Bravo, J., Hervás, R., Rodríguez, M. (eds.) IWAAL 2012. LNCS, vol. 7657, pp. 216–223. Springer, Heidelberg (2012). https://doi.org/10.1007/978-3-642-35395-6_30
3. Becker, M., Lippel, J., Stuhlsatz, A., Zielke, T.: Robust dimensionality reduction for data visualization with deep neural networks. Graph. Models **108**, 101060 (2020)
4. Chan, D., Rao, R., Huang, F., Canny, J.: T-SNE-CUDA: GPU-accelerated t-SNE and its applications to modern data. In: Proceedings of SBAC-PAD, pp. 330–338 (2018)
5. Cunningham, J., Ghahramani, Z.: Linear dimensionality reduction: survey, insights, and generalizations. JMLR **16**, 2859–2900 (2015)
6. Dempster, A.P., Laird, N.M., Rubin, D.B.: Maximum likelihood from incomplete data via the EM algorithm. J. Roy. Stat. Soc. Ser. B (Methodological) **39**(1), 1–22 (1977)

7. Donoho, D.L., Grimes, C.: Hessian eigenmaps: locally linear embedding techniques for high-dimensional data. Proc. Natl. Acad. Sci. **100**(10), 5591–5596 (2003)
8. Engel, D., Hattenberger, L., Hamann, B.: A survey of dimension reduction methods for high-dimensional data analysis and visualization. In: Proceedings of IRTG Workshop, vol. 27, pp. 135–149. Schloss Dagstuhl (2012)
9. Espadoto, M., Falcao, A., Hirata, N., Telea, A.: Improving neural network-based multidimensional projections. In: Proceedings of IVAPP (2020)
10. Espadoto, M., Hirata, N., Telea, A.: Deep learning multidimensional projections. J. Inf. Vis. (2020). https://doi.org/10.1177/1473871620909485
11. Espadoto, M., Hirata, N.S., Telea, A.C.: Self-supervised dimensionality reduction with neural networks and pseudo-labeling. In: Proceedings of IVAPP, pp. 27–37. SCITEPRESS (2021)
12. Espadoto, M., Martins, R.M., Kerren, A., Hirata, N.S., Telea, A.C.: Towards a quantitative survey of dimension reduction techniques. IEEE TVCG **27**(3), 2153–2173 (2019)
13. Espadoto, M., Rodrigues, F.C.M., Hirata, N.S.T., Hirata Jr., R., Telea, A.C.: Deep learning inverse multidimensional projections. In: Proceedings of EuroVA, Eurographics (2019)
14. Ester, M., Kriegel, H.P., Sander, J., Xu, X., et al.: A density-based algorithm for discovering clusters in large spatial databases with noise. In: Proceedings of KDD, vol. 96, pp. 226–231 (1996)
15. Fisher, R.A.: The use of multiple measurements in taxonomic problems. Ann. Eugenics **7**(2), 179–188 (1936)
16. Frey, B.J., Dueck, D.: Clustering by passing messages between data points. Science **315**(5814), 972–976 (2007)
17. Glorot, X., Bengio, Y.: Understanding the difficulty of training deep feedforward neural networks. In: Proceedings of AISTATS, pp. 249–256 (2010)
18. He, K., Zhang, X., Ren, S., Sun, J.: Delving deep into rectifiers: surpassing human-level performance on imagenet classification. In: Proceedings of IEEE ICCV, pp. 1026–1034 (2015)
19. Hinton, G.E., Salakhutdinov, R.R.: Reducing the dimensionality of data with neural networks. Science **313**(5786), 504–507 (2006)
20. Hoffman, P., Grinstein, G.: A survey of visualizations for high-dimensional data mining. Inf. Vis. Data Min. Knowl. Disc. **104**, 47–82 (2002)
21. Joia, P., Coimbra, D., Cuminato, J.A., Paulovich, F.V., Nonato, L.G.: Local affine multidimensional projection. IEEE TVCG **17**(12), 2563–2571 (2011)
22. Jolliffe, I.T.: Principal component analysis and factor analysis. In: Principal Component Analysis, pp. 115–128. Springer, New York (1986). https://doi.org/10.1007/978-1-4757-1904-8_7
23. Kaufman, L., Rousseeuw, P.: Finding Groups in Data: An Introduction to Cluster Analysis. Wiley, Hoboken (2005)
24. Kehrer, J., Hauser, H.: Visualization and visual analysis of multifaceted scientific data: a survey. IEEE TVCG **19**(3), 495–513 (2013)
25. Kingma, D.P., Welling, M.: Auto-encoding variational bayes. CoRR abs/1312.6114 (2013), eprint: 1312.6114
26. Kohonen, T.: Self-organizing Maps. Springer, Berlin (1997). https://doi.org/10.1007/978-3-642-97966-8
27. Krogh, A., Hertz, J.A.: A simple weight decay can improve generalization. In: Proceedings of NIPS, pp. 950–957 (1992)
28. LeCun, Y., Cortes, C.: MNIST handwritten digits dataset (2010). http://yann.lecun.com/exdb/mnist
29. Liu, S., Maljovec, D., Wang, B., Bremer, P.T., Pascucci, V.: Visualizing high-dimensional data: advances in the past decade. IEEE TVCG **23**(3), 1249–1268 (2015)

30. Lloyd, S.: Least squares quantization in PCM. IEEE Trans Inf. Theor. **28**(2), 129–137 (1982)
31. Maaten, L.V.D.: Barnes-hut-SNE. arXiv preprint arXiv:1301.3342 (2013)
32. Accelerating t-SNE using tree-based algorithms: Maaten, L.V.d. JMLR **15**, 3221–3245 (2014)
33. Maaten, L.V.D., Hinton, G.: Visualizing data using t-SNE. JMLR **9**, 2579–2605 (2008)
34. Maaten, L.V.d., Postma, E.: Dimensionality reduction: a comparative review. Technical Report, Tilburg University, Netherlands (2009)
35. Martins, R.M., Minghim, R., Telea, A.C., et al.: Explaining neighborhood preservation for multidimensional projections. In: CGVC, pp. 7–14 (2015)
36. McInnes, L., Healy, J.: UMAP: uniform manifold approximation and projection for dimension reduction. arXiv:1802.03426v1 [stat.ML] (2018)
37. Modrakowski, T.S., Espadoto, M., Falcão, A.X., Hirata, N.S.T., Telea, A.: Improving deep learning projections by neighborhood analysis. In: Bouatouch, K., et al. (eds.) VISIGRAPP 2020. CCIS, vol. 1474, pp. 127–152. Springer, Cham (2022). https://doi.org/10.1007/978-3-030-94893-1_6
38. Nonato, L., Aupetit, M.: Multidimensional projection for visual analytics: linking techniques with distortions, tasks, and layout enrichment. IEEE TVCG (2018). https://doi.org/10.1109/TVCG.2018.2846735
39. Paulovich, F.V., Minghim, R.: Text map explorer: a tool to create and explore document maps. In: Proceedings of International Conference on Information Visualisation (IV), pp. 245–251. IEEE (2006)
40. Paulovich, F.V., Nonato, L.G., Minghim, R., Levkowitz, H.: Least square projection: a fast high-precision multidimensional projection technique and its application to document mapping. IEEE TVCG **14**(3), 564–575 (2008)
41. Pedregosa, F., et al.: Scikit-learn: machine learning in python. J. Mach. Learn. Res. (JMLR) **12**, 2825–2830 (2011)
42. Pezzotti, N., Höllt, T., Lelieveldt, B., Eisemann, E., Vilanova, A.: Hierarchical stochastic neighbor embedding. Comput. Graph. Forum **35**(3), 21–30 (2016)
43. Pezzotti, N., Lelieveldt, B., Maaten, L.V.d., Höllt, T., Eisemann, E., Vilanova, A.: Approximated and user steerable t-SNE for progressive visual analytics. IEEE TVCG **23**, 1739–1752 (2017)
44. Pezzotti, N., et al.: GPGPU linear complexity t-SNE optimization. IEEE TVCG **26**(1), 1172–1181 (2020)
45. Roweis, S.T., Saul, L.L.K.: Nonlinear dimensionality reduction by locally linear embedding. Science **290**(5500), 2323–2326 (2000)
46. Salton, G., McGill, M.J.: Introduction to Modern Information Retrieval. McGraw-Hill, New York (1986)
47. Shi, J., Malik, J.: Normalized cuts and image segmentation. IEEE TPAMI **22**(8), 888–905 (2000)
48. Sorzano, C., Vargas, J., Pascual-Montano, A.: A survey of dimensionality reduction techniques (2014). arXiv:1403.2877 [stat.ML]
49. Tenenbaum, J.B., Silva, V.D., Langford, J.C.: A global geometric framework for nonlinear dimensionality reduction. Science **290**(5500), 2319–2323 (2000)
50. Thoma, M.: The Reuters dataset, July 2017. https://martin-thoma.com/nlp-reuters
51. Torgerson, W.S.: Theory and Methods of Scaling. Wiley, Hoboken (1958)
52. Ulyanov, D.: Multicore-TSNE (2016). https://github.com/DmitryUlyanov/Multicore-TSNE
53. Venna, J., Kaski, S.: Visualizing gene interaction graphs with local multidimensional scaling. In: Proceedings of ESANN, pp. 557–562 (2006)
54. Wattenberg, M.: How to use t-SNE effectively (2016). https://distill.pub/2016/misread-tsne
55. Xiao, H., Rasul, K., Vollgraf, R.: Fashion-MNIST: a novel image dataset for benchmarking machine learning algorithms (2017). arXiv:1708.07747

56. Xie, H., Li, J., Xue, H.: A survey of dimensionality reduction techniques based on random projection (2017). arXiv:1706.04371 [cs.LG]
57. Zhang, Z., Wang, J.: MLLE: modified locally linear embedding using multiple weights. In: Advances in Neural Information Processing Systems (NIPS), pp. 1593–1600 (2007)
58. Zhang, Z., Zha, H.: Principal manifolds and nonlinear dimensionality reduction via tangent space alignment. SIAM J. Sci. Comput. **26**(1), 313–338 (2004)

Visualization of Source Code Similarity Using 2.5D Semantic Software Maps

Daniel Atzberger[(✉)], Tim Cech, Willy Scheibel, Daniel Limberger,
and Jürgen Döllner

Hasso Plattner Institute, Digital Engineering Faculty, University of Potsdam, Potsdam, Germany
daniel.atzberger@hpi.uni-potsdam.de

Abstract. For various program comprehension tasks, software visualization techniques can be beneficial by displaying aspects related to the behavior, structure, or evolution of software. In many cases, the question is related to the semantics of the source code files, e.g., the localization of files that implement specific features or the detection of files with similar semantics. This work presents a general software visualization technique for source code documents, which uses 3D glyphs placed on a two-dimensional reference plane. The relative positions of the glyphs captures their semantic relatedness. Our layout originates from applying Latent Dirichlet Allocation and Multidimensional Scaling on the comments and identifier names found in the source code files. Though different variants for 3D glyphs can be applied, we focus on cylinders, trees, and avatars. We discuss various mappings of data associated with source code documents to the visual variables of 3D glyphs for selected use cases and provide details on our visualization system.

Keywords: Source code mining · Software visualization · Glyph visualization

1 Introduction

About 90 % of the entire costs of a software project are related to the maintenance phase [14], i.e., to prevent problems before they occur (preventive maintenance), correct faults (corrective maintenance), improve the functionality or performance (perfective maintenance), or adapt to a changing environment (adaptive maintenance) [23]. There are various visualization techniques to represent aspects related to the structure, the behavior, or the evolution of the underlying software, to assist users in program comprehension tasks during the maintenance phase. Nevertheless, since software has no intrinsic gestalt, software visualization uses suitable *abstractions and metaphors* to depict aspects of and relations within software data to support and, at best, align users in their mental representation of selected software aspects. Interactive visualizations allow users to analyze a software project in an exploratory way and thus support finding information and gaining knowledge. Examples for well-established, interactive software visualization techniques are:

- *Icicle Plots* for representations of trace executions [10,36],
- *Treemaps* depicting the hierarchical structure of software projects [32,41],

© Springer Nature Switzerland AG 2023
A. A. de Sousa et al. (Eds.): VISIGRAPP 2021, CCIS 1691, pp. 162–182, 2023.
https://doi.org/10.1007/978-3-031-25477-2_8

- *Circular Bundle Views* illustrating relations, e.g., include dependencies [11],
- *Software Cities* that reflect the development history of software [45,46], and
- similar approaches based on cartographic metaphors [21,28].

Many specific questions in maintenance are related to the semantic structure of software projects. For example, in the case of perfective maintenance, source code files implementing a specific functionality or concept need to be identified. It is helpful to be aware of other files that share semantics in this context. Such tasks can become intensively time-consuming with long-lasting software systems and with an increasing number of different developers. In order to support such tasks, various layouts exist that can reflect semantic similarities between files, i.e., by placing files with a similar semantic closer to one another [2,4,27,28]. Using 2D or 3D glyphs to represent files with a semantic positioning and additional data mapping, e.g., software metrics mapped to the glyphs' visual variables, facilitates the comprehension of the semantic structure of a software project. For the remainder of this work, we refer to the term *glyphs* as defined by Ward et al.; "In the context of data and information visualization, a glyph is a visual representation of a piece of data or information where a graphical entity and its attributes are controlled by one or more data attributes" [51].

In this work, we present a general approach for placing custom 3D glyphs in a 2D reference space for software visualization tasks, in order to (1) capture the semantic structure of source code files and (2) allow for an additional, inherent visual display of related data, e.g., software metrics. For our layout technique, we assume developer comments and deliberately chosen identifiers to not only provide instructions for compilers but to simultaneously document and communicate intent, function, and context to developers. This assumption motivates the use of techniques from the Natural Language Processing (NLP) domain for mining the semantic structure of source code documents. We apply Latent Dirichlet Allocation (LDA), a probabilistic topic model, to capture the semantic structure of a software structure, which leads to a mathematical description of source code files. By applying Multidimensional Scaling (MDS) as a dimension reduction technique, we generate a two-dimensional layout that reflects the semantic relatedness between the source code files. We represent every source code unit or file as a single 3D glyph. Though plenty of glyphs and metaphors have been applied to software visualization tasks, we focus our discussion on three examples we considered valuable:

Cylinders with their extent, height, and color as visual variables.

Trees with a variety of visual variables, e.g., size, type, leaf color, health, age, and season.

Avatars which can be easily distinguished from each other and clearly identified, e.g., for depicting software developers or teams.

We describe fitting use cases for every glyph and provide examples using popular Open Source projects data. Figure 1 shows one exemplary result of our visualization approach.

The remainder of this work is structured as follows: In Sect. 2 we review existing work related to our approach. We provide an overview of possible layouts for visualizing source code and glyphs and natural metaphors in the software visualization domain.

Fig. 1. Example of a *Software Forest* using handcrafted tree models from *SketchFab* (sketchfab.com) as 3D glyphs. Each tree represents a source code file. Quantitative and qualitative data associated to the files can be mapped to age, type, and health of a tree.

In Sect. 3 we detail the layout approach, which is based on LDA and MDS and applied to comments and identifiers in source code. Section 4 describes use case scenarios and shows how data related to the semantics of source code files can be represented. We further present a detailed explanation of our system and its implementation in Sect. 5 and, finally, conclude this paper in Sect. 6 and present directions for future work.

2   Related Work

Our visualizations are created in two distinct steps. First, we generate a semantic layout that is then used for placing 3D glyphs (representing source code files). Second, we map quantitative and qualitative data of source code files to the available visual variables of the 3D glyphs. With respect to the prior art, we, therefore, focus on these two aspects. We describe existing approaches for placing documents in a reference space in order to reflect their semantic similarity and also describe existing 2.5D approaches based on treemaps for software visualization tasks. We then present relevant work on three widely used visualization metaphors, namely the island metaphor, the tree metaphor, and the city metaphor. Selected glyphs are presented at the end of this section.

Semantic Layouts for Software Visualization. When designing visualizations, one has to consider the placement of data items in the reference space. In the case of document visualization, we call a layout whose goal is to reflect the semantic relatedness between the data items a semantic layout. In a semantic layout, documents that share a common similarity are placed nearby each other. As documents are mostly viewed as Bag-of-Words (BOW), i.e., the order of words within a document is neglected, and only their frequency is taken into account, dimension reduction techniques are used to project the high-dimensional points to a two-dimensional plane or a three-dimensional space.

Skupin et al.proposed an approach for generating two-dimensional visualizations for text documents using cartographic metaphors [44]. The authors applied Self-Organizing Map (SOM) on the BOW [26], as dimension reduction technique, to place abstracts of publications about geography on the plane. Furthermore, dominant terms were displayed, thus showing the semantic content of the region in the visualization.

Kuhn et al.were the first to propose a semantic layout for software visualization tasks [27,28]. First, each source code file is considered as a single document and several preprocessing tasks are undertaken to remove noise from the vocabulary. Then, the high-dimensional BOW is reduced in their dimension in two steps. The topic model Latent Semantic Indexing (LSI) [13] is applied, which describes each document through its expression in the latent topics within a software project, which can already be seen as a dimension reduction of the BOW. After this, MDS [12] is applied on the dissimilarity matrix that captures the pairwise dissimilarities of the documents using the cosine-similarity. The resulting two-dimensional scatterplot is then equipped with height lines, resulting in a cartographic visualization. In addition, two-dimensional glyphs are placed for displaying coding activities, e.g., test tubes.

Linstead et al. [34,35] were the first to propose a semantic software layout based on LDA and its variant, the Author-Topic Model (ATM), which additionally takes information about authorship into account [39]. By applying the topic models on the source code of the Eclipse project, both source code files and authors are described as distributions over latent topics. The final layout is computed by applying MDS on the dissimilarity matrix, which contains the pairwise symmetrized Kullback-Leibler divergence of the authors or files.

Another approach that models the semantic structure of source code files using LDA for visualization tasks was presented by Atzberger et al. [2]. In their approach, the authors first apply MDS on the topic-word distributions to compute two-dimensional vertices, representing the topics, as presented in [43]. The position of a document is then computed as a convex linear combination according to its document-topic distribution. Using this layout, the authors introduced the tree metaphor for software visualization, resulting in the so-called *Software Forest*. In a later work, Atzberger et al.discussed the use of pawns and chess figures as 3D glyphs for visualizing the knowledge distribution across software development teams [3]. In this case, the layout reflects the semantic similarity between developers, additional information about the expertise of each developer can then be mapped on the visual variables of the representing glyph.

In another work, Atzberger et al.applied their layout approach to a 3D reference space, creating a stylized scatter plot for the depiction of software projects [4]. Inspired by a metaphor introduced by Lanza et al. [29], the authors displayed each source code file as a star, thereby creating a *Software Galaxy*. The authors also introduced transparent volumetric nebulae to make use of the metaphor of galactic star clusters or nebulae. Attributes such as cluster density or distribution can subsequently be mapped to the nebulaes' intensities and colors.

The Island Metaphor. The 2.5D approach used by Atzberger allows for the integration of a terrain (based on a dynamically generated heightfield), resulting in visualizations resembling islands. Indeed the island metaphor is a widely used visualization metaphor in the Software Visualization domain. Štěpánek developed *Helveg*, a framework for visualizing C# code as islands, based on a graph-drawing algorithm layout [47]. Their approach also uses 3D glyphs, e.g., bridges representing dependencies and trees depicting classes, for visualizing the structure of a project. *CodeSurveyor* is another approach that makes use on the cartographic metaphor [21]. Based on a hierarchical graph layout algorithm, files are positioned in a 2D reference plane and are aggregated to states, countries, or continents according to the architectural structure of the software project. *CodeSurveyor* shares characterisitcs of treemaps that use non-rectangular shapes [40]. Schreiber et al.proposed *ISLANDVIZ*, another approach using the island metaphor. It enables users to interactively explore a software system in virtual reality and augmented reality alike [42].

Treemap Layouts. Another widely used class of layout algorithms in the software visualization domain are *Treemaps*. Treemaps are inherently capable of reflecting the typically hierarchical structure of software projects [40,41]. Given their 2D layout, they can be extended into the third dimension, thus resulting in a 2.5D visualization. Besides height, color, and texture 2.5D treemaps offer additional visual variables for additional information display [31–33]. An approach that refer to natural phenomena, e.g., fire or rain, for visualizing software evolution in a 2.5D treemap was proposed by Würfel et al. [54]. It is worth mentioning that the class of treemap algorithms includes a large number of shapes other than just rectangles or Voronoi cells [41].

The Tree Metaphor. In our considerations, we use the tree metaphor since trees offer a variety of visual variables. Kleiner and Hartigan were the first to propose a mapping of multivariate data to a 2D tree [25]. Based on hierarchical clustering of variables, for each data point, the geometry of each tree, i.e., the thickness of a branch, the angle between branches, and their orientation, is derived from the data attributes. Erra presented an approach to visualize object-oriented systems using the tree metaphor, thus resulting in a forest [16,17]. For every revision each file is depicted as a tree, whose visual variables reflect properties of the source code, i.e., software metrics, in a predefined way. Later Atzberger et al.applied the tree metaphor for software visualization tasks [2]. The main difference between Atzberger et al.and Erra et al.is the placement of the trees in the reference plane. The approach of Atzberger et al.is not restricted to the case of object-oriented programming languages, as it only uses the natural language in source code. Furthermore, the system of Atzberger et al.allows users to specify custom mappings of data and visual attributes. The authors do not focus on rendering realistic trees but rather apply handcrafted models for their approach. Kleiberg et al.use the tree metaphor for visualizing an entire set of hierarchically structured data. This approach differs from most other approaches because each tree does not represent a single document [24].

The City Metaphor. This metaphor is probably the most popular use of 3D glyphs in the software visualization domain. In their approach *CodeCity*, Wettel and Lanza applied a city metaphor for exploring object-oriented software projects using a 2.5D visualization, referring to real-world cities [52,53]. Each class is represented by a building and packages are grouped into districts that are placed according to a modified treemap algorithm. By mapping software metrics onto the visual variables of the cuboids, e.g., its height and the size of the base, a user can get an overview of the structure of a project. Steinbrückner adopted the idea of the city metaphor and introduced a novel layout approach, based on a hierarchical street system, that captures a project development over time [45,46].

Other Approaches. Beck proposed a mapping between software metrics of object-oriented software projects and geometric properties of figurative feathers, e.g., its size, shape, and texture [5]. Their approach *Software Feathers* is intended to support developers in getting a first overview of a software project and to deticting interesting code entities. Fernandez et al.extended an approach by Lewis et al. [30], that generates 2D glyphs in order to identify classes with the same dependencies and similar set of methods [19]. Chuah and Eick proposed the three glyph visualizations *InfoBUG*, *Time-wheel*, and *3D-wheel* for the task of visualizing project-oriented software data [9].

3   Glyph Placement in a 2D Reference Space

According to Ward et al.there are three general strategies for placing glyphs [51]:

1. **Uniform.** All glyphs are placed in equidistant positions.
2. **Structure-Driven.** The positions of the glyphs arise from the structure of the data set, e.g., a hierarchy or graph structure within the data.
3. **Data-Driven.** The positions of the glyphs are determined by a set of data attributes.

In this section, we present the layout approach presented by Atzberger et al. [2]. In a semantic layout, the relative position between two points on the 2D reference plane should reflect the semantic relatedness between the corresponding data points, i.e., source code files of a software project. For this, the assumption is made that the semantic similarity between source code files is reflected in a shared vocabulary and can therefore be captured using techniques from the NLP domain. The approach for placing 3D glyphs on a plane has three stages. First, the source code files of a software project are preprocessed to get rid of words that carry no semantic information. In the second step LDA is applied to the corpus of preprocessed documents to model each source code file as a high-dimensional vector. Lastly, in the third step, MDS is applied to reduce the vectors in their dimensionality.

3.1   Data Preprocessing

In our considerations each source code file of a project is viewed as a single document, the set of all documents is called the corpus, and the set of all words in the corpus forms the vocabulary. We neglect the ordering of the words within a document and only store their frequencies in the so-called term-document-matrix. In order to remove words from the vocabulary that carry no semantic information, e.g., stopwords of the natural language, it is necessary to perform several preprocessing steps before applying topic models. Moreover, source code often follows naming conventions, e.g., the Camel Case convention, thus requiring additional preprocessing steps [7]. In our experiments, the following sequence of preprocessing steps has turned out to produce a usable vocabulary [2].

1. **Removal of Non-text Symbols:** All special characters such as dots and semicolons are replaced with white spaces to avoid accidental connection of words not meant to be combined. This includes the splitting of identifier names, e.g., the word *foo.bar* gets split into *foo* and *bar*.

2. **Split of Words:** Identifiers are split according to delimiters and the Camel Case convention, e.g., *FooBar* is split into *foo* and *bar*, and stripped from redundant white space subsequently.
3. **Removal of Stop Words:** Stop words based on natural language and programming language keywords are removed as they carry no semantic content. Additionally, we filter the input based on a hand-crafted list comprising domain-specific stop words, e.g., data types and type abstractions.
4. **Lemmatization:** To avoid grammatical diversions, all words are reduced to their basic form, e.g., *said* and *saying* are reduced to *say*.

After applying the four preprocessing steps, we store each document as a BOW. For the remainder of this paper, we refer to a documents' BOW after preprocessing as a document.

3.2 Latent Dirichlet Allocation on Source Code

Topic models are a widely used class of techniques for investigating collections of documents, e.g., for knowledge comprehension or classification tasks [1]. For software engineering tasks, LDA proposed by Blei et al. [6], is the most common technique [7]. Assuming a set of documents $\mathcal{D} = \{d_1, \ldots, d_m\}$, the so-called *corpus*, LDA extracts latent topics $\varphi_1, \ldots, \varphi_K$, underlying the corpus, where the number of topics K is a hyperparameter of the model. As topics are given as multinomial distributions over the vocabulary $\mathcal{V}$, which contains the terms of the corpus $\mathcal{D}$, the "concept" underlying a topic, in most cases can be derived from its most probable words. Table 1 shows an example for three topics with their ten most probable words extracted from the Bitcoin project [2]. From the most probable words, we suggest that topic #1 deals with the internal logic of cryptocurrency. Words like "thread", "time", "queue", and "callback" are related to the general concept of parallel processing in C++, and topic #3 is concerned about the UI.

Besides the topics, LDA learns representations $\theta_1, \ldots, \theta_m$ of the documents as distributions over the topics. The distributions $\theta_1, \ldots, \theta_m$ therefore capture the semantic structure of the documents and allow a comparison between them on a semantic level. LDA makes the assumption of an underlying generative process, which is given by

1. For each document d in the corpus $\mathcal{D}$ choose a distribution over topics $\theta \sim$ Dirichlet(α)
2. For each word w in d
   (a) Choose a topic $z \sim$ Multinomial(θ)
   (b) Choose the word w according to the probability $p(w|z, \beta)$.

The parameter $\alpha = (\alpha_1, \ldots, \alpha_K)$, where $0 < \alpha_i$ for all $1 \leq i \leq K$, is the Dirichlet prior for the document-topic distribution. Its meaning is best understood, when written as the product $\alpha = a_c \cdot m$ of its concentration parameter $a_c \in \mathbb{R}$ and its base measure $m = (m_1, \ldots, m_k)$, whose components sum up to 1. The case of a base measure $m = (1/K, \ldots, 1/K)$ is denoted as symmetrical Dirichlet prior. For small values of a_c, the Dirichlet distribution would favor points in the simplex that are close to one edge, i.e., LDA would try to describe a document with a minimum of topics. The larger the value

Table 1. Three exemplary topics extracted from *Bitcoin Core*(Source code taken from github.com/bitcoin/bitcoin) source code with $K = 50$ and the Dirichlet priors set to their default values.

Topic #1		Topic #2		Topic #3	
Term	Prob.	Term	Prob.	Term	Prob.
Std	0.070	Thread	0.132	Address	0.115
Transaction	0.031	Time	0.070	Model	0.108
Fee	0.027	Queue	0.064	Table	0.065
Tx	0.026	Std	0.054	Label	0.051
Ban	0.024	Callback	0.040	Qt	0.033
Str	0.023	Run	0.037	Index	0.030
Handler	0.016	Call	0.025	Dialog	0.024
Output	0.016	Mutex	0.021	Column	0.024
Bitcoin	0.015	Scheduler	0.020	Ui	0.021
Reason	0.015	Wait	0.018	Role	0.019

of a_c the more likely that LDA is to fit all topics a non-zero probability for a document. Analogous, those considerations hold true for the Dirichlet prior $\beta = (\beta_1, \ldots, \beta_N)$, $0 < \beta_i$ for $1 \leq i \leq N$ for the topic-term distribution, where N denotes the size of the vocabulary $\mathcal{V}$.

Since inference for LDA is intractable, approximation techniques need to be taken into account [6]. Among the most widely used are Collapsed Gibbs Sampling (CGS) [20], Variational Bayes (VB) [6], and its online version (OVB) [22].

3.3 Multidimensional Scaling

LDA applied on the source code files leads to a description of each document as a high-dimensional vector, whose components represent the expression in the respective topic. Therefore using a similarity measure, e.g., the Jensen-Shannon divergence, two documents can be compared on a semantic level, thus forming structures, e.g., clusters and outliers, in the set of all documents. Linstead et al.used this notion of similarity and applied the dimension reduction MDS on the documents to generate a two-dimensional layout. However, this approach implicitly assumes that all extracted topics are "equally different" to each other and neglects the fact that the topics, viewed as distributions over the vocabulary, can be compared among each other themselves. The layout approach by Atzberger et al.addresses this issue and applies the dimension reduction technique MDS on the topics $\varphi_1, \ldots, \varphi_K$, which can be compared to each other using the Jensen-Shannon distance [2,43]. This results in points $\bar{\varphi}_1, \ldots, \bar{\varphi}_K \in \mathbb{R}^2$, whose Euclidean distance reflects the Jensen-Shannon-distance of the high-dimensional topics. A document d, given by its document-topic distribution $\theta = (\theta^{(1)}, \ldots, \theta^{(K)})$, is then represented as the convex linear combination $\bar{d}$, precisely

$$\bar{d} = \sum_{j=1}^{K} \theta^{(j)} \bar{\phi}_j. \tag{1}$$

A document with a strong expression in a topic is subsequently placed next to that topic, taking the similarity of topics into account.

4 Visual Attributes of 3D Glyphs and Use Cases

In Sect. 2, we summarized popular visualization metaphors based on 3D glyphs in the Software Visualization domain. In this section, we review (1) the city metaphor and (2) the forest metaphor together with (3) the island metaphor. We categorize our visualization as $\mathcal{A}^3 \oplus \mathcal{R}^2$, i.e., three-dimensional primitives placed on a two-dimensional reference space pl [2, 15]. We further present a novel idea of placing avatars into the visualization, thus indicating developer activities.

4.1 City Metaphor

The city metaphor, as proposed by Wettel et al., owes its name its visual similarity to modern cities, caused by displaying software files as cuboids [52]. The motivation for choosing this metaphor was to support a user navigating through a software system by adopting a well-known metaphor from everyday life. All existing approaches rely on a layout that captures the hierarchical structure of a software project, thus focusing on the architectural aspect of a project. Therefore, the approaches do not support program comprehension tasks related to the underlying semantic concepts of a software project. One advantage of the city metaphor is that they offer various visual variables. Examples proposed in the literature are:

- Wettel et al.mapped the number of methods to height and the number of attributes to the cuboids' horizontal extent [52].
- Steinbrückner et al.used stacked cylinders, where each cylinder displays the coding activity of a single developer made on a file [46].
- Limberger et al.present various advanced visual variables, e.g., sketchiness or transparency, for cuboids that can be applied for the city metaphor [32]. Recently, Limberger et al.investigated the use of animations for displaying the evolution of source code artifacts measured between two revisions [31].

We adapt the idea of the city metaphor in our considerations by representing each file of a software project as a cylinder. Figure 2 shows a simple example for the project *globjects*, where the height and the color of the cylinders are used as visual variables. The height of the cylinder displays the Lines-of-Code (LOC) of the respective file, thus revealing the impact of underlying concepts for the software project. The color displays the percentage of commented lines in the respective file using a sequential color scheme, which allows drawing conclusions about the code quality in relation to a concept. In most cases, large files are grouped nearby each other, thus indicating their underlying concepts seem to have a large impact on the size of the project in terms of LOC. Furthermore, large files often harbor the risk of non-sufficient documentation in the form of comments. This observation could motivate the project maintainer to focus on that concept, distributed over the individual files, in a future refactoring process.

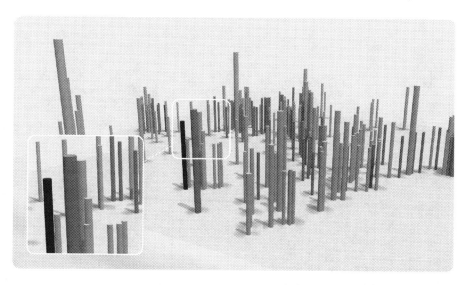

Fig. 2. Example for cylinders placed on a 2D reference plane. Each cylinder represents a single source code file of the project *globjects*[4]. The height displays the LOC of each file, and the color the percentage of commented lines.

4.2 Forest Metaphor

As shown in Sect. 2, the idea of forest islands is two widely used metaphors in the Software Visualization domain, especially as they offer a grouping of files according to some "relatedness". Furthermore, islands and forests are real-world structures, thus making them suitable for creating a mental map for the user to support program comprehension tasks. Our presentation here follows the preceding work of Atzberger et al.closely [2]. We focus our discussion to the following set of visual variables:

- The tree height, e.g., for depicting the size of a file in terms of LOC.
- The color of the tree crown, e.g., displaying software metrics related to the quality or complexity of the respective file.
- The tree type, e.g., to distinguish the source code files by their file endings.
- The health status of a tree, e.g., for displaying failed tests.
- Chopped trees, e.g., for visualizing deleted files.

Figure 3 shows two sets of tree glyphs and demonstrates the visual attributes they inherit [2].

When visualizing a software project using the tree metaphor, we first compute the position of each file as presented in Sect. 3, i.e., each file is represented as a single tree, thus forming an entire forest. Then for each point, the value of a height field is computed as presented in [28]. This has the effect that dense regions are placed on higher ground than regions with fewer trees, but still assuring that single trees stand on a terrain of $30\% - 50\%$ of the maximal height. Furthermore, we integrated the possibility to configure the water height, which can be seen as a height filtering technique.

Fig. 3. Examples of two sets of tree glyphs: the top row inherits the visual variables size, color, and health status. The bottom row shows trees of different types. Both models were purchased on *SketchFab*: "HandPainted Pine Pack" by ZugZug and "Low Poly Nature Pack" by NONE.

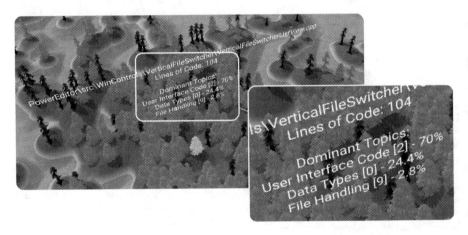

Fig. 4. Software Forest of the *notepad-plus-plus* project. The tooltip shows the underlying topic distribution of the file represented by the selected tree (highlighted). All trees with the same dominant topic are highlighted.

Figure 4 shows the result of applying our approach on the *notepad-plus-plus* project[5] based on the set of pine trees shown in Fig. 3. The underlying visual mapping aimed to represent the document-topic distribution of each file. The tree type is chosen according to the main topic of each file, i.e., the topic that has the highest probability in the file, e.g., documents with the main topic "User Interface Code" are displayed as green pine trees. All trees of the same color are highlighted when hovering over a tree. Here we want to mention that we manually labeled the topics for the project by examining their most probable words. In general, this is a time-consuming task that needs to be done manually [37].

---

[5] Source code taken from https://github.com/notepad-plus-plus/notepad-plus-plus.

Our next application demonstrates the use of Software Forest for the bitcoin project[6]. In Sect. 3 we showed three interesting topics extracted from the source code by applying LDA with $K = 50$ topics and default values for the Dirichlet priors. We map the topic with the highest impact for a document onto the tree type. As the number of tree types is usually limited, this visualization approach does not scale for a large number of topics. The bitcoin project is mainly written in C++, C, and Python. We ignore the other source code files and map the programming language onto the color of the tree. The height of the tree captures the LOC for the respective file (Fig. 5).

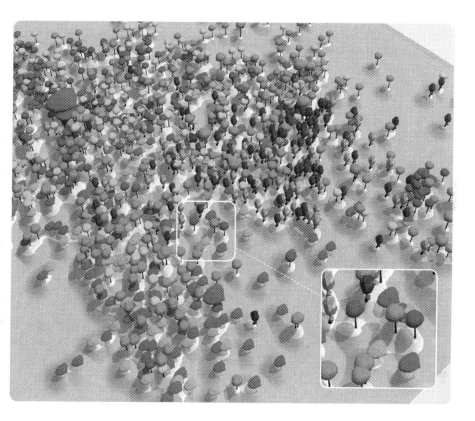

Fig. 5. Part of the software forest for the bitcoin project.

4.3   Developer Avatars

Our last visualization metaphor uses 3D glyphs displaying people for showing coding activities within a software project. Each developer or team is assigned an avatar whose position shows the source code contributed to within a given timespan. One question that could be addressed with this visualization would be the assignment of suitable developers when a bug related to a concept or a file would occur. Figure 6 shows an

---

[6] Source code taken from github.com/bitcoin/bitcoin.

example for placing avatars and cylinders on an island for the example of the *globjects* project. The color of the cylinders displays a complexity metric, whereas each figure represents a single developer. The avatars are placed nearby the file on which they contributed the most. The large red cylinder indicates a considerable risk in a file, as its complexity is very high. Moreover, we can deduce from the visualization that an avatar next to a cylinder might have the required knowledge to maintain or review the risk.

In our example, each team member can choose among a set of given figures, which he would favor as a representation, however the idea of mapping data to glyphs displaying developers has been presented by Atzberger et al.for the task of displaying data related to the skills and expertise of developers [3]. However when using human-looking glyphs for displaying developer related data, various visual attributes become critical and should be considered very carefully. One idea to overcome this issue, would be the use of abstract forms, which only reminds on human faces, as initially presented as the popular Chernoff faces [8].

Fig. 6. Examples using avatars positioned in relation to their coding activities.

5   System Design and Implementation Details

In this section, we present implementation details with respect to the layout computation and the rendering of our visualization prototype, i.e., the tools and libraries we choose for generating a 2D layout based on the vocabulary in the source code files and the visualization mapping and rendering, respectively. We further describe the supported interaction techniques for enabling a user to explore a software project. We use a separation of the layout computation and the interactive rendering component, where the layout computation component computes a visualization dataset from a source code repository that is used as an input of the rendering component (see Fig. 7).

5.1 Layout Computation

Our approach follows the implementation presented by Atzberger et al.in their earlier work about the Software Forest [2]. For preprocessing, the natural language in the source code documents, we apply the *nltk*[7] library for obtaining a list of stopwords for the English language. We further use *spacy*[8] for lemmatization. We used the LDA implementation provided by the library *Gensim*[9]. *Gensim* offers an LDA implementation based on the original implementation by Blei et al. [6] as well as its online version introduced by Hofman et al. [22]. The implementation of MDS is taken from the Machine learning library *scikit-learn*[10]. The result of the layout computation is a 2D layout that is merged with other static source code metrics into a CSV file that is later used for input to the rendering component.

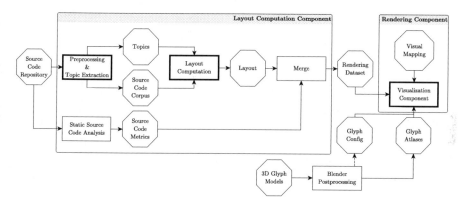

Fig. 7. The data processing pipeline to compute the semantic layouts. The rendering component composes the layouts and glyph atlases based on the visual mapping.

5.2 Rendering

The rendering component is an extension to a scatter plot renderer, written in *TypeScript* and *WebGL* [49]. The main dependency is the open-source framework *webgl-operate*[11], which handles canvas and WebGL context management, as well as labeling primitives and glTF scene loading and rendering. The 3D glyph models are integrated into the rendering component by means of a glyph atlas and a configuration file. The basic designs for our more advanced visualization metaphors, i.e., trees and people, are taken from *SketchFab*[12]. The 3D glyph atlases are constructed manually using *Blender*[13], but

---

[7] https://www.nltk.org/.

[8] https://spacy.io/.

[9] https://radimrehurek.com/gensim/.

[10] https://scikit-learn.org/stable/.

[11] https://webgl-operate.org/.

[12] https://sketchfab.com/feed.

[13] https://www.blender.org/.

every other 3D editor with glTF is a feasible alternative. Together with a glyph atlas, we have to specify its objects within a *JSON* configuration file (an example is given in Listing 1). This rendering component is embedded into a Web page with further GUI elements for the visual mapping and direct interaction techniques on the canvas to support navigation in the semantic software map.

5.3   User Interaction

As basic interaction techniques, a user can choose mappings from data to visual variables of the selected glyphs, navigate through the 2.5D visualization, and retrieve details on demand displayed by tooltips by rotating and zooming. Figure 8 shows the user interface of our web-based implementation prototype. Our system supports basic interaction techniques, e.g., rotating and zoom. Furthermore, a tooltip displaying the entire entries of the respective data point contained in the CSV file shows up. As our approach highly depends on LDA, we highlight all trees with the same dominant topic as the selected one when hovering over it. Furthermore, our system allows the user to define a custom mapping between data columns and the visual variables provided by the selected model. For each model, we ensure that at least the type, the height, and the color are available as visual metaphors. By adjusting the effect of the variable tree size, which depends on a data attribute, the user can further interactively explore the effect of data variables for the source code files. In order to enhance the rendering with visual cues and more fidelity, the user can modify rendering details, e.g., by toggling Anti-Aliasing or soft shadows.

```json
{
    "modelFile": "PeopleCylinders2.glb",
    "attributes": [ "color" ],
    "modelScale": 1.0,
    "types": [
        { "name": "Cylinder",
            "baseModel": "Cylinder_Ax.001",
            "variants": [
                { "name": "Cylinder_Ax.001", "color": 1.0 },
                { "name": "Cylinder_Ax.002", "color": 0.75 },
                { "name": "Cylinder_Ax.003", "color": 0.5 },
                { "name": "Cylinder_Ax.004", "color": 0.25 },
                { "name": "Cylinder_Ax.005", "color": 0.0 }
            ]
        },
        { "name": "People",
            "baseModel": "Person0",
            "variants": [
                { "name": "Person0", "color": 1.0 },
                { "name": "Person1", "color": 0.5 },
                { "name": "Person2", "color": 0.0 }
            ]
        }
    ]
}
```

Listing 1: An example JSON configuration of a mapping from attribute values to 3D model. Two types of glyph categories are defined, namely "Cylinder" and "People". This configuration can be used to display source code files as cylinders and developers as people-looking glyphs in the same semantic software map.

6 Conclusion

6.1 Discussion

Software Visualization techniques support users in program comprehension tasks by displaying images based on data related to software artifacts. In many cases, the questions are about the semantics of a software project, e.g., for locating concepts or functionalities in the source code. Our previous work used a tree metaphor and a semantic layout to create map-like visualizations to support users in program comprehension tasks related to the semantics. In this extended work, we detailed how the topic model LDA and the dimension reduction technique MDS are applied for generating a layout for capturing the semantic relatedness between source code files. We presented mappings between quantitative and qualitative aspects of source code files, e.g., source code metrics or file types, and visual variables of selected 3D glyphs for concrete program comprehension tasks. We applied the city, the forest, and the island metaphor for our use-cases. Our web-based visualization can visualize large data sets and provides a significant degree of freedom to the user by supporting various interaction techniques.

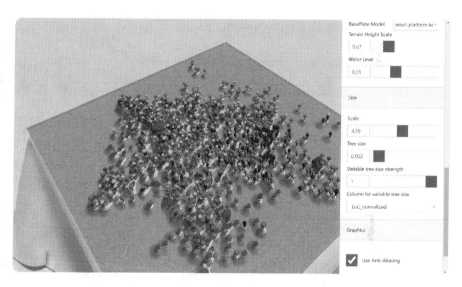

Fig. 8. User interface of our web-based implementation. Besides the full mapping configuration, rendering parameters can be adjusted by the user.

Though LDA has shown great success in modeling the concepts inherent in a software project [38], the possibility of visual indication of misleading or irrelevant relations must not be neglected. For example, the positioning of a document in 2D is not unique as it arises from a convex linear combination of the reduced topic-word distributions. Therefore, two documents with totally different document-topic distributions may be placed next to one another. In practice, however, the choice of the Dirichlet prior α forces LDA to favor document-topic distributions with only a few topics.

For our experiments, we created visualizations for the two Open Source projects *globjects* and *bitcoin*. Both can be seen as representatives for mid-sized software projects. However, a software visualization should also provide insights into large projects as the need for program comprehension increases with project size. Figure 9 shows a 2.5D visualization for the Machine Learning framework *TensorFlow*[14] that comprises a total of 13 154 files, where each file is represented by a cylinder with the same visual mapping as presented in Sect. 4. The data volume makes it difficult to maintain interactive framerates on average machines. Though the island (without glyphs) is a map-like visualization in itself, its capabilities are limited, as its number of visual variables is limited.

Our visual mappings were motivated by common questions in a software development process. However, we do not provide empirical measurements, e.g., provided by a user study, that would demonstrate the actual benefit of our visualizations for users. It is yet unclear whether the choice of visual variables and glyphs is appropriate for users in real-world settings. The ideas presented in Sect. 4 so far only provide a starting point for future investigations. Nevertheless, the given examples of map configurations indicate that our 2.5D software visualization is suitable for depicting aspects of and relations within software data, supports finding information and gaining knowledge, and possibly synchronizes the mental representation of selected software aspects with the actual data.

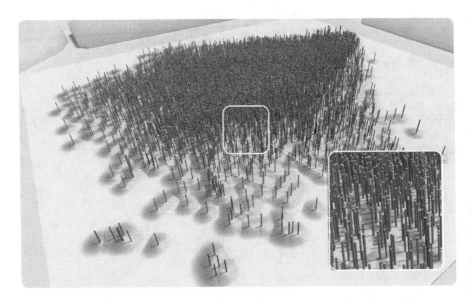

Fig. 9. Visualization of the tensorflow dataset using cylinders. The dataset contains 13 154 files, which shows the limitation in discernible data items of our technique.

---

[14] Source code taken from https://github.com/tensorflow/tensorflow.

6.2   Future Work

Concerning our visualization approach, various possibilities for future work exist. Most importantly, the effectiveness of our approach and the visual mappings should be evaluated in a systematic user study, e.g., to identify visual mappings best-suited for program comprehension tasks in an industrial setting with developers and project managers. Furthermore, we can imagine including more advanced visual mappings, especially in the case of the city metaphor [32].

Our glyph placement strategy is an example of a data-driven approach [50] for that distortion techniques should be considered. Our examples indicate that an increased glyph height tends to increase visual clutter. Therefore, distortion strategies as presented in [50] seem well-suited for mitigation. A modern approach for removing distortion in 2.5D visualizations was presented in [48] and should be applicable for our case. Furthermore, quality metrics associated with the results of dimension reduction techniques can help measure whether the dimension reduction was able to capture local and global structures within a dataset. As our visualization approach mainly builds upon the semantic layout, we plan to implement a feature in our framework that generates the layout for a given software project automatically by evaluating various dimension reduction techniques with respect to selected quality metrics, as presented in [18].

Acknowledgements. This work is part of the "Software-DNA" project, which is funded by the European Regional Development Fund (ERDF or EFRE in German) and the State of Brandenburg (ILB). This work is part of the KMU project "KnowhowAnalyzer" (Förderkennzeichen 01IS20088B), which is funded by the German Ministry for Education and Research (Bundesministerium für Bildung und Forschung). We further thank the students Maximilian Söchting and Merlin de la Haye for their work during their master's project at the Hasso Plattner Institute during the summer term 2020.

References

1. Aggarwal, C.C., Zhai, C.: Mining text data. Springer, New York (2012). https://doi.org/10.1007/978-1-4614-3223-4
2. Atzberger, D., et al.: Software forest: a visualization of semantic similarities in source code using a tree metaphor. In: Proceedings of the 16th International Joint Conference on Computer Vision, Imaging and Computer Graphics Theory and Applications - Volume 3 IVAPP, IVAPP 2021, pp. 112–122. INSTICC, SciTePress (2021). https://doi.org/10.5220/0010267601120122
3. Atzberger, D., et al.: Visualization of knowledge distribution across development teams using 2.5d semantic software maps. In: Proceedings of 13th International Conference on Information Visualization Theory and Applications, IVAPP 2022, INSTICC, SciTePress (2022)
4. Atzberger, D., Scheibel, W., Limberger, D., Döllner, J.: Software galaxies: displaying coding activities using a galaxy metaphor. In: Proceedings of 14th International Symposium on Visual Information Communication and Interaction, VINCI 2021, pp. 18:1–2. ACM (2021). https://doi.org/10.1145/3481549.3481573
5. Beck, F.: Software feathers - figurative visualization of software metrics. In: Proceedings of 5th International Conference on Information Visualization Theory and Applications - Volume 1: IVAPP, IVAPP 2014, pp. 5–16. INSTICC, SciTePress (2014). https://doi.org/10.5220/0004650100050016

6. Blei, D.M., Ng, A.Y., Jordan, M.I.: Latent dirichlet allocation. J. Mach. Learn. Res. **3**, 993–1022 (2003). https://doi.org/10.5555/944919.944937
7. Chen, T.-H., Thomas, S.W., Hassan, A.E.: A survey on the use of topic models when mining software repositories. Empirical Softw. Eng. **21**(5), 1843–1919 (2015). https://doi.org/10.1007/s10664-015-9402-8
8. Chernoff, H.: The use of faces to represent points in k-dimensional space graphically. J. Am. Stat. Assoc. **68**(342), 361–368 (1973). https://doi.org/10.1080/01621459.1973.10482434
9. Chuah, M., Eick, S.: Glyphs for software visualization. In: Proceedings of 5th International Workshop on Program Comprehension, IWPC 1997, pp. 183–191. IEEE (1997). https://doi.org/10.1109/WPC.1997.601291
10. Cornelissen, B., Zaidman, A., van Deursen, A.: A controlled experiment for program comprehension through trace visualization. IEEE Trans. Softw. Eng. **37**(3), 341–355 (2011). https://doi.org/10.1109/TSE.2010.47
11. Cornelissen, B., Zaidman, A., Holten, D., Moonen, L., van Deursen, A., van Wijk, J.J.: Execution trace analysis through massive sequence and circular bundle views. J. Syst. Softw. **81**(12), 2252–2268 (2008). https://doi.org/10.1016/j.jss.2008.02.068
12. Cox, M.A.A., Cox, T.F.: Multidimensional scaling. In: Handbook of Data Visualization, pp. 315–347. Springer, Berlin (2008). https://doi.org/10.1007/978-3-540-33037-0_14
13. Deerwester, S., Dumais, S.T., Furnas, G.W., Landauer, T.K., Harshman, R.: Indexing by latent semantic analysis. J. Am. Soc. Inf. Sci. **41**(6), 391–407 (1990). https://doi.org/10.1002/(SICI)1097-4571(199009)41:6⟨391::AID-ASI1⟩3.0.CO;2-9
14. Dehaghani, S.M.H., Hajrahimi, N.: Which factors affect software projects maintenance cost more? Acta Informatica Medica **21**(1), 63–66 (2013). https://doi.org/10.5455/aim.2012.21.63-66
15. Dübel, S., Röhlig, M., Schumann, H., Trapp, M.: 2d and 3d presentation of spatial data: a systematic review. In: Proceedings of VIS International Workshop on 3DVis, 3DVis '14, pp. 11–18. IEEE (2014). https://doi.org/10.1109/3DVis.2014.7160094
16. Erra, U., Scanniello, G.: Towards the visualization of software systems as 3d forests: the CodeTrees environment. In: Proceedings of 27th Annual ACM Symposium on Applied Computing, SAC 2012, pp. 981–988. ACM (2012). https://doi.org/10.1145/2245276.2245467
17. Erra, U., Scanniello, G., Capece, N.: Visualizing the evolution of software systems using the forest metaphor. In: Proceedings of 16th International Conference on Information Visualisation, iV 2012, pp. 87–92 (2012). https://doi.org/10.1109/IV.2012.25
18. Espadoto, M., Martins, R.M., Kerren, A., Hirata, N.S.T., Telea, A.C.: Toward a quantitative survey of dimension reduction techniques. Trans. Vis. Comput. Graph. **27**(3), 2153–2173 (2021). https://doi.org/10.1109/TVCG.2019.2944182
19. Fernandez, I., Bergel, A., Alcocer, J.P.S., Infante, A., Gîrba, T.: Glyph-based software component identification. In: Proceedings of 24th International Conference on Program Comprehension, ICPC 2016, pp. 1–10. IEEE (2016). https://doi.org/10.1109/ICPC.2016.7503713
20. Griffiths, T.L., Steyvers, M.: Finding scientific topics. Proc. Natl. Acad. Sci. **101**, 5228–5235 (2004). https://doi.org/10.1073/pnas.0307752101
21. Hawes, N., Marshall, S., Anslow, C.: CodeSurveyor: Mapping large-scale software to aid in code comprehension. In: Proceedings of 3rd Working Conference on Software Visualization, VISSOFT 2015, pp. 96–105. IEEE (2015). https://doi.org/10.1109/VISSOFT.2015.7332419
22. Hoffman, M., Bach, F., Blei, D.: Online learning for latent dirichlet allocation. In: Advances in Neural Information Processing Systems. NIPS 2010, vol. 23, pp. 856–864 (2010)
23. Systems and software engineering-Vocabulary: Standard. International Organization for Standardization (2017). https://doi.org/10.1109/IEEESTD.2017.8016712
24. Kleiberg, E., van de Wetering, H., van Wijk, J.J.: Botanical visualization of huge hierarchies. In: Proceedings of Symposium on Information Visualization, INFOVIS 2001, pp. 87–87. IEEE (2001). https://doi.org/10.1109/INFVIS.2001.963285

25. Kleiner, B., Hartigan, J.A.: Representing points in many dimensions by trees and castles. J. Am. Stat. Assoc. **76**(374), 260–269 (1981). https://doi.org/10.1080/01621459.1981. 10477638
26. Kohonen, T.: Exploration of very large databases by self-organizing maps. In: Proceedings of International Conference on Neural Networks, ICNN 1997, pp. 1–6. IEEE (1997). https:// doi.org/10.1109/ICNN.1997.611622
27. Kuhn, A., Loretan, P., Nierstrasz, O.: Consistent layout for thematic software maps. In: Proceedings of 15th Working Conference on Reverse Engineering, WCRE 2008, pp. 209–218. IEEE (2008). https://doi.org/10.1109/WCRE.2008.45
28. Kuhn, A., Erni, D., Loretan, P., Nierstrasz, O.: Software cartography: thematic software visualization with consistent layout. J. Softw. Maintenance Evol. Res. Pract. **22**(3), 191–210 (2010)
29. Lanza, M.: The evolution matrix: recovering software evolution using software visualization techniques. In: Proceedings of 4th International Workshop on Principles of Software Evolution, IWPSE 2001, pp. 37–42. ACM (2001). https://doi.org/10.1145/602461.602467
30. Lewis, J.P., Rosenholtz, R., Fong, N., Neumann, U.: VisualIDs: automatic distinctive icons for desktop interfaces. Trans. Graph. **23**(3), 416–423 (2004). https://doi.org/10.1145/ 1015706.1015739
31. Limberger, D., Scheibel, W., Dieken, J., Döllner, J.: Visualization of data changes in 2.5d treemaps using procedural textures and animated transitions. In: Proceedings of 14th International Symposium on Visual Information Communication and Interaction, VINCI 2021, pp. 6:1–5. ACM (2021). https://doi.org/10.1145/3481549.3481570
32. Limberger, D., Scheibel, W., Döllner, J., Trapp, M.: Advanced visual metaphors and techniques for software maps. In: Proceedings of 12th International Symposium on Visual Information Communication and Interaction, VINCI 2019, pp. 11:1–8. ACM (2019). https://doi. org/10.1145/3356422.3356444
33. Limberger, D., Trapp, M., Döllner, J.: Depicting uncertainty in 2.5d treemaps. In: Proceedings of 13th International Symposium on Visual Information Communication and Interaction, VINCI 2020, pp. 28:1–2. ACM (2020). https://doi.org/10.1145/3430036.3432753
34. Linstead, E., Rigor, P., Bajracharya, S., Lopes, C., Baldi, P.: Mining eclipse developer contributions via author-topic models. In: Proceedings of 4th International Workshop on Mining Software Repositories, MSR 2007, pp. 30:1–4. IEEE (2007). https://doi.org/10.1109/MSR. 2007.20
35. Linstead, E., Bajracharya, S., Ngo, T., Rigor, P., Lopes, C., Baldi, P.: Sourcerer: mining and searching internet-scale software repositories. Data Min. Knowl. Disc. **18**(2), 300–336 (2009). https://doi.org/10.1007/s10618-008-0118-x
36. Malony, A., Hammerslag, D., Jablonowski, D.: Traceview: a trace visualization tool. IEEE Softw. **8**(5), 19–28 (1991). https://doi.org/10.1109/52.84213
37. Markovtsev, V., Kant, E.: Topic modeling of public repositories at scale using names in source code. arXiv CoRR cs.PL (2017). https://arxiv.org/abs/1704.00135
38. Maskeri, G., Sarkar, S., Heafield, K.: Mining business topics in source code using latent dirichlet allocation. In: Proceedings of 1st India Software Engineering Conference, ISEC 2008, pp. 113–120. ACM (2008). https://doi.org/10.1145/1342211.1342234
39. Rosen-Zvi, M., Griffiths, T., Steyvers, M., Smyth, P.: The author-topic model for authors and documents. In: Proceedings of 20th Conference on Uncertainty in Artificial Intelligence, UAI 2004, pp. 487–494. AUAI Press (2004). https://doi.org/10.5555/1036843.1036902
40. Scheibel, W., Limberger, D., Döllner, J.: Survey of treemap layout algorithms. In: Proceedings of 13th International Symposium on Visual Information Communication and Interaction, VINCI 2020, pp. 1:1–9. ACM (2020). https://doi.org/10.1145/3430036.3430041

41. Scheibel, W., Trapp, M., Limberger, D., Döllner, J.: A taxonomy of treemap visualization techniques. In: Proceedings of 15th International Joint Conference on Computer Vision, Imaging and Computer Graphics Theory and Applications - Volume 3: IVAPP, IVAPP 2020, pp. 273–280. INSTICC, SciTePress (2020). https://doi.org/10.5220/0009153902730280

42. Schreiber, A., Misiak, M.: Visualizing software architectures in virtual reality with an island metaphor. In: Chen, J.Y.C., Fragomeni, G. (eds.) VAMR 2018. LNCS, vol. 10909, pp. 168–182. Springer, Cham (2018). https://doi.org/10.1007/978-3-319-91581-4_13

43. Sievert, C., Shirley, K.: LDAvis: a method for visualizing and interpreting topics. In: Proceedings of Workshop on Interactive Language Learning, Visualization, and Interfaces, pp. 63–70. ACL (2014). https://doi.org/10.3115/v1/W14-3110

44. Skupin, A.: The world of geography: visualizing a knowledge domain with cartographic means. Proc. Natl. Acad. Sci. **101**(suppl 1), 5274–5278 (2004). https://doi.org/10.1073/pnas.0307654100

45. Steinbrückner, F., Lewerentz, C.: Representing development history in software cities. In: Proceedings of 5th International Symposium on Software Visualization, SOFTVIS 2010, pp. 193–202. ACM (2010). https://doi.org/10.1145/1879211.1879239

46. Steinbrückner, F., Lewerentz, C.: Understanding software evolution with software cities. Inf. Visual. **12**(2), 200–216 (2013). https://doi.org/10.1177/1473871612438785

47. Štěpánek, A.: Procedurally generated landscape as a visualization of C# code. Technical Report, Masaryk University, Faculty of Informatics (2020). bachelor's Thesis

48. Vollmer, J.O., Döllner, J.: 2.5d dust & magnet visualization for large multivariate data. In: Proceedings of 13th International Symposium on Visual Information Communication and Interaction, VINCI 2020, pp. 21:1–8. ACM (2020). https://doi.org/10.1145/3430036.3430045

49. Wagner, L., Scheibel, W., Limberger, D., Trapp, M., Döllner, J.: A framework for interactive exploration of clusters in massive data using 3d scatter plots and webgl. In: Proceedings of 25th International Conference on 3D Web Technology, Web3D 2020, pp. 31:1–2. ACM (2020). https://doi.org/10.1145/3424616.3424730

50. Ward, M.O.: A taxonomy of glyph placement strategies for multidimensional data visualization. Inf. Visual. **1**(3–4), 194–210 (2002)

51. Ward, M.O., Grinstein, G., Keim, D.: Interactive Data Visualization: Foundations, Techniques, and Applications. CRC Press, Boca Raton (2010)

52. Wettel, R., Lanza, M.: Visualizing software systems as cities. In: Proceedings of International Workshop on Visualizing Software for Understanding and Analysis, VISSOFT 2007, pp. 92–99. IEEE (2007). https://doi.org/10.1109/VISSOF.2007.4290706

53. Wettel, R., Lanza, M.: CodeCity: 3d visualization of large-scale software. In: Companion of the 30th International Conference on Software Engineering, ICSE Companion 2008, pp. 921–922. Association for Computing Machinery (2008). https://doi.org/10.1145/1370175.1370188

54. Würfel, H., Trapp, M., Limberger, D., Döllner, J.: Natural phenomena as metaphors for visualization of trend data in interactive software maps. In: Proceedings of Conference on Computer Graphics and Visual Computing, CGVC 2015, pp. 69–76. EG (2015). https://doi.org/10.2312/cgvc.20151246

Revisiting Order-Preserving, Gap-Avoiding Rectangle Packing

Sören Domrös$^{(\boxtimes)}$ ⓘ, Daniel Lucas ⓘ, Reinhard von Hanxleden ⓘ, and Klaus Jansen ⓘ

Kiel University, 24118 Kiel, Germany
{sdo,stu124145,rvh,kj}@informatik.uni-kiel.de

Abstract. We present an improved 2D rectangle packing heuristic that preserves the initial ordering of the rectangles while maintaining a left-to-right reading direction. We also present an algorithm configuration to fall back to a simpler algorithm that works more reliably for simple packing problems and an option to optimize the result in non-interactive scenarios. This is achieved by checking for stackability, approximating the required width, and using a strip packing algorithm to pack the rectangles with the option to improve the approximated width iteratively. We present still existing Obviously Non-Optimal packings and general problems of packings that preserve the reading direction, and discuss the problem of rectangle packing in hierarchical graphs. Moreover, the algorithm without the width approximation step can solve strip packing problems such that a reading direction is maintained.

Keywords: Automatic layout · Model order · Rectangle packing

1 Introduction

Rectangle packing problems remain in most cases hard problems irrespective of whether the rectangles are packed in a specific area, aspect ratio, width, height, or different bins [6]. Variations of bin packing or strip-packing are often used in the transportation industry. Here packing problems have additional constraints and rectangles, which correspond to packages, have to be packed such that they can be removed in a specific order and a stable packing can be achieved without tilted packages [4].

This work extends the work of [5]. They evaluate the box approach, the LR-rectpacking approach that we will use in its scale measure configuration and just call rectpacking, and a constraint based solution via CP optimizer for flat rectangle graphs.

As in [5], this work is motivated by the placement of *regions* in the graphical language SCCharts [8]. SCCharts are modeled textually in the Kiel Integrated Environment for Layout Eclipse Rich Client (KIELER)[1] [7,9] and are automatically synthesized into a diagram using the open source Eclipse Layout Kernel (ELK)[2]. This allows to use common version management tools for textual modeling and at the same time has the

---

[1] www.rtsys.informatik.uni-kiel.de/en/research/kieler.
[2] https://www.eclipse.org/elk/.

© Springer Nature Switzerland AG 2023
A. A. de Sousa et al. (Eds.): VISIGRAPP 2021, CCIS 1691, pp. 183–205, 2023.
https://doi.org/10.1007/978-3-031-25477-2_9

advantage of transient views of the graphical model [7]. While the textual model is created, we assume that the ordering of regions is intended by the developer. Therefore, we want to generate a diagram that places the regions such that their *model order*, given by the textual input file, is respected in the resulting drawing, while still being able to utilize the screen real estate efficiently. Even though SCCharts do not only consist of rectangles but also node-link diagrams inside the rectangles, we want to focus only on the rectangle packing problem in this paper.

SCCharts regions always require a rectanglular area and can be *collapsed* (see regions **A** - **E**, **G**, **I**, **J**, and **L** in Fig. 1) to make their contents invisible or expanded (see regions **F**, **H**, and **K**). Collapsed regions always have the same height but a width depending on the region name. Expanded regions may have arbitrarily big inner behavior and are usually much bigger than collapsed regions.

In the KIELER tool an SCChart is drawn in a specific window. This window has a specific aspect ratio called the *desired aspect ration* (DAR) defined by its width divided by it height. For simplicity and without loss of generality, we will assume that the DAR is set to 1.3. The generated drawing does not have to fit this aspect ratio exactly but its contents can typically be drawn with a higher zoom level if it is the case, as expressed by the *scale measure* (SM), formally defined later. A bigger scale measure means that regions can be drawn bigger, which means all components and labels can be read more easily.

Regions are placed such that they do not have any "gaps" between them (e. g. compare Fig. 1c to Fig. 1d) since it creates clear rows and is aesthetically more pleasant.

Contributions and Outline. The new contributions are the following:

- We showcase region packing problems for which the Nothing is Obviously Non-Optimal (NONO) principle [11] is difficult to abide, resulting in Obviously Non-Optimal (ONO) packings in Sect. 4.1.
- Additionally to the box and rectpacking algorithm, we present two improvements to the rectpacking algorithm and propose an improved rectpacking algorithm that can be used to solve packings as a result of badly approximated width in Sect. 5.
- We describe the constraints used to solve the region packing problem via an optimization problem that maximizes the scale measure in Sect. 6.
- We compare the improved rectpacking algorithm using the generated region packing problems from [5] in Sect. 7.1.
- Additionally to the evaluation of box, rectpacking, and the constraint-based solution with generated models, we evaluate them with real SCCharts on a local and global level with the new problem class of only expanded regions in Sect. 7.2.
- We evaluate and discuss the problem of local maximum scale measures in hierarchical graphs at the example of SCCharts in Sect. 7.3.

We also cover the following contributions from [5]:

- The presentation and formalization of the region packing problem (Sect. 2), including placement constraints that facilitate a reading direction.
- The box algorithm to solve the region packing problem (Sect. 3, see Fig. 1b).

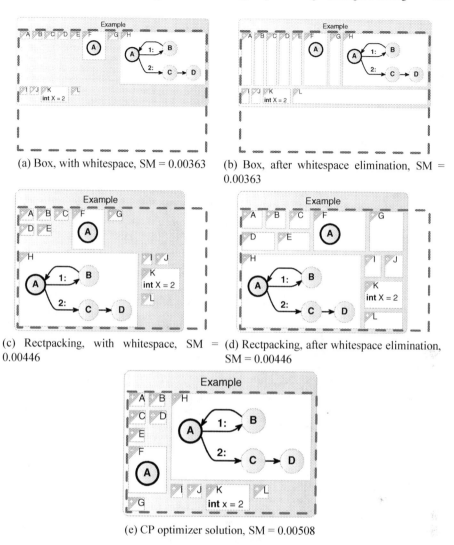

(a) Box, with whitespace, SM = 0.00363

(b) Box, after whitespace elimination, SM = 0.00363

(c) Rectpacking, with whitespace, SM = 0.00446

(d) Rectpacking, after whitespace elimination, SM = 0.00446

(e) CP optimizer solution, SM = 0.00508

Fig. 1. An SCChart with region F, H, and K expanded, desired aspect ratio of 1.6 (red-dashed bounding box), with scale measure SM (larger is better), [5]. (Color figure online)

- The rectpacking algorithm (Sect. 4, see Fig. 1d).

The evaluation of the algorithms can be found in Sect. 7, which is divided into the evaluation of region packing with partly collapsed regions using generated models, and the novel evaluation of the region packing problem with only expanded regions with real SCCharts models. We conclude and present future work in Sect. 8.

Related Work. As also described in [5], the general approach is related to several existing works:

[6] mention several rectangle and strip packing algorithms that do not consider an ordering of the rectangles or a reading direction.

[3] present a strip packing algorithm that considers removal order as an ordering constraint. However, the removal order allows different reading directions, e. g. left-to-right and right-to-left, in the same packing, which we do not allow in our problem.

[1] only restrict the vertical placement of regions in their strip packing with precedence constraints and strip packing with release times algorithm for FPGA programming, which, again, is not equivalent to a reading direction. However, their algorithm allows to eliminate whitespace between different rectangles, which they do not consider to do in their context.

[10] showcase an asymptotic fully polynomial approximation scheme for strip packing that does not consider an ordering. Future work could be to design an approximation scheme for the region packing problem.

[2] introduce a treemap visualization algorithm for file systems or other hierarchical structures. They also form rows and subrows to place the rectangles in. However, they do not consider order and only have a fix area for each rectangle instead of minimum height and width.

[20] present an algorithm to layout wordclouds that preserves the neighborhood of words. While a neighborhood preserving algorithm is indeed interesting it does not preserve a reading-direction, does not create rows and subrows of words to read them easily based on their order, does not have a clear order of words, and does not allow to eliminate whitespace between them.

The second author presented a prototype of the *rectpacking* algorithm in his thesis that also motivates the need to solve the region packing problem better for SCCharts with one big and several small or collapsed regions [12]. The *rectpacking* algorithm as it is now still uses the general idea of the width approximation step that was proposed in this thesis.

2   The Region Packing Problem

Let us formally define the packing problem that we henceforth call the *region packing problem* based on the example of SCCharts regions:

The regions describe an ordered sequence $R = (r_1, r_2, \ldots r_n)$ with $r_i = (w_i, h_i)$ for region r_i, with the minimal width w_i and minimal height h_i. To get the final drawing one wants to compute coordinates x_i and y_i for each region r_i and optionally a new width w_i and height h_i if one wants to eliminate whitespace (see Fig. 1a compared to Fig. 1b). Additional configuration, i. e. spacing between regions, padding, and a minimal width of the parent can be configured, but we will omit these in the following sections for simplicity. Henceforth, we call the regions r_{i-1} and r_{i+1} the *neighbors* of r_i.

A first intuitive requirement is that the resulting drawing has to be free of overlaps. Moreover, we want that the new width w_i and height h_i of each region is not smaller than the minimum width w_i and height h_i. We call these requirements the *correctness requirements* that have to be respected to produce a valid drawing. These requirements are of course founded in aesthetic criteria since we generally want to prevent overlaps of diagram elements [13]. Additionally, we want the regions to be ordered, which introduces layout stability and helps to maintain a mental map, as well as to produce compact drawings by making the best possible use of the drawing area.

Usually one cannot use a mental map during layout creation since no previous depiction of the diagram exist [14]. However, as stated before, we assume that the user generated the textual input file step by step and already knows how regions are ordered in it or at least has a general idea of that. The generated diagram should preserve this order. There might be region placements, such as region A to D in Fig. 1c or Fig. 3a, for which it is unclear whether they are ordered by reading them from left-to-right or top-down. We solve this by introducing a clear left-to-right reading direction to allow the user to trust in this order, which allows to infer the correct order in this case, since it is clear the we read from left to right. Note that this approach is not limited to a left-to-right reading direction, it is just a very common one and for the sake of this paper we only discuss this one.

Regions should be recognizable or discoverable. In SCCharts this is often possible by the inner behavior and the size of the region, e. g. since we know that the inner state machine of region H in Fig. 1a looks the way it does, we will recognize it as such. This does of course not work if we have several similar regions, the user does not know about the inner behavior, or the region is collapsed. A clear ordering of regions can, therefore, help to identify regions by their neighbors and their placement.

2.1   Scale Measure

The scale measure describes how big an element can be drawn compared to the available drawing area. The *original scale measure* OSM $= \min\left(\frac{w_d}{w_a}, \frac{h_d}{h_a}\right)$ expresses how well the drawing uses the given area [16]. E.g., an OSM of 1 means that both the width and the height fit the drawing area, but that the drawing cannot be enlarged anymore without exceeding the drawing area. An OSM of 0.5 means that the drawing has to be shrunk by a factor of 2 to fit the drawing area. Clearly, a larger OSM allows a more readable diagram and is hence better. In the KIELER tool it is not possible to get concrete values for the desired width and height, but we can use the desired aspect ratio instead. By assuming a desired height $h_d = 1$ and a desired width $w_d = 1$, we can define the scale measure based on the desired aspect ratio DAR as SM $= \min\left(\frac{DAR}{w_a}, \frac{1}{h_a}\right)$ [5].

2.2   Region Alignment

If we want to talk about reading direction and placement of regions, we have to introduce proper terminology to describe region placement and alignment.

A region packing consist of *rows*. If regions have different heights, it wastes screen real estate to only align them in rows, as seen in Fig. 1a. It needs to be possible to stack them somehow if one region is much bigger than the other ones. Since we also want to maintain a reading direction in such a stack, we introduce the concept of *subrows* in rows. Additionally, we want to group regions that have a similar height together in *blocks*, since they do not waste much space when they are together in a subrow.

An example for this grouping can be seen in Fig. 2. The drawing has two rows. The first row is divided into three blocks based on the region height. The second row is divided into two blocks. All regions inside their row or subrow have an upper bound for their y-coordinate that we henceforth call the *row level* or *subrow level*. The division of blocks into subrows can be seen in Fig. 2b. Additionally, we can stack blocks on top of each other in so called *stacks*, which is not depicted here.

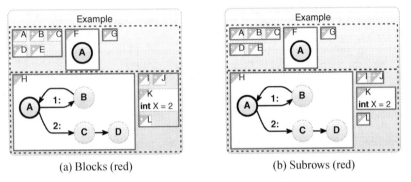

(a) Blocks (red)   (b) Subrows (red)

Fig. 2. Rows, blocks, and subrows (dotted, black) in a rectangle packing, [5]. (Color figure online)

Whitespace elimination further helps to maintain a reading direction by solving the orientation problem in some cases (see Fig. 1c compared to Fig. 1d). Moreover, the absence of gaps makes it easier to continue reading from left to right.

2.3   Ordering Requirements

The most basic ordering constraint is that for regions r_i and r_j with $i < j$, region r_i is horizontally or vertically before region r_j: $x_i + w_i \leq x_j \vee y_i + h_i \leq y_j$. More important, however, is consistency, meaning that subrows and rows are recognizable. E. g. Fig. 6a abides this horizontal and vertical ordering property but has no clear overall ordering.

We further restrict possible positions of region r_{i+1} based on the preceding region r_i by the following rules:

(1) r_{i+1} is directly right of its preceding neighbor r_i and top-aligned, or
(2) r_{i+1} is right of its preceding neighbor and top aligned at the current row level, or
(3) r_{i+1} is in the next subrow in the same stack (or block) of r_i, or
(4) r_{i+1} is in the next row.

Rule (1) applies to region D and E or F and G in Fig. 1c. This describes two cases to position a node: next the the last node in the row or the subrow. Rule (2) applies to E and F and (3) applies to C and D or K and L. In this example rule (4) only applies to G and H.

Note that these constraints do not suffice to get good solutions. The region packing in Fig. 1a only uses rule (1) and (4) and has a clear reading direction but a bad scale measure. Figure 3a does potentially use all rules but does not use (1) often enough. Therefore, we introduce a top-down reading direction inside the rows, as seen in region A to E, that is still ambiguous after whitespace elimination, as seen in Fig. 3b. This kind of drawings can also be produced by the constraints-based packing solution if they yield a better scale measure. Since the rules are prioritized, as described in Sect. 6, this will, however, not be the case in this example, as seen in Fig. 1e.

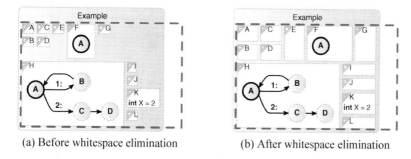

(a) Before whitespace elimination   (b) After whitespace elimination

Fig. 3. No clear reading direction in region packing solution for regions A – E, [5].

Note that the box algorithm will only use rules (1) and (4) to layout the regions in rows. Using only rule (1) and (3) could replicate the trivial approach of the box layouter by having only subrows inside a single row, which is not distinguishable from multiple rows without subrows. For all non-trivial approaches no rule has a clear priority over the others and one can always construct packing problems for which a specific decision is not optimal.

3   The Box Algorithm

All algorithms that we present in this paper consist of two steps: width approximation, which reduces the region packing problem to a strip packing problem, and region placement.

For the box algorithm, the first algorithm we present now, these two steps are shown in Alg. 1 and 2. The box algorithm is a greedy algorithm for layouting regions that only uses the rules (1) and (4), meaning it places regions in a row until they no longer fit and a new row has to be opened, as seen in Alg. 2. The *target width* is approximated using the total area of all regions and its standard deviation (see Alg. 1).

This algorithm fulfills all ordering constraints, has a clear reading direction, and performs reasonably well for regions of similar height, as we will show in Sect. 7. Its inability to stack regions, however, produces ONO drawings such as Fig. 1a that could easily be improved by stacking regions. After whitespace elimination this becomes even more evident since the height increases a lot and abnormally formed regions with an aspect ratio that does not stand in relation to its content are created. This motivates the rectpacking algorithm.

4   The Rectpacking Algorithm

The rectpacking algorithm also consists of a width approximation (see Alg. 3) and a simple placement step (see Alg. 4). After that the regions are compacted (see Alg. 5) by forming stacks, blocks, and subrows, as seen in Fig. 6, Fig. 1c, and Fig. 1d.

Instead of doing a static analysis based on the area of the regions involved, we perform a greedy algorithm that optimizes the scale measure, as seen in Alg. 3. We begin by placing the first region top-left and for each new region we place it such that

Algorithm 1:   boxWidthApproxima-
tion.

Input: Regions rs, DAR
Output: Approximated width
1 $totalArea = \sum area(rs)$
2 $area =$
    $totalArea + |rs| * \text{stddev}(totalArea)$
3 **return** $\max(\text{maxWidth}(rs), \sqrt{area * DAR})$

Algorithm 2: boxPlace.

Input: Regions rs, width w
Output: Placed regions rs
1 $lineX, lineY, lineHeight = 0$
2 **foreach** r *in* rs **do**
3   **if** $lineX + r.width \le w$ **then**
4     $r.x = lineX$
5     $r.y = lineY$
6     $lineX += r.width$
7     $lineHeight =$
        $\max(lineHeight, r.height)$
8   **else**
9     $lineY += lineHeight$
10    $lineX = 0$
11    $lineHeight = r.height$
12    $r.x = 0$
13    $r.y = lineY$

Fig. 4. Box width approximation and placement algorithms, [5].

the succeeding region is placed based on the preceding region and the scale measure is optimal with area and aspect ratio as a secondary and tertiary criterion, which is calculated by the bestPlacement function that greedily selects the best of the following alternatives:

LR Directly right of the preceding region
DR Right of the whole drawing, top aligned
LB Directly below the preceding region
DB Below the whole drawing, left aligned.

The placement step (see Alg. 4) places regions in the same manner as the box heuristic. The step is used to group regions with similar height in blocks and assign each block to its own stack, as illustrated in Fig. 6b. Additionally, the minimum and maximum block width and height are calculated, since they speed up certain compaction steps. These structures will be used during compaction to stack compacted blocks. Moreover, the row height of the placement step is used as the maximum row height. Note that this aspect of the heuristic can produce ONO packings, as seen in Sect. 4.1.

After placement the drawing is compacted, as described in Alg. 5. For each row, we check for each block, whether the next block (in this row or the next) has regions that could be included in the current block if it is compacted. In the next step, we check whether the next block would fit on top of the current, which would visually create a subrow in the current row. If this is not the case, the next block might be placed right of the current one in a new stack. In this case, the current stack is drawn such that the full row height and minimal row width is used since we are sure that no other block in this row can be placed on top of it without compromising the ordering. Placing two stacks next to each other may result in the inevitable stack alignment ONO-case (see Sect. 4.1) that is usually prevented by adding same height regions to the same block. Else, the next block is in the next row and cannot be added to the current one. Therefore, the stack of

Algorithm 4: rpPlace [5].

Input: Regions rs, width w
Output: Placed regions rs
1   Row row = new Row(w)
2   Stack $stack$ = new Stack(row)
3   Block $block$ = new
    Block(row, $stack$)
4   **foreach** r *in* rs **do**
5     $similar$ =
     hasSimilarHeight($block$, r)
6   fit = fitRow($block$, r)
7   **if** $similar \wedge fit$ **then**
8   block.add(r)
9   **else if** fit **then**
10   stack = new Stack(row)
11   block = new
      Block(row, $stack$, $block$)
12   block.add(r)
13   **else**
14   row = new Row(w, row)
15   stack = new Stack(row)
16   block = new
      Block(row, $stack$, $block$)
17   block.add(r)

Algorithm 3: rpWidthApproximation.

Input: Regions rs, DAR
Output: Width w
1   Drawing d
2   **foreach** r *in* rs **do**
3   lr = placeLR(d, r)
4   dr = placeDR(d, r)
5   lb = placeLB(d, r)
6   db = placeDB(d, r)
7   d =
     bestPlacement(lr, dr, lb, db, DAR)
8   **return** getWidth(d)

Fig. 5. Rectpacking width approximation and placement.

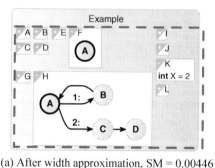

(a) After width approximation, SM = 0.00446

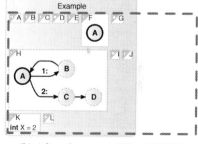

(b) After placement, SM = 0.00371

Fig. 6. Layout with rectpacking heuristic, $DAR = 1.6$ (red-dashed). See also Fig. 1c and Fig. 1d for compaction and whitespace elimination steps, [5]. (Color figure online)

the current block is drawn such that it utilizes the remaining width of the current row. This continues until the last row is compacted.

Whitespace can be eliminated by dividing additional space equally to all rows, then to all stacks, blocks, subrows, and finally regions, as seen in Fig. 1c compared to Fig. 1d. Note that the box algorithm allows to only change the width of the last region in each row and only increase the height for the other ones, as seen in Fig. 1b.

As seen in [5], this solution work reasonably well for graphs with at least one big node, which are graphs were at least two regions can be stacked instead of drawn next to each other. For the case of same height regions with varying width (SH), which represents only collapsed regions in an SCChart, it is outperformed by the box algorithm. To deal with this and other problems, we propose the improved rectpacking algorithm in Sect. 5.

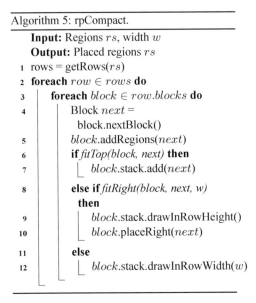

Fig. 7. Compaction of the rectpacking algorithm, [5].

4.1   ONO Cases

There are several ONO cases that may occur in the region packing problem that are not completely avoidable.

Bad Width Approximation. Rectpacking (and also the box algorithm) produces bad scale measures if high and slim region and long and flat regions alternate, as seen in Fig. 8a.

The constraint based solution (see Fig. 8b) yields a compact packing with a better scale measure. However, the region ordering is largely lost. It is unclear whether regions n3 to n7 or only regions n3, n4, n5, and n7 form a stack. Whitespace elimination can solve this problem since it expands the regions such that rows and subrows are visible. However, whitespace elimination can also create wrong alignments. If the row and subrow structure is not part of the algorithm, one can eliminate the whitespace by placement alone. To do this the regions are handled beginning with the last placed region. Its width and height are increased such that the drawing bounds do not change and no overlaps are created. This continues with the second last region until all regions are expanded and results in a drawing such as Fig. 8c. If one begins with the first region the formed rows and subrows might compromise the ordering. In Fig. 8d region n8 is expanded to the bottom of the drawing. Therefore, region n9 is visually be before it and also before region n6. Moreover, no clear rows and subrows are formed.

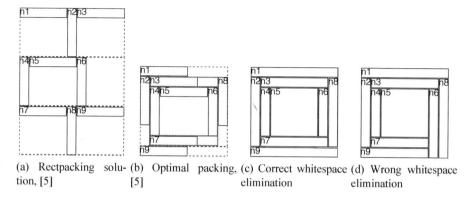

(a) Rectpacking solu- (b) Optimal packing, (c) Correct whitespace (d) Wrong whitespace
tion, [5]   [5]   elimination   elimination

Fig. 8. Example of bad scale measure resulting from rectpacking. Rows are highlighted in dotted black, blocks are highlighted in red if their bounds may be unclear. (Color figure online)

Wrong Stack Alignment. Packings, such as region A to D in Fig. 1c, must not only occur such that one has to primarily read from left-to-right but has to read top-down.

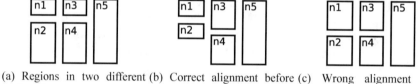

(a) Regions in two different (b) Correct alignment before (c) Wrong alignment after
stacks align   whitespace elimination   whitespace elimination

Fig. 9. Even though regions are correctly placed in rows, stacks, blocks, and subrows, they may still align with regions and create orderings that do not conform with the model order.

This can occur if two stacks such as the ones in Fig. 9a are placed next to each other. Since regions n1 and n2 and regions n3 and n4 have a different height, they may not be placed in the same subrow, but are placed in the same stack instead if the row height allows this. This leads to an unintentional alignment of regions n1 and n3 and regions n2 and n4. This can also occur in lesser extent such that only a few subrow between two stacks are wrongfully aligned.

Another possible cause is whitespace elimination. The wrong alignment is created by enlarging all regions equally and thus visually creating subrows, as seen in Fig. 9b and 9c. Therefore, a packing such as the one in Fig. 9b is prevented by the compaction algorithm (see Alg. 5), which prefers to stack different blocks on top of each other in the same stack instead of next to each other in different stacks.

No Row Height Increase. As mentioned before, the rectpacking heuristic does not increase the height of a row during compaction, which can produce ONO packings such as Fig. 10.

The solution shown in Fig. 10b requires the algorithm to backtrack. After adding n5 to the first row, it is also necessary to reevaluate all stacks and blocks in the current

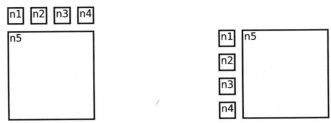

(a) n5 cannot be added to the same row.   (b) n5 can be added to the same row, which produces a compact drawing.

Fig. 10. Allowing to revise the row height after placement can create better drawings at the cost of computation time.

row and draw them such that they utilize the new height. Refusing to do this creates another ONO packing in which the user can clearly see that the regions could be stacked to improve the drawing.

Consider a region packing as the one in Fig. 6b. Even if region H, which is initially placed in the next row, would be in the target width of the first row after compacting region A – G, it would not fit in the height. Since H is much higher than the current highest region F, this would result in a packing which seems unintuitive and like an error of the algorithm. This can be solved by backtracking and stacking regions A – G better to fit the new higher height.

Since this potentially increases computation time significantly, the solution is not suitable for interactive scenarios and will not be considered here, but can be implemented as part of future work.

5   The Improved Rectpacking Algorithm

The main problem of the rectpacking algorithm is that its width approximation step is often not correct. Especially for regions that are not stackable, the approximated width is generally too small. In other cases, the width approximation does not clearly underestimate or overestimate the required width, as described in [5].

5.1   Checking for Stackability

We propose a heuristic to check in linear time whether a region packing problem has the potential to stack regions to improve the scale measure. For each three region r_i, r_{i+1}, and r_{i+2} we check whether two neighboring regions stacked onto each other are smaller than the third region by checking whether $h_i \geq h_{i+1} + h_{i+2}$ or $h_{i+2} \geq h_i + h_{i+1}$. If this is not the case, we know that the box heuristic will most likely perform better and execute it instead.

Note that this is only a heuristic for stackability. There are still cases left for which regions cannot be stacked, e. g. if the width of one of the smaller regions defines the target width and it is, therefore, in its own row, which also means that it should define its height, which does not allow to place another region on top of it.

5.2 Revising the Width

Even if the regions are stackable the approximated width might just a little bit too small or too big such that a suboptimal packing is created. Therefore, we propose to revise it. The initial rectpacking run yields an aspect ratio that may be either bigger or smaller than the desired aspect ratio and we can revise the target width as follows:

We want to find a new target width based on the previous approximation. Since we do not want to do this blindly, we need the find a minimal decrease or increase of the width that is guaranteed to change the packing.

We check for each row how much the width has to be increased to fit the next block of the next row, as seen in Fig. 11a. Here the width of region H has to be added to the width of the first row up to region G to be able to place H in there.

The same can be done on subrow level if the region packing consist of only one row. Similarly, we can collect for each row the width of the last block to the current row Fig. 11b. Here the first row must be shortened to not fully include G to decrease the row width. The second row must be shortened to not fully include the block I – L.

We get a range of values that is guaranteed to influence the region packing. We choose the minimum value that influenced the packing to not miss a potentially optimal packing and executed rectpacking a second time with a revised target width by skipping the width approximation step. In Fig. 11b the second row width deduction is smaller than the first, we choose the second width to revise the target width.

Note that if we are not in an interactive scenario, this approach can be used to configure an iterative algorithm to find the best width to achieve the best scale measure.

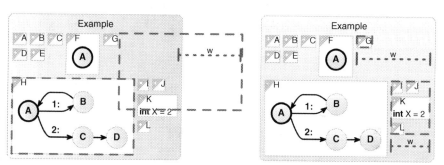

(a) Additional width **w** per row that results in a wider row.

(b) Decreasing the row width by **w** would create a narrower row and, therefore, drawing.

Fig. 11. The width that has to be considered as additional or deducted width is marked in dotted-blue and the responsible block in red-dashed lines. (Color figure online)

6 A Constraint-Based Approach

Recall that our goal is to maximize the scale measure and to maintain a reading direction. Formalizing a maximization problem for the scale measure is relatively easy. By adding the correctness requirements for a packing (see Sect. 2), we make sure that the packing is free of overlaps and no rectangles change their size. Whitespace can be eliminated after the layout completed, as explained in Sect. 4.1, therefore, it is not included in the approach itself.

A basic ordering constraint such as the one discarded in Sect. 2.3 is not enough to limit the search space to a reasonable size. Therefore, we use the constraints defined as rules (1) to (4) in Sect. 2.3, which we already identified as reasonable positions to facilitate on order and a reading direction. As a result the following variables are introduced based on the drawing after placing region i:

- $maxHeight_i$: The current maximum height of the drawing (necessary for rule (1))
- $rowLevel_i$: The current row level (necessary for rule (2))
- $startXCurrentStack_i$: The x-coordinate of the current stack (necessary for rule (3))
- $endYCurrentSubrow_i$: The end y-coordinate of the current subrow (necessary for rule (3))
- $endXCurrentStack_i$: The end x-coordinate of the current stack (necessary to calculate the x-coordinate of the next stack)

These allow to specify the possible positions of a region based on their preceding region as follows:

Rule (1), right of preceding, in current subrow:

$$x_i = x_{i-1} + w_{i-1}$$
$$endXCurrentStack_i = \max(endXCurrentStack_{i-1}, x_i + w_i)$$
$$startXCurrentStack_i = startXCurrentStack_{i-1}$$
$$rowLevel_i = rowLevel_{i-1}$$
$$endYCurrentSubrow_i = \max(endYCurrentSubrow_{i-1}, y_i + h_i)$$
$$maxHeight_i = \max(maxHeight_{i-1}, endYCurrentSubrow_i)$$
$$y_i = y_{i-1}$$

Rule (2), right of preceding region in a new stack:

$$x_i = endXCurrentStack_{i-1}$$
$$endXCurrentStack_i = x_i + w_i$$
$$startXCurrentStack_i = endXCurrentStack_{i-1}$$
$$rowLevel_i = rowLevel_{i-1}$$
$$endYCurrentSubrow_i = rowLevel_i + h_i$$
$$maxHeight_i = \max(maxHeight_{i-1}, endYCurrentSubrow_i)$$
$$y_i = rowLevel_i$$

Rule (3), in a new subrow:

$$x_i = startXCurrentStack_{i-1}$$
$$endXCurrentStack_i = \max(endYCurrentStack_{i-1}, x_i + w_i)$$
$$startXCurrentStack_i = startXCurrentStack_{i-1}$$
$$rowLevel_i = rowLevel_{i-1}$$
$$endYCurrentSubrow_i = \max(currentSubrowEnd_{i-1} + h_i)$$
$$maxHeight_i = \max(maxHeight_{i-1}, endYCurrentSubrow_i)$$
$$y_i = endYCurrentSubrow_{i-1}$$

Rule (4), in a new row:

$$x_i = 0$$
$$endXCurrentStack_i = w_i$$
$$startXCurrentStack_i = 0$$
$$rowLevel_i = maxHeight_{i-1}$$
$$endYCurrentSubrow_i = rowLevel_i + h_i$$
$$maxHeight_i = endYCurrentSubrow_i$$
$$y_i = rowLevel_i$$

Additionally, $maxWidth$ is defined as $max(x_i + w_i)$ for all region r_i. This allows to maximize the scale measure by maximizing $\min(\frac{DAR}{maxWidth}, \frac{1}{maxHeight_n})$.

Since a fixed prioritization of the rules (1) to (4) does not always produce the best scale measure nor the best drawing regarding reading direction there is nothing to add here and we prioritize the solution by rule number. E. g. if two solutions yield the same scale measure the solution is chosen that used a lower rule number for a first region for which the decisions were different. This allows us to maintain a left-to-right reading direction, as seen in region A – E in Fig. 1e. However, it does not limit the row height by the highest element in it, as seen in Fig. 1e.

Note that one can achieve the same result using different rules. For a packing problem with same height regions it might be irrelevant whether one creates only one row with several subrows or several rows without subrows.

7   Evaluation

The box and rectpacking layout algorithm were implemented in the ELK framework[3].

The graphs are drawn and evaluated for four different algorithm configurations with a DAR of 1.3 and a spacing of 1 between regions. SCCharts can be hierarchical, we here use a bottom-up layout strategy. This means region H in Fig. 1c knows its minimum size that is defined by its content as described in Sect. 2.

---

[3] https://www.eclipse.org/elk/reference/algorithms.html.

The algorithm configurations are:

- B: Using the box layouter with set priorities to enforce region order.
- R: The rectpacking heuristic as proposed by [5].
- IR: The improved rectpacking algorithm with both optimizations proposed in Sect. 5 and configured such that the width is revised only once.
- C: The solved constraint-based maximization problem proposed in Sect. 6.

The run time of the box algorithm is clearly in $\mathcal{O}(n)$. Rectpacking solves the placement problem in $\mathcal{O}(n \log(n))$, as reported by [5]. IR behaves as box or rectpacking depending on the input graph. In practice the run time of B, R, IR seem linear in the problem size and are in our experiments in millisecond range.

7.1   Generated Models

We evaluated the performance of the algorithms using the GrAna tool [15] with 200 graphs for each graph class taken from [5]. The number of regions in the generated graphs is between 20 and 30 to make the instances solvable by CP optimizer.

Normal regions have a height of 20 and a width with the mean of 100 and a standard deviation of 20. The big nodes class (BN) has 2 to 5 big regions with a width and height between 300 and 1000. The one big node class (OB) has only one big region. The same height class (SH) has no big regions.

The box heuristic (B) handles regions of same height (SH) very good. The main reason for this is that the width approximation (see Alg. 1) is very accurate in this case, as seen in Fig. 12a, since it is near the ideal aspect ratio and produces a good scale measure, as seen in Fig. 12g. The width approximation and the inability to stack regions results in worse results for the one big region (OB) and big regions (BN) cases, as seen in Figure Fig. 12b, 12e, 12h, 12c, 12f, and 12i. In Fig. 12g, it is clear that the constraint-based solution (C) gets a clear advantage from breaking the reading direction and taking time to optimize the scale measure.

The rectpacking heuristic is better than the box algorithm and near the optimal solution in all OB and BN cases but its approximation step falls short when regions are not stackable, as it is the case for SH problems since the width is overestimated, as seen in Fig. 12a, 12d, and 12g.

The IR heuristic solves this problem by using the box layouter for these cases. For BN problems the box algorithm is not used but the revised width improves the solution significantly, as seen in Fig. 12c, 12f, and 12i. For OB graphs the initially approximated width seems to be good enough to not change after being revised. This means the initial scale measure was good and, therefore, the approximated width was good enough to rarely leave room for improvement after one iteration of width revision, as seen in Fig. 12h and Fig. 12l. For SH graphs IR falls back to the box layouter that improves at most times upon the rectpacking solution, as seen in Fig. 12g and 12l.

The whitespace did not have much impact on the quality of the solution, however, less whitespace generally means the area is used more efficiently, which results often in a better scale measure.

When we compare the improvement to the rectpacking approach in detail, we see that for most SH and the slightly more of the OB problems, the initial width is overestimated since the resulting aspect ratio is lower, as seen in Fig. 12j. For BN cases an improvement could be made in both directions equally.

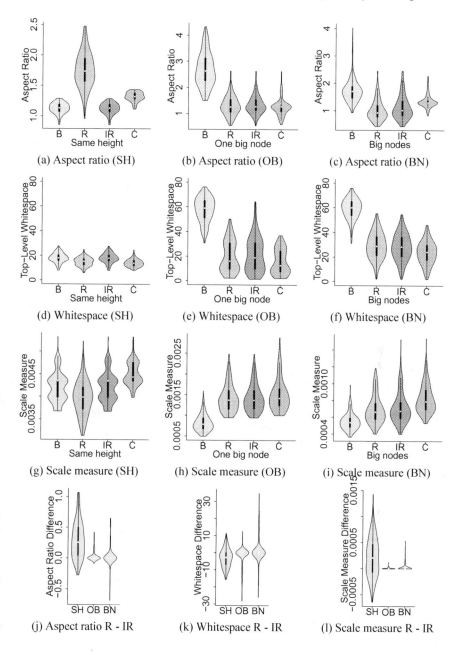

(a) Aspect ratio (SH)   (b) Aspect ratio (OB)   (c) Aspect ratio (BN)

(d) Whitespace (SH)   (e) Whitespace (OB)   (f) Whitespace (BN)

(g) Scale measure (SH)   (h) Scale measure (OB)   (i) Scale measure (BN)

(j) Aspect ratio R - IR   (k) Whitespace R - IR   (l) Scale measure R - IR

Fig. 12. Aspect ratio, whitespace, scale measure, and comparison of SH, OB, and BN problems.

7.2   Real World Models (SCCharts)

We take 372 real world SCCharts from papers such as [17, 18], as well as student models developed during lectures, and projects such as the Railway Project '14 and '17

[19], which need 2719 region packing problems to solve. A quantitative analysis of the complexity of these models can be seen below. For real world examples, we limit the computation time to one hour per graph, which was only needed for the biggest three SCCharts from the railway projects.

For sake of evaluation all SCCharts are expanded, meaning we introduce a new category next to SH, OB, BN. Moreover, we layout state machines (see the inner behavior of region H in Fig. 1c) from left to right and shorten edge labels to their priority.

Table 1 shows how many layout problems exist per hierarchy level. For example Fig. 13 does have 9 states at depth 0, 5 layered problems at depth 1, 4 trivial rectpacking problems at depth 2, 2 layered problems at depth 3, and 1 rectpacking problems at depth 4. Note that rectpacking problems are at an even depth, and layered problems (node link diagrams) have to be solved at odd depth levels. Figure 13 also serves as an example were the width is revised to produce a better drawing. However, since the box algorithm also produces this drawing it is not counted towards the problems improved by width revision in Tab. 1.

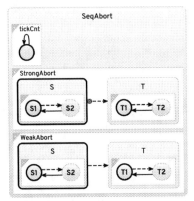
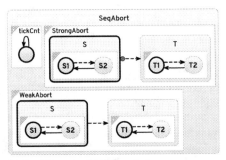

(a) Since the row height is not revised the drawing becomes too high.

(b) Revising the width produces a more compact drawing that would also be produced by the box algorithm.

Fig. 13. The SeqAbort SCChart.

Most SCCharts do not have stackable expanded regions in them. One can see one outlier at depth 10 where most regions are stackable. Of all region fewer than 5% are stackable, which means that most of the SCCharts expanded region packing problems are simple problems that most likely are better solved by the box layouter.

The packing problems seem to get more complex in models with more hierarchy, which generally are bigger models, since they are more complex and more likely to reduce this complexity by introducing parallel regions of execution. Only very few models were improved by revising the width via the improved rectpacking algorithm. At depth 2, 16 models increased the approximated width and 16 decreased it. At depth 12, 11 models increased the width. Since most problems are trivial or nearly trivial, this was expected to be the case. The complexity of the state machines in an SCChart peaks at a depth between 5 and 7 with on average over 9 nodes with more than 13 edges between them. The state machines at lower depth seem to be less complex on average, which again might be the case since less complex models seem to be smaller.

Since only very few models can be improved by guessing a better target width and since this step is rather expensive and has to be fully evaluated in future work, we propose to not use that per default but only check for stackability.

Table 1. Layout problems per depth in the used SCCharts models.

Depth	Algorithm	Instances	Mean #children	Mean #edges	Stackable	Improved by Sect. 5.2
0		13534	0	0		
1	Layered	3130	3.77	5.71		
2	Rectpacking	2001	1.5	0	105	32
3	Layered	675	3.59	3.5		
4	Rectpacking	542	1.36	0	7	0
5	Layered	131	9.65	15.45		
6	Rectpacking	126	1.08	0	3	0
7	Layered	33	9.58	13.39		
8	Rectpacking	33	2.27	0	2	0
9	Layered	25	2.32	3.4		
10	Rectpacking	14	3.42	0	11	11
11	Layered	12	1	0		
12	Rectpacking	2	6	0	0	0
13	Layered	1	3	2		
14	Rectpacking	1	4	0	1	0

First, we have a look at the individual region packing problems and not at the whole SCChart. If one only looks at all non-trivial region packing problems, which are region packing problems with at least two children, one sees that all approaches perform more or less the same, as seen in Fig. 14. These problems can also be solved by a minimization problem, however, it performs nearly the same as all other approaches, therefore, we omitted it. The width and height are more or less the same, as seen in Fig. 14a and Fig. 14b. The box algorithm performs better than rectpacking, however, there are still cases were rectpacking is better than the box algorithm, as seen in Fig. 14e. The improved rectpacking algorithm is on average better than rectpacking and the box algorithm, as seen in Fig. 14e. Overall SCCharts with only expanded regions seems to be in most cases a trivial problem and even non-trivial problems can be solved well by the simple box algorithm.

7.3 Hierarchical Graphs

An SCChart does not necessarily have only one level of hierarchy, as seen in Fig. 1, but can have multiple, as seen in Fig. 13. The example has a maximum depth of four, the outermost state SeqAbort has three inner regions (potentially it could be arbitrarily many). This region could have arbitrarily many states. The state S in the StrongAbort region also has one inner region, which again has states. Since an SCChart is layouted bottom-up, each region packing problem needs a fixed aspect ratio that cannot be approximated based on the top-level elements and is, therefore, set to the fixed value 1.3. This causes problems, as seen in Fig. 15.

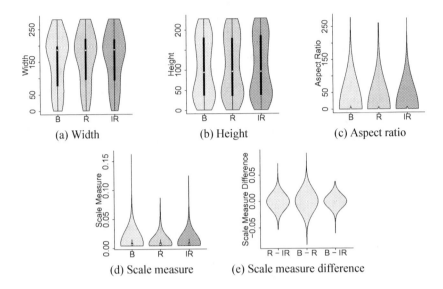

(a) Width   (b) Height   (c) Aspect ratio

(d) Scale measure   (e) Scale measure difference

Fig. 14. Width, height aspect ratio, scale measure, and comparison of non-trivial region packing problems.

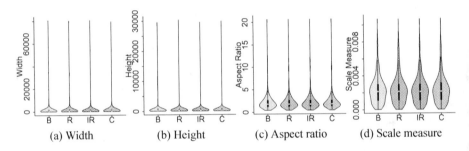

(a) Width   (b) Height   (c) Aspect ratio   (d) Scale measure

Fig. 15. Width, height, area, aspect ratio, and scale measure of SCCharts models.

The constraint based approach does not result in the best aspect ratio. One can see that only a few graphs are actually layouted differently and that the overall width and height of the drawing stays nearly the same for SCCharts with only expanded regions. Solving an inner region packing problem optimally means the local scale measure of each packing problem is optimal. However, this does not necessarily have a positive impact on the overall scale measure, as seen in Fig. 15d.

For SCCharts the global scale measure is more important, which must not correlate with the locally optimized scale measure. Nevertheless, it is important to produce compact drawings, even on a local level.

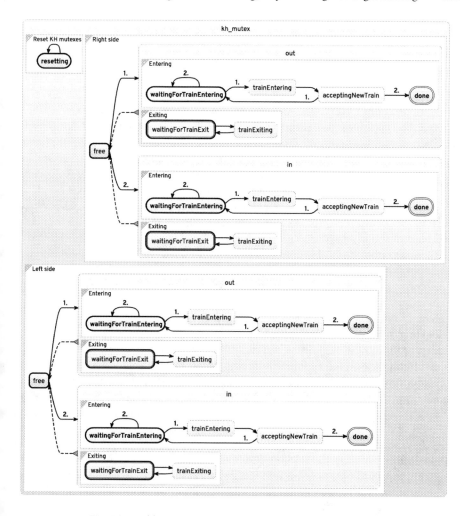

Fig. 16. The kh_mutex SCChart from the Railway Project '14.

8   Conclusion and Future Work

The rectpacking algorithm achieves better results than the simple box algorithm for packing problem in which regions are stackable. However, the width approximation step lacks accuracy if this is not the case, for example if all regions have the same or similar height, as it is the case for SCCharts with only collapsed or only expanded regions. This can be improved if one uses the box layouter and regions are not stackable.

In hierarchical graphs the local scale measure is not as important as the compactness of the packing. Therefore, all algorithms perform similar and sometimes better than the locally optimal solution (C). The rectpacking and improved rectpacking solutions do, therefore, perform also better for hierarchical graphs if the packing problems allow to stack regions, as it is the case for OB and BN problems.

Revising the width may be expensive, since it needs at least double the time of the original approach, however, it can significantly improve the packing for problems with many stackable regions. In real world models this does not occur very often since most real models have few regions that are most times not stackable if all regions are expanded. Checking for stackability is easily done and allows to solve such problems by the much simpler box algorithm, therefore, we suggest to only add the stackability check to the improved rectpacking algorithm and to use it for the SCCharts region packing problem in the future.

Even though the improved rectpacking improves upon rectpacking, there are still several ONO-cases it cannot handle. As part of future work a backtracking rectpacking algorithm that solves the problem of a fixed row height (see Sect. 4.1) can be implemented. Moreover, the iterative width revision approach (see Sect. 5.2) would be evaluated with more than one iteration as well as its impact on SCCharts models and the resulting computation time.

The problem of hierarchical models remains unsolved for bottom-up layout, which could be solved as follows:

First, an initial packing has to be created to see whether the aspect ratio has to be increased or decreased. Second the packing problems that result in a too high width or height must be changed. The height or width *critical packing problems* can be identified by looking at the highest layer in the node link diagrams and which region packing problems define the width of a layer. The SCChart in Fig. 16 is too high. When looking at the different levels, the regions Right side and Left side are the limiting factors in terms of height. Their height on the other hand is defined by the states in and out in the second layer. Additionally these states define the width of that layer and, therefore, the width of the whole region and the whole packing. Using the width revision improvement proposed in Sect. 5.2 the local drawing is changed and the overall aspect ratio and, therefore, scale measure is changed. This is done by placing region Exiting right of region Entering by increasing the target width, which results in a wider and less high drawing with a better scale measure. Even though one can identify the width or height critical regions, it remains a complex problem that will be dealt with as part of future work.

A top-down layout algorithm could change this particular problem but it would be necessary to estimate the width and height of each state machine, which also reduces the size at which elements can be drawn.

References

1. Augustine, J., Banerjee, S., Irani, S.: Strip packing with precedence constraints and strip packing with release times. In: Proceedings of the Eighteenth Annual Acm Symposium on Parallelism in Algorithms and Architectures (SPAA'06), pp. 180–189. ACM, New York, NY, USA (2006)
2. Bruls, M., Huizing, K., Van Wijk, J.J.: Squarified treemaps. In: de Leeuw, W.C., van Liere, R. (eds.) Data visualization 2000, pp. 33–42. Springer, Vienna (2000). https://doi.org/10.1007/978-3-7091-6783-0_4
3. Da Silveira, J.L., Miyazawa, F.K., Xavier, E.C.: Heuristics for the strip packing problem with unloading constraints. Comput. Oper. Res. **40**(4), 991–1003 (2013)

4. Da Silveira, J.L., Xavier, E.C., Miyazawa, F.K.: Two-dimensional strip packing with unloading constraints. Discrete Appl. Math. **164**, 512–521 (2014)
5. Domrös, S., Lucas, D., von Hanxleden, R., Jansen, K.: On order-preserving, gap-avoiding rectangle packing. In: Proceedings of the 13th International Conference on Information Visualization Theory and Applications (IVAPP'21), part of the 16th International Joint Conference on Computer Vision, Imaging and Computer Graphics Theory and Applications (VISIGRAPP'21), pp. 38–49. INSTICC, SciTePress (2021). https://doi.org/10.5220/0010186400380049
6. Dowsland, K.A., Dowsland, W.B.: Packing problems. Eur. J. Oper. Res. **56**(1), 2–14 (1992). https://doi.org/10.1016/0377-2217(92)90288-K
7. Choppy, C., Sokolsky, O. (eds.): Monterey Workshop 2008. LNCS, vol. 6028. Springer, Heidelberg (2010). https://doi.org/10.1007/978-3-642-12566-9
8. von Hanxleden, R., et al.: SCCharts: sequentially constructive Statecharts for safety-critical applications. In: Proceedings of ACM SIGPLAN Conference on Programming Language Design and Implementation (PLDI 2014), pp. 372–383. ACM, Edinburgh, UK, June 2014
9. von Hanxleden, R., Fuhrmann, H., Spönemann, M.: KIELER–The KIEL integrated environment for layout eclipse rich client. In: Proceedings of the Design, Automation and Test in Europe University Booth (DATE 2011), Grenoble, France, March 2011
10. Kenyon, C., Rémila, E.: A near-optimal solution to a two-dimensional cutting stock problem. Math. Oper. Res. **25**(4), 645–656 (2000)
11. Kieffer, S., Dwyer, T., Marriott, K., Wybrow, M.: HOLA: human-like orthogonal network layout. IEEE Trans. Vis. Comput. Graph. **22**(1), 349–358 (2016). https://doi.org/10.1109/TVCG.2015.2467451
12. Lucas, D.: Order- and drawing area-aware packing of rectangles. Bachelor thesis, Christian-Albrechts-Universität zu Kiel, Faculty of Engineering, September 2018
13. Purchase, H.C.: Metrics for graph drawing aesthetics. J. Vis. Lang. Comput. **13**(5), 501–516 (2002)
14. Kaufmann, M., Wagner, D. (eds.): GD 2006. LNCS, vol. 4372. Springer, Heidelberg (2007). https://doi.org/10.1007/978-3-540-70904-6
15. Rieß, M.: A graph editor for algorithm engineering. Bachelor thesis, Kiel University, Department of Computer Science, September 2010
16. Rüegg, U., von Hanxleden, R.: Wrapping layered graphs. In: Chapman, P., Stapleton, G., Moktefi, A., Perez-Kriz, S., Bellucci, F. (eds.) Diagrams 2018. LNCS (LNAI), vol. 10871, pp. 743–747. Springer, Cham (2018). https://doi.org/10.1007/978-3-319-91376-6_72
17. Schulz-Rosengarten, A., von Hanxleden, R., Mallet, F., de Simone, R., Deantoni, J.: Time in SCCharts. In: Proceedings of Forum on Specification and Design Languages (FDL 2018), Munich, Germany, September 2018
18. Schulz-Rosengarten, A., Smyth, S., Mendler, M.: Towards object-oriented modeling in SCCharts. In: Proceedings of Forum on Specification and Design Languages (FDL 2019), Southampton, UK, September 2019
19. Smyth, S., et al.: SCCharts: the mindstorms report. Technical Report 1904, Christian-Albrechts-Universität zu Kiel, Department of Computer Science, December 2019. ISSN 2192–6247
20. Wang, Y., et al.: Edwordle: consistency-preserving word cloud editing. IEEE Trans. Vis. Comput. Graph. **24**(1), 647–656 (2017)

Exploratory Data Analysis of Population Level Smartphone-Sensed Data

Hamid Mansoor[✉], Walter Gerych, Abdulaziz Alajaji, Luke Buquicchio,
Kavin Chandrasekaran, Emmanuel Agu, and Elke Rundensteiner

Worcester Polytechnic Institute, MA, USA
{hmansoor,wgerych,asalajaji,ljbuquicchio,kchandrasekaran,
emmanuel,rundenst}@wpi.edu

Abstract. Mobile health involves gathering smartphone-sensor data passively from user's phones, as they live their lives 'In-the-wild", periodically annotating data with health labels. Such data is used by machine learning models to predict health. Purely Computational approaches generally do not support interpretability of the results produced from such models. In addition, the interpretability of such results may become difficult with larger study cohorts which make population-level insights desirable. We propose **P**opulation **L**evel **E**xploration and **A**nalysis of smartphone **DE**tected **S**ymptoms (PLEADES), an interactive visual analytics framework to present smartphone-sensed data. Our approach uses clustering and dimension reduction to discover similar days based on objective smartphone sensor data, across participants for population level analyses. PLEADES enables analysts to apply various clustering and projection algorithms to several smartphone-sensed datasets. PLEADES overlays human-labelled symptom and contextual information from in-the-wild collected smartphone-sensed data, to empower the analyst to interpret findings. Such views enable the contextualization of the symptoms that can manifest in smartphone sensor data. We used PLEADES to visualize two real world in-the-wild collected datasets with objective sensor data and human-provided health labels. We validate our approach through evaluations with data visualization and human context recognition experts.

Keywords: Interactive visual analytics · In-the-wild smartphone-sensed data · Exploratory data analysis

1 Introduction

Ubiquitous devices like smartphones are increasingly being used to monitor their users' health [33]. Smartphones are equipped with several sensors such as accelerometers, gyroscopes, GPS, light, sound and activity detectors. Data from such sensors can be used to infer several health markers such as Circadian Rhythms (sleep-wake cycles) [1,58], depression [22,33,50] and infectious diseases like the flu [35]. To build computational models for such inferences, researchers rely on conducting "In-the-Wild" data collection studies to gather data that mimics real life as closely as possible. Such studies require subjects to install an application on their smartphones that continuously

© Springer Nature Switzerland AG 2023
A. A. de Sousa et al. (Eds.): VISIGRAPP 2021, CCIS 1691, pp. 206–231, 2023.
https://doi.org/10.1007/978-3-031-25477-2_10

and passively gather sensor data as they live their uninterrupted lives "in-the-wild". The subjects are periodically asked to provide ground truth health status data (quality of sleep, stress levels, activities performed etc.) by answering questionnaires on their devices [57].

This approach results in realistic but imperfect data. Such data often contains missing labels (i.e. objective sensor data with no corresponding human provided labels) and missing periods of data collection [3,56] due to participants turning off the application, or the application crashing. The data from smartphone sensors is complex, multivariate and is difficult to analyze without pre-processing. It is difficult to meaningful associations between the sensor data and reported health symptoms. Having a way to group data similar in terms of smartphone sensor *features values* and overlaying human provided symptom and wellness reports may be a useful way to increase *explainability*. For example, showing the links between poor sleep and late night phone usage [1] may enable an analyst to understand causes behind the symptom/wellness reports. Another example is showing changes in reported sleep duration and quality along with smartphone-sensed sleep location (e.g. main residence [normal] vs. at a workplace [abnormal]) may help contextualize and explain sleep disruptions.

As the breadth and scope of such data gathering studies increases to larger populations, it is useful to have visual views that can represent information about multiple participants at the same time. It can also enable analysts to understand, compare and contextualize various sub-populations with the participants. For instance, finding groupings of people based on their location presence across different times of day may indicate important differences in life circumstances such as different shift workers i.e. night vs. day shifts etc. Visualizations over longer time periods may also enable analysts to distinguish between one-off behaviors from longer term patterns. For example visualizing sleep disruptions and poor sleep along with mobility over a significant period of time can differentiate between mentally healthy participants who travel often and have occasional sleep disruptions from mentally ill participants who stay mostly at a single location and report frequent sleep disruptions [43]. This enables the analyst to filter participants who report days with concerning symptoms and use their data to build classification models to assess other participants who may be exhibiting similar manifestations of smartphone sensed data.

Unsupervised clustering is effective for sense-making of complex and multi-variate, data [30]. The high-dimension results that are produced by clustering algorithms can be effectively visualized on a 2-D plane using Dimension Reduction. Examples of such dimension reduction methods include t-SNE [34], Multi-dimensional Scaling [41] and Isomap [54]. These approaches work with a large number of features across vast numbers of data points. Clustering and projection along with dimension reduction are often used in *Exploratory Data Analysis*. Working with large scale multi-dimensional data can become overwhelming due to the availability of several clustering and projection algorithms [30]. Using multiple algorithms and parameter configuration makes it important to keep track of the various outcomes. In addition, analysts may want to assign semantic labels to various data points based on their domain knowledge. Data visualizations can also provide interactive and connected views that show the importance of different smartphone-sensed features for the clustering and projection outcome.

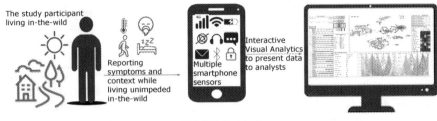

PLEADES Approach

Fig. 1. Our interactive data visualization approach for exploratory data analysis.

We researched, designed and implemented **P**opulation **L**evel **E**xploration and **A**nalysis of smartphone **DE**tected **S**ymptoms (PLEADES), an interactive data visualization framework to analyze smartphone-sensed data. PLEADES enables the analysts to select and define the smartphone-sensed data features that are used for clustering. This lets them use their domain knowledge to find relevant patterns that they may want to focus on for specific categories of smartphone-sensed behavior (e.g. mobility) and reduce the confounding effect of features that are not relevant. PLEADES enables analysts to select various clustering and projection algorithms, along with the features for that are used for clustering. It allows the analyst to filter and select multiple participants and cluster the usable study days from their data. This enables the analysts to compare multiple sub-populations for further intuition. PLEADES visualizes clustering results as color-coded horizontally stacked bars to show the proportion of study across the different participants that fall into each cluster. We use three quality metrics to order the clustering results. PLEADES presents aggregated summaries for different clusters to enable a clearer understanding of the semantic differences that may manifest in the smartphone-sensed data. For example, participants who travel often will have much more variable location data than stay-at-home participants, and clustering and projecting data based on location features allows analysts to contextualize reported symptom/wellness reports.

This work is an extension of our previous work on using interactive clustering and projections of smartphone-sensed data for exploratory data analysis [39]. This version is a significant extension as we add

- An extended domain analysis of the state of the art in the fields of visual exploratory data analysis of complex data and visualization approaches to analyze and understand data from ubiquitous devices like smartphones
- A detailed requirements analysis with experts in data science - specifically in training and classifying machine learning models for health and context detection using smartphone data
- Detailed discussions of use cases, along with an additional use case to show the utility of our approach
- Insightful and detailed discussion of our findings and future research directions including preliminary sketches of our proposed approach

Overall, the specific contributions of our work include:

- A detailed domain analysis to present the state-of-the-art in visualizing complex human behavioral data from ubiquitous devices.
- A thorough expert-led requirements, goal and task analysis to understand the workflow of analyzing smartphone-sensed data.
- PLEADES, an interactive visualization analytics tool for reproducible and flexible population-level exploratory data analysis of smartphone-sensed data along with symptom reports. PLEADES allows analysts to select from multiple clustering and dimension reduction algorithms and provides multiple connected views for insightful analysis.
- Demonstration of the utility of PLEADES through intuitive use cases concerning the analysis of in-the-wild collected health and wellness related smartphone data.
- Evaluation of PLEADES with four experts in the fields of smartphone sensed health and data visualizations.
- Discussion and proposal of future research directions.

2 Related Work

2.1 Health and Context Detection Using Smartphone-Sensed Data

Smartphone-sensed data, along with human provided health and context labels has been shown to accurately detect a diverse variety of ailments. Madan et al. [35] collected symptom data such as coughing and sneezing during a flue season for a group of college students and were able to make models to predict infectious diseases like influenza. Smartphone sensed data also contains semantically important information and can provide insight into abnormal behaviors like mobility patterns that can be indicative of mental illness like depression [22, 33, 44, 50]. GPS sensed mobility has also been linked to general wellness measures such as loneliness, anxiety, affect, stress and energy [45]. Screen interactions to detect disruptions in Circadian Rhythms (sleep-wake patterns) [1], which have health ramifications [58]. Smartphone sensor data has also been shown to be predictive of college students' academic performance [59] and social functioning in schizophrenia patients [60]. All these approaches relied on well labelled data that the analysts can use to build predictive models. However, data quality becomes an issue on a larger scale and longer term studies. Data visualizations can provide analysts with multiple contextualizing views to help analysts understand their participants better and also the results of their classification models.

2.2 Clustering Multivariate Data for Exploratory Data Analysis

Unsupervised clustering, dimension reduction and projection are useful techniques for exploratory analysis of large and complex datasets [63]. Such approaches enable analysts to use their domain knowledge to perform important analytic tasks for flexible understanding of the data. Such tasks can include assigning data points to specific clusters, and using domain knowledge to merge or separate various clusters [62] [4, 61]. No computational models can find perfect solutions to separate complex data into meaningful groupings which is why interactive approaches that utilize domain expertise in addition to interactive analysis are valuable. Typically, researchers use such approaches to find groupings that support their research goals or to prove or disprove any conclusions [2,23]. Interactive clustering, dimension reduction and projection have been used exploratory data analyses in many diverse domains such as health [11,30], crime [21], parallel and distributed computing usage [31] and clinical data [24,32].

Exploratory data analysis requires tweaking with several clustering algorithms, projections, parameters and results which can become overwhelming. Clustervision [30] by Kwon et al. is a visualization tool that presents ranked results across multiple dimension reduction and clustering algorithms for intuitive analysis of complex data. It uses multiple context providing linked visualizations across selectable data points. Clustrophile [19] and Clustrophile 2 [10] by Cavallo and Demiralp, are a family of interactive visual analytics tools to perform *Exploratory Data Analysis* of complex datasets by allowing analysts to fine tune dimension reduction parameters. They introduced a novel concept called the "Clustering Tour", to present visualizations like feature-average heatmaps and enabled the comparison of different features across different grouping of the data. Chatzimparmpas et al. [12] created t-viSNE, an interactive visual analytics tool for analyzing t-SNE results using multiple linked panes with bar charts and parallel coordinate plots. Their approach was to enable a comprehensive control of the various parameters and inputs to visualize clustering results of t-SNE across multiple linked panes. Li et al. [32] used interactive clustering and projection to help analysts devise accurate classification models of using health records. All these approaches the wide-scale applicability of interactive clustering and projection approaches to analyze, contextualize and understand complex data.

Our contribution is to utilize these visual clustering, dimension reduction and projection techniques to the exciting new domain of complex smartphone-sensed data. These approaches are particularly well-suited for analysis of smartphone-sensed data and health and wellness reports due to the many issues with such data including labelling and contextualization. In addition, traditional non-visual approaches become infeasible for exploratory data analysis as the population size of participants grows. Clustering and projection are well-suited to show overlaid human-supplied labels along with important semantic information such as the prevalence of weekdays and weekends against objective smartphone-sensed data. This allows the analysts to find important relationships in such data that can then guide their model building process. Mansoor et al. implemented COMEX [36] and DELFI [37], data visualization framework that present smartphone sensed data across multiple connected panes and used visual encodings of metrics like anomaly scores to guide analysts in finding mislabelled data and apply labels to unlabelled data.

2.3   Visual Analysis of Data Gathered In-the-Wild Using Ubiquitous Devices

Data visualizations are particularly well suited to understand smartphone-sensed data, as such data tends to be complex, multivariate and in need to additional analysis before any inferences can be made about health and context [40]. There are several examples of works that have utilized smartphone and smartwatch data to present data to everyday users for personal tracking and goal setting [14–16,25,28,65]. In addition, such data is also used to provide analysts, both healthcare analysts and data scientists, with the tools to make sense of such data [40]. Location data through phone connections with cell towers is one of the most commonly used data streams to analyze human behaviors and is often visualized for urban planning [29,47,51]. More granular person level GPS locations is also one of the most commonly collected data stream in in-the-wild studies [42] and can reveal a lot about about potential physical and mental health issues [5,6]. Shen et al. created MobiVis [52], an interactive visualization analytics tool to understand individual and group behaviors such as movements, communications etc. and helped analysts to visually mine data by semantic filtering for analysis of "social-spacial-temporal" smartphone data, using an intuitive glyph called the "Behavior ring". Intuitive glyph design can compactly present multiple important aspects of smartphone-sensed data. Mansoor et.al. [38] created ARGUS, an interactive visual analytics tool to help analysts not only identify but explain breakages in behavioral rhythms, detected from smartphone-sensed data. They used a version of the z-glyph [8] to highlight presence of levels of behavioral rhythms and breakages therein. Data visualizations can also be used to fix issues with the data quality since automatically sensed data can include mislabelled and unlabelled data, which makes it difficult to improve machine learning classification accuracy.

These works show the utility of interactive visual analytics approaches to help analysts at the various stages of smartphone-sensed health model building. Our work adds to this field by utilizing intuitive visual analytics techniques for unsupervised exploratory data analysis to guide model building. Specifically, our work aims to highlight important associations between reports of certain contexts and health symptoms with objective sensor data.

3   Goal and Task Analysis

We conducted internal workshops with four experts in data science, at our department. The experts all had experience in building health and human context classifiers using in-the-wild collected smartphone-sensed data. We asked them about their requirements when working with such in-the-wild data. They stressed the need to have an interactive analysis approach for early exploration of the data, before they started training and testing classification models. The experts were focused on having ways to investigate information of study participants at a **Population Level** for scalability. From this high level view, they wanted to have the ability to drill down on specific groups of study participants, along with specific participants. They wanted flexible ways to use different statistical features and analyze their relationships with any human reported health and wellness symptoms. We discussed the high-level requirements that any interactive approach would need to fulfill. Here we abstract out the four main requirements:

- R1: Ability to see data at a bird's eye level i.e. at a population level rather than individual analysis.
- R2: Design features from objective smartphone-sensed data that have been shown to have health/context predictive capabilities. For e.g. staying at primary location (usually deemed to be home more than usual has been associated with depression [22,50]).

- R3: Get an overview of the relationships (or lack thereof) of between objective sensor features and behaviors (detected and reported).
- R4: Apply different algorithms and methods to the feature data to find interesting patterns and relationships in data.

Interactive visual analytics approaches that let analysts experiment with clustering and projection algorithms fulfill the requirements that were expressed by the experts and have been reported to be very useful for exploratory data analysis [12, 30] in many domains. The experts were aware of clustering and projection and showed a lot of interest in having an interactive visualization interface that would help them fulfill their requirements, discussed above. The specific types of data points that the analysts were interested in clustering and projecting were day level aggregations of data across all the users. The analysts wanted to use a window of 24 h to divide up the data per user as human behaviors are highly influenced by daily cycles like sleep wake patterns [58]. In addition, several studies to collect in-the-wild data often asked participants to provide labels for days such as number of hours slept, quality of sleep and stress levels [6, 59]. After selecting interactive clustering, dimension reduction and projection as the visual approach, we asked the experts to specify the goals that they would have while using interactive clustering and projection. We summarize a list of goals that the experts had and the tasks to accomplish them:

Goal 1: *Grouping similar days:* Segmenting every participant's data into days and then grouping them in terms of similarity of features of sensor data to show important differences between days such as higher activity clusters vs. sedentary clusters etc.

- Task 1: Specifying sensor features for smartphone data for clustering, to understand and analyze different behaviors.
- Task 2: Applying clustering and dimension reduction techniques to display similar days on a 2D plane. Clusters will be color-coded.
- Task 3: Display multiple possible iterations of the clustering and projection algorithms for interpretation, along with measures of to display the quality of clustering results.

Goal 2: *Understand the causative factors that lead to the clustering results:* Analyze the summary of underlying objective sensor data that comprise the various clusters.

- Task 4: Showing the calculated importance of smartphone-sensed features with regard to clustering results to understand cluster separation. For example, a result may assign screen interaction levels higher importance and the clusters may be separated by high screen interaction vs. low screen interaction.
- Task 5: Show the variation in feature values between clusters to help analysts to assign semantic meaning to them.

Goal 3: *Compare individuals to populations and sub-populations:* This lets analysts find interesting groupings of users.

- Task 6: Show a selectable and filterable list of all participants for clustering analysis.
- Task 7: Show the distribution of clusters for each participants's data to help analysts assign semantic meaning. For instance, showing if a participant has more days in a cluster with lower mobility, activity levels etc.

Goal 4: *Overlay human-labelled health and wellness symptoms on objective smartphone-sensed data:* This helps analysts to assign semantic labels to data. For instance, clusters with days that have higher night screen usage also having poorer reported sleep and higher stress levels etc.

– Task 8: Present summaries of human-labelled symptom data such as stress levels, average sleep hours and quality etc. for every cluster, along with enabling filtering and selection of specific days for analysis.
– Task 9: Show external day-level factors that may explain the symptoms present (e.g. weekend vs weekdays, academic deadlines etc.)

Goal 5: *Saving exploration results for reproducible analysis:*

– Task 10: Storing results on the local machine from analysis sessions to share with other analysts and colleagues for reproducibility and to save time as clustering is computationally intensive.

4 Our Visual Approach: PLEADES

After conducting the requirements, goals and task analysis, we designed and implemented an interactive visual analytics framework called **P**opulation **L**evel **E**xploration and **A**nalysis of smartphone **DE**tected **S**ymptoms (PLEADES), to enable analysts to perform exploratory data analysis. We based our approach on the "Information Seeking Mantra" by Shneiderman et.al. [53] which states: "Show the important, zoom and filter, details on demand". Using this principled approach, we designed the various views of PLEADES. Here we describe the main views and the rationale behind our designs.

4.1 Data Description and Clustering and Dimension Reduction Algorithm Selection and Features View

The participant data was divided into days and the features were calculated for sensor values across multiple epochs such as day (9am-6pm or 8am-4pm), evening (6pm-12am or 4pm-12am) and night (12am-9am or 12am-8am), similar to [59]. The analyst can select different datasets (we provide access to two datasets: ReadiSens and StudentLife [59]) and can also specify the features that will be used for clustering (G1. T1). The analyst can also filter the participants whose data is used (all participants are included by default). The analyst can select from three dimension reduction (t-SNE, Isomap and multi-dimensional scaling) and three clustering (kMeans, agglomerative and spectral) techniques in (Fig. 2 H). Clicking on the "Features View" (FV) button shows a pane (Fig. 2 I) with all the available sensor values for the chosen dataset. This pane also allows the analyst to choose multiple epochs that the chosen sensor values can be averaged by. These features are then input into the clustering and projection algorithms (G1, T1). Cavallo and Demiralp [10] conducted thorough user studies for exploratory data

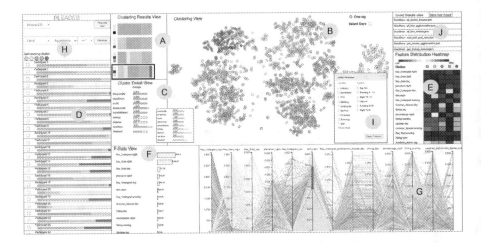

Fig. 2. PLEADES (Image from our earlier paper [39]): A) Every multi-colored bar is a clustering result for the chosen algorithms and number of clusters k. The results are ordered by the average "quality" score, of three different scores. The width of each colored bar in the represents the proportion of days in that cluster. B) Selecting a result projects it with every circle representing one day, color coded by cluster. C) Hovering over any day in the Clusters View shows its cluster's details in the Cluster Detail View. D) Every study participant is a row in the Users View and the bars represent distribution across the clusters for their days. E) The feature value intensities across all clusters is shown in the Feature Distribution Heatmap. F) The F-Stats View shows the most important features for the selected clustering result, determined by the ANOVA F-Statistic. G) Every polyline is a day with the color representing the cluster. The axes represent features and are brushable i.e. analysts can select ranges of values. H) Analysts can select the clustering and dimension reduction algorithms. I) Selecting features and their epochs for averaging. These features will be calculated for all days which will then be clustered. J) Pre-computed clustering results from previous sessions are displayed to save analysts' time.

analysis using clustering and projection and they reported that analysts showed particular focus on feature selection during their analyses as they explained that it was very important for the outcomes.

4.2   Clustering Results View (CRV)

The Clustering Results View (CRV) displays the clustering results after the analyst has selected the various parameters and clicked "Compute" in 2 H). Our approach was inspired by Kwon et.al. who designed and implemented Clustervision [30] a visualization framework for exploring complex data through clustering and projection. They also displayed multiple clustering results that were ordered by quality in addition to allowing for specification of clustering and projection algorithms. The CRV displays the results as horizontally stacked bars and the colors within those bars represent the cluster along with the widths representing the proportion of total days (across all participants) that belong to those cluster (Fig. 2 A). We used an 8 color palette from ColorBrewer [27] to assign each cluster a discernible color (G1, T2). The results are ordered by quality

(G1, T2, T3). We calculated the average across the three clustering quality measures: Silhouette score [49], Davies-Bouldin score [18] and Calinski-Harabasz score [7]. The quality scores are presented in the aforementioned order as squares on the left of the clustering results. The score value is encoded as opacity - higher quality ∎) vs. low quality: ▨. Presenting various results of clustering and projection algorithms allows analysts to perform flexible exploration of the data for greater insight and intuition.

4.3 Clusters View (CV)

The analyst can select a result in the CRV by clicking on it which shows the projection of the selected clustering result on a 2-Dimensional view in the Clusters View (CV). Every point is a day and the color encoding the cluster (Fig. 2 B), consistently throughout every other view of PLEADES. This view aims to give a view of days that are similar according to the clustering result, in addition of overlaps between different clusters (G1, T2). Using this view along with the CRV guides the analyst to dive deeper into specific clusters or days. The analyst can drill down on specific days by checking the "Select Days" (Fig. 2 B) box. They can then brush over the days of interest in the CV, which will show their details in the Cluster Details View (explained later) and highlight them in the Daily Values View (explained later). The analyst can also make a note by saving these days along with the participants associated with them, by giving their selection a name in a dialog that appears after the days are brushed (G5, T10). This enables analysts to apply their domain knowledge to understand whether certain days belong in a cluster, that have not been clustered by the automated approach. This also assists analysts in understanding the types of days that can be used for classification models. For example, they can assign meaningful semantic information, such as low stress and better sleep on days that are typically weekends and train and test a classifier on such days.

4.4 Users View (UV)

The User's View (UV) (Fig. 2 D) shows a list of the participants in the smartphone-sensed symptoms studies. The colored bars within every participant's row represent the distribution of that participant's days across the different clusters (G3, T7). The user list can be sorted by the prevalence of days in a specific cluster, by clicking on that cluster's respective color under *"Sort users by cluster"* (G3, T6) (Fig. 2 H). Hovering the mouse cursor over a user's row highlights their days in the CV and the Daily Values View (explained later) while hiding others users' days (G3, T7). The user can be filtered/selected for re-clustering by clicking on the checkboxes in their rows(G3, T6).

4.5 F-Stats View (FSV)

The F-Stats View (FSV) (Fig. 2 F) displays the most important features for creating the clusters in the clustering chosen in CRV. We performed the Analysis Of Variance (ANOVA) test for every clustering result to obtain the f-statistic. We only show the features that have a statistically significant relationship i.e. p less than 0.05. We used a simple bar chart to show this ranked list of the most important features. This enables an analyst to reason about the chosen clustering result in terms of the proportion of importance given to each features and consequently the reasons for the separation between the different clusters (G2, T4).

4.6   Cluster Details View (CDV)

The Cluster Details View (CDV) (Fig. 2 C) visualizes aggregated data for the days in a cluster that are being hovered over in the CV. The CDV shows the information for the hovered over cluster against the averages across all clusters (G4, T8, T9). This bar with the gray stroke ▭ represents the average across all days. The color of the fill inside the gray bar represents the cluster of the day being hovered over in the CV. If the analyst has brushed over specific days in the CV, the fill color is: �(icon). The aggregated information depends on the daily measures that were contained in the dataset and can include comparisons such as the average incidence of occurrence of weekends in that cluster/ selected days, the average distance travelled and average sleep quality reported.

4.7   Daily Values View (DVV)

The Daily Values View (DVV) contains a parallel coordinates plot where every polyline represents a day and the Y-axes represent feature values (Fig. 2 G). The Y-axes are brushable and allow analysts to filter days based on specific ranges of features values. The lines are color-coded consistently to represent the cluster they belong to. This view lets analysts filter down on specific features and assign semantic meaning to clusters (G4, T8).

4.8   Feature Distribution Heatmap (FDH)

The Feature Distribution Heatmap (FDH) (Fig. 2 E) visualizes the average values of the features across the clusters with a gradient of dark blue to dark red, representing low and high values respectively (G2, T5). The features are shown ordered from top to bottom based on their importance (shown in FSV). This view is important as it shows the distributions of feature values across all clusters to help analysts compare between clusters and understand the representative characteristics of the days within clusters. This helps the analyst in quickly assigning semantic meaning to different clusters.

4.9   Saved Results View (SRV)

The Saved Results View (SRV) lets the analysts save the results of data exploration sessions. Clustering complex data is computationally time-consuming and intense. Constantly re-running clustering algorithms may not be scalable or reproducible and may disadvantage researchers with limited access to the latest computing hardware [9]. The analyst can save results from a data analysis session they performed by clicking on the **"Save New Result"** button in the SRV (Fig. 2 J). The clustering results along with all

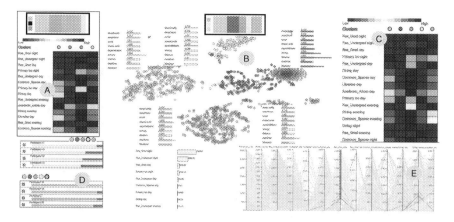

Fig. 3. (Image from our earlier paper [39]) kMeans clustering of every day across every participant based on the similarity of their geo-location features. The results are then projected using t-SNE. A) A clustering result with k=3 and high quality (Davies-Bouldin score) and the associated Feature Distribution Heatmap. B) Selecting a result with k=5. Cluster details are shown for the five clusters. The yellow cluster has high presence in "Res_Grad_night" and "Res_Grad_day", where as the green and purple clusters have high values for presence in the "Res_Undergrad_ day, evening and night", possibly indicating two different student populations i.e. graduate students and undergraduate students. E) Brushing over "Res_Grad_night" shows no purple or green lines. (Color figure online)

other associated data will be stored for quick future access. The analyst can provide a descriptive name for the session which will then be displayed in the list every time PLEADES is started and can be selected to show the earlier session (G5, T10).

5   Evaluation with Use Cases

We introduce Nina, a PhD candidate in computational psychology. Nina wants to build machine learning models that can accurately identify health symptoms like bad sleep and stress levels using objective smartphone-sensed data, with some human labels. Nina has two datasets (ReadiSens and StudentLife [59])and she would like to perform exploratory data analysis on them using PLEADES, before she start building her classifiers. She wants to get a high level understanding of relationships between symptoms and sensor data.

5.1   StudentLife (Dataset 1)

The first dataset was collected by the StudentLife [59] project. This project collected data for 49 Dartmouth University (USA) students throughout a 10-week term. The students were required to install a smartphone application which passively gathered sensor data including:

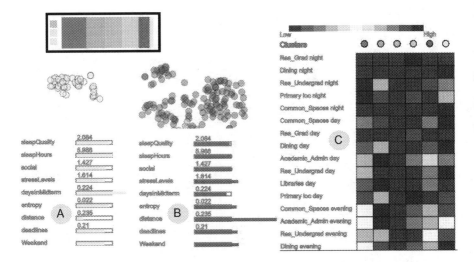

Fig. 4. (Image from our earlier paper [39]) After clustering potential grad and undergrad students, there are four clusters of undergraduate students. This can help insights by observing how undergraduates differ in their behaviors and how their smartphone labelled symptoms manifest in objective sensor data.

- Screen interactions
- Light
- Conversations (automatically detected)
- Activities (stationary, walking, running and unknown)
- On-campus location (detected through WiFi)
- GPS locations.

The buildings are binned into categories such as undergraduate-residential, graduate-residential, dining, academic and admin-services. The application also gathered GPS coordinates that we clustered using DBSCAN [20]. Unlike clustering approaches like k-means, DBSCAN does not need a predefined number of clusters, which is useful in our use cases as individuals can have varying travel patterns. DBSCAN is a density-based method with two hyperparameters: min_points and $min\_distance$. A point x is a core point if there are at least min_points number of points - set as five - in a distance of $min\_distance$ from a point - set as 300m. We used the primary and secondary location only, which are defined as the geo-cluster where the participants spent most and the second most time in. Students were asked to respond to daily surveys about their sleep quality, hours of sleep and stress levels.

The data was divided into days for every participant and analyst-specified features are also calculated per day. We calculated mobility statistics for the days in every cluster in the clustering result including the average distance travelled and the location entropy i.e. how many **different** geo-clusters were visited. These features are linked to symptoms [22]. We also visualize the proportion of weekends in every cluster in addition to the proportion of days in the "midterm". This refers to a time period in the study that was academically demanding.

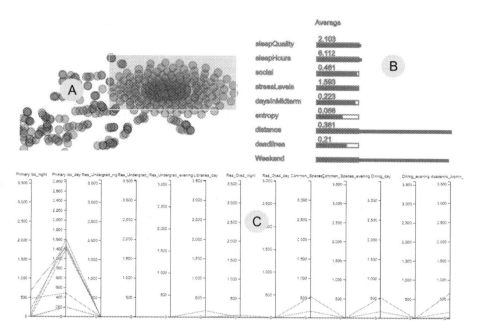

Fig. 5. (Image from our earlier paper [39]) Days in the selected clump have little presence on campus and are more likely to be weekends, along with higher than average distance being travelled.

5.2   Use Case 1: Gaining a Quick Overview of the Data

To get a high level view of the data, Nina first selects all of the sensor and chooses across 3 epochs (day, evening and night) (Fig. 2 I). These features are used to cluster and project using agglomerative clustering (k = 6 clusters) and t-SNE respectively (G1, T1). The clustering results with three and four clusters (second and third highest quality) (G1, T3) are selected. Nina interacts with them in the CV and finds nothing particularly interesting in the CDV. She then selects fourth highest quality clustering result (k = 5) (Fig. 2 A), that has good quality according to the Davies-Bouldin score (G1, T3). She sees in the FSV that on-campus building presence related features (Res_Undergrad, Common_Space, Dining) are very important for this clustering result (G2, T4). She hovers over the mouse over the clusters in the CV to view their details in the CDV. She sees that days in cluster ⬤ (Fig. 2 B), have a higher amount of deadlines, higher stress levels, poorer sleep and generally fall on weekdays (Fig. 2 C) (G4, T8, T9). This makes intuitive sense as deadlines cause behavioral changes. In contrast to this cluster, ◯ has more days that are weekends, slightly better sleep duration and quality, fewer deadlines, and more distance traversed. Such contrasts clusters makes Nina curious and she decides to save this clustering session using the SRV and name it "More deadlines with less sleep" (G5, T10).

5.3   Use Case 2: Examining Student Characteristics that Can Be Helpful for Insightful Comparisons

Nina realizes that features for presence in on campus residences were important across several clustering results. For the next clustering results, she only selects the location features (on-campus buildings and GPS locations) (Fig. 2 H) and re-computes the clustering results using K-Means (k = 6) and t-SNE across all participants. She selects a clustering result with k = 4 (Fig. 3 A). She sees in the FDH that there is one cluster with high presence in Res_Grad and two clusters for which the constituent days had high levels of presence in Res_Undergrad. She wants to see if she can find clusters with clearer feature distribution and selects a result with k = 5 (Fig. 3 B). Cluster ⬤ (Fig. 3 B) has higher incidence of being in Res_Undergrad across all times of day (Fig. 3 C) and cluster ◍ has a higher value of being in other on-campus buildings such as Libraries, Academic etc. (G2, T5). The days in cluster ○ have few to no incidence of being in Res_Undergrad. There are also few incidences of being in other on-campus building, with the exception being Res_Graduate (Fig. 3 C). Sorting the UV (Fig. 3 D) using these three clusters and brushing on the "Res_Grad_night" axis in the DVV reveals that there are no users who have days in both clusters ⬤ ◍ and cluster ○ (G3, T6).

This seems to be an indication that there are two sub-populations (G3, T7) in this dataset. Nina is aware that the StudentLife [59] study included both undergraduate and graduate students. Nina thinks that the users with days in clusters ⬤ and ◍ are undergraduates whereas the users with days in ○ are graduate students. This is an important finding for her as one of the goals at the start of the analysis session that she had for was to compare the behavior patterns and symptoms between different populations. Undergraduate and graduate students generally differ in several life circumstances such as their ages along with course-loads, familial commitments etc. She examines the details for these three clusters in the CDV to see if there are any significant difference. She sees that for ⬤ (Fig. 3 B), the students reported slightly slightly more stress and slightly worse sleep along with more deadlines (G4, T8). Interestingly, for cluster ○ (Fig. 3 B), the students reported average sleep quality, slightly lower stress levels and fewer than average deadlines. The students in with days in cluster ◍ did not report any concerning symptoms (Fig. 3 B). Nina wants ti discuss these findings with other students in her lab and proceeds to save the results from this analysis session in the SRV , calling it "Geo analysis of StudentLife dataset" (G5, T10).

Nina found the overlaying of semantically understandable information like the different kinds of on-campus buildings with the objective sensor-data features to be useful. She liked having the ability to sort users by clustering prevalence that made it easy for her to discover these two populations of students. She also notices in the FDV that there are fewer days of presence in any on-campus building (Fig. 3 C) for the days in cluster ⬤. She hovers the mouse over a day in that cluster and notices in the CDV that the students travelled much more distance (Fig. 3 B) than usual for these days. Interestingly, these days were much more likely to be weekends, which makes intuitive sense to Nina (G4, T9). Nina notices a odd shape in ⬤ (Fig. 5 A) and proceeds to select those days by clicking on *"Select Days"* (Fig. 2 B) and then brushing over the days in that clump.

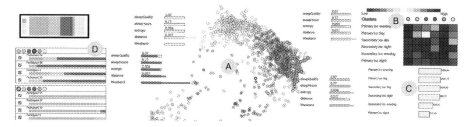

Fig. 6. (Image from our earlier paper [39]) Visualizing ReadiSens data (dataset 2). A) Clustering the geo-features of the ReadiSens data with kMeans and projecting it using Isomap. The yellow cluster has a much higher proportion of weekdays than other clusters along with higher levels of distance travelled, perhaps indicating work-life routine. The pink cluster has days that are more likely to be weekends and with lower sleep quality and little time spent in either the primary or the secondary locations. (Color figure online)

She sees in the CDV (Fig. 5 B) that these days are much more likely to be weekends when compared with the overall cluster ●, in addition to having much higher distance travelled. She also notices (Fig. 5 C) that there is little to no presence for all these days in on-campus buildings in the DVV. She is quite confident that the students travelled for these days. Additionally, she sees more hours of sleep, slightly better sleep quality and fewer deadlines. This is interesting for Nina as she is now able to assign semantic context to objective sensor data. She also plans to build classification models using these days, which can then enable her to find similar days in other clusters. She makes a note for future analysis by labeling these days "Travelling off campus" (G5, T10).

5.4   Use Case 3: Analyzing Graduate Vs. Undergraduate Students

Nina wants to analyze the two distinguishable sub-populations and compare them to each other. She selects the students that she is reasonably confident belong to either group (15 undergraduates and 8 graduates) in the UV and re-runs the clustering and projection (same algorithms) for their data and k = 6 (G3, T6, T7). She chooses a result with k = 6 and looks at the FDH to gain a similar understanding to the last use case. She is particularly interested in viewing the distribution of incidences of presence in on-campus buildings. She notices four clusters ● ○ ● ○ where the participants had a high incidence of being present in Res_Undergrad and a single cluster ◐ with higher Res_Graduate (Fig. 4 C). Hovering the mouse over ○ shows more than average number of days in the midterm with poorer sleep quality (Fig. 4 A). Interestingly, the students reported less stress and sociability issues (G4, T8) for ○. For ●, Nina noticed higher than average distance travelled with slightly worse stress and sleep quality levels (Fig. 4 B). She was able to gain a finer level of view for a population she identified earlier using PLEADES. She save the results to show her analysis to her research partners (G5, T10).

5.5   ReadiSens (Dataset 2)

The second dataset that Nina has access to is called ReadiSens, which was provided to our team by a third party data collector. It contains data for 76 participants in a large

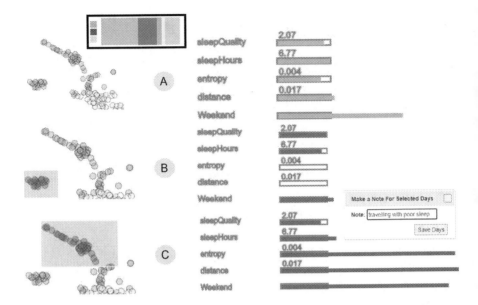

Fig. 7. (Image from our earlier paper [39]) A) More likely to be weekends and the sleep quality is poorer. B) Average weekends with average sleep quality and little travel. C) The clump on the right has poorer sleep quality and more travelling. In addition the days in this clump are much more likely to be weekends.

scale smartphone sensed data study. The dataset also contains reported symptoms such as sleep duration and quality. The participants installed the ReadiSens data collection application that ran passively in the background and administered surveys daily and weekly to collect health and wellness symptom reports. The participants were completely anonymized. The sensors include:

- GPS locations (anonymized while still keeping spatial relevance)
- Activity levels
- Screen interactions
- Sound levels.

We derived the mobility features from the GPS location data was using the same methodology as the previous dataset. We also used the same methodology (DBSCAN clustering) to derive participant's primary and secondary locations. The participants provided daily answers about sleep quality and duration through an app administered survey. There was variance in the level of compliance for providing labels. The sensor data was divided per day across all users and we calculated the same contextual and mobility features (e.g. proportion of weekends, distance travelled etc.) as the previous dataset.

5.6 Use Case 4: Patterns of Presence in Primary Vs. Secondary Location

Nina selects all the data features across all epochs. She chooses kMeans and Isomap and selects k = 6. She goes through a few clustering results but does not seem to find insight that stands out (G1, T2, T3). She decides to specify a single feature type (geo-location) and drill down on it (G1, T1). Nina is aware of research that shows that GPS detected location patterns can accurately identify semantically important location like "home" [22,50] vs. "work" which in turn have important health ramifications [26,48]. She selects primary and secondary geo-clusters across the 3 epochs and clusters the data using the same algorithms as before with k = 6.

Nina selects a clustering result with k = 6 and interacts with some clusters (Fig. 6 A) and sees that for the days in cluster ⬤, the participants typically stayed in their primary location for all 3 epochs. These days were more likely to be weekends, with more than average sleep hours and less distance travelled (G4, T8, T9). Nina thinks that ⬤ represents times where the participant stayed "home". Having multiple connected visualizations make this intuition easier since she does not have access to actual GPS location for which she can get a human understandable location type from services like [46]. She assigns the days in this cluster with a label for this semantic information.

Next she hovers over the cluster ⬤. These days are less likely to be weekends (Fig. 6 A). In addition, the participants are typically in their secondary location more during the evening and the day with much less presence in their secondary location at night (Fig. 6 B). Participants are also typically not at their primary location during the day and are a slightly more present there during evening. However, they are usually there for the night (Fig. 6 B). These days also had higher distance travelled reports of fewer than average sleep hours. Nina can confidently guess that these days are part of a home vs. work routine. She saves this clustering session in the SRV at "Home vs. work". This is important for her as shift work behavior has long term health ramifications [48,55]. Additionally, this is an ongoing project and the machine learning classifiers that Nina builds using these days can be deployed to identify future work patterns.

Nina hovers over the cluster ⬤ and notices that these days are much more likely to be weekends. She sees in the FDH that there are few instances of participants being present in their primary location or secondary location for ⬤ (Fig. 6 B). There is also a drop in the quality of sleep (G4, T8). This along with the fact that this cluster ⬤ is relatively small leads Nina to think that this cluster has days where participants travelled and stayed away from either home or work. However, the clustering result is of poor quality (Fig. 6 A) and the projection on the plane is scattered. Nina is unable to see a clear spatial grouping of ⬤ and decides to tweak the clustering parameters.

She selects location features and selects t-SNE, kMeans and k = 6. A result (k = 5) has a better quality than the previous selection (G1, T2, T3) (Fig. 7). The ⬤ cluster (Fig. 7 A) has a higher number of weekend days and interestingly lower sleep quality. Nina sees two clumps of ⬤ and selects those days separately. She can see that days in first clump (Fig. 7 B) are more likely to be weekends, with fewer hours of sleep, little movement across geo-locations and average sleep quality(G4, T8, T9). Nina sees that (Fig. 7 C) are more likely to be weekends, have higher distance travelled and also have poorer quality of sleep (G4, T8, T9). She is now confident that these days represent travel. Nina to wants to make classifiers that can detect this behavior in data that may not contain any human provided labels. She makes a note for these days as "Travelling with poor sleep scores" in the dialog that appears after the their selection the CV (G5, T10).

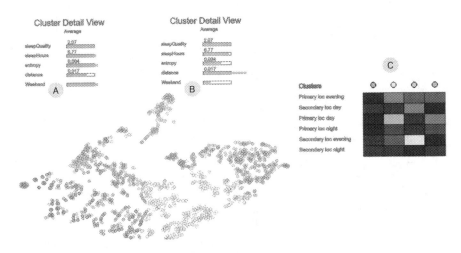

Fig. 8. The participants with days in ⬤ cluster appear to stay at primary location most of the time, whereas the the participants with days in ⬤ tend to stay at at secondary location during later hours of the day.

5.7 Use Case 5: Understanding Variances in Behaviors of Potentially Different Shift Workers

After use case 4, Nina is interested to see if she can find different kinds of shift workers in the anonymized Readisens data. Nina is aware of research that shows strong correlations between shift work and mental health [17,55]. The location data has been anonymized which means she is unable to rely on services like Foursquare [46] to find out what the human understandable type of location. She chooses k = 6, location features, t-SNE and kMeans for dimension reduction and clustering algorithms respectively (G1, T2, T3). She selects a clustering result with average scores. She notices in CDV that for the days in ⬤ cluster, the participants tend to stay at primary location ((Fig. 8 C)) with little distance travelled and roughly the average amount of days in being weekends (Fig. 8 A) (G4, T8, T9). In contrast, the days in the ⬤ cluster tend to much more likely to be weekdays (Fig. 8 B). Nina notices that ⬤ days have slightly fewer sleep hours. She also sort by both the clusters in the UV and notices that there is a small number of participants with days in both ⬤ and ◯. Nina wonders whether these days are representative of shift work (particularly later in the evening) vs. stay-at-home careers. She is interested in looking further into these days and the participants with days in these clusters, to see if she can find further differences in health markers. She makes a note of the days in both the clusters (G5, T10).

6   Evaluation with Experts

To evaluate our interactive visual analytics approach, we invited three experts in implementing health predictive models using machine and deep learning using smartphone-sensed data. They were all PhD candidates in data science. We also invited one expert in interactive data visualizations, who had a master's degree in computer science and extensive experience in designing and implementing data visualizations. Due to COVID-19 restrictions, we held the evaluation session using video screen-sharing to demonstrate PLEADES. The experts were asked to feel free to contribute any feedback at any point of the evaluation session. After a brief walk-through tutorial, the experts were shown the same use cases as Nina. They were all very familiar with the concept of unsupervised clustering and projection as a useful way for performing exploratory data analysis. They found the ability to select sensor features and along with epochs to be quite useful. They mentioned that during early stage exploration of such data, they would require several iterations of parameters and algorithms before discovering interesting results. They also like the ability to save results from previous analysis sessions they were well aware that clustering and projection are computationally intensive tasks and that having the ability to save results would enable them to revisit prior insights in addition to fostering collaboration since they can share the results with their colleagues.

One expert (in smartphone-sensed data model building) found our approach of separating out the raw sensor-level data from contextual data such as the proportion of days in weekends for specific clusters, the average amount of sleep for days in the cluster etc. in the CDV as *"it shows two types of information like features that are maybe more granular and only smartphone detectable and then you have this contextual information that adds more semantic meaning."* The experts suggested interesting potential groupings of the participants that we had not considered, while walking through the use cases. For the ReadiSens dataset (Sect. 5.6), one expert wanted to compare regular travellers with stay-at-home people as both these have been shown to be predictive of health issues [64]. He ordered the users by ⬜ and ⬤ (Figure   6 D). After seeing the ordered lists, he wanted to select a sub-sample of the participants in the two extremes of movements patterns and then compute a machine learning classification model to analyze those users and whether they can be clearly separated. For the StudentLife dataset, the experts found an interesting grouping when going through use case 2 (Sect. 5.3). They noticed that for the days in ⬜ cluster, there was very little presence in on-campus residences but there was more presence in other on-campus buildings. There was also relatively larger presence in the primary location. The experts made an informed guess that the students with days in this cluster may have off-campus residences. One expert suggested that they would like to filter and group on-campus and off-campus students and using PLEADES, analyze the clustering and projection results of that data to observe changes in symptoms. On the whole, the experts found our approach to be valid and PLEADES useful. They demonstrated interest in using PLEADES to perform exploratory data analysis on smartphone sensed health and wellness data and to assign understandable semantic labels to objective sensor data.

7   Discussion, Limitations and Future Directions

An important aspect that the evaluators with research experience in machine learning model building, brought up was the learning curve behind using such a tool. They were all familiar utilizing data visualizations in other projects but felt that it would be very helpful to create a clear guide on how the views are connected and what specifically is being visualized by every pane.

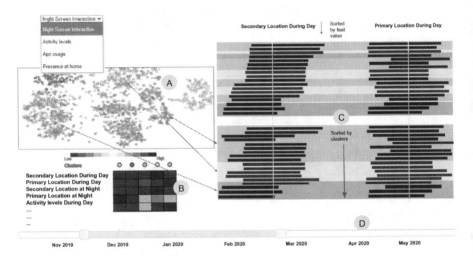

Fig. 9. A) Clustering participants to form cliques of users. B) Understanding the feature characteristics of the group C) Multiple sort-able axes to understand feature value distributions across different groups. D) Select-able time windows for seasonal analyses.

In addition, research in smartphone-sensed health monitoring is focusing more on longer term deployment for capturing data passively with minimal human labelling burden for health labels. Interactive visual analytics for health analyses of large populations challenging especially for a complex domain like smartphone-sensed health. Day level data analysis (which we have performed so far) of thousands of users is not scalable. In addition, external factors cause a large amount of diversity in populations: E.g.: comparing sleep patterns between night vs. day various shift workers, or comparing activity levels between laborers vs. desk workers etc. There also needs to be taken into account Intra-group differences as well. In addition, large scale changes in behaviors such as seasonal changes around winter breaks or large scale societal changes like COVID-19 may also be important to account for in any population level analysis. We will be investigating visual analytics approaches like multi-level visual aggregation, grouping and clustering to present such data for future work (Fig. 9).

We performed a preliminary goal and task analysis for visual analytics-enabled population-level analysis of smartphone-sensor data. The first goal that we came up with was to allow analysts to define groups and make comparisons between those groups based on different health behaviors and data feature values. To enable this, the first task is to cluster smartphone users into visual groups or *cliques* that can be color coded (Fig. 9 A and C). Such groupings of users can differentiate between laborers vs. desk workers vs. stay at home people etc. and can enable analysts to compare individuals more meaningfully. The second task is to enable Semantic Feature Definition for e.g. defining active screen use as not sleeping, different locations as home etc. based on temporal patterns of stays. Such Human-understandable features rather than sensor-values can enable health experts to make sense of such data on a larger scale. The second goal is to determine distinct smartphone-sensed group signature and phenotype. To achieve that, we propose presenting feature distributions for color coded cliques (Fig. 9 C). Showing feature distributions across user cliques can facilitate the discovery of various inter and intra-clique correlations. The third goal is to facilitate interactive temporal analysis of health behaviors across different cliques (Fig. 9 D). We propose adding Interactive timeline window selection to calculate the data features over. This can enable analysts to take into account the various large level changes that can be expected at different times of the year.

In addition to exploratory data analysis, data visualizations have been shown to be effective in fostering *Explainable Machine Learning* [13]. An important future direction for this research is to integrate machine learning pipelines for such exploratory data analyses that can enable analysts to run classification models. Analysts may plug and play different machine learning architectures, algorithms and parameters to optimize classification accuracy and computation expense [9]. For example, selecting days in a cluster with higher than average stress or poor sleep labels and using a visual interface to specify the machine learning algorithm, parameters and architecture to train a classifier using data from those days. The interface can show various metrics from the classification results such as accuracy, loss etc. and allow the analyst to tweak various parameters to see if the results can be improved incrementally.

8   Conclusion

We researched, designed and implemented PLEADES, an interactive visual analytics tool to help analysts perform exploratory data analysis of smartphone-sensed data along with reported health and wellness measures. PLEADES helps analysts contextualize the factors that lead to the manifestation of smartphone detected and reported health and wellness symptoms. Our approach enables the analysts to select clustering parameters including the number of clusters desired, along with the ability to specify multiple clustering and dimension reduction techniques. PLEADES used multiple intuitively linked panes with interactive visualizations like heatmaps, bar charts and brushable parallel coordinated plots to help analysts understand different clustering results. This allows analysts to make important semantic links between human reported data and objective smartphone sensed-data. We validated our approach with intuitive use cases that visualized two real world datasets along with feedback from experts in smartphone-health detection and data visualizations.

References

1. Abdullah, S., Murnane, E.L., Matthews, M., Choudhury, T.: Circadian computing: sensing, modeling, and maintaining biological rhythms. In: Rehg, J.M., Murphy, S.A., Kumar, S. (eds.) Mobile Health, pp. 35–58. Springer, Cham (2017). https://doi.org/10.1007/978-3-319-51394-2_3

2. Andrienko, G., Andrienko, N., Rinzivillo, S., Nanni, M., Pedreschi, D., Giannotti, F.: Interactive visual clustering of large collections of trajectories. In: 2009 IEEE Symposium on Visual Analytics Science and Technology, pp. 3–10. IEEE (2009)

3. van Berkel, N., Goncalves, J., Wac, K., Hosio, S., Cox, A.L.: Human accuracy in mobile data collection (2020)

4. Boudjeloud-Assala, L., Pinheiro, P., Blansché, A., Tamisier, T., Otjacques, B.: Interactive and iterative visual clustering. Inf. Vis. 15(3), 181–197 (2016)

5. Boukhechba, M., Chow, P., Fua, K., Teachman, B.A., Barnes, L.E.: Predicting social anxiety from global positioning system traces of college students: feasibility study. JMIR Mental Health 5(3), e10101 (2018)

6. Boukhechba, M., Daros, A.R., Fua, K., Chow, P.I., Teachman, B.A., Barnes, L.E.: Demonicsalmon: Monitoring mental health and social interactions of college students using smartphones. Smart Health 9, 192–203 (2018)

7. Caliński, T., Harabasz, J.: A dendrite method for cluster analysis. Commun. Stat. Theory Methods 3(1), 1–27 (1974)

8. Cao, N., Lin, Y.R., Gotz, D., Du, F.: Z-glyph: Visualizing outliers in multivariate data. Inf. Vis. 17(1), 22–40 (2018). https://doi.org/10.1177/1473871616686635

9. Cashman, D., Perer, A., Chang, R., Strobelt, H.: Ablate, variate, and contemplate: Visual analytics for discovering neural architectures. IEEE Trans. Visual Comput. Graphics 26(1), 863–873 (2019)

10. Cavallo, M., Demiralp, Ç.: Clustrophile 2: Guided visual clustering analysis. IEEE Trans. Visual Comput. Graphics 25(1), 267–276 (2018)

11. Cavallo, M., Demiralp, Ç.: A visual interaction framework for dimensionality reduction based data exploration. In: Proceedings of the 2018 CHI Conference on Human Factors in Computing Systems, pp. 1–13 (2018)

12. Chatzimparmpas, A., Martins, R.M., Kerren, A.: t-visne: Interactive assessment and interpretation of t-sne projections. IEEE Trans. Visual Comput. Graphics 26(8), 2696–2714 (2020)

13. Chatzimparmpas, A., Martins, R.M., Jusufi, I., Kerren, A.: A survey of surveys on the use of visualization for interpreting machine learning models. Inf. Vis. 19(3), 207–233 (2020)

14. Chen, C., Wu, R., Khan, H., Truong, K., Chevalier, F.: Vidde: Visualizations for helping people with copd interpret dyspnea during exercise. In: The 23rd International ACM SIGACCESS Conference on Computers and Accessibility, pp. 1–14 (2021)

15. Choe, E.K., Lee, B., Kay, M., Pratt, W., Kientz, J.A.: Sleeptight: low-burden, self-monitoring technology for capturing and reflecting on sleep behaviors. In: Proceedings of the 2015 ACM International Joint Conference on Pervasive and Ubiquitous Computing, pp. 121–132 (2015)

16. Choe, E.K., Lee, B., Zhu, H., Riche, N.H., Baur, D.: Understanding self-reflection: how people reflect on personal data through visual data exploration. In: Proceedings of the 11th EAI International Conference on Pervasive Computing Technologies for Healthcare, pp. 173–182 (2017)

17. Costa, G.: Shift work and health: current problems and preventive actions. Saf. Health Work 1(2), 112–123 (2010)

18. Davies, D., Bouldin, D.: A cluster separation measure. IEEE Trans. Patter Anal. Mach. Intell. (1979)

19. Demiralp, Ç.: Clustrophile: A tool for visual clustering analysis. arXiv preprint arXiv:1710.02173 (2017)
20. Ester, M., Kriegel, H.P., Sander, J., Xu, X., et al.: A density-based algorithm for discovering clusters in large spatial databases with noise. In: Kdd, vol. 96, pp. 226–231 (1996)
21. Fujiwara, T., Kwon, O.H., Ma, K.L.: Supporting analysis of dimensionality reduction results with contrastive learning. IEEE Trans. Visual Comput. Graphics 26(1), 45–55 (2019)
22. Gerych, W., Agu, E., Rundensteiner, E.: Classifying depression in imbalanced datasets using an autoencoder-based anomaly detection approach. In: 2019 IEEE 13th International Conference on Semantic Computing (ICSC), pp. 124–127. IEEE (2019)
23. Guo, P., Xiao, H., Wang, Z., Yuan, X.: Interactive local clustering operations for high dimensional data in parallel coordinates. In: 2010 IEEE Pacific Visualization Symposium (PacificVis), pp. 97–104. IEEE (2010)
24. Guo, R., et al.: Comparative visual analytics for assessing medical records with sequence embedding. Visual Informat. 4(2), 72–85 (2020)
25. Gupta, A., Tong, X., Shaw, C., Li, L., Feehan, L.: FitViz: a personal informatics tool for self-management of rheumatoid arthritis. In: Stephanidis, C. (ed.) HCI 2017. CCIS, vol. 714, pp. 232–240. Springer, Cham (2017). https://doi.org/10.1007/978-3-319-58753-0_35
26. Harrington, J.M.: Health effects of shift work and extended hours of work. Occup. Environ. Med. 58(1), 68–72 (2001)
27. Harrower, M., Brewer, C.A.: Colorbrewer. org: an online tool for selecting colour schemes for maps. Cartographic J. 40(1), 27–37 (2003). https://doi.org/10.1179/000870403235002042
28. Heng, T.B., Gupta, A., Shaw, C.: Fitviz-ad: A non-intrusive reminder to encourage non-sedentary behaviour. Electron. Imaging 2018(1), 1–332 (2018)
29. Krueger, R., et al.: Birds-eye - large-scale visual analytics of city dynamics using social location data. Comput, Graphics Forum 38(3), 595–607 (2019). https://doi.org/10.1111/cgf.13713
30. Kwon, B.C., et al.: Clustervision: Visual supervision of unsupervised clustering. IEEE Trans. Visual Comput. Graphics 24(1), 142–151 (2017)
31. Li, J.K., et al.: A visual analytics framework for analyzing parallel and distributed computing applications. In: 2019 IEEE Visualization in Data Science (VDS), pp. 1–9. IEEE (2019)
32. Li, Y., Fujiwara, T., Choi, Y.K., Kim, K.K., Ma, K.L.: A visual analytics system for multi-model comparison on clinical data predictions. Visual Informat. 4(2), 122–131 (2020)
33. Liang, Y., Zheng, X., Zeng, D.D.: A survey on big data-driven digital phenotyping of mental health. Inf. Fusion 52, 290–307 (2019)
34. Maaten, L.v.d., Hinton, G.: Visualizing data using t-sne. J. Mach. Learn. Res. 9, 2579–2605 (2008)
35. Madan, A., Cebrian, M., Moturu, S., Farrahi, K., et al.: Sensing the "health state" of a community. IEEE Pervasive Comput. 11(4), 36–45 (2011)
36. Mansoor, H., Gerych, W., Buquicchio, L., Chandrasekaran, K., Agu, E., Rundensteiner, E.: Comex: Identifying mislabeled human behavioral context data using visual analytics. In: 2019 IEEE 43rd Annual Computer Software and Applications Conference (COMPSAC), vol. 2 (2019). https://doi.org/10.1109/COMPSAC.2019.10212
37. Mansoor, H., Gerych, W., Buquicchio, L., Chandrasekaran, K., Agu, E., Rundensteiner, E.: Delfi: Mislabelled human context detection using multi-feature similarity linking. In: 2019 IEEE Visualization in Data Science (VDS) (2019). https://doi.org/10.1109/VDS48975.2019.8973382
38. Mansoor, H., et al.: Argus: Interactive visual analysis of disruptions in smartphone-detected bio-behavioral rhythms. Visual Informat. 5(3), 39–53 (2021)

39. Mansoor., H., et al.: Pleades: Population level observation of smartphone sensed symptoms for in-the-wild data using clustering. In: Proceedings of the 16th International Joint Conference on Computer Vision, Imaging and Computer Graphics Theory and Applications - IVAPP: IVAPP, vol. 3, pp. 64–75. INSTICC, SciTePress (2021). https://doi.org/10.5220/0010204300640075
40. Mansoor, H., et al.: Visual analytics of smartphone-sensed human behavior and health. IEEE Comput. Graphics Appl. **41**(3), 96–104 (2021)
41. Mead, A.: Review of the development of multidimensional scaling methods. J. Royal Stat. Soc. Ser. D (The Statistician) **41**(1), 27–39 (1992)
42. Melcher, J., Hays, R., Torous, J.: Digital phenotyping for mental health of college students: a clinical review. Evid. Based Ment. Health **23**(4), 161–166 (2020)
43. Mendes, E., Saad, L., McGeeny, K.: (2012). https://news.gallup.com/poll/154685/stay-home-moms-report-depression-sadness-anger.aspx
44. Mohr, D.C., Zhang, M., Schueller, S.M.: Personal sensing: understanding mental health using ubiquitous sensors and machine learning. Annu. Rev. Clin. Psychol. **13**, 23–47 (2017)
45. Müller, S.R., Peters, H., Matz, S.C., Wang, W., Harari, G.M.: Investigating the relationships between mobility behaviours and indicators of subjective well-being using smartphone-based experience sampling and gps tracking. Eur. J. Pers. **34**(5), 714–732 (2020)
46. NPR: https://developer.foursquare.com/
47. Pu, J., Xu, P., Qu, H., Cui, W., Liu, S., Ni, L.: Visual analysis of people's mobility pattern from mobile phone data. In: Proceedings of the 2011 Visual Information Communication-International Symposium, p. 13. ACM (2011)
48. Ravesloot, C., et al.: Why stay home? temporal association of pain, fatigue and depression with being at home. Disabil. Health J. **9**(2), 218–225 (2016)
49. Rousseeuw, P.J.: Silhouettes: a graphical aid to the interpretation and validation of cluster analysis. J. Comput. Appl. Math. **20**, 53–65 (1987)
50. Saeb, S., et al.: Mobile phone sensor correlates of depressive symptom severity in daily-life behavior: an exploratory study. J. Med. Internet Res. **17**(7), e175 (2015)
51. Senaratne, H., et al.: Urban mobility analysis with mobile network data: a visual analytics approach. IEEE Trans. Intell. Transp. Syst. **19**(5), 1537–1546 (2017)
52. Shen, Z., Ma, K.L.: Mobivis: A visualization system for exploring mobile data. In: 2008 IEEE Pacific Visualization Symposium, pp. 175–182. IEEE (2008)
53. Shneiderman, B.: The eyes have it: A task by data type taxonomy for information visualizations. In: Proceedings of the IEEE Symposium on Visual Languages, pp. 336–343. IEEE (1996)
54. Tenenbaum, J.B., De Silva, V., Langford, J.C.: A global geometric framework for nonlinear dimensionality reduction. Science **290**(5500), 2319–2323 (2000)
55. Torquati, L., Mielke, G.I., Brown, W.J., Burton, N.W., Kolbe-Alexander, T.L.: Shift work and poor mental health: a meta-analysis of longitudinal studies. Am. J. Public Health **109**(11), e13–e20 (2019)
56. Vaizman, Y., Ellis, K., Lanckriet, G., Weibel, N.: Extrasensory app: Data collection in-the-wild with rich user interface to self-report behavior. In: Proceedings of the 2018 CHI Conference on Human Factors in Computing Systems, pp. 1–12 (2018)
57. Van Berkel, N., Ferreira, D., Kostakos, V.: The experience sampling method on mobile devices. ACM Comput. Surv. (CSUR) **50**(6), 1–40 (2017)
58. Vetter, C.: Circadian disruption: What do we actually mean? Euro. J. Neurosc.(2018)
59. Wang, R., et al.: Studentlife: assessing mental health, academic performance and behavioral trends of college students using smartphones. In: Proceedings of the 2014 ACM International Joint Conference On Pervasive And Ubiquitous Computing, pp. 3–14 (2014)

60. Wang, W., et al.: Social sensing: Assessing social functioning of patients living with schizophrenia using mobile phone sensing. In: Proceedings of the 2020 CHI Conference on Human Factors in Computing Systems, pp. 1–15 (2020)
61. Wenskovitch, J., Dowling, M., North, C.: With respect to what? simultaneous interaction with dimension reduction and clustering projections. In: Proceedings of the 25th International Conference on Intelligent User Interfaces, pp. 177–188 (2020)
62. Wenskovitch, J., North, C.: Pollux: Interactive cluster-first projections of high-dimensional data. In: 2019 IEEE Visualization in Data Science (VDS), pp. 38–47. IEEE (2019)
63. Wenskovitch Jr., J.E.: Dimension Reduction and Clustering for Interactive Visual Analytics. Ph.D. thesis, Virginia Tech (2019)
64. Weston, G., Zilanawala, A., Webb, E., Carvalho, L.A., McMunn, A.: Long work hours, weekend working and depressive symptoms in men and women: findings from a uk population-based study. J. Epidemiol. Community Health **73**(5), 465–474 (2019)
65. Zhao, Y., et al.: Visual analytics for health monitoring and risk management in CARRE. In: El Rhalibi, A., Tian, F., Pan, Z., Liu, B. (eds.) Edutainment 2016. LNCS, vol. 9654, pp. 380–391. Springer, Cham (2016). https://doi.org/10.1007/978-3-319-40259-8_33

Towards Interactive Geovisualization Authoring Toolkit for Industry Use Cases

Jiří Hynek[1]([⊠]) [iD] and Vít Rusňák[2] [iD]

[1] Faculty of Information Technology, Brno University of Technology,
Brno, Czech Republic
hynek@fit.vut.cz

[2] Institute of Computer Science, Masaryk University, Brno, Czech Republic
rusnak@ics.muni.cz

Abstract. Interactive visualizations of geospatial data are commonplace in various applications and tools. The visual complexity of these visualizations ranges from simple point markers placed on the cartographic maps through visualizing connections, heatmaps, or choropleths to their combination. Designing proper visualizations of geospatial data is often tricky, and the existing approaches either provide only limited support based on pre-defined templates or require extensive programming skills. In our previous work, we introduced the Geovisto toolkit – a novel approach that blends between template editing and programmatic approaches providing tools for authoring reusable multilayered map widgets even for non-programmers. In this paper, we extend our previous work focusing on Geovisto's application in the industry. Based on the critical assessment of two existing usage scenarios, we summarize the necessary design changes and their impact on the toolkit's architecture and implementation. We further present a case study where Geovisto was used in the production-ready application for IoT sensor monitoring developed by Logimic, a Czech-US startup company. We conclude by discussing the advantages and limitations of our approach and outlining the future work.

Keywords: Geospatial data · Geovisualizations · Visual Authoring tools

1 Introduction

Interactive geovisualizations are used in various use cases, ranging from simple choropleths in newspaper articles to specialized analytical applications for disaster management [9] or ornitology [19]. The underlying *geospatial data* can combine location information, descriptive attributes (categorical, numerical, or even textual), and optionally also temporal dimensions (e.g., timestamp, duration). The interactive geovisualizations can display data in multiple layers and enable users to explore them at different detail levels through zooming and panning. The right choice of visual geospatial data representation is not always straightforward. When done wrong, it might lead to obscuring data perspectives that are essential

ⓒ Springer Nature Switzerland AG 2023
A. A. de Sousa et al. (Eds.): VISIGRAPP 2021, CCIS 1691, pp. 232–256, 2023.
https://doi.org/10.1007/978-3-031-25477-2_11

for the users [3]. Moreover, creating efficient interactive geovisualizations usually requires programming skills.

In the last decade, we can observe growing efforts toward developing visualization authoring systems enabling the creation of such interactive visualizations for non-programmers [7,13]. Shortcomings of these tools include the focus on 2D charts, only a few types of available geovisualizations, and limited capabilities in terms of input data or support for multi-layered geovisualization interaction.

Our work aims to provide the geovisualization authoring toolkit, which has an extensible API for programmers and allows authoring various use cases through a user-friendly interface for users without programming skills. In this paper, we: a) summarize the feedback acquired from the two usage scenarios in which the early Geovisto prototype introduced in [10]; b) introduce the architectural and implementation changes of the redesigned version; c) present a novel use case of Geovisto in the production-ready application for IoT sensor monitoring.

The paper is structured as follows. Section 2 overviews the related work and summarizes the shortcomings of current geovisualization authoring approaches. Section 3 summarizes the Geovisto prototype and the two use cases described in detail in our previous work [10]. Section 4 presents the design requirements revisions and proposed changes to Geovisto's architecture and implementation. Sections 5 and 6 show the novel architecture of the toolkit and the implementation respectively. The case study of Geovisto's application in the context of IoT sensor monitoring is in Sect. 7. Finally, Sect. 8 discusses the advantages and disadvantages of our approach, and Sect. 9 summarizes the paper and outlines future work.

2 Related Work

In this section, we first overview several widely-used 2D geovisualization types. Next, we present the *visualization authoring methods* with a particular focus on authoring tools and their limitations.

2.1 Geovisualization Types

Geovisualizations often take advantage of combining multiple layers where each layer presents only a subset of data. The typical base layer is a cartographic map that provides a spatial context for visualized data. The geographic information systems (e.g., QGIS[1] or ArcGIS[2] and the web mapping applications available to the general public (e.g., Google Maps, Bing Maps, Open Street Maps) provide the cartographic layers through public APIs, which can be used in the 3rd party applications.

Further, we list the most common geospatial data visualization types. *Point distribution maps* represent the simplest geovisualizations used for visualizing datasets of elements containing only the location information (1 a)). If the

---

[1] https://qgis.org/en/site/.

[2] https://www.arcgis.com/index.html.

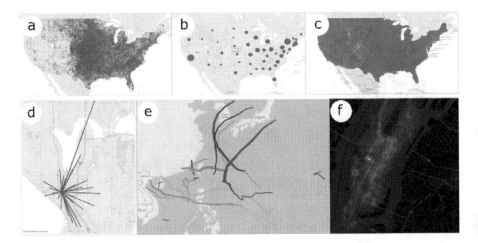

Fig. 1. Common geovisualization types: a) point distribution maps; b) proportional symbol map; c) choropleth; d) spider map; e) flow map; f) heatmap. Source: Tableau Software LLC.

elements contain the location and one descriptive numerical value, they could be plotted as *(proportional) symbol maps* (1 b)). The symbol can be a circle or a glyph whose physical size determines the value. Symbol maps are also useful when the element has two or three descriptive attributes since we can distinguish their size, shape, and color. More advanced modifications enable us to show even more data, e.g., when the glyph symbol is replaced by small 2D charts (e.g., pie/donut/bar charts). When the dataset contains information, not for single locations but the whole regions, *choropleth maps* (or filled maps) are the best option. The color fill of the region represents value (1 c)). Another type of spatial visualization is *heatmaps* (or density maps) that are common, e.g., from weather maps showing the measured temperature or precipitation (1 f)). A particular category is geovisualizations showing routes and paths. Well-known from navigations, the basic *path maps* show direction between two points. However, in the case of flight monitoring websites or computer network visualizations, we can naturally extend the point-to-point to multipoint connections, also known as *spider maps* (1 d)). Finally, by adding the temporal dimension, we can visualize *flow maps*, enabling traffic visualization on the edges (1 e)).

2.2   Geovisualization Authoring Approaches

The interactive visualizations can be authored in three general ways: by programming, template editing, or authoring tools and applications.

Programmatic approaches are the most demanding in terms of users' skills and learning curve but offer the most versatility for fine-tuning of visual appearance and interaction capabilities. The frameworks for developing interactive visualizations are usually designed for web applications. D3 [2] is one of the most popular imperative frameworks nowadays, and many other libraries use it. It allows mapping the input data to a Document Object Model (DOM) and transforms it via data-driven operations. ProtoVis [1] toolkit, also leveraging the imperative paradigm, is based on the idea of decomposing visualizations into hierarchies of visual primitives whose visual properties are data functions. The declarative paradigm frameworks represent Vega [17] and Vega-lite [16]. They both provide a set of building blocks for interactive visualization designs. They differ in the level of abstraction and primary use cases. Vega-lite is a high-level grammar built on top of Vega and was designed for prototyping standard chart types rapidly. Backward compatibility allows programmers to implement more advanced use cases in Vega. There are also several widely-used geovisualization libraries for the web development such as Mapbox GLJS[3], OpenLayers[4] or Leaflet[5]. The latter one we utilize in Geovisto.

Template editing is the exact opposite of programmatic approaches. It is a well-established way to create simple charts in spreadsheet applications like Microsoft Excel or Apache OpenOffice. The main characteristics are limited functionality in terms of interaction and the ability to visualize tabular-based data in a pre-defined set of charts (e.g., pie charts, bar charts, or choropleths). Users can modify only a basic set of parameters such as color, font, chart shape, or legend position. Template editing is also available in dashboard platforms like Grafana [6]), data analysis tools such as Tableau [18], or analytical frameworks such as ElasticSearch in the form of extension library [4]. They allow the users to connect their dataset through API. On the other hand, their main disadvantage is that they centralize their platform's visualization with limited support for their export.

The *authoring tools* build on the advantages of the former two. We can imagine them as advanced graphics software focusing on designing interactive charts. They allow users to create visualizations from basic building blocks that can be widely customized in visual appearance and interaction capabilities through GUI. The output visualizations can be exported as web components and published still without programming skills. The visualization community introduced several projects in the last couple of years. Lyra [15], Data Illustrator [12], or Charticulator [14] represents such tools or systems. However, their primary focus is on authoring 2D charts, and geospatial data visualization is often limited to data presentation in a single layer. Another downside is that the tools require specific visual design knowledge, limiting some users. There are also examples of domain-specific visualization authoring applications. For example, NewsViews [5] targets data journalists to help them create interactive geovisualizations for online news articles. GeoDa Web [11] platform leverages the cloud storage and computing capabilities and enables data analysts to visualize and publish maps and plots to social media in a user-friendly way. Unlike the general visualization authoring systems, the domain-specific ones are simpler and reduce the need for specific visual design knowledge.

---

[3] https://www.mapbox.com/mapbox-gljs.

[4] https://openlayers.org.

[5] https://leafletjs.com.

2.3   Limitations of Current Authoring Tools

We aim to generalize the geovisualization authoring tool while focusing on ease of use for professional and novice users. In general, we identified three limitations of the current tools that we address in our work.

Tabular data as the primary input format. Most of the tools expect the data in a tabular format (e.g., CSV), where columns are attributes (or domains) of elements in rows. However, many of the recent data sets are in hierarchical object formats such as JSON or NoSQL databases. For these, additional data transformation or preprocessing is necessary before their use in visualizations. Our goal is to allow users to upload arbitrary geospatial data in an object-oriented format and select the visualization attributes.

Limited number of configuration options. Since the existing tools focus mainly on general 2D chart visualizations, the list of available geovisualization types and their configuration options are narrow. The most frequent are choropleths, heatmaps, or spider maps. As a result, the user can often display only a few data attributes. Our goal is to enable a combination of visualization types in multiple layers and let users decide which suits their needs.

Limited interaction capabilities. Finally, current tools provide only limited interaction capabilities with visualized geospatial data such as their filtering or region-based selection. Our goal is to let users configure the output geovisualization in line with the expected usage and allow them to set multi-layer interaction capabilities and cross-layer data linkage.

We propose Geovisto – the geovisualization authoring toolkit, which enables configuring geospatial data visualizations for use in web-based dashboard applications or as a part of visual analytics workflows. In the reminder, we present its design and prototype implementation. Two usage scenarios demonstrate its applicability.

3   Geovisto Prototype

In this section, we outline the Geovisto prototype and two usage scenarios described in detail in our earlier paper [10]. The usage scenarios that were used to demonstrate Geovisto's features also served for further revision of the requirements.

Geovisto prototype is a standalone ReactJS[6] component, using Leaflet and D3.js JavaScript libraries. Thus, it can be shared and included as a widget in third-party web applications. The implementation is based on the four design requirements: a) it has a component-based *architecture*; b) the input data are transformed to a flat *data model*; c) its *user interface* enable user-defined data mapping to multiple configurable layers; d) users can export and import *map configurations*.

Geovisto renders the base map with one or more predefined layers when loaded. Users can specify their dataset and import or export map configurations. Available layers are choropleth, marker, and connection layer. The layers

---

[6] https://reactjs.org/.

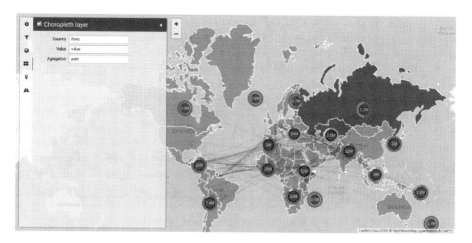

Fig. 2. An example of the Geovisto prototype map widget. It contains the sidebar (on the left) used for the configuration of layers, the definition of filter rules, and the map's general setting. The map contains the choropleth, marker, and connection layers. The example shows the configuration of the choropleth layer. It links the 'from' data domain with the 'country' visual dimension, the 'value' data domain with the 'value' visual dimension, and uses the 'sum' function to aggregate the values.

can be managed from the user interface (e.g., show/hide the layer, define the data visualized in each layer, apply basic filtering on the visualized data). The Geovisto prototype also provides functions for projecting geographic features onto the map and interaction capabilities with the base map. It handles events invoked by the map layers (user interaction) and ships them to other layers, which can process them (since the map layers are independent). Figure 2 shows an example Geovisto prototype map widget.

We further demonstrated the Geovisto prototype on two distinct usage scenarios: Covid-19 pandemic open data, and DDoS attack analysis.

Covid-19 Pandemic Open Data: We used the map to visualize the worldwide spread of the COVID-19 disease to demonstrate the widget's general applicability. We used the data from the rapidapi.com[7] service and converted them to the JSON format to import them into the map widget. Since the map allows the users to change the data domains, the users can compare the countries from different aspects (sum of confirmed cases, numbers of recoveries, and deaths). They can also combine these views using the choropleth and marker layers. Figure 3 shows an example of the use case.

---

[7] https://rapidapi.com/.

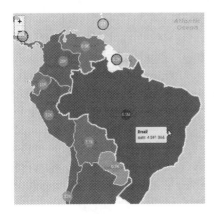 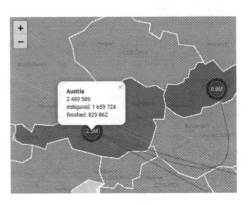

Fig. 3. Covid-19 pandemic data. The choropleth layer compares the number of confirmed cases with the disease. The marker layer shows the number of deaths caused by the disease.

Fig. 4. DDoS attack analysis usage scenario. The example shows the share of mitigated and finished attacks for selected countries.

DDoS Attack Analysis: The scenario was performed in cooperation with Flowmon Networks a.s.[8], a company providing complex tools for automated monitoring, analysis, and network traffic protection. Figure 4 shows a DDoS monitoring component. It provides an overview of all DDoS attacks and the source and destination countries. The connections between the countries visualize the relations of the traffic flows. A country's details show specific aspects of the attacks, such as the state of the attacks (active, mitigated, finished) and their numbers (in pop-up windows). The multilayer map meets the requirements. It contains either the information about the source of DDoS attacks or their destinations. Then, the connection layer can display the relations between the countries. The users can filter the data to display only a specific subset. Finally, they can select a particular country in the choropleth and highlight all the related data presented in the same or other map layers.

While the former usage scenario focused on demonstrating Geovisto's features and general applicability, the latter demonstrated its utilization in the real-world example from the cybersecurity domain. We further analyzed and evaluated the usage scenarios to revise the design requirements and identify the shortcomings limiting Geovisto's applications in the industry.

4 Design Requirements Revision

The main area of Geovisto's deployment is industrial applications. In order to meet the requirements of the industry, we reformulated the initial design requirements based on the Geovisto prototype assessment in the presented scenarios. The revised requirements focus on five main aspects:

---

[8] https://www.flowmon.com/en.

- **Usability**: Geovisto should utilize the concept of authoring systems and provide map layers representing ready-to-use thematic maps to decrease the effort to prototype visual projections of geographical data quickly;
- **Modularity**: Geovisto should not be served as a monolith but in the form of independent modules which would provide particular functionality such as map layers and map controls; these modules could be used only when needed in order to decrease the size of the result;
- **Configurability**: Geovisto's basemap and its layers and controls might be customized with generic datasets, geographical data, appearance, and behavior; users might capture the current map state and reload this state later;
- **Extensibility**: Geovisto should provide a core with programming API to customize the map programmatically, allow further extensions of the existing modules of the library, or implement new own modules concerning the current requirements;
- **Accessibility**: the library (and modules of the library) should be available through a known package manager software to support versioning and improve integration into its own system infrastructure, build and deliver the solution as a part of its system.

The following subsections list these aspects reflecting the initial prototype and identify required modifications to the original prototype design that have driven the re-implementation of the Geovisto toolkit.

4.1   Usability

One of the crucial problems during the design and implementation of user interface and visualization is to overcome the communication barrier between customers providing requirements and programmers delivering the final product for them. Usually, salespeople, UX designers, or data analysts try to break this barrier. However, their lower knowledge of the system architecture and underlying data models might skew the description of the requirements to the programmers. These specifications are usually vague, and they do not consider actual data representation (e.g., data types and relations between data entities) and effort (e.g., complexity and price of database queries) to map the data into the UI components. The main goal of the Geovisto toolkit is to blend the programmatic and template editing approaches known from contemporary mapping libraries to improve user experience during the prototyping phase.

The idea of Geovisto is to provide a UI layer composed of ready-to-use map layers and controls, which would allow the UI designer to project the actual data and prototype the map views corresponding to the end-user requirements. Then, a snapshot of the map state could be exported and shared in a serialized format. Such a configuration might help the programmer who implements a new map widget into the production version of the application or service used by the end-users, as illustrated in Fig. 5.

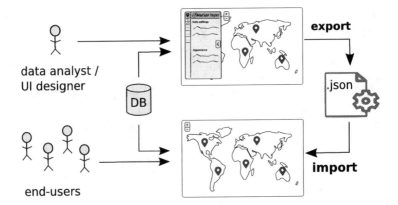

Fig. 5. Geovisto's authoring and configuration sharing workflow. First, the UI designer creates a data projection into the map layers and exports the configuration into a JSON file. The configuration can be shared with end-users or programmers developing the web front-end.

The authoring tools could have been used while clarifying the user requirements and possible use cases of the Flowmon UX team. Since Geovisto can work with custom datasets, the UX team members used the prototype independently, generating multiple map configurations providing perspectives of their custom data without any coding knowledge. This approach improved mutual communication between them and programmers and rapidly increased the ability to generate new geovisualization use cases.

While the Geovisto prototype provided decent authoring tools to prepare the map drafts, export, and import the map state, the programmatic definition of the state as properties of map and map layers was rather cumbersome. Since the Geovisto prototype was implemented in JavaScript, the property types were unclear, leading to occasional crashes and debugging requests. One of the most needed requirements was to re-implement the project into TypeScript[9], which only emphasizes the importance of statically typed languages in the industry and even the front-end and data visualization.

4.2 Modularity

When implementing the prototype, our initial goal was to design a clear code structure and decompose the library into the so-called *Geovisto tools* representing particular map layers and controls and the map core handling communication between the tools. Although we fulfilled the modular approach, the main drawback stood for how the library was delivered – in the form of one JavaScript repository. Thus, programmers using Geovisto needed to load the whole library,

---

[9] https://www.typescriptlang.org.

although they wanted to use only a subset of Geovisto's tools. To fully accomplish the proposed modularity, it was necessary to break apart the repository into standalone packages to be included as project dependencies when needed. The crucial task to handle this was to solve the problem of possible dependencies between the tools (e.g., one tool needed to know the type of event object sent by another tool).

4.3   Configurability

The Geovisto prototype worked with the following types of inputs:

- **Geographical Data:** the specification of polygons and their centroids represented in GeoJSON format. The prototype used the specification of world countries published by J. Sundstrom[10] but it should be replaceable with generic specifications. The only requirement was that every GeoJSON feature had to contain a polygon identifier (e.g., country code), which is needed to connect the geographical data with the dataset.
- **Datasets:** the values stored in a serialized format (JSON). The data needs to contain at least one data domain representing an identifier of the geographical feature (e.g., country code).

Since there are various models representing the data, it was essential to create a mechanism for processing such models – choosing the data domains and binding them to the map layers' visual dimensions. Hence, every map layer provides a list of visual dimensions, which can be associated with data domains. The users can select the data domains manually using the layer settings provided by the map sidebar. In contrast to existing authoring tools, this approach focuses only on geospatial data. Users can work with multiple data domains representing geographic location formats (such as the ISO 3166 country codes) and use them in various use cases.

Since the dataset can represent non-tabular data structures (e.g., JSON or XML formats), recursive data preprocessing was needed to construct a valid data model representing data domains. Only then, the list of the data domains was served to the UI. Figure 6 shows an example demonstrating the principle. The Geovisto prototype provides a basic flattening algorithm that expands all nested arrays into a combination of flat data visual projections and aggregations.

---

[10] https://github.com/johan/world.geo.json.

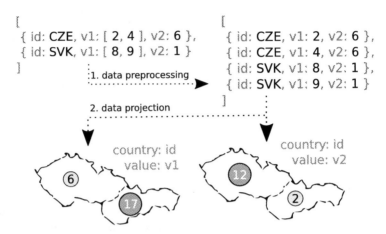

Fig. 6. An example of data composed of two records stored in the pseudo-JSON format. Since the records contain nested lists, they need to be preprocessed first. They are expanded into four records represented by all combinations of the values. This representation is characterized by data domains that can be mapped into visual dimensions. The figure shows two different projections and aggregation of data.

Another requirement from the Flowmon evaluation was to implement different flattening strategies. For instance, some of the nested lists might represent specific qualitative characteristics of network traffic which should not be preprocessed as described in the example of Fig. 6. For this purpose, the Geovisto prototype lacked a solid mechanism to deliver custom data preprocessing algorithms.

Similarly, overriding the default Geovisto behavior and settings was cumbersome and required decent knowledge of the library architecture. For instance, Flowmon needed to integrate the map instances into its own environment, which is characterized by specific appearance (e.g., types of controls familiar to the company's customers). Hence, the requirement to completely redesign the map layers and controls has a high priority for future deployment of the map instances to corporate environments.

4.4   Extensibility

Another requirement from the Flowmon evaluation was to implement different flattening strategies. For instance, some of the nested lists might represent specific qualitative characteristics of network traffic which should not be preprocessed as described in the example of Fig. 6. For this purpose, the Geovisto prototype lacked a solid mechanism to deliver custom data preprocessing mechanisms.

Similarly, overriding the default Geovisto behavior and settings was cumbersome and required decent knowledge of the library architecture. For instance, Flowmon needed to integrate the map instances into its environment, characterized by specific appearance (e.g., types of controls familiar to its customers). Hence, the requirement to completely redesign the map layers and controls has a high priority for future deployment of the map instances to corporate environments.

4.5 Accessibility

Since our goal is to deliver Geovisto in compact modules, it is essential to maintain modules versioning. These modules should be available in package management systems, such as npm (Node.js Package Manager), and the modules users (i.e., programmers) should decide on their own when to switch to a higher version. It is another essential requirement in the industry when delivering new product releases. In order to deliver a stable product to its customers, the dependent libraries must be reliable.

Flowmon develops its user interfaces in the React.js library. It helps organize the user interface into logical parts (React components) and manage its rendering lifecycle and UI events. The Geovisto prototype was wrapped in the React component, but we decided to leave this abstraction in future versions and provide the React extension as a standalone package. We kept Geovisto as a Leaflet-based TypeScript library that can be integrated into any web application by the companies which might use different UI frameworks (such as Angular or Vue.js).

5 Architecture

We updated the Geovisto prototype's architecture concerning the listed requirements, which decomposes the library into the map core and map layers. We designed a revised architecture reflecting the new aspects of Geovisto. The idea of new Geovisto architecture is similar to the old one. However, it generalizes the Geovisto modules as so-called *Geovisto Tools*, representing map layers, map controls (e.g., sidebar), or utilities (e.g., filters and themes). Map layers are a particular type of tool (Fig. 7).

The reason behind the decomposition was to provide standalone npm packages that can be included in a project when needed. Every *Geovisto Tool* is a TypeScript project with a package.json file containing the npm metadata[11]. It contains two peer dependencies – *Geovisto Core* and Leaflet – which force the programmer to include *Geovisto Core* and Leaflet library in own project. Hence, the built packages of *Geovisto Tools* do not include the code of these libraries in order to minimize the size of the packages and prevent conflicts in dependencies.

5.1 Core

The management of the *Geovisto Tools'* life cycle, inputs, and map state is provided by the *Geovisto Core*. It is an npm package[12] which represents an abstraction of the Leaflet library, and it needs to be (together with Leaflet) included in every project which utilizes *Geovisto Tools*.

---

[11] Metadata required by the Node.js Package Manager when resolving the tree of package dependencies, running, building, and publishing the package.

[12] https://www.npmjs.com/package/geovisto.

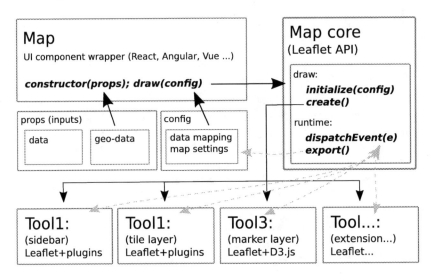

Fig. 7. Geovisto architecture overview. The map component takes props and config and renders a Leaflet-based map composed of map tools – usually SVG elements generated via the Leaflet API or D3.js library. The map tools are independent of each other and communicate via events. They represent map layers, map controls, and utilities.

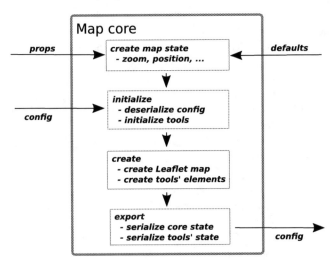

Fig. 8. Map core life-cycle. First, the map state is initialized by default values of the Geovisto toolkit and props given by the programmer. Then, the user can override the state using config (such as data mapping or appearance). The map and tools are rendered based on the combination of values given by Leaflet, programmer, and user. Finally, the user can use the map, change the state and export the config.

Figure 8 describes the workflow of the *Geovisto Core*. First, it processes the inputs and initializes the state of the map and instances of the required *Geovisto*

Tools. Then, based on the initial state, it creates and renders the Leaflet map and instances of *Geovisto Tools*. The phase of state initialization is crucial, and it determines the data projection and appearance of the map and tools. It is based on the following inputs:

- **Default Values (*defaults*)** – the state defined by Geovisto: the implicit values and functions representing the map's default behavior and appearance. They make the initial state of the map and the tools.
- **Properties (*props*)** – the state defined by the programmer: the default state can be overridden programmatically by using props. The programmer might influence either the map's appearance (static values) or override the default behavior (functions). Some of the props are optional (e.g., initial map zoom); however, there are several important mandatory props that are essential to render the map:
  - *Geo-data manager* providing geographical data (available GeoJSON definitions), which can be used across the tools.
  - *Data manager* providing dataset and strategy for data preprocessing into a suitable list data records which can be used across the tools.
  - *Tool manager* providing tool instances that should extend the *Geovisto Core*. Every tool might accept its own props and config to override its default state.
- **Configuration (*config*)** – the state defined by the user: the ability of the user to override default values and properties defined by the programmer. Config is defined by serialized format data (e.g., JSON) and manager, which processes this format and transforms it to the *Geovisto Core* model and tools. It can also be exported during the map runtime to capture the snapshot of the current map state. In contrast to the props, it represents only the static characteristics of the map, not the procedural characteristics of the map. Config usually defines map appearance and data mapping (projections of data domains to the dimensions of map layers).

All of the inputs are wrapped in so-called *input managers*, which process the inputs and transform them into Geovisto models. This approach gives the programmer the opportunity to work on their own input format and provide their own strategies to process these formats. It makes the library more generic and applicable in different environments.

5.2   API

In contrast to the Geovisto prototype, the new Geovisto version (Core and selected tools) was reimplemented using the TypeScript language. Using static types allowed us to describe the exact model of all map objects. The code structure was split into two parts representing:

- **Types and Interfaces:** declaration of all Geovisto objects, their properties, and methods (e.g., map, tool, layer, state, defaults, props, config, events, geo-data, data domains, layer dimensions, aggregation functions, filters, etc.)

– **Classes:** internal default definitions of map objects which provide implicit behavior, ready to use

Both the declarations and definitions of Geovisto objects are exported using ES6 module exports, so they can be used to design new Geovisto objects or extend the existing ones. In order to allow comfortable overriding of implicit map objects, the Factory design pattern was applied. Besides that, the programmer can approach low-level Leaflet objects and utilize all capabilities of this library.

The architecture of *Geovisto Core* is used in *Geovisto Tools* implementing the interfaces and types and extend the classes of *Geovisto Core API*. Since the tools might also be extended or used by each other, they export their own declarations and definitions of tool objects, similarly to the *Geovisto Core*. Then, the tools might communicate with each other using events and the Observer design pattern and the types of event objects are be known by the observers (e.g., the change of preferred style in the themes tool).

The tools are represented as standalone npm packages. In order to avoid direct dependencies between the npm packages, only the types and interfaces can be imported, and so-called devDependecies[13] are used.

6   Implementation

The *Geovisto Core* is distributed along with eight already published *Geovisto Tools* in the npm repository[14] under the MIT license. The source codes are available on Github[15]. Several other tools are in the development. Further, we present the published ones.

6.1   Layers

Layer tools represent thematic map layers. Besides *Tile layer*, each of the following layers allows defining a GeoJSON describing geographical objects of the layer (e.g., polygons, or points based on the type of thematic map). In contrast to the prototype, Geovisto accepts multiple definitions of GeoJSON directly in the props. Then, a data mapping needs to be set to connect the data domains with the layer's dimensions (e.g., geographical dimension, value dimension, or aggregation function) as illustrated in Fig. 2. The following map layer tools are already available in the npm repository.

– **Tile Layer Tool** represents the base map layer which utilizes Leaflet Tile layer API to show underlying maps of existing tile providers[16]. This might be required when the data needs to be connected with real geographical places.
– **Choropleth Layer Tool** allows to use GeoJSON specifications of polygons representing geographic regions and link them with the data. Unlike basic choropleth widgets, our implementation can process custom definitions of

---

[13] https://nodejs.dev/learn/npm-dependencies-and-devdependencies.
[14] https://www.npmjs.com/search?q=geovisto.
[15] https://github.com/geovisto.
[16] https://github.com/leaflet-extras/leaflet-providers.

geographic areas. Primarily, we work with the specification of world countries. However, different GeoJSON files can be used, as described in Sect. 5. The advantage of this approach is the higher scalability of the layer. We can use the layer in different situations and detail (e.g., countries, districts, custom areas). We can also adjust it according to the foreign policy of specific countries (e.g., visualization of disputed territories).

- **Marker Layer Tool** works with GeoJSON specification of points and visualizes the data related to exact geographic locations via *markers*. Similar to the choropleth polygons, every marker has a unique identifier and geographic position (e.g., country code and country centroid). Since marker visualization could be problematic when many are close to each other (clutter of markers), we use Leaflet.markercluster plugin[17] to overcome this issue by clustering the close markers into groups and aggregating the values.
- **Connection Layer Tool** visualizes relations between geospatial locations in the form of edges. The layer enables the user to select two required dimensions: *from* and *to*, representing nodes of the rendered edges (by default, we work with the country centroids identified by country codes). Optionally, the user can set the *value*, which affects the strength of the lines.

A common problem of connection maps is their complexity and poor edge placement. Holten and Van Wijk [8] proposed a force-directed edge bundling rendering technique that significantly reduces the clutter of edges. S. Engle demonstrated its application[18] on a flight map in the US. The example implements the technique using the d3-force[19] module of the D3.js library, which "implements a velocity Verlet numerical integrator for simulating physical forces on particles." In Geovisto, we implemented an SVG overlay layer using the Leaflet API and rendered the SVG elements representing edges using the D3.js library and the d3-force module according to Engle's approach. It was necessary to implement correct projections of the SVG elements into the Leaflet map concerning the map's zoom and current position. The result provides a comprehensive view of edges that can be zoomed in/out.

6.2   Controls and Utilities

The second type of tool adds additional controls and functionality to the map layers. Currently, Geovisto provides the support for adding custom UI controls in the sidebar, filtering and selection of data, and changing style themes:

- **Sidebar Tool** provides a collapsible sidebar control and the API allowing other tools to add custom sidebar tabs or sidebar tab fragments. The map layer tools utilize this to provide controls for their customization and changing data mapping.
- **Filters Tool** provides either UI controls to filter visualized data records and the API to define custom advanced filter operations. The users specify filter rules as conditional expressions evaluating selected data domains' values.

---

[17] https://github.com/Leaflet/Leaflet.markercluster.
[18] https://bl.ocks.org/sjengle/2e58e83685f6d854aa40c7bc546aeb24.
[19] https://github.com/d3/d3-force.

- **Selection Tool** provides a mechanism for connecting map layers with selected map layer geographical objects. The communication between the layers is implemented via the observer design pattern. Every event passed to the layers contains information about the source element selected by the user. It consists of the identifier of the geographic element (e.g., country code) and the layer. The identifiers of geographic elements can be used in more than one layer (e.g., choropleth country, country marker, connection node). Then, the filtering is based on the search of these identifiers through the map layer elements. The search algorithm avoids the cyclic event invocation. The elements found on the map are highlighted (Fig. 9).
- **Themes Tool** provides a set of predefined styles (e.g., colors), which are delivered to other tools via events and API, which allows defining own custom style themes.

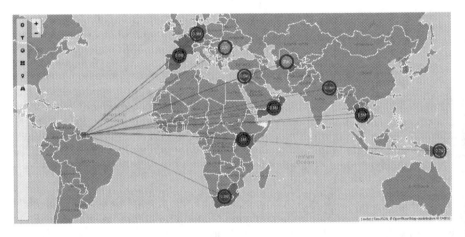

Fig. 9. Geographic element selection. The selection of Suriname in the choropleth layer invokes an event that is passed to other map layers. The connection layer handles the event, finds, and highlights all the edges which connect Suriname with other countries. This selection invokes another event which contains all the countries connected with Suriname. It affects the choropleth and marker layer, which highlights appropriate countries. Further invocations of events are stopped.

7   Case Study: Logimic

We demonstrated Geovisto's applicability in a case study that was done in cooperation with Logimic – the Czech-US startup company that brings innovative IoT solutions to industry.[20]

---

[20] Logimics' products include smart city dashboards for monitoring billions of sensors, street lighting control systems, indoor monitoring of temperature and humidity with small battery-operated wireless sensors, wireless control of industrial heaters, and many others (https://www.logimic.com/).

One of Logimic's products is a user-friendly web application implemented in TypeScript and Angular framework. It processes and aggregates large-scale cloud data gathered from devices and provides monitoring and analytic tools to end-users (e.g., administrators of smart devices, service workers, or inhabitants of smart cities). Its main strength is the simplicity of data presentation delivered in the form of several dashboards, systematically organized in different levels of detail. For instance, basic users can monitor devices using high-level views with simple indicators presenting key performance indicators (KPIs). On the other hand, analysts could utilize drill-down actions to watch KPI alerts, detect device problems and analyze the reasons behind these problems to create service requests for service workers. Due to devices' geographic locations, KPI alerts and related device problems are problematic. Since many devices might be distributed in the city, such information is crucial to navigating the service worker to the device. It should be comprehensively displayed when an alert is focused. Geovisto was used for this purpose. Figure 10 shows an example of a device KPI alert selection and map focus.

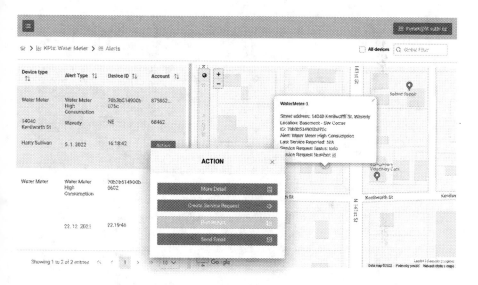

Fig. 10. Device alerts view. The user can click on an alert in the list (on the left) and the corresponding device is zoomed in on the map with description popup. Then, the user can create a service request.

In order to include the Geovisto map into the Logimic application, it was necessary to create an Angular component that serves as a wrapper for the Logimic map. The principle was similar to the React component created for Flowmon (Sect. 3). Since the *Geovisto Core* library is delivered as an npm package and it was reimplemented to TypeScript, it was easy to set this library as the npm dependency and import the library in the Angular component written in

TypeScript. Geovisto creation and API functions calls were integrated into the Angular lifecycle callbacks, similarly as it can be done by using React lifecycle hooks. We expect the library to be used either in pure JavaScript/Typescript projects or in various advanced UI frameworks (such as Vue.js or Svelte).

For the purposes of Logimic, we tested the following existing tools, currently provided by Geovisto:

- **Tile layer tool** displays a real-world map which is vital to locate the devices. Also, the satellite view is beneficial when the service worker is in the field and needs to quickly locate the devices (e.g., actual positions of lamps, entrance to buildings) as shown in Fig. 11. The tool itself does not provide a map tiles server. It only provides the ability to connect the tool with a chosen mapping provider service[21] using the Leaflet API. Logimic purchases API keys concerning the policy of the chosen map providers.

Fig. 11. Satellite perspective using Google maps. It can provide the service worker with a detailed view of the focused neighborhood and help associate the device marker with the actual location.

- **Filters tool** allows to select only the devices that might be important either for the desktop user to analyze a map region or the service worker for navigation across the series of same devices (e.g., the distribution of lamps in the street – Fig. 12).

---

[21] https://github.com/leaflet-extras/leaflet-providers.

Fig. 12. Device filtering. In this example, service workers can only see one device type (lamps) to unclutter the view and remove unneeded markers.

- **Themes tool** enables the widget appearance customization, so it fits the surrounding environment.
- **Sidebar tool** allows to add new controls for customization of mentioned tools. Currently, the controls are displayed as a part of the map widget, but with the planned redesign of the application, it might be required to move these controls outside the map widget and include them in the global menu. This was also one of Flowmon's requirements. Since the *Geovisto Core* and *tools* provide API for their customization, it is possible to control them externally.

Regarding the visualization of device markers, we integrated the Geovisto toolkit as part of the Logimic environment to demonstrate the possibility of extending Geovisto externally. The tool is similar to the Marker layer provided by Geovisto, but it adds some new Logimic-specific functionality:

- The tool is connected to the list of device alerts and listens to the selection changes in order to focus the device on the map when an alert is clicked.
- It extends marker popups for additional device metadata and allows to invoke service requests dialogs directly.

This tool can be published as an npm package; however, it represents an internal extension applicable in the Logimic application.

8   Discussion

As confirmed by the evaluation with Logimic, Geovisto's attributes (usability, modularity, configurability, extensibility, and accessibility) improved vastly. The multilayered map appeared to be an excellent way to display the geographic locations of IoT devices distributed in the cities. Satellite view, filter, and focus tools help locate the devices that alert KPI problems and navigate service workers to these devices. We expect that Geovisto might be used with different use cases of different industrial systems. Further, we present Geovisto's advantages and disadvantages.

8.1 Advantages

One of Geovisto's main advantages is that it provides UI tools to prototype map instances without implementing much code. Then, the state of a map instance can be serialized and exported. Even though the prototyping possibilities are limited, this functionality might be beneficial for a programmer trying to find the best map configuration. Also, it might improve the communication between the UX team, which can find an appropriate map configuration, and the programmers, which can use this configuration to implement the production version of the map.

Geovisto can work with generic datasets and project them onto custom geographical objects (concerning the capabilities of chosen map layers). Users can select various data domains, which allows them to explore the information further. Showing more layers at the same time helps the users to see the data in context. The interactive data filtering emphasizes the relations between geographical locations. The selection of map layer objects can be propagated to other layers, focusing the important details better with a combination of highlighting tools.

When the programmers need to create an unusual data projection, they can either choose from the existing *Geovisto Tools* or implement their own using the *Geovisto Core API*. The second version of the library was rewritten in the statically typed TypeScript language, improving code readability and decreasing the number of runtime errors caused by the wrong API application.

The library does have a modular architecture. It provides a thin core layer delivered as an npm package providing the core API. Then, additional *Geovisto Tools* extend the Core and provide particular map layers, controls, and utilities. Programmers can import additional npm packages in their projects only when required, which decreases the size of the result.

8.2 Limitations

Geovisto is an open-source library that is still under development. The usage scenarios showed only a fragment of geospatial data types that could be visualized. More usage scenarios and case studies are needed to validate the generalization of our approach. We should focus more on processing the large-scale data and the performance and profiling of the library.

Another limitation relates to data preprocessing that has to be done to gain a flat data structure. Our implicit approach causes enlargement and redundancy of the data. Thanks to that, the data can be processed quickly. However, it would be helpful to design an algorithm that can work with the data without preprocessing and more efficiently. The new version of Geovisto offers the possibility to override these algorithms. However, a more extensive set of implicit data processing strategies would improve its usability.

Last but not least, the lack of proper usability evaluation is another drawback of our work. For instance, selecting colors and combining several map layers is limited by people's comprehensibility of the widget. The users might be overwhelmed by the data, mainly when chosen inappropriate color combinations. The z-index of the layers is hardcoded, and users cannot change it. Usually, the users should not need to change the default settings (e.g., the marker and connection layers are above the choropleth), but they should control their ordering in the future with more layers added.

9   Conclusion and Future Work

There are three general approaches to authoring interactive geovisualizations: programmatic, template editing, and authoring tools. The existing authoring tools, however, are mainly focusing on 2D charts and diagrams, and their capabilities for authoring geovisualizations are limited. In our work, we focus on designing and implementing an authoring tool specifically focused on delivering interactive geovisualizations.

Earlier, we implemented a prototype version of the Geovisto toolkit based on JavaScript and Leaflet and demonstrated it on two usage scenarios (DDoS Attack Analysis and Covid 19 Pandemic open data) in [10]. In this paper, we followed up with an analysis of usage scenarios, identified prototype limitations, and revised the design requirements for the new version in terms of *usability, modularity, configurability, extensibility,* and *accessibility.*

Modular architecture allows to include only necessary parts of the library and decrease the size of the product. Configurability allows customization of included parts to integrate the map into the company's environment. Improved extensibility offers the creation of new map tools specific to companies. We re-implemented the Geovisto toolkit in TypeScript – a statically-typed language – that improves further development and decreases runtime errors.

The library has been published in the form of npm several packages[22]. The source codes are available on Github under MIT license[23].

The requirements reflected the intended industrial use and invoked changes in Geovisto's architecture and implementation. We presented the case study where Geovisto was used in the production-ready application for visualizing IoT sensor devices on the map developed by Logimic startup company. The case study confirmed that the Geovisto toolkit fulfills our goal of creating a programmatic mapping library that provides template editing known from mapping authoring systems.

---

[22] https://www.npmjs.com/search?q=geovisto.
[23] https://github.com/geovisto.

9.1   Future Work

There are also several sub-projects we are currently working on. One of them is a web service enabling non-programmers to prototype map instances using the Geovisto toolkit and include them as widgets on their websites. We are developing an infrastructure that will manage map configurations, datasets, and GeoJSONs. The system will provide the front-end application wrapper, including the UI tools to manage user-defined maps. The back-end will provide a configuration database and API for remotely fetching the configurations. We also plan to support loading data from third-party relational and non-relational database systems.

The second area deals with layer improvements and creating new ones. We have already implemented the bubble map, spike map, and heatmap layers, which play an essential role in the comprehensive data distribution visualization. Another almost finished tool provides animated geospatial data visualization with the time dimensions (i.e., timestamps). It enables the animation of spatio-temporal data domains and seeks them to the defined time frame. As a result, it will allow the user to see the evolution of values in individual geographic regions in time. Also, we plan to improve the visual appearance of the layers and add interactive map legends. Since the users can show multiple layers in the map simultaneously, we will pay closer attention to the color pallets used in the layers (e.g., sufficient color contrast, color-blind safe palette combinations). Lastly, we will add further visual dimensions to the layers and controls for manipulating the layers.

The third area focuses on quality assurance. Since the project is getting larger and composed of several packages that might use the API of others, it is necessary to do proper testing before publishing new versions. We will also pay attention to the documentation to better describe the API, including usage examples.

Acknowledgements. Jiří Hynek was supported by The Ministry of Education, Youth and Sports from the National Programme of Sustainability (NPU II) project "IT4Innovations excellence in science – LQ1602". Vít Rusňák was supported by ERDF "CyberSecurity, CyberCrime and Critical Information Infrastructures Center of Excellence" (No. CZ.02.1.01/0.0/0.0/16_019/0000822) project. We also thank Progress Flowmon and Logimic, which provided usage scenarios and cooperated during the evaluation of the Geovisto toolkit.

References

1. Bostock, M., Heer, J.: Protovis: a graphical toolkit for visualization. IEEE Trans. Vis. Comput. Graph. **15**(6), 1121–1128 (2009)
2. Bostock, M., Ogievetsky, V., Heer, J.: D^3 data-driven documents. IEEE Trans. Vis. Comput. Graph. **17**(12), 2301–2309 (2011). https://doi.org/10.1109/TVCG. 2011.185

3. Degbelo, A., Kauppinen, T.: Increasing transparency through web maps. In: Companion Proceedings of the The Web Conference 2018, WWW 2018, pp. 899–904.International World Wide Web Conferences Steering Committee, Geneva (2018). https://doi.org/10.1145/3184558.3191515

4. Elasticsearch, B.: Maps for Geospatial Analysis (2020). https://www.elastic.co/maps, Accessed 10 Feb 2020

5. Gao, T., Hullman, J.R., Adar, E., Hecht, B., Diakopoulos, N.: NewsViews: an automated pipeline for creating custom geovisualizations for news. In: Proceedings of the SIGCHI Conference on Human Factors in Computing Systems, CHI 2014, pp. 3005–3014. Association for Computing Machinery, New York (2014). https://doi.org/10.1145/2556288.2557228

6. Grafana Labs: Grafana: The Open Observability Platform (2020). https://grafana.com/, Accessed 10 June 2020

7. Grammel, L., Bennett, C., Tory, M., Storey, M.A.: A survey of visualization construction user interfaces. In: Hlawitschka, M., Weinkauf, T. (eds.) EuroVis - Short Papers. The Eurographics Association (2013). https://doi.org/10.2312/PE.EuroVisShort.EuroVisShort2013.019-023

8. Holten, D., Van Wijk, J.J.: Force-directed edge bundling for graph visualization. Comput. Graph. Forum **28**(3), 983–990 (2009). https://doi.org/10.1111/j.1467-8659.2009.01450.x

9. Huang, Q., Cervone, G., Jing, D., Chang, C.: DisasterMapper: a CyberGIS framework for disaster management using social media data. In: Proceedings of the 4th International ACM SIGSPATIAL Workshop on Analytics for Big Geospatial Data, BigSpatial 2015, pp. 1–6. Association for Computing Machinery, New York (2015). https://doi.org/10.1145/2835185.2835189

10. Hynek, J., Kachlík, J., Rusňák, V.: Geovisto: a toolkit for generic geospatial data visualization. In: Proceedings of the 16th International Joint Conference on Computer Vision, Imaging and Computer Graphics Theory and Applications. SCITEPRESS - Science and Technology Publications (2021). https://doi.org/10.5220/0010260401010111

11. Li, X., Anselin, L., Koschinsky, J.: GeoDa web: enhancing web-based mapping with spatial analytics. In: Proceedings of the 23rd SIGSPATIAL International Conference on Advances in Geographic Information Systems, SIGSPATIAL 2015. Association for Computing Machinery, New York (2015). https://doi.org/10.1145/2820783.2820792

12. Liu, Z., Thompson, J., et al.: Data illustrator: augmenting vector design tools with lazy data binding for expressive visualization authoring. In: Proceedings of the 2018 CHI Conference on Human Factors in Computing Systems, CHI 2018, pp. 1–13. Association for Computing Machinery, New York (2018). https://doi.org/10.1145/3173574.3173697

13. Mei, H., Ma, Y., Wei, Y., Chen, W.: The design space of construction tools for information visualization: a survey. J. Visual Lang. Comput. **44**, 120–132 (2018). https://doi.org/10.1016/j.jvlc.2017.10.001

14. Ren, D., Lee, B., Brehmer, M.: Charticulator: interactive construction of bespoke chart layouts. IEEE Trans. Vis. Comput. Graph. **25**(1), 789–799 (2019)

15. Satyanarayan, A., Heer, J.: Lyra: an interactive visualization design environment. In: Proceedings of the 16th Eurographics Conference on Visualization, EuroVis 2014, pp. 351–360. Eurographics Association, Goslar, DEU (2014)

16. Satyanarayan, A., Moritz, D., Wongsuphasawat, K., Heer, J.: Vega-Lite: a grammar of interactive graphics. IEEE Trans. Vis. Comput. Graph. **23**(1), 341–350 (2017)

17. Satyanarayan, A., Russell, R., Hoffswell, J., Heer, J.: Reactive vega: a streaming dataflow architecture for declarative interactive visualization. IEEE Trans. Vis. Comput. Graph. **22**(1), 659–668 (2015)
18. Tableau Software, LLC.: Mapping Concepts in Tableau (2020). https://help. tableau.com/current/pro/desktop/en-us/maps_build.htm, Accessed 10 Feb 2020
19. Xavier, G., Dodge, S.: An exploratory visualization tool for mapping the relationships between animal movement and the environment. In: Proceedings of the 2nd ACM SIGSPATIAL International Workshop on Interacting with Maps, MapInteract 2014, pp. 36–42. Association for Computing Machinery, New York (2014). https://doi.org/10.1145/2677068.2677071

Computer Vision Theory
and Applications

Global-first Training Strategy
with Convolutional Neural Networks to Improve
Scale Invariance

Dinesh Kumar[1]([⊠])[iD] and Dharmendra Sharma[2][iD]

[1] School of Information Technology, Engineering, Mathematics and Physics,
University of the South Pacific, Suva, Fiji
`dinesh.i.kumar@usp.ac.fj`
[2] Faculty of Science and Technology, University of Canberra, ACT, Canberra, Australia
`dharmendra.sharma@canberra.edu.au`

Abstract. Modelled closely on the feedforward conical structure of the primate vision system - Convolutional Neural Networks (CNNs) learn by adopting a local to global feature extraction strategy. This makes them *view-specific* models and results in poor invariance encoding within its learnt weights to adequately identify objects whose appearance is altered by various transformations such as rotations, translations, and scale. Recent physiological studies reveal the visual system first views the scene globally for subsequent processing in its ventral stream leading to a *global-first* response strategy in its recognition function. Conventional CNNs generally use small filters, thus losing the global view of the image. A trainable module proposed by Kumar & Sharma [24] called Stacked Filters Convolution (SFC) models this approach by using a pyramid of large multi-scale filters to extract features from wider areas of the image, which is then trained by a normal CNN. The end-to-end model is referred to as Stacked Filter CNN (SFCNN). In addition to improved test results, SFCNN showed promising results on scale invariance classification. The experiments, however, were performed on small resolution datasets and small CNN as backbone. In this paper, we extend this work and test SFC integrated with the VGG16 network on larger resolution datasets for scale invariance classification. Our results confirm the integration of SFC, and standard CNN also shows promising results on scale invariance on large resolution datasets.

Keywords: Convolutional neural network · Feature map · Filter pyramid · Global feature · Scale invariance · Visual system

1 Introduction

Convolutional Neural Networks (CNNs) are modelled on the physiological understanding of the biological visual system of primates and has its basis firmly grounded to the idea that the visual system extracts and uses local features for classification and recognition of visual objects [25]. Such models have achieved great success in various computer vision tasks such as in image classification, object detection, visual concept discovery, semantic segmentation and boundary detection. Algorithms purely

© Springer Nature Switzerland AG 2023
A. A. de Sousa et al. (Eds.): VISIGRAPP 2021, CCIS 1691, pp. 259–278, 2023.
https://doi.org/10.1007/978-3-031-25477-2_12

based on CNNs or used as a basis of other complicated algorithms such as R-CNN [9], ResNet [12], DenseNet [13], SegNets [2] etc. are applied in various practical application domains such as in self-driving cars, facial recognition authentication systems such as in mobile phones, no-checkout shopping such as Amazon Go store, fashion and textile, medical image processing and quality assurance in manufacturing industries [21].

One of the reasons for the success of CNNs is its ability to extract features automatically from image and video data, thus eliminating the need for requiring prior hand-crafted features which is needed in the case of traditional Machine Learning (ML) methods. This makes CNNs excellent *view-specific* evaluators, meaning they are able to generalise well to objects drawn from the train data distribution. Though they successfully extract local features for object detection, they are not able to learn *invariant features*. This means if the same objects are presented to the CNN for classification for example, in a different size, CNNs do not perform well [15, 17, 27]. Invariance refers to the ability of recognising objects even when the appearance varies in some ways as a result of transformations such as translations, scaling, rotation or reflection.

Recent neuronal and physiological studies have provided new insights into the workings of the brain and Visual Information Processing System (VIPS) in general. These studies are showing the importance of global features towards classification and recognition tasks and suggest the visual system uses both local and global features in its recognition function. More importantly, there are suggestions of a *global-first* response strategy of the visual system to speed-up recognition [11, 14, 44] whereby cells tuned to global features respond to visual stimuli prior to cells tuned on local features. This theory provides the potential for using global features combined with local features to solve transformation invariance problems in CNNs. By design, CNNs employ a *local-to-global* feature extraction strategy using local patch-wise convolution operation using mostly small kernels. This allows the model view localised patches of the image, but unable to consider global views of the image, thus losing out on spatial relationships between features which may be relevant to improving invariance property in the model architecture.

There are some studies that show a combined use of global features with CNN features such as in [22, 23, 55], however, the models are designed to use global features in parallel with CNN features and therefore do not present the CNN networks to train using global features of the images. To extract a *global-first* view of the image to train a CNN is studied in the work of [24]. The authors developed a technique called Stacked Filters Convolution (SFC) to extract features from wider areas of the image by using a pyramid of large multi-scale filters in parallel. The extracted features are then further upscaled in order to a) enhance the extracted features, and b) make the feature map size equivalent to the input image size. The resultant features are then combined and trained on a normal CNN. This end-to-end model is referred to as Stacked Filter CNN. The experiments were performed on small resolution datasets (CIFAR10 [20] and Fashion-MNIST (FMNIST) [52]) and using small CNN (LeNet [25]) as backbone. Their results on small resolution datasets showed effectiveness of the integration of SFC module with the CNN backbone on classification of scaled images sampled from the validation sets of the same datasets. The model however, lacked validation on larger resolution datasets.

In this paper, we extend the work of [24] and test SFC integrated with the pretrained VGG16 network on larger resolution datasets for scale invariance classification. We select PASCAL VOC [7] and ImageHoof [42] datasets for this purpose. We use large multi-scale filters to first extract global features from input images which are upscaled and then combined (similar to the process defined in [24]). However, before training on the VGG16 network, we use a convolutional operation to downsample the combined features depth-wise so that the feature maps have the same dimensions as the input image. Our results confirm the integration of SFC, with CNN also shows promising results on scale invariance on large resolution datasets.

The main contributions of this paper are to extend the work of [24] by

(a) demonstrating the applicability of training CNN's with global features instead of using larger resolution images directly as input;
(b) showing the use of large multi-view filters as an effective way to extract global spatial information from larger resolution images and to serve as global features for learning by CNNs; and
(c) showing the effectiveness of the integration of the SFC module with CNNs on larger resolution images.

The rest of the paper is organised as follows: Sect. 2 reviews related work while Sect. 3 describes the SFC module architecture. Section 4 describes our experiment design and results are presented in Sect. 5. We summarise and point to future directions in Sect. 6.

2 Background

Given this paper is related to topics on global feature extraction using CNNs, use of large kernels to extract multi-scale features from input images and pyramid based methods in CNNs for scale invariant classification, they are reviewed briefly in the following subsections.

2.1 Global Features in Computer Vision

The term *global features* in computer vision refers to describing an image as a whole [30]. They are used to generalise the distribution of the visual information in the object through various statistics that represent information on contours, shape and texture in the image and are useful for tasks such as object detection and classification. *Local features* are used to describe image patches (key points in the image) of an object [4]. These features, represented as lines and curves are basic building blocks of object shapes and are useful for tasks such as object recognition. While local features are effectively extracted in CNNs using small filters performing a patch-wise operation with the target image, extracting global features requires studying the whole image or spatially larger areas of the target image. Several work has been proposed to extract global features from images. This paper considers two categories of global feature extractor methods and their application with CNNs. These categories are:

(a) global feature descriptors; and
(b) large kernels (filters) in CNNs.

Global Feature Descriptors. Several studies report use of global feature descriptors to solve image classification and object detection problems such as HOG [5, 34], invariant moments [51, 54], uniform local-binary patterns (LBP) and discrete cosine transform (DCT) [33], discrete fourier transform (DFT) [44], color and entropy statistics [4], Gabor filters for texture analysis [4], and shape index [30] but mostly without combining with CNNs. In one study, Scale-Invariant Feature Transform (SIFT) is combined with CNN [57] but we note SIFT is classified as a local feature descriptor [49].

A neural network model is proposed by Zhang *et al.* [55] called Histogram of Gradients (HOG) improved CNN (HCNN) that combines texture features from traditional CNNs and global structural features from HOG [5] to cover for the shortness of CNNs in recognising fooling images (where some local features are chaotically distributed). Fusion of global with local features made their network become more sensitive to fooling images despite recording a slight decrease in classification accuracy. The MNIST [26] and a subset of the ImageNet [6] datasets were used to evaluate the performance of HCNN. Figure 1 describes the architecture of HCNN. The model however, was not tested on scale invariance classification. A similar approach is followed in the work of [23] where the authors use a color histogram in addition to HOG as global feature extractors. Their end-to-end network called Global features improved CNN (GCNN) was tested on classification of scaled images. The results showed improved performance of GCNN over well established VGG16 and LeNet5 CNNs on classification of scaled images from the Tiny Imagenet [28] and FMNIST datasets. The GCNN model showed the potential of using global features from input images for training with CNNs to improve scale invariance. However, the global feature extractors HOG and color histogram are non-trainable thus, non-updatable when used with a CNN during the training phase. Furthermore, the models present the fusion of global and local features in a parallel pipeline structure rather than using global features as a priori which is the goal of the SFCNN model.

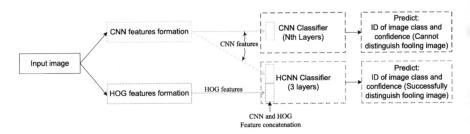

Fig. 1. The HCNN architecture [55]. The HCNN classifier processes concatenated CNN and HOG features (image reproduced from [21]).

Large Kernels (filters) in CNNs. The use of large kernels to extract features from spatially broader areas of the target image have been studied in some work. In the area of semantic segmentation, Peng et al. [36] proposed a Global Convolutional Network (GCN) in which they studied the use of large kernels. Two important design principles were followed for GCN. Firstly, to retain localisation performance, the model structure comprised of only fully convolutional and deconvolutional layers. Secondly, to enable densely connections between feature maps and per-pixel classifiers, large kernel size was adopted in the network architecture. This enhanced the networks capability to handle different transformations. They conducted their experiments on PASCAL VOC dataset and concluded that large kernels play an important role in both classification and localisation tasks. In another piece of work Park and Lee [35] inform extracting information from a large area surrounding the target pixel is essential to extract for example texture information.

The use of large kernels in CNNs also reduces the number of convolutions required to scan the entire image, and thus, requiring less computations. However, with increasing kernel sizes increases the number of parameters (weights) in the network that will require gradient updates. This will potentially slow the back propagation process. Moreso, given additional parameters to process may require additional training cycles to allow the model to reach convergence. These problems can be mitigated by carefully choosing kernel sizes in relation to the input image size and choosing a higher learning rate at the beginning of model training to speed-up convergence. Also, given the improvements in processing capabilities of modern computers and the availability of GPUs provide an opportunity to use large kernels in CNNs. The SFC module in SFCNN uses large kernels to extract features from effectively larger areas of the image.

2.2   Pyramid Based Methods in CNNs for Scale-Invariant Classification

Pyramid based methods have been used to address scale invariance in CNNs to some extent but have been limited to either generating image pyramids, feature map pyramids or filter pyramids.

Image Pyramids. In image pyramid based CNN, copies of the input image are generated at multiple scales forming a pyramid of images. Each scaled image is then processed by a series of convolution and pooling layers independently. These series form a columnar architecture dedicated to processing the original image at multiple resolutions. The final output is computed as an ensemble of outputs from all scale columns [50]. This process is described in Fig. 2. Image pyramid based technique has been practised in the works of [5, 8, 16, 31, 32, 39].

An obvious advantage of image pyramid based methods is the input image is seen by the model at multi-scale levels; hence, allowing the model to develop a representation for the given scale levels. However, scaling the target image to generate image pyramids is similar to applying scale augmentation. In our work, we present no augmentation of the input images.

Feature Pyramids. In feature pyramids methods, some or all levels of feature maps are used towards generating a prediction. The basic feature pyramid based model, referred to as *pyramidal feature hierarchy*, uses all feature maps; hence, all scales for prediction. The final prediction is computed as an ensemble of all feature maps. Figure 3 illustrates this technique. Whilst pyramidal feature hierarchy methods allow use of features from different scales towards prediction, the flow of signals from one feature layer to another remain sequential and one-directional.

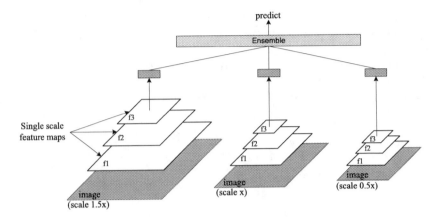

Fig. 2. Image pyramid CNN architecture [50] (image reproduced from [21]).

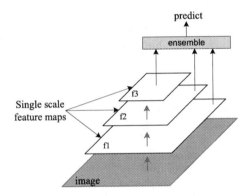

Fig. 3. Pyramidal Feature Hierarchy architecture [19].

For example, [29] exploit the pyramidal hierarchy of feature maps in deep convolutional networks by developing lateral connections from each feature map in the pyramid to build high-level semantic feature maps at all scales. They argue the feature maps of different spatial resolutions produced in the standard CNN introduces semantic gaps caused by different depths. In their work the higher-resolution maps were shown to be important for detecting smaller objects. In the end, they proposed a CNN architecture called Feature Pyramid Network (FPN) in which they developed lateral connections from each feature map in the standard CNN feature pyramid via a top-down pathway. They argued that by developing such lateral connections between feature maps makes CNN scale-invariant, as a change in an object's scale is offset by shifting its level in the pyramid. The FPN architecture allowed them to combine rich semantics from all levels of the feature hierarchy by reusing the original feature maps. Since the feature maps are reused, FPN does not incur much computational overhead. Similar architectures are proposed in works of [18,19,56].

Feature pyramids capitalise on the feature maps of the CNN; hence, come at no extra computation overhead and have been argued to be useful for detecting small objects.

However, the limitation of feature pyramid is that it is built on inherent multi-scale, pyramidal structure of the base CNN networks, which are originally designed for classification tasks [56]. Hence, the features are only limited to the task the base CNN was designed for and may not be suitable for other image processing tasks.

Filter Pyramids. The works of [40,41] claim that visual processing is hierarchical and that along the hierarchy, receptive field sizes of the neurons increases. This structure of the vision system is claimed to build invariance - first to position and scale and then to viewport and other transformations. Inspired by these models the approach of using differently sized convolutional filters in parallel to capture more context is increasingly being explored by researchers [10,22,53]. Google's INCEPTION family of models uses this approach [45–47]. The design of the INCEPTION module [46] is based heavily on the intuition that visual information should be processed at various scales and then aggregated so that subsequent levels can extract abstract features from different scales.

Similarly, based on the concept of large kernels and pyramid based methods, [22] propose a distributed information integration CNN model called D-Net by combining local and global features from images. To extract global features, they developed a trainable layer called Filter Pyramid Convolutions (FPC). In FPC layer, various scale filters (from small to large filters) are applied to progressively cover broader areas of an image. The features extracted are then pooled, resulting compact sized feature maps as output in terms of its spatial dimension. This design however, limited the output of the FPC layer to be used as input in subsequent convolution layers. The design of the FPC layer is adopted in the SFC module. However, to overcome the problem of small scaled output feature maps from FPC layer, the feature maps in SFC module are instead upscaled. The upscaled feature maps allows SFC module output to be used as input in subsequent feature extraction layers of a CNN.

The advantage of using filter pyramids or multi-scale filters such as in the INCEPTION module is that it allows the network to make larger spatial views of the image or feature maps. This allows the network to draw in more semantic information and discriminative features from the input than the conventional small filter sizes in standard CNNs. The limitations of this approach are that larger filter sizes mean more parameters for the network to update, and thus, take longer for network to converge.

3 Stacked Filter CNN (SFCNN)

In this section we describe the trainable module called Stacked Filters Convolution (SFC) proposed in [24] that allows a CNN network take advantage of large kernels to extract global features to improve classification of scaled images. The design of SFC module is inspired by the work of [14] who show that biological visual system utilizes global features prior to local features in detection and recognition. The integration of SFC module with an existing CNN is referred to as Stacked Filter CNN (SFCNN). The SFCNN model is shown in Fig. 4. The core part of SFCNN - SFC is described in the following sub-section.

3.1   Stacked Filters Convolution (SFC) Module

The SFC module contains a collection of filters of varying sizes. This is unlike a traditional CNN where normally a small filter is applied for each convolution in a convolution layer. The multi-scale filters form a pyramidal structure of stacked filters and operate on the target image using the same standard sliding window convolution technique (Fig. 4(a)).

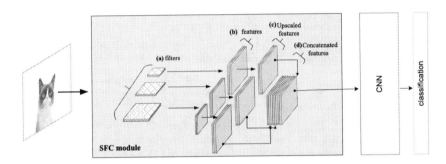

Fig. 4. Architecture of SFCNN with $k = 3$ filters in SFC module (adapted from [24]). In SFC module, multi-scale filters (a) generate multi-scale feature pyramids (b) which are upscaled using bilinear upscaling method. These feature maps are upscaled to a the same resolution (h, w) as the input image, concatenated (d) and then passed to the CNN network for further feature extraction.

The main aim of each filter with dimensions (k_h, k_w) in the filter-stack is to produce a feature map as output with dimensions (f_h, f_w) which can be upscaled (in its height and width dimensions only using a non-recurring scale factor (u)), to same size as the input image I; that is, $(f_{(h*u)}, f_{(w*u)}) = (I_h, I_w)$. The value of hyper parameters *stride* and *padding* are also considered for selection of the dimensions of each filter. Subsequently, sizes of other filters are identified using a similar process.

Since each filter produces multi-scale feature maps (Fig. 4(b)), these maps are then normalised to produce a uniform size final feature maps equivalent to the size of the input image (Fig. 4(c)). Here, the technique of *bilinear* upscaling method is used. Finally all upsampled feature maps are concatenated and passed to the next layer (Fig. 4(d)). Since the SFC module is the only layer that gets to inspect the target image, [24] proposes the inclusion of a small filter in the filter-stack. This is to allow extracting local features from the target image which would otherwise be lost. In this way, the SFC module also allows local features to be collected and packed together with global features for onward processing. In our implementation of the SFC module, we further downsample the concatenated features (in the depth dimension) using a convolution operation so that the final output feature maps are the same size as the input image.

3.2   Forward and Backward Propagation in SFC Module

A forward pass is achieved by passing an input image to the SFC module which applies convolutions with each filter from a filter stack and outputs a stack of feature maps as a result. This process repeats for all stacks of filters in the layer resulting in stacks of output feature maps of different scales accordingly. The stack of output feature maps are then upsampled to generate uniform-sized outputs in terms of height and width of the feature maps in all stacks. The shape of each stack of upscaled features is saved for use in backward propagation. The upscaled stack of features are finally concatenated for forward propagation into the traditional CNN network (described in [25]).

The backward function in SFC module receives gradients from the network. The gradients are then unstacked or slices in the exact same dimensions and shape of the individual stack of feature maps that were concatenated during the forward pass. This results in stacks of gradients maps corresponding to each stacked upscaled feature maps (during forward pass). Each stack of gradient is max pooled by the same factor that was used to upscale the feature maps initially during the forward pass. Using chain rule derivative algorithm these gradients are then used to update the weights of filters in the corresponding filter stacks.

4   Experiments

In Kumar and Sharma [24], experiments to test the efficacy of SFC integrated with a CNN is conducted using CIFAR10 and FMNIST datasets trained with LeNet5 as the CNN module. Their experiments however, were performed on small resolution datasets and using small CNN. In this paper we extend their work by testing SFCNN on larger resolution datasets. This section describes the selected large resolution datasets, the VGG16 architecture and SFC parameters.

4.1   Datasets

ImageHoof. A subset of the ImageNet dataset, ImageHoof contains images of all dog breeds. The dataset is freely available from *fastai* DL library [42]. This dataset consists of 12,954 training images and 3929 test images in color. There is no validation set. The images are divided into 10 mutually exclusive classes representing names of ten dog breeds. The original ImageHoof dataset is highly imbalanced and contains images of various resolutions. This dataset is therefore preprocessed prior to usage. First, ratio of train and test images is adjusted to 80%/20% respectively from the initial 67%/43%. This was done to shift more images to the training batch. Secondly, images from the training set were transferred to the test set for classes which had fewer images in population. Post preprocessing, the ImageHoof dataset contained a total of 13500 images consisting of 10800 and 2700 in the train and test set respectively.

PASCAL VOC. The PASCAL Visual Object Classes (VOC) 2012 dataset is widely used as a benchmark dataset for object detection, semantic segmentation, and classification tasks [7]. The images are divided into 20 mutually exclusive classes representing names aeroplane, bicycle, boat, bus, car, motorbike, train, bottle, chair, dining table, potted plant, sofa, TV/monitor, bird, cat, cow, dog, horse, sheep, and person. The dataset is split into three subsets containing pixel-level segmentation annotations, bounding box annotations and object class annotations. For the purpose of this research we combine images from all three subsets resulting in 13351 for training and 3477 for testing.

4.2   VGG16 Network

Since our goal is to test large resolution datasets on the SFC module and train on a CNN network, we select the VGG16 network for this purpose. Here, the VGG16 network is utilised for benchmarking and also for integrating global features extracted through SFC to a CNN network. Proposed by Simonyan & Zisserman [43], VGG16 is a popular CNN model used by researchers in the computer vision field for image classification and segmentation tasks. It was originally trained on ImageNet dataset that contains over 14 million images categorised into 1000 classes. Several configurations of the VGG CNN exist, ranging from 11, 13, 16 and 19 weight layers. These configurations are labelled A-E and differ only in the depth. In this work, configuration D is used that contains 16 weight layers comprising of 13 convolution and 3 hidden layers in the fully connected part of the network. All convolution layers are configured with 3×3 filter sizes. The network also uses maxpooling layers and is used in several work such as in [1,37,38]. In this work, VGG16 network is trained on PASCAL VOC and ImageHoof datasets. The architecture of VGG16 is described in Table 1. This includes information on network structure and hyper-parameter settings. Since the VGG16 architecture is unchanged in our implementation provided us with the opportunity to use transfer learning, where we use the pretrained weights of the VGG16 implementation trained on the ImageNet dataset from PyTorch v1.2.0 deep learning library.

Table 1. VGG16 - Configuration D - CNN architecture.

VGG16 - Configuration D - 16 weight layers					
Input image size: 224×224 RGB image					
Layer	Layer type	# of filters/neurons	Filter/pool size	Padding	stride
1	convolution	64	3×3	1	1
2	convolution	64	3×3	1	1
	maxpool		2×2		2
3	convolution	128	3×3	1	1
4	convolution	128	3×3	1	1
	maxpool		2×2		2
5	convolution	256	3×3	1	1
6	convolution	256	3×3	1	1
7	convolution	256	3×3	1	1
	maxpool		2×2		2
8	convolution	512	3×3	1	1
9	convolution	512	3×3	1	1
10	convolution	512	3×3	1	1
	maxpool		2×2		2
11	convolution	512	3×3	1	1
12	convolution	512	3×3	1	1
13	convolution	512	3×3	1	1
	maxpool		2×2		2
14	fully connected	4096			
15	fully connected	4096			
16	fully connected	1000			
	softmax				

4.3   SFC Hyper-Parameters

We follow a similar approach for selection of the hyper-parameters for the SFC module as described in [24]. For training on ImageHoof and PASCAL VOC datasets, the SFC module in our implementation was constructed with 4 stacks of filters ($k\_stacks = 34$) having filters of sizes (3×3), (25×25), (65×65) and (113×113) respectively. The filter sizes are selected so that using appropriate upscaling factor, the resultant feature maps can be upscaled to (224×224) which is the input image size for the VGG16 network. Each stack is initialised with 16 filters ($n\_filters = 16$). We set $stride = 1$ for all stacks, $padding = 1$ for stack with 3×3 filters, $padding = 0$ for the rest of the stacks and upscaling factors $1, 2, 1.4, 1.12$ respectively for each filter stack. The final shape of the concatenated stacks of feature maps on the datasets is $(64 \times 224 \times 224)$ where $64 = k\_stacks \times n\_filters$. Table 2 describes the hyper-parameters in detail.

Table 2. Description of hyper-parameters and calculation of final output feature map sizes in the SFC module. The output size of the intermediate feature map in column (E) is dependent on the filter size (column (B)), *stride* and *padding* and must satisfy the condition that multiplied with a non-recurring upscaling factor must equal to the image size (column G) where $(I_h, I_w) = (O_h, O_w)$. The same SFC module parameters are applied to both ImageHoof and PASCAL VOC datasets.

(A) image size (I_h, I_w)	(B) filter size k_h, k_w	(C) stride s	(D) padding p	(E) feature map output size (f_h, f_w) $(f_h = (I_h + 2p) - k_h + 1)/s$ $(f_w = (I_w + 2p) - k_w + 1)/s$	(F) up-scaling factor	(G) final output map size (O_h, O_w)
224×224	113×113	1	0	112×112	2	224×224
224×224	65×65	1	0	160×160	1.4	224×224
224×224	25×25	1	0	200×200	1.12	224×224
224×224	3×3	1	1	224×224	1	224×224

4.4   The SFCNN Network

The complete SFCNN network used for training and evaluation on the task of scale invariance classification in this paper is given in Fig. 5. The network architecture is similar to the SFCNN architecture proposed in [24]. However, batch normalisation is applied to the output of SFC module in order to reduce generalisation error and to speed up training, without increasing overfitting [3]. Before training on the pretrained VGG16 network, the SFC module output is further downsampled in the *depth* dimension using a convolution operation. This was done to make the resolution of the SFC feature maps equivalent to a standard image resolution so that it can be accepted by the VGG16 network as input. This step was required in order to use transfer learning on the SFC output.

4.5   Training Process

First we establish benchmark results by training the pretrained VGG16 network on ImageHoof and PASCAL VOC datasets separately. This establishes our benchmark

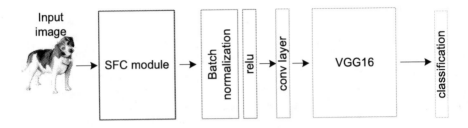

Fig. 5. Architecture of the SFCNN network used on ImageHoof and PASCAL VOC datasets.

results against which we compare results of the respective SFCNN networks. Then we integrate SFC module with the VGG16 network as shown in Fig. 5 and retrain on ImageHoof and PASCAL VOC datasets respectively. Hence, we obtain a total of four trained models for comparison (two models per dataset). The training parameters for our models are described in Table 3. We abbreviate the VGG16 trained networks on ImageHoof and PASCAL VOC datasets as *VGG16-Imh* and *VGG16-voc* respectively, and *SFCNN-Imh* and *SFCNN-voc* for SFCNN trained networks.

Table 3. Summary of training parameters for the benchmark CNNs and SFCNN models.

	Dataset			
	ImageHoof		PASCAL VOC	
Network name	VGG16-Imh	SFCNN-Imh	VGG16-voc	SFCNN-voc
Learning rate	0.001 (epochs 1–20)	0.001 (epoch 1) 0.0001 (epochs 2–20)	0.0001 - epochs 1–20	
Training epochs	20			
CNN activation function	relu			
FC activation function	sigmoid			
Transfer learning	yes			
Momentum	0.9			
Weight decay	0.0001			
Optimiser	Stochastic gradient decent			
Loss function	Cross-entropy			
Train batch size	16			
Test batch size	1			
DL library	PyTorch v1.2.0			
Hardware	Dell Precision T7910 64 GB RAM Nvidia Geforce Titan X 12 GB GPU			

4.6   Scaled Images for Testing

Scaled images are prepared from the test set of each dataset for testing respective VGG16 and SFCNN netwirks. This process is described in detail in [24]. 7 scale categories - $[150, 140, 120, 100, 80, 60, 50]$ are established to test the models. Numbers > 100 indicate enlargement while < 100 indicate reduction in the size of an image. 50 test images per class from ImageHoof and PASCAL VOC datasets, are selected at random. Each image is then scaled according to the scale percentage defined in the scale category list, resulting in an additional 6 scaled images per class in addition to the original image (of scale 100%). In this way, for each class in each dataset, 7 scale category folders are created and respective scaled images stored in them accordingly. Using this process, 350 scaled images per class are sampled from each dataset. Furthermore, an *ensemble* dataset is created by combining all scaled images from all classes for each dataset. This resulted in a total of 3500 scaled images for testing on ImageHoof dataset (10 *classes* $\times 350$) and 7000 scaled images on PASCAL VOC dataset (20 *classes* $\times 350$) respectively. Figure 6 shows an example image from each dataset and its corresponding scaled versions for testing. The models are analysed on scaled images from each of these scale categories independently as well as on the ensemble dataset.

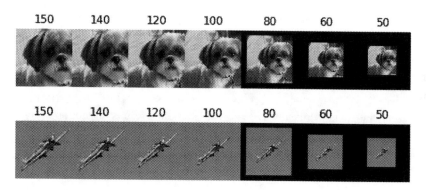

Fig. 6. An example of scaled test images from datasets PASCAL VOC - aeroplane (*bottom*) and ImageHoof - n02086240 (Shih-Tzu) (*top*). The numbers indicate percentage image is scaled to. 100 indicates no scaling.

4.7 Evaluation Metrics

The *accuracy* metric is used to evaluate the trained models on scale categories. Accuracy is an intuitive performance measure to simply evaluate the generalisation capability the models by finding out the total number of scaled images that were correctly classified in the respective scale categories. The top-1 and top-5 accuracy of each network on the scale categories is evaluated.

5 Results and Discussion

In this section we discuss the results of SFCNN in two specific areas. First, we compare the train and test statistics of SFCNN with the benchmark VGG16 trained models. Second, the models trained are evaluated on scaled images.

5.1   Comparing Train and Test Statistics on Non-scaled Images

The convergence of deep learning models are usually influenced by the choice of hyper-parameters and the number of trainable parameters. Networks with a large parameter base usually converge slowly and take a longer time to train. In addition to the inclusion of a benchmark CNN within the SFCNN network, the SFC module contains components that directly increase the size of the network parameters. This mainly refers to the large multi-scale filters introduced in SFC. It is therefore expected that the SFCNN network would require more epochs to train to reach the level of results obtained by the VGG16 network given similar training environment. Despite this challenge, we attempted to train the models for the same number of epochs by carefully choosing the learning rates.

Table 4 compares the train and test statistics (accuracy and loss) for all the networks. These statistics are evaluations on the raw train and test images without any form of scale jittering. Whilst the pretrained *VGG16-Imh* model overfits the ImageHoof dataset, *SFCNN-Imh* reveals a stable train and test results despite the increase in parameters in the network and when trained for the same number of epochs. While *SFCNN-Imh* train losses are higher, the network achieves the same test result of 92.1% as the *VGG16-Imh* network using pretrained weights. On the other hand, significant results are obtained on PASCAL VOC dataset where *SFCNN-voc* outperforms the *VGG16-voc* network on train and test statistics. Here, *SFCNN-voc* achieved a difference in accuracy of 2.5% higher than the *VGG16-voc* network indicating that SFCNN network performs better on datasets that are non-ImageNet based. These baseline results provide some evidence that training CNN networks on features extracted from larger areas of the input image using large kernels is useful in improving the generalisation capability of the models studied in this paper.

Table 4. Train and test statistics of SFCNN and benchmark CNNs.

Model	Train acc	Train loss	Test acc	Difference (loss)	Difference (test acc)
ImageHoof					
VGG16-Imh	1.000	0.001	0.921		
SFCNN-Imh	0.996	0.015	**0.921**	**0.014**	**0.0%**
PASCAL VOC					
VGG16-voc	0.665	0.616	0.572		
SFCNN-voc	**0.665**	**0.547**	**0.597**	**−0.069**	**+2.5%**

5.2   Evaluation of SFCNN on Scaled Images

The classification results of the models on different scale categories and on different datasets can be viewed in Table 5. The column *hit rate* indicates the number of scale categories SFCNN outperformed the benchmark. Similar to [24], for this study, hit rate of $>= 50\%$ is desirable, that is, SFCNN should at least perform better on 50% of the scale categories compared to the benchmark VGG16 only networks. Since the ensemble test dataset combines all scaled images in one batch it is excluded from this ratio.

Classifications accuracies are obtained by testing the studied models on scaled images from each scale category.

Compared with the benchmark CNNs, the performance of SFCNN is evaluated on scaled images in two categories as follows:

(i) Generalisation on larger resolution datasets, and
(ii) Effect on enlarged and reduced image scales

Table 5. Performance summarisation (top-1 and top-5 accuracy) of SFCNN and benchmark CNNs on all the scale categories. The difference in accuracy between SFCNN and benchmark CNNs are shown as percentages in brackets. A positive figure indicates higher accuracy of SFCNN over the benchmark CNN on the respective scale category.

| Model | Metric | Enseble | Scale categories (scale size in (%)) | | | | | | | |
			150	140	120	100	80	60	50	hit rate
ImageHoof										
VGG16-Imh	Top-1 acc	0.889	0.880	0.900	0.926	0.926	0.892	0.872	0.820	
SFCNN-Imh		0.871	**0.892**	**0.914**	0.924	**0.928**	**0.904**	0.844	0.760	0.571
		(−1.8%)	(+1.2%)	(+1.4%)	(−0.2%)	(+0.2%)	(+1.2%)	(−2.8%)	(−6.0%)	(4/7)
ImageHoof										
VGG16-Imh	Top-5 acc	0.991	0.984	0.992	0.988	0.992	0.994	0.992	0.988	
SFCNN-Imh		0.987	**0.986**	**0.994**	**0.994**	**0.992**	0.986	0.978	0.980	0.571
		(−0.4%)	(+0.2%)	(+0.2%)	(+0.6%)	(0.0%)	(−0.8%)	(−1.4%)	(-0.8%)	(4/7)
PASCAL VOC										
VGG16-voc	Top-1 acc	0.440	0.513	0.513	0.519	0.543	0.406	0.323	0.270	
SFCNN-voc		**0.497**	**0.566**	**0.588**	**0.587**	**0.585**	**0.551**	**0.334**	0.240	0.857
		(+5.7%)	(+5.3%)	(+7.5%)	(+6.8%)	(+4.2%)	(+14.5%)	(+1.1%)	(−3.0%)	(6/7)
PASCAL VOC										
VGG16-voc	Top-5 acc	0.825	0.875	0.883	0.902	0.900	0.797	0.736	0.662	
SFCNN-voc		**0.858**	**0.908**	**0.917**	**0.929**	**0.926**	**0.896**	**0.757**	**0.666**	1.000
		(+3.3%)	(+3.3%)	(+3.4%)	(+2.7%)	(+2.6%)	(+9.9%)	(+2.1%)	(+0.4%)	(7/7)

Generalisation on Larger Resolution Datasets. The performance of SFCNN on small resolution datasets - CIFAR10 and FMNIST has been studied in the work of [24]. When tested on scaled images on various scale categories, their results revealed that the SFCNN network performed better on color images (CIFAR10) than on grey-scale images (FMNIST). They concluded that spatial features extracted from larger areas of the target image during training helped improve scale invariance in CNN networks, in particular for color images. This research has aimed to further extend the work of [24] by testing SFCNN on larger resolution datasets. ImageHoof and PASCAL VOC were selected for this purpose. Here, the hit rates of SFCNN on both datasets are > 50% indicating higher accuracy on majority of the scale categories than the benchmark VGG16 only networks. Significant results are obtained on PASCAL VOC dataset where the *SFCNN-voc* network outperforms the *VGG16-voc* network on 6 out of the 7 scale categories (top-1 accuracy) and on all scale categories considering top-5 accuracy (hite rate = 100%).

Images from the various scale categories are combined in the ensemble test set. The average of the test accuracies on all scale categories determines the accuracy of the ensemble category. The higher classification accuracy score (both top-1 (49.7%) and top-5 (85.8%)) on the PASCAL VOC ensemble test set is directly contributed by the individual scale category accuracies. For example, the top-1 accuracy score of *SFCNN-voc* network is higher than the benchmark *VGG16-voc* network by 5.7% which amounts to 399 more scaled images classified correctly. Furthermore, SFCNN top-5 accuracies indicate the model is able to predict the correct class of the scaled image in its top 5 predictions. For ImageHoof dataset, whilst the *SFCNN-Imh* network produces better results on majority of the scale categories, its performance on the ensemble dataset is lower than the benchmark *VGG16-Imh* networks. This means that the difference in accuracy (both top-1 and top-5) of the *SFCNN-Imh* networks on reduced scaled images was much lower than the benchmark *VGG16-Imh* networks.

From the above results we observe that pretrained networks such as the VGG16 would produce competitive results when trained on datasets sampled from the ImageNet distribution such as the ImageHoof dataset. However, when non-ImageNet based datasets are used, SFCNN networks perform better. Our results also indicate that regardless of the source of data, training CNNs with spatial global features improves network generalisation and its ability to classify scaled images.

Effect on Enlarged and Reduced Image Scales. Accuracy scores of SFCNN are compared with VGG16 networks on scaled up images (categories $[150, 140, 120]$). For these categories the best performing SFCNN is on PASCAL VOC dataset (*SFCNN-voc*) recording an average accuracy of $+6.3\%$ more than the benchmark *VGG16-voc* network (top-1 accuracy). A possible reason presented to explain this is the process of upscaling feature maps in the SFC module blurs the features thus smoothing edges and removing noise from an image in the process, thus improving classification accuracy. Though *SFCNN-Imh* records an average top-1 accuracy of $+1.2\%$ on ImageHoof dataset, it underperforms on scale category $[120]$. Upon investigation, the lower accuracies recorded on ImageHoof dataset were found to be attributed to a possible overfitting of the *VGG16-voc* and *SFCNN-voc* model given that the dataset is already seen by the pretrained VGG16 CNN.

Comparing accuracy scores on scaled down images (categories $[80, 60, 50]$), promising performance of SFCNN is noted over VGG16 network trained on PASCAL VOC dataset. Here, average accuracy score is higher by 4.2% considering top-1 accuracy. However, there is poor performance of SFCNN on reduced scaled down Imagehoof images. Relating the feature map upscaling method with inter-class similarities of images of dogs revealed that whilst blurring helped smooth edges and remove noise, it also resulted in low-variation in feature maps as a result of similarities that existed in the original Imagehoof dataset such as color of dogs.

Scale category $[100]$ is where images are in their original state (unscaled). In this category test accuracy of SFCNN surpasses benchmark CNNs by 0.2% on ImageHoof dataset and 4.2% on PASCAL VOC dataset respectively.

6   Conclusion

In this paper, we extend the work of [24] and test SFC module integrated with the pretrained VGG16 network on larger resolution datasets for scale invariance classification.

The SFC module is developed to model the *global-first* feature extraction strategy of the primate vision system proposed by [14]. In SFC module, global spatial features are extracted from the target image using large multi-scale kernels resulting in multi-scale feature maps. The multi-scale feature maps are upscaled to a uniform resolution and then combined. A convolution operation downsamples the feature maps which is then trained using a pretrained VGG16 network. The end-to-end network is referred to as SFCNN.

We study the effects of *global-first* feature extraction on scale invariance by evaluating SFCNN's ability to classify test images subjected to scale transformations and compare with established benchmarks results obtained in this research. Our results confirm SFCNN also generalises well on larger resolution datasets in addition to improving the network's ability to classify scaled images. From our experimental results we conclude that spatial features extracted from larger areas of the target image during training help in improving the scale invariance capability of CNN based networks.

The advantage of SFCNN lies in its ability to extract features from spatially larger areas of the input image using larger kernels. This overcomes the shortcomings of standard CNNs that usually apply smaller kernels which are more effective in extracting local features. The introduction of large multi-scale kernels in SFC module however, increases the network parameters. Furthermore, the SFC module generates larger feature maps as a result of upscaling which in turn requires more convolution operations in subsequent layers in the network. The concatenation of upscaled features further increases the volume of the feature maps. These limitations ultimately lead to increased computation time for SFCNN.

Problems and opportunities that require further investigations are to a) test SFCNN on the ImageNet dataset, b) test on image resolutions larger than 224×224, c) trial other upscaling methods to upscale feature maps in SFC module, d) test SFCNN on other forms of transformations such as rotations and translations, and e) integrate SFC module with other benchmark CNNs such as ResNet and EfficientNet [48].

References

1. Alippi, C., Disabato, S., Roveri, M.: Moving convolutional neural networks to embedded systems: the alexnet and vgg-16 case. In: 2018 17th ACM/IEEE International Conference on Information Processing in Sensor Networks (IPSN), pp. 212–223. IEEE (2018)
2. Badrinarayanan, V., Kendall, A., Cipolla, R.: Segnet: A deep convolutional encoder-decoder architecture for image segmentation. IEEE Trans. Pattern Anal. Mach. Intell. **39**(12), 2481–2495 (2017)
3. Bjorck, N., Gomes, C.P., Selman, B., Weinberger, K.Q.: Understanding batch normalization. In: Advances in Neural Information Processing Systems 31 (2018)
4. Bosch, M., Zhu, F., Khanna, N., Boushey, C.J., Delp, E.J.: Combining global and local features for food identification in dietary assessment. In: 2011 18th IEEE International Conference on Image Processing, pp. 1789–1792. IEEE (2011)
5. Dalal, N., Triggs, B.: Histograms of oriented gradients for human detection. In: 2005 IEEE Computer Society Conference on Computer Vision and Pattern Recognition (CVPR 2005), pp. 886–893 (2005)
6. Deng, J., Dong, W., Socher, R., Li, L.J., Li, K., Fei-Fei, L.: ImageNet: A Large-Scale Hierarchical Image Database. In: CVPR 2009 (2009)

7. Everingham, M., Van Gool, L., Williams, C.K.I., Winn, J., Zisserman, A.: The pascal visual object classes (voc) challenge. Int. J. Comput. Vis. **88**(2), 303–338 (2010)
8. Felzenszwalb, P.F., Girshick, R.B., McAllester, D., Ramanan, D.: Object detection with discriminatively trained part-based models. IEEE Trans. Pattern Anal. Mach. Intell. **32**(9), 1627–1645 (2009)
9. Girshick, R., Donahue, J., Darrell, T., Malik, J.: Rich feature hierarchies for accurate object detection and semantic segmentation. In: Proceedings of the IEEE Conference On Computer Vision And Pattern Recognition, pp. 580–587 (2014)
10. Gong, Y., Wang, L., Guo, R., Lazebnik, S.: Multi-scale orderless pooling of deep convolutional activation features. In: Fleet, D., Pajdla, T., Schiele, B., Tuytelaars, T. (eds.) ECCV 2014. LNCS, vol. 8695, pp. 392–407. Springer, Cham (2014). https://doi.org/10.1007/978-3-319-10584-0_26
11. Han, Y., Roig, G., Geiger, G., Poggio, T.: Is the human visual system invariant to translation and scale? In: 2017 AAAI Spring Symposium Series (2017)
12. He, K., Zhang, X., Ren, S., Sun, J.: Deep residual learning for image recognition. In: Proceedings of the IEEE Conference On Computer Vision And Pattern Recognition, pp. 770–778 (2016)
13. Huang, G., Liu, Z., Van Der Maaten, L., Weinberger, K.Q.: Densely connected convolutional networks. In: Proceedings of the IEEE Conference On Computer Vision And Pattern Recognition, pp. 4700–4708 (2017)
14. Huang, J., et al.: Rapid processing of a global feature in the on visual pathways of behaving monkeys. Front. Neurosci. **11**, 474 (2017). https://doi.org/10.3389/fnins.2017.00474
15. Jaderberg, M., Simonyan, K., Zisserman, A., Kavukcuoglu, K.: Spatial transformer networks. In: Advances in Neural Information Processing Systems 28, pp. 2017–2025. Curran Associates, Inc. (2015)
16. Kanazawa, A., Sharma, A., Jacobs, D.W.: Locally scale-invariant convolutional neural networks. CoRR abs/ arXiv: 1412.5104 (2014)
17. Kauderer-Abrams, E.: Quantifying translation-invariance in convolutional neural networks. arXiv preprint arXiv:1801.01450 (2017)
18. Kim, S.-W., Kook, H.-K., Sun, J.-Y., Kang, M.-C., Ko, S.-J.: Parallel feature pyramid network for object detection. In: Ferrari, V., Hebert, M., Sminchisescu, C., Weiss, Y. (eds.) ECCV 2018. LNCS, vol. 11209, pp. 239–256. Springer, Cham (2018). https://doi.org/10.1007/978-3-030-01228-1_15
19. Kong, T., Sun, F., Huang, W., Liu, H.: Deep feature pyramid reconfiguration for object detection. In: Ferrari, V., Hebert, M., Sminchisescu, C., Weiss, Y. (eds.) ECCV 2018. LNCS, vol. 11209, pp. 172–188. Springer, Cham (2018). https://doi.org/10.1007/978-3-030-01228-1_11
20. Krizhevsky, A., Hinton, G., et al.: Learning multiple layers of features from tiny images. Tech. rep, Citeseer (2009)
21. Kumar, D.: Multi-modal Information Extraction and Fusion with Convolutional Neural Networks for Classification of Scaled Images. Ph.D. thesis, University of Canberra, Canberra, Australia (2020)
22. Kumar, D., Sharma, D.: Distributed information integration in convolutional neural networks. In: Proceedings of the 15th International Joint Conference on Computer Vision, Imaging and Computer Graphics Theory and Applications - VISAPP, vol. 5, pp. 491–498. SciTePress (2020). https://doi.org/10.5220/0009150404910498
23. Kumar, D., Sharma, D.: Multi-modal information extraction and fusion with convolutional neural networks. In: 2020 International Joint Conference on Neural Networks (IJCNN), pp. 1–9. IEEE World Congress on Computational Intelligence (IEEE WCCI) (2020). https://doi.org/10.1109/IJCNN48605.2020.9206803

24. Kumar, D., Sharma, D.: Feature map upscaling to improve scale invariance in convolutional neural networks. In: Proceedings of the 16th International Joint Conference on Computer Vision, Imaging and Computer Graphics Theory and Applications, vol. 5, pp. 113–122 (Febuary 2021). https://doi.org/10.5220/0010246001130122

25. LeCun, Y., Bottou, L., Bengio, Y., Haffner, P., et al.: Gradient-based learning applied to document recognition. Proc. IEEE **86**(11), 2278–2324 (1998)

26. LeCun, Y., Cortes, C., Burges, C.J.: The mnist database of handwritten digits, vol. 10(34), p. 14 (1998). http://yann.lecun.com/exdb/mnist/

27. Lenc, K., Vedaldi, A.: Understanding image representations by measuring their equivariance and equivalence. In: CVPR (2015)

28. Li, F.F., Karpathy, A., Johnson, J.: Tiny ImageNet Visual Recognition Challenge (2019). https://tiny-imagenet.herokuapp.com/. (Accessed 30-Dec-2019)

29. Lin, T.Y., Dollár, P., Girshick, R., He, K., Hariharan, B., Belongie, S.: Feature pyramid networks for object detection. In: Proceedings of the IEEE Conference On Computer Vision And Pattern Recognition, pp. 2117–2125 (2017)

30. Lisin, D.A., Mattar, M.A., Blaschko, M.B., Learned-Miller, E.G., Benfield, M.C.: Combining local and global image features for object class recognition. In: 2005 IEEE Computer Society Conference on Computer Vision and Pattern Recognition (CVPR 2005)-Workshops, p. 47. IEEE (2005)

31. Lowe, D.G.: Distinctive image features from scale-invariant keypoints. Int. J. Comput. Vision **60**(2), 91–110 (2004)

32. Marcos, D., Kellenberger, B., Lobry, S., Tuia, D.: Scale equivariance in cnns with vector fields. arXiv preprint arXiv:1807.11783 (2018)

33. Margae, S., Ait Kerroum, M., Fakhri, Y.: Fusion of local and global feature extraction based on uniform lbp and dct for traffic sign recognition. In: International Review on Computers and Software (IRECOS) vol. 10 (January 2015). https://doi.org/10.15866/irecos.v10i1.5051

34. Nguyen, T.K., Coustaty, M., Guillaume, J.L.: A combination of histogram of oriented gradients and color features to cooperate with louvain method based image segmentation. In: VISIGRAPP 2019 (2019)

35. Park, H., Lee, K.M.: Look wider to match image patches with convolutional neural networks. IEEE Signal Process. Lett. **24**(12), 1788–1792 (2016)

36. Peng, C., Zhang, X., Yu, G., Luo, G., Sun, J.: Large kernel matters-improve semantic segmentation by global convolutional network. In: Proceedings of the IEEE Conference On Computer Vision And Pattern Recognition, pp. 4353–4361 (2017)

37. Ren, S., He, K., Girshick, R., Sun, J.: Faster r-cnn: Towards real-time object detection with region proposal networks. In: Advances in Neural Information Processing Systems, pp. 91–99 (2015)

38. Saqib, M., Khan, S.D., Sharma, N., Blumenstein, M.: A study on detecting drones using deep convolutional neural networks. In: 2017 14th IEEE International Conference on Advanced Video and Signal Based Surveillance (AVSS), pp. 1–5. IEEE (2017)

39. Sermanet, P., Eigen, D., Zhang, X., Mathieu, M., Fergus, R., LeCun, Y.: Overfeat: Integrated recognition, localization and detection using convolutional networks. arXiv preprint arXiv:1312.6229 (2013)

40. Serre, T.: Hierarchical models of the visual system. In: Jaeger, D., Jung, R. (eds.) Encyclopedia of Computational Neuroscience, pp. 1–12. Springer, New York (2013). https://doi.org/10.1007/978-1-4614-6675-8_345

41. Serre, T., Wolf, L., Bileschi, S., Riesenhuber, M., Poggio, T.: Robust object recognition with cortex-like mechanisms. IEEE Trans. Pattern Anal. Mach. Intell. **29**(3), 411–426 (2007). https://doi.org/10.1109/TPAMI.2007.56

42. Shaw, A.: Imagehoof dataset (2019). https://github.com/fastai/imagenette/blob/master/README.md. (Accessed 10-Dec-2019)

43. Simonyan, K., Zisserman, A.: Very deep convolutional networks for large-scale image recognition. arXiv preprint arXiv:1409.1556 (2014)
44. Su, Y., Shan, S., Chen, X., Gao, W.: Hierarchical ensemble of global and local classifiers for face recognition. IEEE Trans. Image Process. **18**(8), 1885–1896 (2009)
45. Szegedy, C., Ioffe, S., Vanhoucke, V., Alemi, A.A.: Inception-v4, inception-resnet and the impact of residual connections on learning. In: Thirty-First AAAI Conference on Artificial Intelligence (2017)
46. Szegedy, C., et al.: Going deeper with convolutions. In: Proceedings of the IEEE Conference On Computer Vision And Pattern Recognition, pp. 1–9 (2015)
47. Szegedy, C., Vanhoucke, V., Ioffe, S., Shlens, J., Wojna, Z.: Rethinking the inception architecture for computer vision. In: Proceedings of the IEEE Conference On Computer Vision And Pattern Recognition, pp. 2818–2826 (2016)
48. Tan, M., Le, Q.V.: Efficientnet: Rethinking model scaling for convolutional neural networks. arXiv preprint arXiv:1905.11946 (2019)
49. ping Tian, D., et al.: A review on image feature extraction and representation techniques. Int. J. Multimedia Ubiquitous Eng. **8**(4), 385–396 (2013)
50. Wang, H., Kembhavi, A., Farhadi, A., Yuille, A.L., Rastegari, M.: Elastic: Improving cnns with dynamic scaling policies. In: Proceedings of the IEEE Conference on Computer Vision and Pattern Recognition, pp. 2258–2267 (2019)
51. Wu, J., Qiu, S., Kong, Y., Chen, Y., Senhadji, L., Shu, H.: Momentsnet: a simple learning-free method for binary image recognition. In: IEEE International Conference on Image Processing (ICIP), pp. 2667–2671. IEEE (2017)
52. Xiao, H., Rasul, K., Vollgraf, R.: Fashion-MNIST: a Novel Image Dataset for Benchmarking Machine Learning Algorithms. Tech. rep., arXiv (2017)
53. Zagoruyko, S., Komodakis, N.: Learning to compare image patches via convolutional neural networks. In: Proceedings of the IEEE Conference On Computer Vision And Pattern Recognition, pp. 4353–4361 (2015)
54. Zekovich, S., Tuba, M.: Hu moments based handwritten digits recognition algorithm. In: Recent Advances in Knowledge Engineering and Systems Science (2013)
55. Zhang, T., Zeng, Y., Xu, B.: Hcnn: A neural network model for combining local and global features towards human-like classification. Int. J. Pattern Recognit Artif Intell. **30**(01), 1655004 (2016)
56. Zhao, Q., et al.: M2det: A single-shot object detector based on multi-level feature pyramid network. In: Proceedings of the AAAI Conference on Artificial Intelligence, vol. 33, pp. 9259–9266 (2019)
57. Zheng, L., Yang, Y., Tian, Q.: Sift meets cnn: A decade survey of instance retrieval. IEEE Trans. Pattern Anal. Mach. Intell. **40**(5), 1224–1244 (2017)

Spline-Based Dense Medial Descriptors for Image Simplification Using Saliency Maps

Jieying Wang[4]([⊠]) [ID], Leonardo de Melo[2] [ID], Alexandre X. Falcão[2] [ID], Jiří Kosinka[1] [ID], and Alexandru Telea[3] [ID]

[1] Bernoulli Institute, University of Groningen, 9747 AG Groningen, The Netherlands
j.kosinka@rug.nl
[2] Department of Information Systems, Institute of Computing, University of Campinas, São Paulo 13083-852, Brazil
afalcao@ic.unicamp.br
[3] Department of Information and Computing Sciences, Utrecht University, 3584 CC Utrecht, The Netherlands
a.c.telea@uu.nl
[4] Bernoulli Institute, Shandong University of Science and Technology, 579 Qianwangang Road, Huangdao District, Qingdao 266590, Shandong Province, P.R. China
jieying.wang@rug.nl

Abstract. Medial descriptors have attracted increasing interest in image representation, simplification, and compression. Recently, such descriptors have been separately used to (a) increase the local quality of representing salient features in an image and (b) globally compress an entire image via a B-spline encoding. To date, the two desiderates, (a) high local quality and (b) high overall compression of images, have not been addressed by a single medial method. We achieve this integration by presenting Spatial Saliency Spline Dense Medial Descriptors (3S-DMD) for saliency-aware image simplification-and-compression. Our method significantly improves the trade-off between compression and image quality of earlier medial-based methods while keeping perceptually salient features. We also demonstrate the added-value of user-designed, as compared to automatically-computed, saliency maps. We show that our method achieves both higher compression and better quality than JPEG for a broad range of images and, for specific image types, yields higher compression and similar quality than JPEG 2000.

Keywords: Medial descriptors · Saliency maps · B-splines · Image simplification · Image compression

1 Introduction

Image simplification and compression are essential in many applications in science, engineering, and consumer contexts. *Compression* methods, such as the well-known JPEG [44] and the newer JPEG 2000 [39] and BPG [5] efficiently reduce the cost of storing and/or transmitting an image, typically in a lossy manner, by discarding certain image features or details. *Simplification* keeps image structures deemed important while eliminating less-important ones, to ease the analysis and processing of the former structures.

© Springer Nature Switzerland AG 2023
A. A. de Sousa et al. (Eds.): VISIGRAPP 2021, CCIS 1691, pp. 279–302, 2023.
https://doi.org/10.1007/978-3-031-25477-2_13

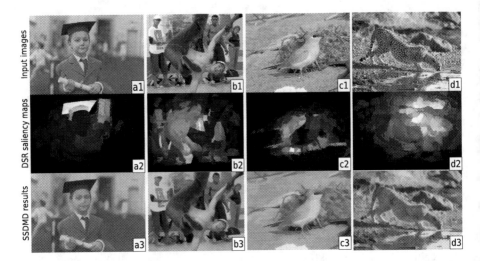

Fig. 1. Examples of the DSR saliency estimator failing to detect salient objects: (a3–d3) show the SSDMD results using the saliency maps (a2–d2) for images (a1–d1).

A particular class of simplification-and-compression methods models images as a set of luminance threshold-sets [58] and encodes these by their Medial Axis Transforms (MATs). Wang *et al.* [50] followed this approach to propose Dense Medial Descriptors (DMD), a lossy image compression method. While DMD showed promising quantitative and qualitative results, it cannot yet compare in *both* visual quality and compression ratio (CR) with state-of-the-art compression methods like JPEG or similar. Two lines of research tried to address this issue.

Improving Quality: DMD simplifies an image *globally*, making it hard to preserve fine details in some areas while strongly simplifying the image in other areas. The SSDMD method [49] addressed this by adding a saliency map to DMD, allowing users to specify different spatial simplification levels over an image. SSDMD delivers higher local quality than DMD (as specified by the saliency map) but has two key limitations. First, it only marginally improves CR when compared to DMD, since highly-salient image areas actually increase the MAT information needed to be stored. Secondly, SSDMD uses *automatically* computed saliency maps to control simplification. Such maps can significantly fail to capture what users perceive as salient (thus, to be preserved) *vs* non-salient (thus, to be simplified). Figure 1 outlines this problem for four images (a1–d1) with saliency maps (a2–d2; bright=salient; dark=non-salient) automatically computed by the DSR method [25]. SSDMD compression results (a3–d3) arguably lose details that humans would find salient, such as blurred faces (a3, b3, c3) and nearly complete loss of the leopard skin texture (d3).

Improving Compression: DMD stores the MATs of an image's threshold sets as pixel chains, which is exact, but inefficient storage-wise. The Spline Dense Medial Descriptors (SDMD) method [47] improved CR by representing MATs with accurate and compact-storage B-spline descriptors for each threshold set [48]. Yet, just as DMD,

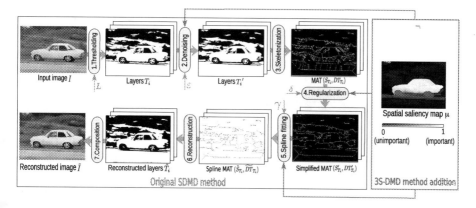

Fig. 2. Spline-based dense medial descriptors pipeline with free parameters in green. Elements added by 3S-DMD method proposed in this paper are marked in red. (Color figure online)

SDMD simplifies images only *globally*, thus increasing CR but achieving limited visual quality.

Our Contributions: We jointly address the visual quality *and* CR goals of all above earlier MAT-based image compression methods by a single method:

- We combine the strengths of SSDMD [49] (*spatial* control of image simplification) with SDMD [47] (*compact* encoding of MATs with B-splines);
- We allow users to interactively tune parameters of the joint method, including full control over the saliency map design;
- We evaluate our proposal on additional image types and compare it, with favorable results, with state-of-the-art methods (JPEG and JPEG 2000).

We organize this paper as follows. Section 2 presents related work on medial descriptors for image compression. Section 3 details our Spatial Saliency Spline-based Dense Medial Descriptor (3S-DMD) method. Section 4 evaluates our results. Section 5 discusses 3S-DMD. Section 6 concludes the paper.

2 Related Work

Our 3S-DMD method (Fig. 2) adapts SDMD to use saliency maps to further simplify less important regions while preserving salient ones (new contributions marked red in the figure). We next discuss related work: dense medial descriptors (Sect. 2.1), spline-based DMD (Sect. 2.2), and saliency maps (Sect. 2.3).

2.1 Dense Medial Descriptors (DMD)

The key idea of DMD [50] is to use medial axes to efficiently encode luminance threshold-sets of an image. Let $I : \mathbb{R}^2 \to [0, 255]$ be the 8-bit Y channel in the YUV space of a color image. DMD splits I in $n = 256$ threshold sets or *layers*

$$T_i = \left\{ \mathbf{x} \in \mathbb{R}^2 \mid I(\mathbf{x}) \geq i \right\}, 0 \leq i < n. \tag{1}$$

Since adjacent layers often contain highly similar information, DMD uses only a subset $D \subset \{T_i\}$ of $L = |D| < 256$ layers to encode I (Fig. 2, step 1). Here and next, $|\cdot|$ denotes set size. In some layers, small-size islands (connected components in the foreground T_i or background $\overline{T}_i$) can appear, due to small local intensity variations. DMD fills in, respectively removes, islands smaller than a fraction ε of $|T_i|$, respectively $|\overline{T}_i|$, which contribute little to the image I (Fig. 2, step 2). Next, DMD extracts medial axis transforms (S_{T_i}, DT_{T_i}) from these L layers (Fig. 2, step 3), where

$$DT_{T_i}(\mathbf{x}) = \min_{\mathbf{y} \in \partial T_i} \|\mathbf{x} - \mathbf{y}\| \tag{2}$$

is the distance transform [15] of the boundary ∂T_i of layer T_i, and

$$S_{T_i} = \{\mathbf{x} \in T_i | \exists \mathbf{f}_1 \in \partial T_i, \mathbf{f}_2 \in \partial T_i, \mathbf{f}_1 \neq \mathbf{f}_2 : \|\mathbf{x} - \mathbf{f}_1\| = \|\mathbf{x} - \mathbf{f}_2\| = DT_{T_i}(\mathbf{x})\} \tag{3}$$

is the medial axis, or skeleton, of T_i. In Eq. 3, $\mathbf{f}_1$ and $\mathbf{f}_2$ are called feature points [19] of skeletal point $\mathbf{x}$. Computing MATs of binary images is a well-studied topic, described in detail in classical work [21, 23, 31, 35, 36, 38].

The medial axes S_{T_i} contain many so-called *spurious branches* caused by small perturbations along ∂T_i. Storing such branches takes significant space but contributes little to the reconstruction quality. To address this, DMD uses the salient-skeleton metric [40] defined as

$$\sigma(\mathbf{x}) = \frac{\rho(\mathbf{x})}{DT_{T_i}(\mathbf{x})}, \tag{4}$$

where $\rho(\mathbf{x})$ is the fraction of the boundary ∂T_i that the skeletal point $\mathbf{x}$ encodes [42]. Saliency-based regularization removes all pixels $\mathbf{x} \in S_{T_i}$ where $\sigma(\mathbf{x})$ is below a user-specified threshold $\delta > 0$, yielding a simplified skeleton S'_{T_i} and corresponding distance transform DT'_{T_i} (Fig. 2, step 4). From the regularized MAT (S'_{T_i}, DT'_{T_i}), one can reconstruct a simplified version $\widetilde{T}_i$ of each layer T_i as the union $\cup_{\mathbf{x} \in S'_{T_i}} B(\mathbf{x}, DT'_{T_i}(\mathbf{x}))$ of discs B centered at pixels $\mathbf{x} \in S'_{T_i}$ and with radii given by $DT'_{T_i}(\mathbf{x})$. An approximation $\widetilde{I}$ of the input image I is finally obtained by drawing all reconstructed layers $\widetilde{T}_i$ atop each other in increasing order of luminance i (Fig. 2, step 7).

DMD uses the fast GPU implementation of [7], which is pixel-exact and linear in the number of pixels in T_i [19, 28]. Full implementation details are available at [50]. DMD provides an *accurate* encoding of grayscale and color images. However, DMD stores the MATs (S'_{T_i}, DT'_{T_i}) using pixel chain delta encoding, which is inefficient and leads to a *poor compression ratio*.

2.2   Spline-Based Medial Descriptors (SDMD)

Compactly encoding MATs has attracted interest in binary shape representation [22, 45]. B-splines were found effective for this as they store fewer (control) points than all pixels in an MAT. Zhu et al. [57] and Yushkevich *et al.* [55] accurately modeled MATs of 2D binary shapes with multiple cubic B-splines. Yet, they require vector representations of the input shape and its MAT and also require a Voronoi-based MAT method [4] which is slow for complex shapes.

Spline-based Medial Axis Transform (SMAT) [48] extended the above B-spline idea to use *raster* representations for T_i, S_{T_i}, and DT_{T_i}, to directly handle any binary raster image. In detail, MAT branches (S'_{T_i}, DT'_{T_i}), seen as 3D pixel curves, and fitted with 3D B-splines. Each control point $c_j = (\mathbf{p}_j, DT_{T_i}(\mathbf{p}_j)) \in \mathbb{R}^3$ consists of a 2D position $\mathbf{p}_j$ and its corresponding DT value. Fitting uses the least-squares method [13] aiming to get (1) a minimal number of control points and (2) an approximation error γ between the MATs and B-splines below a user-given value γ (Fig. 2, step 5). Reconstruction first rasterizes the B-splines using de Casteljau's algorithm [34] and next creates the layers $\widetilde{T}_i$ by the disc-union method outlined in Sect. 2.1 (Fig. 2, step 6).

Wang *et al.* [47] proposed Spline Dense Medial Descriptors (SDMD) that uses the SMAT method to encode color images. SDMD applies SMAT to all luminance threshold sets of an image but also proposes three improvements to increase CR and quality: adaptively encoding upper or lower threshold-sets, treating chrominance and luminance separately, and removing Y-structures from the skeletons. For details, we refer to [47]. SDMD achieves much higher compression ratios at similar or even better quality to JPEG.

Compared with DMD, which proved to faithfully represent an image, SDMD encodes images both faithfully and *compactly*. Yet, both DMD and SDMD work *globally*: High simplification easily removes small, but visually important, details, leading to poor quality. Conversely, low simplification allocates storage to unimportant image areas, leading to poor compression.

2.3 Saliency Maps

Saliency maps encode the relative importance of various parts of an image for a given task or perceptual standpoint. A saliency map $\mu : \mathbb{R}^2 \to [0, 1]$ gives, for each image pixel $\mathbf{x}$, its importance or saliency, between totally irrelevant ($\mu = 0$) and maximal importance ($\mu = 1$). Such maps have been used for image quality assessment [27], content-based image retrieval [8], context-aware image resizing [18], and saliency-based image compression [3,59]. Saliency maps can be created either in supervised mode—by users via manual annotation (see next Sect. 3.1)—or in unsupervised mode, automatically computed from images.

Supervised methods use ground-truth images to learn discriminant features of salient objects [29]. The most accurate supervised methods use deep-learning [6,51] and typically outperform unsupervised methods. Ywt, they need large amounts of human-annotated training data, and the generalization of training models across image domains usually requires adaptation and retraining [29].

Unsupervised methods use prior knowledge about salient objects and local image characteristics. Most methods start by finding image regions (*e.g.* superpixels) with high color contrast relative to neighbors [20,25,56]. Besides contrast, objects in focus [20], near the image center [10], or having red and yellow tones, important for human vision [33], are all considered as salient factors. Conversely, regions similar to the boundary will have low saliency as most image boundaries are background in natural images [10,20,25,56]. In our work, we use the DSR [25] unsupervised bottom-up saliency estimation method which provides reliable saliency maps without requiring parameter tuning and is fast. Any other saliency estimators can be directly used instead as long as users find the produced maps suitable for their tasks at hand.

3   Proposed 3S-DMD Method

As stated above, an important limitation of SDMD is that it simplifies an image *globally*. Our earlier work, Spatial Saliency DMD (SSDMD) [49], addressed this by simplifying the DMD MAT's using a spatial saliency map. We next present both SSDMD and our new method, 3S-DMD, which improves SSDMD in several respects. Section 3.1 shows how 3S-DMD benefits from manually-designed saliency maps via an interactive application. Section 3.2 presents SSDMD's saliency-map-based simplification of the MAT and how we improved this by saliency-based spline fitting. Finally, Sect. 3.3 shows how we measure the quality of the results of our new 3S-DMD method.

3.1   User-Driven Saliency Map Generation

Section 2.3 reviewed a variety of techniques to automatically compute saliency maps from an image. As mentioned in Sect. 1, such automatically-computed maps may not fully meet user needs (*cf.* Fig. 1 (a2, b2)) or even fail to detect salient objects (*cf.* Fig. 1 (c2, d2)). Even when such maps fit with what users expect, the simplification they induce can lead to unwanted results due to the hard-to-predict shapes that skeletons have. To handle all such issues, we developed an interactive application that allows users to create their *custom* saliency maps or *adjust* maps created by automatic methods. Figure 3a shows the user interface, in which one can draw the saliency map using tools listed in the toolbar, tune all the method's parameters, run the end-to-end pipeline, and check the obtained results. A video of our tool is provided in the supplementary material [46].

We provide three ways for users to manually design saliency maps, as follows.

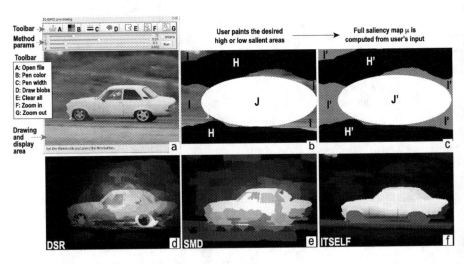

Fig. 3. Directly saliency drawing. (a) Interface with a loaded image. (b) User drawing to specify the saliency. (c) Computed saliency map. (d–f) Generated saliency maps.

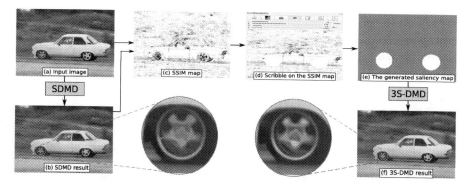

Fig. 4. SSIM-guided user-specified saliency map generation.

Direct Drawing: Users can directly paint a saliency map with various brushes, whose brightness gives the desired saliency (black=0, white=1). Figure 3b shows the drawing of a map for the car image in Fig. 3a. The user marked the car area as highly salient (white ellipse, region J) and background areas farther from the car as zero salient (black scribbled bands, region H). Figure 3c shows the computed saliency map μ. Regions where the user painted saliency are taken over from the drawing (H' and J' are copies of H and J, respectively). Unpainted areas carry no hints that the user found them important or not (Fig. 3b, region I). We set here the saliency to the average value $\mu = 0.5$ (Fig. 3b, region I').

Adjust Precomputed Saliency Map: Fully painting a custom saliency map can be cumbersome, especially when one wants to use multiple saliency values. We support this use-case by allowing users to draw to modify a precomputed saliency map. Figures 3d–f show three such precomputed maps obtained with the DSR method [25], structured matrix decomposition (SMD) method [33], and the recent ITerative Saliency Estimator fLexible Framework (ITSELF) [29] method.

SSIM-guided User-specified Saliency: Users may be unfamiliar with, or unable to run, existing saliency estimation methods. Also, they may not know how to tweak saliency to get the best quality-compression balance. We address these issues by computing the saliency map in a *corrective* way, *i.e.*, by comparing the compression method's output with its input. Figure 4 shows how this works. Given an input image (a), we first run SDMD without a saliency map. Next, we evaluate the quality of the output (b) by the Structural SIMilarity (SSIM) metric [52]. The generated SSIM map (c) shows the per-pixel structural similarity between the original (a) and the output (b), with darker pixels indicating less similar regions. Figure 4 (c) shows that SDMD yields poorer quality over several car details, especially its two wheels. Having this insight, we scribble bright colors on the two wheels to tell their importance (Fig. 4 (d)). We now use this quite simple saliency map (e) to run 3S-DMD to generate a new result (f). As visible in the last image, the quality of the left front wheel has improved.

(a1) Original image (300kB)   (a2) SDMD compression (23.1kB)   (a3) 3S-DMD compression (21.6kB)

(b1) T_{127} (b2) SDMD $T'_{127}(\varepsilon = 0.04)$ (b3) 3S-DMD $T'_{127}(\varepsilon = 0.04)$ (c) Saliency map μ

Fig. 5. Pigeon image (a1) encoded with SDMD (a2) and 3S-DMD (a3) with saliency map (c) computed by the DSR [25] method. Images (b1–b3) show details in layer 127.

3.2   Saliency-Based Parameter Control

We next show how to use the saliency maps created by the various methods in the denoising (step 2), regularization (step 4), and spline fitting (step 5) of our end-to-end pipeline (Fig. 2).

Salient Islands Detection: As explained in Sect. 2.1, (S)DMD only keeps islands, or connected components C_i, which meet the condition $|C_i| \geq \varepsilon|T_i|$. This can remove small but salient features (see Fig. 5): For $\varepsilon = 0.04$, the pigeon's eyes, visible in the original image (a1), are removed (a2). We confirm this by verifying that the small islands in region A in the threshold-set T_{127} (b1) get lost in T'_{127} (b2). Lowering ε can alleviate this, but this allocates more information to encode the less important background, thereby increasing image size. To address this, we use the saliency map μ to compute a saliency-aware metric

$$C_i^\mu = \sum_{\mathbf{x} \in C_i} k_1^{2\mu(\mathbf{x})-1}, \qquad (5)$$

and next remove only islands for which $C_i^\mu < \varepsilon$. The factor k_1 in Eq. 5 controls how much μ affects island removal. For $k_1 = 1$, $C_i^\mu = |C_i|$, so our method behaves like the original (S)DMD. In practice, we set $k_1 = 5$, which means that the most salient pixels ($\mu(\mathbf{x}) = 1$) are given five times their original unit weight; the least important pixels ($\mu(\mathbf{x}) = 0$), in contrast, get one-fifth of their original unit weight. This keeps small-size, but salient, details in the compressed image. Figure 5 (b3) shows this for a saliency map computed with the DSR method [25]. Islands in region A, while small, have a high μ, so they are retained. In contrast, although large, the island in region B has a low saliency, so it is removed. This ends up with a smaller size, but perceptually better, result (a3).

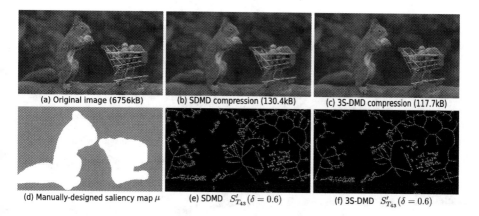

Fig. 6. Salient skeleton detection on a squirrel image (a) with SDMD (b, e) and 3S-DMD (c, f) using a manually-designed saliency map (d).

Saliency-aware Skeleton Simplification: As Sect. 2.1 outlined, (S)DMD regularizes skeletons S'_{T_i} by keeping only pixels $\mathbf{x} \in S_{T_i}$ where $\sigma(\mathbf{x})$ exceeds a user-set threshold δ (Fig. 2, step 4). The SSDMD method [49] further simplifies S'_{T_i} by removing points $\mathbf{x} \in S'_{T_i}$ whose saliency $\mu(\mathbf{x})$ is smaller than a *new* threshold. This not only increases the number of thresholds users have to deal with but also yields poor quality as low-saliency areas get completely removed. SSDMD alleviates this by using various heuristics such as selective layer keeping and interpolation tricks. However, this makes the end-to-end method quite complex.

In contrast to SSDMD, we blend σ with the saliency map μ by computing

$$\sigma'(\mathbf{x}) = \sigma(\mathbf{x}) \cdot k_2^{(\mu(\mathbf{x})-1)} \tag{6}$$

and then obtain S'_{T_i} by upper-thresholding $\sigma'(\mathbf{x})$ with the user-set value δ, *i.e.*,

$$S'_{T_i} = \{\mathbf{x} \in S_{T_i} | \sigma'(\mathbf{x}) > \delta\}. \tag{7}$$

The value k_2 in Eq. 6 controls how much μ affects the skeleton simplification. For $k_2 = 1$, our new metric σ' equals the original σ from (S)DMD. In practice, we set $k_2 = 2$. Hence, the salient-skeleton values $\sigma'(\mathbf{x})$ of the least important pixels ($\mu(\mathbf{x}) = 0$) become half of their original $\sigma(\mathbf{x})$ values; in contrast, the σ values of the most important pixels ($\mu(\mathbf{x}) = 1$) stay unchanged. Figure 6 shows the improvement given by our new metric σ'. Images (e, f) show the regularized skeletons $S'_{T_{43}}$ of one layer, T_{43}, computed with SDMD's σ metric and 3S-DMD's σ' metric, for the same user-set $\delta = 0.6$, and a simple manually-designed saliency map, for illustration purposes (image d). We see how 3S-DMD (image f) simplifies skeletons in the image background more, since the saliency is low there, than SDMD (image e), which has no notion of a low-importance background. In contrast, in the foreground image areas (white areas in the saliency map μ), the 3S-DMD and SDMD skeletons are identical. As a result, 3S-DMD yields the same image quality as SDMD, but with about 10% extra compression.

compression artifacts   low-SSIM foreground areas   artifacts are gone   low-SSIM background areas

Fig. 7. DMD compression has artifacts (a) found as low-SSIM regions (b). SSDMD (c) removes these but marks subtle background differences important for quality (d). Image taken from [49].

Saliency-Based Spline Fitting: Section 2.2 stated that SDMD finds the minimal number of B-spline control points needed to reach a user-given fitting error γ between a skeleton branch B_i and the B-spline C_i. This error is given by the Hausdorff distance $H(B_i, C_i)$ computed over all pixels $\mathbf{x} \in B_i$. We modify the fixed user-set threshold γ to involve the saliency map μ by

$$\gamma' = \gamma \frac{\sum_{\mathbf{x} \in B_i} k_3^{(1-\mu(\mathbf{x}))}}{|B_i|}, \tag{8}$$

where k_3 controls how much μ influences the spline fitting. For $k_3 = 1$, γ' equals the original γ. We set $k_3 = 2$ in practice. Hence, when a branch is fully within a zero-saliency region ($\mu(\mathbf{x}) = 0$), $\gamma' = 2\gamma$, *i.e.*, we allow a double fitting error as compared to the original SDMD. For branches located in a maximum saliency regions ($\mu(\mathbf{x}) = 1$), the fitting error stays the same, *i.e.*, $\gamma' = \gamma$.

3.3   Saliency-Aware Quality Metric

Quality metrics $Q(I, \tilde{I}) \in \mathbb{R}^+$ measure how close a compressed image $\tilde{I}$ is to the original image I. Such metrics include the mean squared error (MSE) and peak signal-to-noise ratio (PSNR). While simple to compute and with clear physical meanings, these metrics do not match well *perceived* visual quality [53]. The SSIM index [52] alleviates this by measuring, pixel-wise, how perceptually similar two images are. Wang et al. [54] proposed Multiscale SSIM (MS-SSIM), which is an advanced top-down interpretation of how the human visual system comprehends images considering variations of image resolution and viewing conditions.

While MS-SSIM models human perception well, it handles focus (high $\mu(\mathbf{x})$) and context (low $\mu(\mathbf{x})$) areas identically. Figure 7 illustrates this: Image (a) shows the DMD result of a car image and (b) shows the SSIM map. Image (a) shows some artifacts on the car roof, also visible as dark areas in the SSIM map (b). Image (c) shows the SSDMD result [49] of the car image, with strong background simplification and detail retention in the focus (car) area. The car-roof artifacts are removed, so (c) matches better the original image than (a). Yet, the MS-SSIM score of (c) is much *lower* than for DMD (0.9088 *vs* 0.9527). The large dark regions in the SSIM map background (d) explain this: While the saliency map μ clearly says that background is unimportant, MS-SSIM considers it *equally* important to foreground.

Given the above, saliency data should be considered by a perception-aware quality metric. This is also reflected by saliency-based objective metrics [2,14,24,26,27]

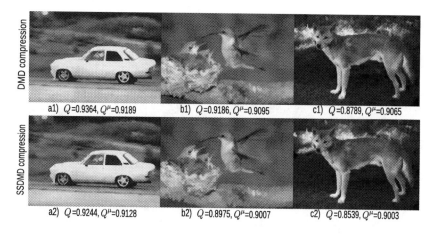

Fig. 8. Comparison of DMD (a1–c1) with SSDMD (a2–c2) for three focus-and-context images. For each image, we show the standard MS-SSIM quality Q, and spatial-saliency-aware MS-SSIM Q^μ. Image taken from [49].

which integrate a visual saliency map into the quality metric as a weighting map, thereby improving image-quality prediction performance. We follow the same idea by integrating the saliency map μ into the MS-SSIM [54] pooling function, as follows. Take the MS-SSIM metric for a reference image I and a distorted image $\tilde{I}$

$$Q(I,\tilde{I}) = \left(\mathrm{SSIM}(I,\tilde{I})\right)^{\beta_M} \prod_{j=1}^{M-1} \left(c_j(I,\tilde{I})\right)^{\beta_j}, \qquad (9)$$

where c_j is the contrast map $c(I,\tilde{I})$ iteratively downsampled by a factor of 2 on scale $1 \leq j \leq M$; $\mathrm{SSIM}(I,\tilde{I})$ is the structural similarity of I and $\tilde{I}$ on scale M [52]; and the factor β_j models the relative importance of different scales. We weigh Q by the saliency map μ yielding the saliency-aware quality metric

$$Q^\mu = \left(\frac{\sum_{\mathbf{x}\in I}\mu(\mathbf{x})\mathrm{SSIM}(\mathbf{x})}{\sum_{\mathbf{x}\in I}\mu(\mathbf{x})}\right)^{\beta_M} \prod_{j=1}^{M-1}\left(\frac{\sum_{\mathbf{x}\in I}\mu_j(\mathbf{x})c_j(\mathbf{x})}{\sum_{\mathbf{x}\in I}\mu_j(\mathbf{x})}\right)^{\beta_j}, \qquad (10)$$

where μ_j is the saliency map at scale j. For notation brevity, the arguments I and $\tilde{I}$ are omitted in Eq. 10. Using Q^μ instead of Q allows in-focus values (high $\mu(\mathbf{x})$) to contribute more to similarity than context values (low $\mu(\mathbf{x})$).

Figure 8 compares the results of DMD (a1–c1) and SSDMD (a2–c2) for three focus-and-context images, using the standard MS-SSIM quality Q and our spatial-saliency-aware quality Q^μ. The Q values for SSDMD are lower than those for DMD, which suggests that SSDMD has a poorer quality than DMD. Yet, we see that SSDMD creates images that are visually almost the same as DMD, in line with the almost identical Q^μ values for SSDMD and DMD. Thus, we argue that Q^μ is a better quality measure for focus-and-context simplification than Q. We consider Q^μ next for evaluating the image quality.

4 Results

Section 3 proposed 3S-DMD, a method that incorporates three schemes for users to create a spatial saliency map, three ways for adjusting the original SDMD with these maps, and a saliency-aware quality metric Q^μ to measure how well the reconstructed image $\tilde{I}$ captures the input image I. We next evaluate 3S-DMD's results in detail, as follows.

- First, we describe our evaluation methodology (Sect. 4.1).
- We show how 3S-DMD depends on its free parameters (Sect. 4.2).
- We compare 3S-DMD with DMD [50] and SDMD [47] (Sect. 4.3).
- Atop [49], we also compare with the JPEG and JPEG 2000 methods (Sect. 4.4).

4.1 Evaluation Methodology

The 3S-DMD encoding consists of a tuple $(w, h, \{l_i\})$, *i.e.*, the pixel width w and height h of the input image I, and the L selected layers l_i. A layer $l_i = (i, f, \{\mathbf{b}_i^k\})$ has an intensity value i, a flag f that tells if it uses upper- or lower-thresholding (for details, see [47]), and a B-spline set $\{\mathbf{b}_i^k\}$ encoding its MAT. Each B-spline $\mathbf{b}_i^k = (d_i^k, \{\mathbf{c}_j\})$ has a degree $d_i^k \in \mathbb{N}$ and control points $\mathbf{c}_j \in \mathbb{R}^3$ (see Sect. 2.2).

Sizes of the images $\tilde{I}$ and I are typically measured by bits per pixel (bpp), *i.e.*, the number of bits used to encode a pixel's grayscale or color value [12]. Yet, in an encoding context, we want to *compare* the sizes of $\tilde{I}$ and I, rather than measure their absolute sizes. For this, we define $CR = |I|/|3SDMD(\tilde{I})|$. Here, $|3SDMD(\tilde{I})|$ is the byte-size of the 3S-DMD storage scheme outlined above, while $|I|$ is the size (in bytes) of the original image I.

The quality Q^μ (Sect. 3.3) and compression ratio CR of 3S-DMD depend on four parameters (Fig. 2): the number of selected threshold-sets L, the size of removed islands ε, the skeletal saliency threshold δ, and the spline fitting tolerance γ. We establish *ranges* for these parameters based on results of previous work [47,49,50], as follows: $L \in [1, 60]$, $\varepsilon \in [0.001, 0.1]$, $\delta \in [0.01, 3]$, and $\gamma \in [0.001, 0.005]$. We further sample these ranges by the following representative values: $L \in \{15, 25\}$, $\varepsilon = 0.02$, $\delta \in \{0.3, 0.8\}$, and $\gamma = 0.0015$. We use these values to compare DMD, SDMD, and 3S-DMD (Sect. 4.3) and 3S-DMD with JPEG and JPEG 2000 (Sect. 4.4). We test all these methods on a 50-image database, which is selected randomly from the MSRA10K [9], SOD [30], and ECSSD [37] benchmarks. In addition to these real-world pictures, we also tested 3S-DMD on several artificially-designed images (Sect. 4.4). All test images have a resolution between 1000^2 to 2000^2 pixels.

4.2 Effect of Parameters

To intuitively illustrate how 3S-DMD performs for different parameter values, we first group these into *weighting factors* and *user thresholds*, and show the effect of these for a specific image.

Fig. 9. Progressive simplification of a flower image (a) using a saliency map (b) for different weight values k_1, k_2, and k_3 (c1–c4).

Weighting Factors Effect: As explained in Sect. 3.2, the k_1, k_2, and k_3 factors control how much the saliency map μ affects the island detection, skeleton simplification, and spline fitting, respectively. We call these weighting factors—in contrast to the user parameters discussed next—since they are more technical parameters, which do not arguably need to be exposed to end users. Secondly, their effect is strongly related to the way 3S-DMD treats image areas of different saliency. Let 'foreground' and 'background' describe areas of high, respectively, low saliency map μ values. Simply put, increasing all (or any) of these three weighting factors progressively simplifies the image background, similarly to a (soft) blurring effect, but keeps the image foreground relatively untouched. Figure 9 shows this for a flower image under different values for k_1, k_2, and k_3. The user parameters are fixed to the default values $L = 25, \varepsilon = 0.02, \delta = 0.3, \gamma = 0.0015$.

The setting $k_1 = k_2 = k_3 = 1$, shown in Fig 9 (c1), corresponds to the original SDMD method since, for this setting, μ has no effect on island detection, skeleton regularization, and spline fitting (see Eqs. 5, 6, and 8). As we increase k_1, k_2, and k_3, the image background gets progressively more simplified; see Figs. 9 (c2–c4). However, the flower in the foreground stays roughly the same in all images. The CR and Q^μ values shown below the images match the above observations: as the weights increase, Q^μ drops only slightly decreases, but CR increases strongly. In practice, as stated in Sect. 3.2, we found $k_1 = 5, k_2 = 2$, and $k_3 = 2$ to be a good default for balancing CR and Q^μ.

User Thresholds Effect: 3S-DMD depends on four thresholds, as follows:

– L controls how smoothly the simplified image captures *color gradients*; larger values yield smoother gradients;

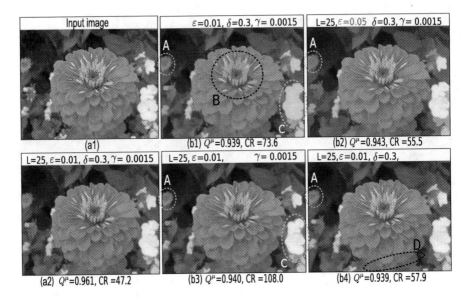

Fig. 10. 3S-DMD results for a flower image (a) using the saliency map of Fig. 9(b) for different combinations of parameters L, ε, δ, and γ.

- ε gives the scale of *details* that are kept in the image; larger values remove larger details;
- δ controls the scale of *corners* that are kept in the image; larger values round off larger corners;
- γ tells how accurately B-splines fit skeleton branches; larger values yield more distorted results.

In contrast to the weighting factors discussed earlier, these four thresholds significantly influence the 'style' of the simplified image. Hence, we believe they are best left under the direct control of the end users.

Figure 10 shows the effect of the thresholds L, ε, δ, and γ by showing the 3S-DMD results on the same flower image, using the same saliency map, as in Fig. 9. Image (a2) shows the results of 3S-DMD when setting user thresholds. The remaining images (b1–b4) are each the effect of a single user threshold change (red in the legend). If we decrease L(image (b1)), even if we select only $L = 15$ layers, we still get a visually convincing result. Yet, the stamens in region B and the flowers in regions A and C look duller than in image (a). Image (b2) uses a higher ε value, which removes many large islands in the image background, *e.g.*, the one corresponding to the yellow flower in region A. Image (b3) uses a higher δ, which rounds off corners of background shapes, *e.g.* the flowers in regions A and C. Finally, image (b4) uses a higher γ, which distorts the boundaries of the flower in region A and creates subtly false colors in region D.

4.3   Comparison with DMD and SDMD

Figure 11 compares the Q^{μ} and CR values of DMD (blue markers), SDMD (red markers), and our proposed 3S-DMD (green markers), for the four user-parameter settings

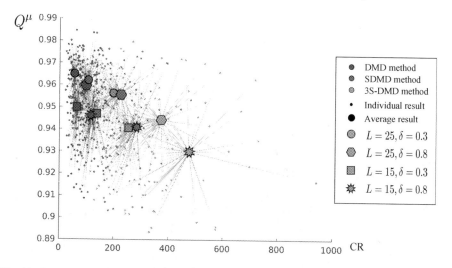

Fig. 11. Star plots of DMD (blue markers), SDMD (red markers), and 3S-DMD (green markers) for 50 real-world images. The actual image data (smaller dots) are connected to the corresponding average value (star center markers) for each method. Marker shapes indicate the four parameter settings being used. (Color figure online)

listed in Sect. 4.1, using a star plot. Small dots indicate metric values for a run involving a method-and-parameter-setting on a single image. Markers at the 'star centers' show average values for all runs over the 50 images in the benchmark for one parameter setting and one method. For each method (color), there are four stars, one for each of the four parameter-settings used, as indicated by the four glyph types in the figure's legend. The star center triples depicted using the same glyph show runs that use the same parameter settings. We fixed $\varepsilon = 0.02$ and $\gamma = 0.0015$ so these user parameters are not listed in the figure's legend.

Figure 11 offers several insights. Small stars show little variance in CR and Q^{μ} from the average for a given method-and-parameter-set. Large stars indicate more variance as a function of the actual images. The sizes and shapes of the stars in the figure are quite similar. Hence, DMD, SDMD, and 3S-DMD show a similar dependency of CR and Q^{μ} on the real-world image type. This is due to the fact that SDMD and 3S-DMD inherit the thresholding and skeletonization used by DMD. Yet, the green stars are slightly larger and more spread horizontally, indicating that 3S-DMD can produce greater changes in CR for similar Q^{μ}.

For each color (method), its four stars show an inverse correlation of CR with Q^{μ}. Indeed, more layers and smaller δ yield higher quality but less compression; conversely, fewer layers and larger δ slightly reduce quality, but strongly increase compression. The axes ranges show this too: CR varies roughly from 50 to 700, while quality varies between 0.91 and 0.98. The three large dots of the same glyph types let us compare the DMD, SDMD, and 3S-DMD methods under the same parameter setting. We see a clear inverse correlation pattern going from high Q^{μ} and low CR (DMD, blue dots) to average Q^{μ} and CR (SDMD, red dots) and then to lower Q^{μ} and highest CR (3S-DMD, green dots). Hence, 3S-DMD always gets higher CR than DMD and SDMD for only a small quality loss. On average, 3S-DMD increases CR by 234.2% relative to DMD, while Q^{μ} drops by only 0.014. Compared with SDMD, 3S-DMD increases CR on average by 53.8%, while Q^{μ} drops by a tiny 0.009. More importantly, when we compare CR and Q^{μ} for different parameter settings, *e.g.*, comparing the large round green marker with the star-shaped blue marker and square red marker, 3S-DMD not only yields a higher CR but also better quality.

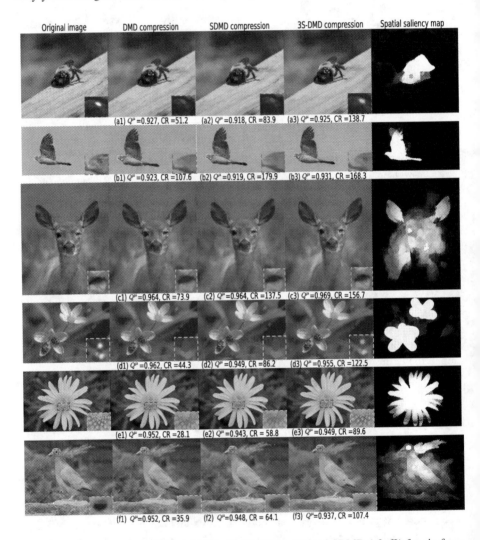

Fig. 12. Comparison of 3S-DMD (a3–f3) with DMD (a1–f1) and SDMD (a2–f2) for six focus-and-context images. For each result, we show the saliency-aware MS-SSIM Q^{μ} and CR. The rightmost column shows the manually-modified DSR saliency map.

Figure 12 further compares the three methods for six focus-and-context images of insects, birds, animals, and plants from the MSRA10K benchmarks [9]. More results are given in the supplementary material [46]. The zoomed-in areas show that, compared with DMD (a1–f1) and SDMD (a2–f2), 3S-DMD (a3–f3) preserves well important features marked as such by the saliency maps, like highlights (a, d), animals' eyes (b, c, f), and the flower stamen (e). For background areas, all three methods perform visually roughly the same. The quality values Q^μ are also similar for the three methods, with 3S-DMD scoring twice as best, three times as second-best, and once in the third place. CR values show that 3S-DMD achieves (significantly) higher compression than DMD and SDMD, except for image (b), where it scores slightly below SDMD. On the other hand, 3S-DMD retains for this example more details than SDMD for the foreground area, such as the bird's eye, as also reflected by its higher quality score.

4.4   Comparison with JPEG and JPEG 2000

Tens of image compression exist, see *e.g.* [1,11,43] and methods cited therein. Comparing 3S-DMD with all of them is not feasible in the scope of this work. However, we provide a comparison with JPEG [44] and JPEG 2000 (J2K) [39] which are arguably among the most well-known, frequently-used, and generic, image compressors.

Comparison with JPEG: Figure 13 compares 3S-DMD with JPEG on our image benchmark. The parameter setting of 3S-DMD (green dots) follows Sect. 4.3. JPEG (blue dots) is run under five quality settings: 10%, 30%, 50%, 70%, and 90%. As in Fig. 11, we use star plots for both 3S-DMD and JPEG: small dots are individual runs and large dots are averages. We see that 3S-DMD cannot reach the same Q^μ values as when JPEG uses its 90% quality setting: the topmost blue dot is above the topmost green dot. However, the vertical spread of the blue *vs* green dots shows that the difference in quality (Q^μ) is small, about 4% on average. If we accept this small quality loss, 3S-DMD always gets higher compression rates than JPEG. In the limit, compared to JPEG with a quality of 10% (point A), 3S-DMD (point B) gets both higher CR and better quality.

Figure 14 refines the above insights by showing six real-world images (building, plant, animal, natural scene, man-made structure, and people), compressed by 3S-DMD (a1–f1), JPEG (a2–f2), and J2K (a3–f3). We see that JPEG with a 10% quality creates obvious artifacts: checkerboarding (b2, c2, e2, f2), banding (a2, c2), and color faking (d2). 3S-DMD yields better quality (Q^μ) and does not exhibit such artifacts. Yet, 3S-DMD loses small-scale, faint, details in the background, like the gravel in the sea (c1) and the red color of the traffic sign (f1). We argue that these are acceptable losses since these details are located in low-saliency areas. Separately, 3S-DMD always achieves higher CR than JPEG.

Comparison with J2K: Figure 13 shows J2K (red dots) run under five fixed compression ratios: 100, 200, 300, 400, and 500. As CR increases, J2K has only a slightly quality loss and performs practically always better than JPEG. Figure 14 also verifies this: J2K's quality Q^μ is always higher than 0.99 and the compressed results are indistinguishable from the originals. 3S-DMD cannot (yet) achieve such quality. However, 3S-DMD can obtain comparable, and sometimes higher, CR values. We further refine the comparison with J2K by considering a narrower class of artificially made images,

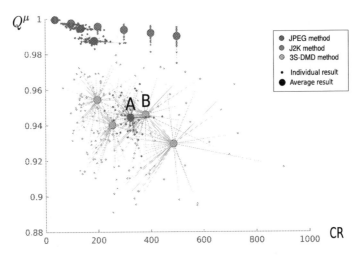

Fig. 13. Comparison of JPEG (blue dots), J2K (red dots), and 3S-DMD (green dots) for 50 images. The actual image data (smaller dots) are connected to the corresponding average value (larger dots) for each parameter setting of the three methods. (Color figure online)

such as graphics art (logos, graphics design), scientific visualization images, synthesized images using graphics rendering and vectorization methods [32], and cartoon images. For such images, 3S-DMD produces both higher CR *and* quality than J2K and JPEG. Figure 15 shows four representative images, one from each of the above four categories, compressed with 3S-DMD (a1–d1), JPEG (a2–d2), and J2K (a3–d3). As in earlier cases, JPEG with a quality of 10% generates obvious artifacts such as blocking (a2, b2, c2, d2), banding (c2), and color faking (c2), and has a CR well below the other two methods. When compared with J2K, our method yields similar Q^μ values. We show some zoomed-in areas to expose a few subtle differences: For the graphics design example (a), 3S-DMD achieves visually much better results, without the checkerboarding and blur artifacts of J2K. This is also seen in the first image in Fig. 15 where 3S-DMD got a higher Q^μ than J2K. For the second image (b) in Fig. 15, 3S-DMD captures the smooth luminance gradient in the shadow area quite well. In contrast, J2K causes a slight amount of false color artifacts. For the strong-contrast images (c) and (d), J2K creates some small-scale blur artifacts. 3S-SDMD does not have such problems but suffers from a slight color change issue due to its selection of threshold-sets to be encoded. Most importantly, with a similar or better quality, 3S-DMD always yields higher compression than J2K for such synthetic images.

We conclude that, for real-world images, 3S-DMD gets both higher CR and quality than JPEG but cannot match J2K's quality at the same CR. Yet, for synthetic images, 3S-DMD gets both much higher CR and quality than JPEG, and also achieves higher CR at similar quality but with fewer artifacts than J2K.

Original image   3S-DMD compression   JPEG-10% compression   J2K compression

(a1) Q^μ =0.959, CR =366   (a2) Q^μ =0.959, CR =346.1   (a3) Q^μ =0.992, CR =400

(b1) Q^μ =0.947, CR =334.8   (b2) Q^μ =0.937, CR =333.7   (b3) Q^μ =0.991, CR =400

(c1) Q^μ =0.966, CR =588.0   (c2) Q^μ =0.945, CR =443.2   (c3) Q^μ =0.992, CR =500

(d1) Q^μ =0.946, CR =508.2   (d2) Q^μ =0.945, CR =379.9   (d3) Q^μ =0.993, CR =500

(e1) Q^μ =0.963, CR =718.3   (e2) Q^μ =0.943, CR =353.7   (e3) Q^μ =0.994, CR =500

(f1) Q^μ=0.945, CR =350.4   (f2) Q^μ=0.945, CR =288.2   (f3) Q^μ=0.992, CR =400

Fig. 14. Comparison of 3S-DMD (a1–f1) with JPEG -10% (a2–f2) and J2K (a3–f3) for six real-world images. For each image, we show the saliency-aware metric Q^μ and CR.

5   Discussion

We now discuss several aspects of our 3S-DMD image compression method.

Genericity and Ease of Use: 3S-DMD is a general-purpose compression method for generic grayscale and color images. It relies on well-tested and robust algorithms such as the skeletonization method in [17,42] and the least-squares B-spline fitting algorithm [13]. In contrast to segmentation tasks [16], 3S-DMD does not require precise saliency maps. Any saliency map that encodes which image areas are more important and which less for an application at hand can be used. 3S-DMD has four user parameters: the number of selected layers L, island size ε, skeleton saliency threshold δ, and spline fitting error γ. These parameters have intuitive effects and default values, as detailed in Sect. 4.2.

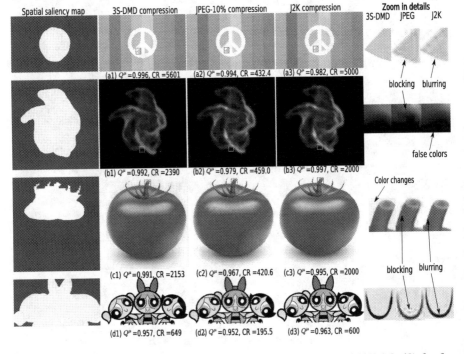

Fig. 15. Comparison of 3S-DMD (a1–d1) with JPEG-10% (a2–d2) and J2K (a3–d3) for four synthetic images. For each image, we show the saliency-aware Q^μ and CR. The leftmost column shows the saliency map obtained by directly scribbling on the input image. The rightmost three columns show zoomed-in areas for 3S-DMD, JPEG, and J2K for detailed comparison.

Speed: We compute the most complex step in 3S-DMD, skeletonization, on the GPU [7,41]. On a Linux PC with an Nvidia RTX 2060, this takes a few hundred milliseconds for images up to 1024^2 pixels. Spline fitting uses about 1 s per color channel, yielding a total of about 3 to 4 s for the compression.

Replicability: We provide our full C++ source code and data for replication purposes, as well as a demo video and additional comparisons with DMD and SDMD, in the supplementary material [46].

Limitations: Image layer components that are one or two pixels thin cannot be encoded by MATs, so 3S-DMD cannot deal optimally with images with many thin-and-long details, such as animal fur, fine textures, and greenery. Figure 16 shows this for two such images. For smooth regions in the background (red boxes), 3S-DMD yields results that are indistinguishable from the originals. However, 3S-DMD cannot capture all the fine-grained details present in the foreground (green boxes). One way to handle such cases is to artificially upscale the images, leading to fine details thicker than a few pixels, which next can be skeletonized with no problems. Studying how to perform this efficiently and with good CR values is an interesting topic for future work.

Fig. 16. Poor performance for 3S-DMD when handling images with many small-scale details, such as animal furs (a) and fine textures (b).

6   Conclusion

We have presented 3S-DMD, a method for saliency-aware image simplification and compression. 3S-DMD combines the strengths of two of its precursors: SSDMD [49] that allows spatial control of image simplification, and SDMD [47] that compactly encodes MATs with B-splines. We have developed an interactive application for users to set parameters and customize saliency maps in three ways. We have illustrated how saliency maps involved in the SDMD pipeline offer spatially-dependent simplification. We have shown graphically and intuitively how 3S-DMD performs under different parameter combinations. To study the effectiveness of 3S-DMD, we have considered a database of 50 real-world images. Quantitative evaluation showed that 3S-DMD greatly improves the compression of SSDMD and SDMD at only a small quality loss. Our method delivers both higher CR and quality than JPEG. While we cannot reach the same high quality at the same CR values as J2K, our method yields similar quality, higher CR, and fewer artifacts for a wide class of synthetic images.

We next aim to consider more extensive comparisons with additional compression techniques, *e.g.*, deep neural network methods. Separately, we aim to extend 3S-DMD beyond grayscale or color image simplifications to simplify 3D scalar fields in scientific visualization, weighted with uncertainty-encoding maps.

Acknowledgments. The first author acknowledges the China Scholarship Council (Grant number: 201806320354) for financial support.

References

1. Agustsson, E., Tschannen, M., Mentzer, F., Timofte, R., Van Gool, L.: Generative adversarial networks for extreme learned image compression. In: ICCV, pp. 221–231 (2019)
2. Alaei, A., Raveaux, R., Conte, D.: Image quality assessment based on regions of interest. Signal Image Video Process. **11**, 673–680 (2017)
3. Andrushia, A., Thangarjan, R.: Saliency-based image compression using Walsh and Hadamard transform. In: Lect Notes Comp Vision Biomech, pp. 21–42 (2018)
4. Attali, D., Montanvert, A.: Computing and simplifying 2D and 3D continuous skeletons. Comput. Vision Image Understand. **67**(3), 261–273 (1997)
5. Ballard, F.: Better portable graphics (2018). https://bellard.org/bpg
6. Borji, A., Cheng, M., Jiang, H., Li, J.: Salient object detection: a benchmark. IEEE TIP **24**(12), 5706–22 (2015)
7. Cao, T.T., Tang, K., Mohamed, A., Tan, T.S.: Parallel banding algorithm to compute exact distance transform with the GPU. In: Proceedings ACM I3D, pp. 83–90 (2010)
8. Chen, T., Cheng, M., Tan, P., Shamir, A., Hu, S.: Sketch2photo: Internet image montage. ACM TOG **28**(5) (2009)
9. Cheng, M.: MSRA10K salient object database (2014). mmcheng.net/msra10k
10. Cheng, M., Mitra, N.J., Huang, X., Torr, P.H., Hu, S.: Global contrast based salient region detection. IEEE TPAMI **37**(3), 569–582 (2014)
11. Choi, Y., El-Khamy, M., Lee, J.: Variable rate deep image compression with a conditional autoencoder. ICCV pp. 3146–3154 (2019)
12. Daintith, J., Wright, E.: A Dictionary of Computing. Oxford Univ, Press (2008)
13. Eberly, D.: Least-squares fitting of data with B-spline curves (2014). geometric Tools. www.geometrictools.com/Documentation/BSplineCurveLeastSquaresFit.pdf
14. Engelke, U., Le Callet, P.: Perceived interest and overt visual attention in natural images. Image Commun. **39**(PB), 386–404 (2015)
15. Fabbri, R., Costa, L.D.F., Torelli, J.C., Bruno, O.M.: 2D Euclidean distance transform algorithms: a comparative survey. ACM Comput Surv **40**(1), 1–44 (2008)

16. Falcão, A., Bragantini, J.: The role of optimum connectivity in image segmentation: can the algorithm learn object information during the process? In: Couprie, M., Cousty, J., Kenmochi, Y., Mustafa, N. (eds.) DGCI 2019. LNCS, vol. 11414, pp. 180–194. Springer, Cham (2019). https://doi.org/10.1007/978-3-030-14085-4_15

17. Falcão, A., Stolfi, J., Lotufo, R.: The image foresting transform: theory, algorithms, and applications. IEEE TPAMI 26, 19–29 (2004)

18. Goferman, S., Zelnik, L., Tal, A.: Context-aware saliency detection. IEEE TPAMI 34(10), 1915–1926 (2011)

19. Hesselink, W.H., Roerdink, J.B.T.M.: Euclidean skeletons of digital image and volume data in linear time by the integer medial axis transform. IEEE TPAMI 30(12), 2204–2217 (2008)

20. Jiang, P., Ling, H., Yu, J., Peng, J.: Salient region detection by UFO: Uniqueness, focusness and objectness. In: Proceedings of the ICCV, pp. 1976–1983 (2013)

21. Kimmel, R., Shaked, D., Kiryati, N., Bruckstein, A.M.: Skeletonization via distance maps and level sets. CVIU 62(3), 382–391 (1995)

22. Kresch, R., Malah, D.: Skeleton-Based morphological coding of binary images. IEEE TIP 7(10), 1387–1399 (1998)

23. Lam, L., Lee, S., Suen, C.Y.: Thinning methodologies - a comprehensive survey. IEEE TPAMI 14(9), 869–885 (1992)

24. Le Callet, P., Niebur, E.: Visual attention and applications in multimedia technologies. Proc. IEEE 101(9), 2058–2067 (2013)

25. Li, X., Lu, H., Zhang, L., Ruan, X., Yang, M.: Saliency detection via dense and sparse reconstruction. In: Proceedings of the ICCV, pp. 2976–2983 (2013)

26. Liu, H., Engelke, U., Wang, J., Callet, Le, P., Heynderickx, I.: How does image content affect the added value of visual attention in objective image quality assessment? IEEE Signal Proc. Let. 20, 355–358 (2013)

27. Liu, H., Heynderickx, I.: Visual attention in objective image quality assessment: Based on eye-tracking data. IEEE TCSVT 21(7), 971–982 (2011)

28. Meijster, A., Roerdink, J., Hesselink, W.: A general algorithm for computing distance transforms in linear time. In: Proceedings ISMM, pp. 331–340 (2002)

29. de Melo Joao, L., de Castro Belem, F., Falcao, A.X.: Itself: Iterative saliency estimation flexible framework. Available at https://arxiv.org/abs/2006.16956 (2020)

30. Movahedi, V., Elder, J.: Design and perceptual validation of performance measures for salient object segmentation. In: IEEE Computer Society Conference (2010)

31. Ogniewicz, R., Kübler, O.: Hierarchical voronoi skeletons. Patt. Recogn. 28(3), 343–359 (1995)

32. Orzan, A., Bousseau, A., Barla, P., Winnemöller, H., Thollot, J., Salesin, D.: Diffusion curves: a vector representation for smooth-shaded images. Commun. ACM 56(7), 101–108 (2013)

33. Peng, H., Li, B., Ling, H., Hu, W., Xiong, W., Maybank, S.J.: Salient object detection via structured matrix decomposition. IEEE TPAMI 39(4), 818–832 (2016)

34. Piegl, L., Tiller, W.: The NURBS Book (2nd Ed.). Springer-Verlag (1997). https://doi.org/10.1007/978-3-642-59223-2

35. Pizer, S., Siddiqi, K., Székely, G., Damon, J., Zucker, S.: Multiscale medial loci and their properties. IJCV 55, 155–179 (2003)

36. Saha, P.K., Borgefors, G., Sanniti di Baja, G.: A survey on skeletonization algorithms and their applications. Patt. Recogn. Lett. 76, 3–12 (2016)

37. Shi, J., Yan, Q., Xu, L., Jia, J.: Hierarchical image saliency detection on extended CSSD. IEEE TPAMI 38(4D) (2016)

38. Siddiqi, K., Pizer, S.: Medial representations: mathematics, algorithms and applications (1nd Ed.). Springer (2008). https://doi.org/10.1007/978-1-4020-8658-8

39. Taubman, D.S., Marcellin, M.W.: JPEG 2000: Image compression fundamentals, standards and practice. Kluwer Academic Publishers (2001)
40. Telea, A.: Feature preserving smoothing of shapes using saliency skeletons. In: Proc. VMLS, pp. 153–170 (2012)
41. Telea, A.: CUDASkel: real-time computation of exact Euclidean multiscale skeletons on CUDA (2019). webspace.science.uu.nl/~telea001/Shapes/CUDASkel
42. Telea, A., Wijk, van, J.: An augmented fast marching method for computing skeletons and centerlines. In: Eurographics, pp. 251–259 (2002)
43. Toderici, G., et al.: Variable rate image compression with recurrent neural networks. In: 4th ICLR (2016)
44. Wallace, G.K.: The JPEG still picture compression standard. IEEE TCE **38**(1), xviii-xxxiv (1992)
45. Wang, H., Schuster, G.M., Katsaggelos, A.K., Pappas, T.N.: An efficient rate-distortion optimal shape coding approach utilizing a skeleton-based decomposition. IEEE TIP **12**(10), 1181–1193 (2003)
46. Wang, J.: 3S-DMD supplementary material (2021). https://github.com/WangJieying/3S-DMD-resources
47. Wang, J., Kosinka, J., Telea, A.: Spline-based dense medial descriptors for lossy image compression. J. Imag. **7**(8), 153 (2021)
48. Wang, J., Kosinka, J., Telea, A.: Spline-based medial axis transform representation of binary images. Comput. Graph. **98**, 165–176 (2021)
49. Wang, J., de Melo Joao, L., Falcão, A., Kosinka, J., Telea, A.: Focus-and-context skeleton-based image simplification using saliency maps. In: Proceedings of the VISAPP, pp. 45–55. SciTePress (2021)
50. Wang, J., Terpstra, M., Kosinka, J., Telea, A.: Quantitative evaluation of dense skeletons for image compression. Information **11**(5), 274 (2020)
51. Wang, W., Lai, Q., Fu, H., Shen, J., Ling, H.: Salient object detection in the deep learning era: An in-depth survey. IEEE TPAMI PP (2021)
52. Wang, Z., Bovik, A., Sheikh, H., Simoncelli, E.: Image quality assessment: from error visibility to structural similarity. IEEE TIP **13**, 600–612 (2004)
53. Wang, Z., Bovik, A.: Mean squared error: Love it or leave it? a new look at signal fidelity measures. IEEE Signal Proc. Mag. **26**, 98–117 (2009)
54. Wang, Z., Simoncelli, E., Bovik, A.: Multiscale structural similarity for image quality assessment. In: ACSSC, pp. 1398–1402 (2003)
55. Yushkevich, P., Thomas Fletcher, P., Joshi, S., Thall, A., Pizer, S.M.: Continuous medial representations for geometric object modeling in 2D and 3D. Image Vision Comput. **21**(1), 17–27 (2003)
56. Zhang, J., et al.: Hypergraph optimization for salient region detection based on foreground and background queries. IEEE Access **6**, 26729–267241 (2018)
57. Zhu, Y., Sun, F., Choi, Y.K., Jüttler, B., Wang, W.: Computing a compact spline representation of the medial axis transform of a 2D shape. Graphical Models **76**(5), 252–262 (2014)
58. Zwan, M.V.D., Meiburg, Y., Telea, A.: A dense medial descriptor for image analysis. In: Proceedings of the VISAPP, pp. 285–293 (2013)
59. Zünd, F., Pritch, Y., Sorkine-Hornung, A., Mangold, S., Gross, T.: Content-aware compression using saliency-driven image retargeting. In: IEEE ICIP, pp. 1845–1849 (2013)

BS-GAENets: Brain-Spatial Feature Learning Via a Graph Deep Autoencoder for Multi-modal Neuroimaging Analysis

Refka Hanachi[1]([✉]) [ID], Akrem Sellami[2] [ID], and Imed Riadh Farah[1,3] [ID]

[1] RIADI Laboratory, ENSI, University of Manouba, Manouba 2010, Tunisia
refka.hanachi@ensi.u-manouba.tn, riadh.farah@ensi.rnu.tn
[2] CRIStAL Laboratory, University of Lille, 59655 Villeneuve-d'Ascq, France
akrem.sellami@univ-lille.fr
[3] ITI Department, IMT Atlantique, 655 Avenue du Technopôle, 29280 Plouzané, France

Abstract. The obsession with how the brain and behavior are related is a challenge for cognitive neuroscience research, for which functional magnetic resonance imaging (fMRI) has significantly improved our understanding of brain functions and dysfunctions. In this paper, we propose a novel multi-modal spatial cerebral graph based on an attention mechanism called MSCGATE that combines both fMRI modalities: task-, and rest-fMRI based on spatial and cerebral features to preserve the rich complex structure between brain voxels. Moreover, it attempts to project the structural-functional brain connections into a new multi-modal latent representation space, which will subsequently be inputted to our trace regression predictive model to output each subject's behavioral score. Experiments on the InterTVA dataset reveal that our proposed approach outperforms other graph representation learning-based models, in terms of effectiveness and performance.

Keywords: Spatial-cerebral features · Graph deep representation learning · Multi-modal MRI · Regression

1 Introduction

In cognitive neuroscience, analyzing and characterizing the complex human brain activity has gained considerable interest over the past few decades, whether that it is driven experimentally, or clinically, and whose main debate consists on how to effectively make such a relationship between a brain characteristic and a behavioral score, reflecting its performance for instance, in an intelligence task or assessing the magnitude of the disease. This leads them to subsequently be able to interpret the brain regions responsible for these cognitive functions. Hence, the advent of powerful new brain imaging has provided valuable information and has brought us insights into the dynamic neural features.

Magnetic Resonance Imaging (MRI) has recently proved to be useful and tends to be the most suitable method, providing, in particular, a true structural and functional

© Springer Nature Switzerland AG 2023
A. A. de Sousa et al. (Eds.): VISIGRAPP 2021, CCIS 1691, pp. 303–327, 2023.
https://doi.org/10.1007/978-3-031-25477-2_14

mapping of the brain, such that both its anatomy (structural MRI (sMRI)) and its functions (functional MRI (fMRI)) can be observed. More crucially, fMRI has been used to visualize brain activity by detecting changes in cerebral hemodynamics. Moreover, it has expanded our understanding of healthy humans' brain organization by mapping the brain activity induced by a set of tasks that the participant performs in a controlled manner in the scanner (task-fMRI) as well as the mapping of functional connectivity from fMRI recordings of resting participants (rest-fMRI). Therefore, examining each voxel's time series and detecting whether the oxygen change in blood flow known as Blood-Oxygen-Level Dependent (BOLD) signal, is altered when responding to a given stimulus is the general aim of the fMRI method to infer the human brain's neuronal activity. In this context, several studies have been conducted for which standard approaches used by neuroscientists [1,2], are focused on the univariate correlational analysis between a selected cerebral characteristic or such a single MRI modality and a behavioral score to determine individual differences. However, this method is very limiting in terms of future observations, since the study of each voxel is carried out in isolation. Therefore, no single modality has yet become the preferred alternative to address all brain function neuroscience issues. In fact, collecting multi-modal brain MRI from the same subject can effectively capitalize on the intensity of each imaging modality, and provide a comprehensive perspective into the brain [3,4], for which fMRI has enabled a wide-ranging analysis in numerous application areas including reading exception words [5], face selectivity [6], and substantial clinical initiative to classify individual subjects either as patients or as controls [7].

Nevertheless, the study of multi-modal brain images is highly complex, involving the use of advanced experimental methods from raw data acquisition to image processing and statistical analysis in order to get the finished output presented typically as statistical maps showing which regions of the brain have reacted to any specific cognitive functions. The General Linear Model (GLM), for instance, is the most commonly used method in fMRI data analysis as part of the Statistical Parametric Mapping (SPM) analysis pipeline. In addition, as a single acquisition of fMRI results in a huge amount of noisy data measured in voxels per session, numerous computational method challenges are required. To approach this high dimensionality problem, dedicated methods to increase comprehensibility and improve the model's performance were emphasized including three key groups: Feature Selection (FS) by disposing of uninformative and irrelevant features, Feature Extraction (FE) to create new features based on the existing ones, and Representation Learning (RL) by learning a function for a better data representation. Various methods like Principal Component Analysis (PCA), Independant Component Analysis (ICA) were applied in the literature, operating on regular data in a grid-sampled structure. However, by considering the brain spatial information between voxels (sMRI), one delicate issue links the nature of these data accentuating the intricate graph structure for which several challenges have been raised in handling the irregular data, and extending deep learning approaches to the graph domain. These considerations were addressed in our previous work [8], where we proposed a multi-modal graph deep learning method that fuses both fMRI modalities based on Brain Adjacency Graph (BAG) generated from sMRI to quantify each subject's performance in voice recognition and identification.

In the present work, an in-depth study of related multi-view representation learning models based on regular data has been carried out. Furthermore, the method was enhanced by developing one extra cerebral graph. In fact, in addition to retaining the spatial information between the brain voxels, we developed a spatial-cerebral graph that aims to handle both fMRI cerebral features estimated at each vertex of the brain and its adjacent neighbors. Accordingly, a new multi-modal graph autoencoder network structure is proposed. Three main contributions are defined:

1. An adaptive dimensionality reduction of two fMRI modalities by using both the 3-D mesh spatial information and the cerebral brain features to preserve the related information using a Graph Autoencoder (GAE) model which allows to project each feature vector of each modality, associated with each vertex of the spatial-cerebral graph in a new representation space.
2. A fusion of the complementarity resulting from two previous feature vectors. It will thus be performed by the multi-modal GAE model receiving the two graph input pairs of two reduced feature vectors using different fusion operators in the fusion layer.
3. Once we get fused the compressed representation Z of both fMRI modalities, a predictive trace regression model to output the scalar score of each subject is designed.

Besides that, experiments were also improved in which unimodal and multi-modal comparative studies between the different representation learning methods, including PCA, ICA, and AE were conducted.

The rest of this paper is organized as follows. Section 2 describes related multi-modal graph deep learning models. Section 3 reveals in detail our proposed method based on the multi-modal spatial-cerebral graph autoencoder and the predictive trace regression model. In Sect. 4, our experimental results over the InterTVA dataset are presented. Finally, in Sect. 5, a conclusion is provided.

2 Existing Work

In this section, we briefly review some of the numerous models dedicated to studying multi-modal representation learning relying both on regular and irregular data, and explore their mathematical concepts.

2.1 Feature Extraction (FE)

Experimentally determined, fMRI is often arranged in 3-D, and each its application results in a huge amount of data measured in voxels (3-D pixels). Each of which contains one value that represents the mean signal (BOLD) computed at a given location. Therefore, learning this series of brain data poses various challenges to accurate analysis and interpretation in order to achieve the best results, one of which is the extremely high dimensional features. In this regard, numerous studies rely on FE methods that refer to the mapping process of an n-dimensional point into a lower p-dimensional space to better fit a predictive model and improve learning performance. Typically, it seeks to extract relevant features denoted by $Z \in \mathbb{R}^{n \times p}$ from a high dimensional MRI data $X \in \mathbb{R}^{n \times D}$, where n is the number of pixels, D is the number of initial features, and p is the number of extracted features. Formally, the main goal of the FE is given as follows:

$$Z = f(X) \tag{1}$$

where f is an extraction function that can be either linear or non-linear through PCA [9], locality-preserving projection (LPP) [10], Locally Linear Embedding (LLE) [11], Laplacian Feature Mapping (LFM) [12], etc. Years later, neural network research has had significant success in data representation, to which many state-of-the-art models have contributed by learning a function that simplifies the extraction of relevant features known as RL or Feature Learning. Hence we discern two major groups as shown in Fig. 1: one based on Euclidean data, where the datatypes are in a regularly structured 1–2 dimensional domain and the other based on non-Euclidean data with irregular structure, commonly called graphs. The group on the left which focuses on structured data requires three key analytical approaches: AutoEncoder (AE), Convolutional Neural Network (CNN), and Canonical Correlation Analysis (CCA). For the other group, various approaches have been proposed in the literature, which maps nodes into a latent representation space in which such p-dimensional space is considered to be sufficiently informative to preserve the original network structure. To do so, some of them use random walks [13–15] to directly obtain the embeddings for each node, while others are defined under the Graph Neural Network (GNN) model which addresses the network embedding problem based on adjacency matrix computation, through the Graph AE (GAE) model [16] as well as GraphSage [17] : a Convolutional Graph Neural Networks (ConvGNNs) spatial-based model.

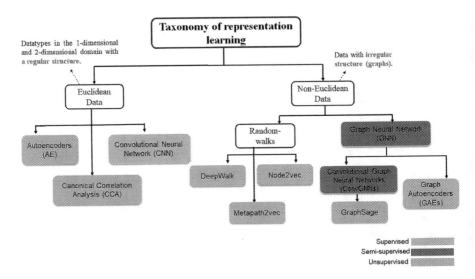

Fig. 1. A taxonomy of representation learning based on Euclidean and non-Euclidean data.

2.2   Muti-view Representation Learning

It is a critical research topic that combines the information acquired from particular unimodal data into a single compact representation. Several approaches have been used to justify the use of complementarity in existing data, highlighting significant dependencies that are difficult to track with a single modality. In this regard, CNN, CCA, and AE go for the most dedicated shared representation methods.

Multi-view Representation Learning Based on CNN. CNN is a specialized Deep Neural Network (DNN) that has shown successful results for computer vision and image processing, which includes the feature extractor in the learning process to automatically learn high level features through backpropagation by using multiple learning blocks. Unlike unimodal CNN, multi-view CNN is dedicated to learning features over multiple modalities, allowing separate representation learning for each view and then mapping them into a shared space where mid-level fusion (features level) is involved (at the convolution layer) to learn multi-view correspondence feature maps [19]. Given two modalities a and b, each associated with a learned feature map X^a and X^b. Basically multi-view feature fusion at convolution layer includes Sum, Max and Concatenation operations, where

- *Sum Operation*: computes the sum of the two feature maps $X^a + X^b$,
- *Max Operation*: takes the maximum of the two feature map max $\{X^a, X^b\}$,
- *Concatenation Operation*: that concatenates the two set of feature maps $[X^a, X^b]$.

Multi-view Representation Learning Based on CCA. CCA was proposed in 1936 and it is one of the most popular multi-view representation learning techniques of connecting two sets of features by finding a linear combination among these sets that are maximally correlated. Comparing to PCA, CCA describes the coordinate system that describes the maximum *cross-covariance* between *two data sets*.

Formally explained, given a pair of observations, denoted from two points of view $(x_1, y_1)..(x_n, y_n)$, each view of which is associated with a matrix respectively $X \in \mathbb{R}^{d_x}$ and $Y \in \mathbb{R}^{d_y}$, CCA aims to find direction vectors u_j, w_j, with $j \in \{1, ..., ..., k\}$ that maximize the correlation between the projections $u_j^T X$ and $w_j^T Y$ in the projected space:

$$u_j w_j = arg_{u,w} max corr(u_j^T X w_j^T Y) \tag{2}$$

A few years later, the success of CCA and DNN in representation learning has motivated many researchers to develop a model that benefits from their complementarity and allows CCA to be expanded to take into account the non-linearity of data, for which, Deep Canonical Correlation Analysis (DCCA) [20] has gained more attention. It's a non-linear extension of the linear method CCA which requires multiple views of data. Moreover, it consists of multiple stacked layers of two DNN f and g to compute representations and extract non linear features for each view, where the canonical correlation between the extracted features $f(X)$ and $g(Y)$ is maximized:

$$max_{W_f, W_g, U, V} = \frac{1}{N} tr(U^T f(X) g(Y)^T V) \tag{3}$$

$$s.t. \qquad U^T(\frac{1}{N}f(X)f(X)^T + r_x I)U = I,$$

$$V^T(\frac{1}{N}g(Y)g(Y)^T + r_y I)V = I,$$

$$u_i^T f(X)g(Y)^T v_j = 0, \quad for \quad i \neq j,$$

where $U = [u_1, \dots , u_L]$ and $V = [v_1, \dots , v_L]$ presents the CCA directions, f and g are non-linear transformations of the two DNNs and (r_x, r_y) are regularization parameters for sample auto-covariance matrices.

Multi-view Representation Learning Based on AE. It is an unsupervised neural network algorithm which learns latent representation through input reconstruction by reducing the reconstruction error. It consists of two networks : the first is called *encoder:* $AE_{Enc(X)}$ that automatically extracts useful features from an input $X \in \mathbb{R}^{n \times D}$ and aims to map them into a latent space representation $Z \in \mathbb{R}^{n \times p}$. The second is called *decoder:* $AE_{Dec(Z)}$ which reconstructs and recovers the original data $\hat{X}$ based on a learning function essentially used Mean Squared Error (MSE) :

$$\frac{1}{N}\sum_{i=1}^{N}(X_i - \hat{X}_i) \qquad (4)$$

where X and $\hat{X}$ are ideally identical ($X \approx \hat{X}$) and $X > Z$. Then, to learn features over multiple modalities, Split AE, and multi-modal Deep Autoencoder (MDAE) have been proposed [18].
Split AE attempts to extract the common representation from a single view which can be used to reconstruct all views where it is presumed that the reconstruction networks are distinct for each view.

MDAE [21], unlike Split AE, it requires multiple modalities as inputs to find a shared representation of them via training a bimodal deep AE. It consists of two separate inputs and outputs, where each view is allocated separate hidden layers and then uses the concatenated final hidden layer of both views as input and maps them to a common embedding layer. The loss function on input pairs X, Y, is defined as follows :

$$\mathcal{L}(x_i, y_i; \theta) = \mathcal{L}_I(x_i, y_i; \theta) + \mathcal{L}_T(x_i, y_i; \theta) \qquad (5)$$

where $\mathcal{L}_I, \mathcal{L}_T$ are the generally perceived squared error loss caused by data reconstruction for the given inputs X and Y :

$$\mathcal{L}_I(x_i, y_i; \theta) = \|x_i - x_i'\|_2^2$$
$$L_T(x_i, y_i; \theta) = \|y_i - y_i'\|_2^2$$

Furthermore, and to sum up, while previous models are effective to capture hidden patterns of Euclidean data, there has been an increasing interest in learning about non-Euclidean data with undefined structures and unknown properties. As a result, they are unable to handle the complicated structure of graphs, posing various challenges in applying deep learning approaches to graph data. Hence, graph RL has attracted considerable research attention over the past few years.

2.3 Graph Representation Learning

Two major groups can be defined as mentioned previously: Random walks, and GNN based approaches. We present a complete description of these methods in the following sections.

Random Walk Based Approaches. The key idea behind these approaches is to optimize node embedding by quantifying similarity between nodes by their co-occurrence over the graph on short, random walks [22]. The three popular methods are:

DeepWalk [13]: It is based on two major steps. The first addresses the neighborhood relations by randomly selecting the first node and traverses then the network to identify its related nodes. The second step uses a SkipGram algorithm [23] to update and learn node representations by optimizing node similarities that share the same information.

Node2vec [15]: Representation Learning based on CNN an advanced version of Deep-Walk, that considers two biased random walks p and q to identify the neighborhood of nodes. p controls the likelihood of immediately revisiting a node in the walk [15] and q controls the likelihood of exposed parts of the graph is not explored.

Metapath2vec [14]: Representation Learning based on CNN it was proposed to handle the network's heterogeneity by maximizing its probability. It uses a meta-path random walk that determines the node type order within which the random walker traverses the graph to ensure that the semantic relationships between nodes type are incorporated into SkipGram.

GNN Based Approaches. Both surveys [16] and [24] define various models based on GNN such as ConvGNNs and GAE, etc.

ConvGNNs: It was proposed to manage convolution operations on graph domains in generating a node v's representation by aggregating neighbors' features x_u with its own features x_v, where $u \in N(v)$ [16]. It covers two main approaches: spectral-based in which, the convolution operation is defined over the entire graph, and spatial-based that defines convolution by taking each node into account, and aggregates neighborhood information. One of the most applied spatial-based approaches is namely, GraphSage (SAmple and aggreGatE) [17]. It first defines the set of the neighborhood for each node by fixing a parameter $k \in \{1, ..., K\}$ that controls the neighborhood depth, then, it trains a set of aggregator functions to learn the node's representation given its feature and local neighborhood: for each node, it generates a neighborhood representation with an aggregator function and concatenates it to the current node representation through which a fully connected layer is fed with a nonlinear activation function [17].

GAE: It encodes nodes/graphs into a latent vector space and reconstructs graph data from the encoded information [16]. Its architecture consists of two networks: an encoder *enc()* to extract a node's feature information by using graph convolutional layers and a decoder *dec()* to reconstruct the graph adjacency matrix $\hat{A}$ while preserving the graph topological information [16] based on a learning function which computes the distance between a node's inputs and its reconstructed inputs.

3 Proposed Approach

In this section, we present our proposed method including the multi-modal graph autoencoder based on attention mechanism (MSCGATE), and the predictive model. Figure 2 reports the general overview of the proposed methodology.

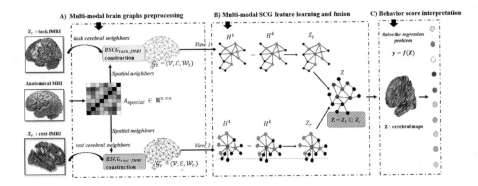

Fig. 2. General overview of the proposed multi-modal graph deep learning method.

Three key phases are defined:

A) **Multi-modal Brain Graphs Preprocessing:** the goal is to use common pipelines to analyze both task-, and rest-fMRI fMRI modalities, that provide 3-D brain scans with 20–40 thousand voxels in a three-dimensional rectangular cuboid, whose dimensions are in the range of millimeters, each of which has an associated time-series of as many time-points as volumes acquired per session. Each brain slice has been processed using SPM12 for slice-timing correction and motion's correction of both data. Then, statistical analysis based on GLM has been performed on all voxels to identify activated brain areas as well as Region Of Interest (ROI) definitions.

(a) *task-fMRI preprocessing:* the estimation of the parameters of the GLM model results in a set of features which consist of the pattern of β-values computed on each pixel per subject in a cognitive task, that allows then, constructing the activation matrix $X_t \in \mathbb{R}^{n \times D_t}$ where n the number of pixels $i \in \{1, 2, ..., n\}$ and D the initial dimension of features.

(b) *rest-fMRI preprocessing:* it requires the participants to remain quiet while lying in the scanner to evaluate functional connectivity. It was performed using FreeSurfer to identify the set of pixels whose time series correlated with the time series of each ROIs in the regions of the Destrieux atlas, i.e. how much the pixel X_i relates the region ROI_j. Therefore, we compute the average matrix of All ROIs, and the correlation between the pixel and the mean of each ROI using a correlation coefficient such as Pearson coefficient :

$$\mathcal{P}(X_i, ROI_j) = \frac{cov(X_i, ROI_j)}{\sigma X_i \sigma ROI_j} \tag{6}$$

These correlations constitute then the feature vector $X_r \in \mathbb{R}^{D_r > 100 features}$ estimated on each pixel per subject. Moreover, two cerebral graphs $\mathcal{G}_{task\_cerebral}$ and $\mathcal{G}_{rest\_cerebral}$ are defined from these two matrices, each of which takes into account the cerebral related task-, and rest fMRI features estimated at each vertex of the brain with a feature vector ($X_{ti} \in \mathbb{R}^{D_t}$ and $X_{ri} \in \mathbb{R}^{D_r}$) respectively, where D_t and $D_r > 100$ features. Similarly, for the sMRI modality, we extract the cortical surface by obtaining the 3-D mesh incorporating the voxels. From this 3-D mesh, we therefore create the two spatial graphs $\mathcal{G}_{task\_spatial}$ and $\mathcal{G}_{rest\_spatial}$ in which, each voxel specifies its adjacent neighbors. Furthermore, we obtain then two spatial-cerebral graphs $\mathcal{G}_t$ and $\mathcal{G}_r$ by combining the two previous graphs for each fMRI modality to better handle the related cerebral features and the spatial connectivity.

B) **Multi-modal SCG Feature Learning and Fusion:** it consists of building an MSC-GATE model, which takes as input two spatial-cerebral graphs, i.e., $\mathcal{G}_t$ and $\mathcal{G}_r$. The goal is to learn locally a latent representation of the multi-modal information by considering the neighborhood information between voxels.

C) **Behavior Score Interpretation:** it involves solving the regression problem, that is, predicting the behavioral score measuring each subject's performance in a cognitive task using the latent representation Z with a trace regression model operating at the subject level.

3.1   Multi-modal Brain Graphs (BGs) Construction

We now explore the Brain Graphs (BGs) construction from both the triangulated mesh 3-D and the activation, and correlation matrices as illustrated in Fig. 3.

Brain Spatial Graph (BSG). sMRI was used to present the connections of each brain vertex from which we obtain a triangulated 3-D mesh representing the cortex surface denoted $\mathcal{G}(\mathcal{V}, \mathcal{E})$ where $\mathcal{V}$ refers to the set of vertices $\{v_1, ..., v_n\}$, $\mathcal{E}$ represents its connectivity with respect to the edges of the graph $\{e_1, ..., e_{\mathcal{E}}\}$ ($e_i \in \mathcal{V} \times \mathcal{V}$). Motivated by the need for a structural representation of the basic topological information provided by $\mathcal{G}$ to traverse the triangulation, an efficient approach is to store the set of edges $\mathcal{E}$ in an adjacency matrix $\mathbf{A}_{spatial} \in \mathbb{R}^{n \times n}$ where n the number of pixels. Therefore, it is generated using the following formula :

$$\mathbf{A}_{spatial}(v, e_i) = \begin{cases} 1, & \text{if } v \in e_i \\ 0, & \text{otherwise} \end{cases} \tag{7}$$

Additionally, $\mathbf{A}_{spatial}$ allows each connection between pixels to be projected in a 2-D structure and where each pixel specifies its five vertices from $\mathcal{V}$ for a current neighborhood size $k = 1$ and six vertices with the added self-loops. Therefore, increasing the neighborhood size can introduce unnecessary sharing of information between pixels. Moreover, getting too big k can also trigger all pixels to have the same representation.

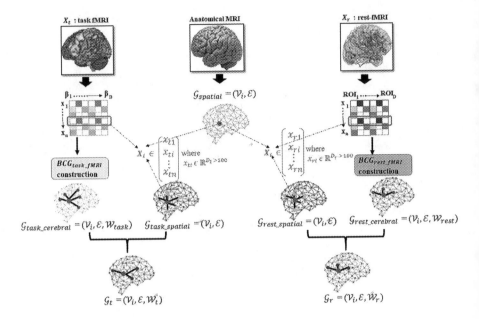

Fig. 3. Multi-modal Brain Graphs (BGs) construction.

More formally, Algorithm 1 provides a computational demonstration from the 3-D triangulated mesh to the resulted of two BSGs, i.e., $\mathcal{G}_{task\_spatial}$ and $\mathcal{G}_{rest\_spatial}$.

Input: 3-D mesh M, scalar k, activation matrix X_t, and correlation matrix X_r,
/* Generate $\mathbf{A}_{spatial}$ from the *mesh*   */
initialization;
$\mathbf{A}_{spatial} = 0, k = 1$;
for $i \leftarrow 1$ **to** n **do**
    for $j \leftarrow 1$ **to** n **do**
        if $M_{i,j} \in \mathcal{N}_k(M)$ *are connected* **then**
            $\mathbf{A}_{spatial}(i,j) \leftarrow 1$;
        end
    end
end
/* Generate $\mathcal{G}_{task\_spatial}$, $\mathcal{G}_{rest\_spatial}$ using $\mathbf{A}_{spatial}$, X_t and
   X_r */
$\mathcal{G}_{task\_spatial} \leftarrow (\mathcal{V}, \mathcal{E}, X_t)$;
$\mathcal{G}_{rest\_spatial} \leftarrow (\mathcal{V}, \mathcal{E}, X_r)$
Algorithm 1. BSG construction Algorithm.

Brain Cerebral Graph (BCG). The aim here is to integrate the pixels' neighboring cerebral features. Therefore, we construct from the two activation, and correlation matrices, two graphs $\mathcal{G}_{task\_cerebral} = (\mathcal{V}, \mathcal{E}, \mathcal{W}_{task})$ and $\mathcal{G}_{rest\_cerebral} = (\mathcal{V}, \mathcal{E}, \mathcal{W}_{rest})$, respectively. $\mathcal{V}$ is a set of vertices, $\mathcal{E}$ are the edges of the corresponding graph, $\mathcal{W}_{task\_cerebral}$, and $\mathcal{W}_{rest\_cerebral}$ are the weighted matrices. Moreover, the weight $w_{i,j}$ for the edge $e_{i,j}$ is computed as follows :

$$\mathcal{W}_{cerebral}(e_i) = \frac{1}{\lambda + dist(v_i, v_j)} \tag{8}$$

where λ is a heat kernel, $dist(v_i, v_j) = \|v_i - v_j\|_2^2$ is the euclidean distance, v_i and v_j are the activation, or/and the correlation coordinates with respect to the corresponding matrix. In order to take the nearest neighbors to v_i, we controlled the neighborhood size k based on a well defined threshold s. Then, the adjacency matrix $\mathbf{A}_{cerebral}$, i.e., $\mathbf{A}_{task\_cerebral}$, and $\mathbf{A}_{rest\_cerebral}$ is obtained:

$$\mathbf{A}_{cerebral}(v, e_i) = \begin{cases} 1, & \text{if } w_{i,j} < s \\ 0, & \text{otherwise} \end{cases} \tag{9}$$

Brain Spatial-Cerebral Graph (BSCG). To reveal the intrinsic relations between voxels of the brain, we mix here the two constructed graphs, i.e., the spatial and cerebral graphs into a fused graph brain for each fMRI modality to be inputted then into the designed GAE for training. Therefore, we obtain $\mathcal{G}_t = (\mathcal{V}, \mathcal{E}, \mathcal{W}_t)$, and $\mathcal{G}_r = (\mathcal{V}, \mathcal{E}, \mathcal{W}_r)$. The weighted matrix $\mathcal{W}$ of each corresponding graph: $\mathcal{W}_t$, and $\mathcal{W}_r$ is therefore defined as follows:

$$\mathcal{W}(e_i) = \varrho \mathcal{W}_{cerebral}(e_i) + (1 - \varrho)\mathcal{W}_{spatial}(e_i) \tag{10}$$

where ϱ defines a compromise between spatial and cerebral fMRI features of each voxel at each graph location. Moreover, the adjacency matrix $\mathbf{A}$, i.e., $\mathbf{A}_t$, or/and $\mathbf{A}_r$ is generated :

$$\mathbf{A}(v, e_i) = \begin{cases} 1, & \text{if } \mathcal{W}(e_i) > 0 \\ 0, & \text{otherwise} \end{cases} \tag{11}$$

3.2 Multi-modal Graph Auto-Encoder Based on the Attention Mechanism (MSCGATE)

Once the BSCG is constructed, our aim is to learn locally a multi-modal latent representation from both modalities task-, and rest-fMRI by aggregating for each voxel the information of its neighborhood. Therefore, we firstly, present the SCGATE feature extractor model. Then, we describe the multi-modal SCGATE (MSCGATE) with different fusion layers.

Feature Learning with SCGATE Model. The main analysis keys, in our approach, target the noisy nature and vast amount of multi-modal imaging data with regard to the number of features per voxel from the pre-processed brain scans in each subject which greatly surpassed the number of training samples. While, it is now crucial to admit only the relevant features contributing to a better data interpretability, hence we choose to

design a graph representation learning network based on AE and the attention mechanism as a feature extractor method simply called SCGATE. The key reason behind it, is
the projection of a graph into a latent representation space based on encoding-decoding
networks in which such low-dimensional space is considered to be sufficiently informative to preserve the original graph structure. Its main architecture includes two networks: Graph Encoder $G_{Enc()}$ and Graph Decoder $G_{Dec()}$ for each modality.

Graph Encoder Network $G_{Enc()}$: It seeks to build new latent representations of vertices
by taking the graph structure into account through stacked layers. Each single graph
encoder layer attempts to aggregate the information from the neighboring vertices of a
target vertex yielding a richer node representations according to their relevance. To allocate learnable weights to the aggregation, an attention mechanism is implemented. The
weights can therefore be directly expressed by attention coefficients between nodes and
provide interpretability. Formally, a single graph layer of $G_{Enc()}$ based on the attention
mechanism can be defined as follows

$$h_i^l = \sigma((\sum_{j \in \mathcal{N}_i} \alpha_{ij}^{(l)} W^{(l)} h_j^{(l-1)})) \tag{12}$$

where h_i^l is the new representation of vertex i in the $l - th$ layer. $\mathcal{N}_i$ is the set of vertex
i's neighbors. α_{ij} is the aggregation weight, which measures how important vertex j to
vertex i, and σ denotes the activation function. In our case, we use the attention mechanism in order to compute aggregation weight, i.e., to measure the relevance between
vertices and their neighbors. Formally, it can be expressed as:

$$\alpha_{ij} = \frac{exp(\sigma(\vec{a}^T [W \vec{h}_i || W \vec{h}_j]))}{\sum_{k \in \mathcal{N}_i} exp(\sigma(\vec{a}^T [W \vec{h}_i || W \vec{h}_k]))} \tag{13}$$

where $\vec{a}$ denotes the weigh vector of the mechanism attention, and $||$ is the concatenation
operation.

Graph Decoder Network $G_{Dec()}$: It allows to reconstruct and recover the input data,
$\hat{X} = G_{Dec}(X, (\mathbf{A}))$. Each graph decoder layer seeks to reconstruct the node representations by considering the representations of their neighbors according to their importance and relevance, which allows capturing the hidden representation of vertices containing the rich features. As $G_{Enc()}$, the $G_{Dec()}$ specifies the same number of layers
in which each graph decoder layer seeks to reverse the process of its corresponding
graph encoder layer. Formally, a single graph layer of $G_{Dec()}$ based on the attention
mechanism can be defined as follows:

$$\hat{h}_i^l = \sigma((\sum_{j \in \mathcal{N}_i} \alpha_{ij}^{(l)} \hat{W}^{(l)} h_j^{(l-1)})) \tag{14}$$

Loss function $\mathcal{L}$: Node features and graph structure are included in the graph-structured
data for which both should be encoded by high-quality node representations. Hence,

we use the MSE loss function to minimize the reconstruction error of node features as follows:

$$\mathcal{L} = \sum_{i=1}^{N} ||X_i - \hat{X}_i||_2 \tag{15}$$

MSCGATE with Fusion Layer. In order to learn a better representation from multiple input modalities, i.e., both fMRI modalities based on BSCG, an MSCGATE is designed which shares with the SCGATE model, the two networks: $G_{Enc()}$ and $G_{Dec()}$ per modality, i.e., $SCGATE_t$ and $SCGATE_r$. In fact, they take as inputs their correspond BSCG, i.e., $\mathcal{G}_t = (X_t, A_t)$, and $\mathcal{G}_r = (X_r, A_t)$ respectively. The two SCGATEs: $SCGATE_t$ and $SCGATE_r$ transform the multi-modal inputs into a basically lower-dimensional representation (every cortical locations in both fMRI modalities) $X_t \in \mathbb{R}^{n \times D_t}$ and $X_r \in \mathbb{R}^{n \times D_r}$ and project them into a latent space representation $Z_t \in \mathbb{R}^{n \times p_t}$ and $Z_r \in \mathbb{R}^{n \times p_r}$. Moreover, both latent representations Z_t and Z_r will be fused in order to find a common shared space. In this context, various types of fusion operations can be used to get compressed latent representations of both input modalities. These operations include *max-pooling()* which takes the maximum of Z_t and Z_r, *mean-pooling()* which is the average between Z_t and Z_r, *concat()* which concatenates Z_t and Z_r, and *inner-product()* that is a generalization of the dot product operation between samples in both Z_t and Z_r. The MSCGATE seeks then to reconstruct each modality using the common latent representation Z, i.e., $\hat{X}_t = MSCGATE_{Dec}(Z)$, and $\hat{X}_r = MSCGATE_{Dec}(Z)$. Figure 4 reports the main architecture of the proposed MSCGATE.

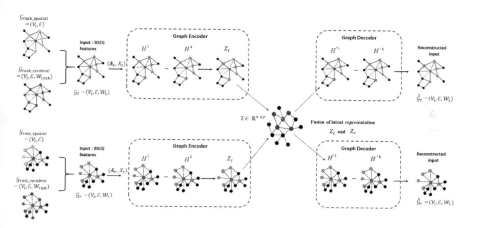

Fig. 4. MSCGATE architecture that learns a better representation from the fused multiple input views Z.

The MSCGATE is trained using MSE loss function which is defined as follows, taking into account for example, the *concat* operator to get fused both latent representations :

$$\mathcal{L}(X_t, X_r; \theta) = \mathcal{L}_t(X_t, X_r; \theta) + \mathcal{L}_r(X_t, X_r; \theta) \tag{16}$$

where

$$\mathcal{L}_t(X_t, X_r; \theta) = \frac{1}{N} \| MSCGATE_{Dec_t}(concat(MSCGATE_{Enc_t}(X_t), MSCGATE_{Enc_r}(X_r))) - \hat{X}_t \|^2$$

$$\mathcal{L}_r(X_t, X_r; \theta) = \frac{1}{N} \| MSCGATE_{Dec_r}(concat(MSCGATE_{Enc_t}(X_t), MSCGATE_{Enc_r}(X_r))) - \hat{X}_r \|^2$$

More formally, Algorithm 2 summarizes the entire generation of multi-modal representation $Z \in \mathbb{R}^{n \times p}$ from the combination of both fMRI modalities based on BSCG.

Input: Pair of $\mathcal{G}_t(\mathbf{A}_t, X_t)$, $\mathcal{G}_r(\mathbf{A}_r, X_r)$ where $X_t \in \mathbb{R}^{n \times D_t}$, $X_r \in \mathbb{R}^{n \times D_r}$, $\mathbf{A}_t \in \mathbb{R}^{n \times n}$, and $\mathbf{A}_r \in \mathbb{R}^{n \times n}$.

for $enc \leftarrow 2$ **to** 100 **do**
　　/* Learn both latent representations from $(\mathbf{A}_t, X_t)$ and
　　　$(\mathbf{A}_r, X_r)$　　　　　　　　　　　　　　　　　　　*/
　　$Z_t = MSCGATE_{Enc_t(\mathbf{A}_t, X_t)}$;
　　$Z_r = MSCGATE_{Enc_r(\mathbf{A}_r, X_r)}$;
　　/* Fusion of Z_t and Z_r　　　　　　　　　　　　　　*/
　　$Z \in \mathbb{R}^{n \times p} = concat(Z_t, Z_r)$;
　　/* From Z, reconstruct the original input pairs　　*/
　　$(\mathbf{A}_t, \hat{X}_t) = MSCGATE_{Dec_t}(Z)$;
　　$(\mathbf{A}_r, \hat{X}_r) = MSCGATE_{Dec_r}(Z)$;
end

Algorithm 2. MSCGATE pipeline.

3.3 Trace Regression Predictive Model

After applying the MSCGATE model upon both fMRI modalities based on BSCG, the objective now is to predict the behavioral score of each subject reflecting its performance in a cognitive task (in a voice recognition task) using the fused latent representation $Z \in \mathbb{R}^{n \times p}$. This prediction is carried out to solve the regression problem basically performed with the well-known linear regression model to predict a scalar response from a vector-valued input, which can be defined as follows :

$$y_i = \beta^T Z_i + \epsilon_i, \qquad i = 1, ..., N \tag{17}$$

where y is the predicted variable, β refers to the regression coefficients, Z is the independent variable, ϵ is a vector of values ϵ_i that add noise to the linear $y - Z$ relation, and $\beta^T Z_i$ is the inner product between Z_i and β. Although this approach was a reasonable compromise when predicting a scalar behavioral score from a vector-valued fMRI data input, it is nevertheless necessary, in our case, to learn a model capable of handling the explanatory variables of the matrix provided by the fused latent representation Z for which the trace regression model has gained rising interest. It is a generalization of the linear regression model that operates on matrix-valued input and attempts to project it into real-valued outputs [25], defined as follows [8]

$$y = tr(\hat{\beta}^T Z) + \epsilon \tag{18}$$

where $tr(.)$ is the trace and $\hat{\beta}$ is the matrix of regression coefficients. Numerous studies [26,27] opted for the regularized least squares to determine an estimation of $\hat{\beta}$ as follows :

$$\hat{\beta} = argmin_\beta \left\{ \sum_{i=1}^{n} (y_i - tr(\beta^T z_i))^2 + \lambda(\beta) \right\} \tag{19}$$

where $\lambda(\beta)$ is a matrix regularizer to explore the low-rank structure of $\hat{\beta}$. In our case, by considering the 3-D mesh, we use a manifold regularization based on Graph Laplacian **G**. To empower the nodes with the same importance as their neighbors, we use two regularization terms where the first is defined based on the *Laplace matrix* **L** of **G**

$$\lambda_1(\beta) = \eta tr(\beta^T \mathbf{L}\beta) \tag{20}$$

where

$$\mathbf{L} = \mathcal{D} - \mathcal{W} \tag{21}$$

$\mathcal{D}$ is a diagonal matrix of node degrees, $\mathcal{D} = \text{diag}(d_1, ..., d_n)$, $\mathcal{W}$ is the weighted adjacency matrix of **G** defined as $\mathcal{W} = (w_{ij})_{i,j=1,...,n}$ with $w_{ij} = w_{ji} \geq 0$, where $w_{ij} = 0$ refers that the vertices v_i and v_j are disconnected. The second lies on the group-sparsity regularization strategy which takes the form

$$\lambda_2(\beta) = \alpha \sum_j \|\beta_j\|^2 \tag{22}$$

Hence, the predictive model is carried out to solve the trace regression problem with the two previous regularization terms

$$\lambda(\beta) = \eta tr(\beta^T \mathbf{L}\beta)/2 + \alpha \sum_j \|\beta_j\|^2 \tag{23}$$

4   Experimental Results

This section discusses the experimental protocol of our proposed method to illustrate its efficiency in the clinical initiative for predicting individual differences in new subjects. It first presents the applied InterTVA dataset to address then the relative results of our predictive model providing both quantitative and qualitative evaluation.

4.1   InterTVA Data Description

Our experiments were conducted on the InterTVA dataset[1], which aims at studying the inter-individual differences using multi-modal MRI data on 40 healthy subjects.

---

[1] https://openneuro.org/datasets/ds001771.

We used an event-related voice localizer in which participants were invited to close their eyes while passively listening to 72 vocal sounds and 72 non-vocal sounds of a fixed duration of 500 ms, with inter-stimulus intervals in the range of 4–5 s. For the rest-fMRI, subjects were asked to rest quit while lying in the scanner for a duration of 12mn. Moreover, anatomical scans (3D T1 images) were acquired for each subject. The main pipeline for analysis of both fMRI modalities (task- and rest-fMRI) includes slice-timing correction and motion's correction using SPM12 (www.fil.ion.ucl.ac.uk/spm). Then, statistical analysis based on GLM has been performed on all voxels. For task-fMRI, the estimation of the parameters of the GLM model results in a set of features that consist of the pattern of β-values induced by hearing each of 144 sounds. This allows therefore, constructing the feature vector $X_t \in \mathbb{R}^{D_t}$ where $D_t = 144$. Rest-fMRI was performed using FreeSurfer to identify the set of voxels whose time series correlated with the time series of each ROIs. These correlations constitute therefore, the feature vector $X_r \in \mathbb{R}^{D_r}$ where $D_r = 150$. These two features are then used as inputs of our graph representation learning model trained with 36×20484 samples. Moreover, four functional runs were performed, each including 36 trials (12 words $\times$ 3 speakers) in which, subjects had to be familiar with three speakers by initially listening to their stories while memorizing the association between the voice and the speaker's name printed on the screen (Anne, Betty and Chloe). The aim here, is not to pay attention to the content of the stories, but rather to try to memorize the voice of the speaker and the connection with his name by pressing one of the three keys on the keyboard built for the experiment to recognize the correct speaker. At the end, a behavioral score is measured which shows the average of the Percentage of correct responses (PC) answered during the 4 runs, in which a total of 144 identification trials were presented (36 trials $\times$ 4 runs):

$$\overline{PC} = \frac{\sum_{i=1}^{m} PC_i}{m} \tag{24}$$

$$= \frac{PC_1 + ... + PC_m}{m} \tag{25}$$

where m is the number of runs.

4.2   Parameters Tuning

Both unimodal SCGATE and multi-modal SCGATE were implemented using the *Keras* framework and learned over 500 epochs with a batch size of 300 training samples. After several tests, we choose the Adam optimizer with a learning rate is equal to 10^{-5}. Moreover, each model was built using three hidden layers for each fMRI modality: $[D_t, 130, 110, \text{enc}, 110, 130, D_t]$ for task-fMRI and $[D_r, 130, 110, \text{enc}, 110, 130, D_r]$ for rest-fMRI in which ten dimensions of the latent representation enc have been developed from 2 to 100 features. In addition, we opted for (*relu, linear*) as an activation functions for the hidden layers and the output layer respectively. Furthermore, we split the whole samples into training and testing sets over 10-fold-cross-validation where each fold consists of 36 subjects for training (36×20484 samples), and 4 subjects for testing (4×20484 samples).

4.3 Performance Evaluation Metrics

In order to evaluate our trace regression model, three performance metrics were computed, i.e., Mean Absolute Error (MAE), MSE, and R-squared score, i.e., R^2 (coefficient of determination):

- MAE seeks to measure the average magnitude of the errors in a series of predictions, without considering their direction. It is defined as follows:

$$MAE = \frac{1}{N} \sum_{i=1}^{N} |y_i - \hat{y}_i| \tag{26}$$

- MSE basically measures the average squared error of our predictions which takes the form:

$$MSE = \frac{1}{N} \sum_{i=1}^{N} (y_i - \hat{y}_i)^2 \tag{27}$$

- R^2 which is the percent of variance explained by the model. It is always going to be between $-\infty$ and 1. Usually, it shows how closely the model estimations match the true values.

$$R^2 = 1 - \frac{MSE(model)}{MSE(baseline)} = 1 - \frac{\sum_{i=1}^{N}(y_i - \hat{y}_i)^2}{\sum_{i=1}^{N}(y_i - \bar{y}_i)^2} \tag{28}$$

where N is the number of subjects, y is the true values (score of behavior), $\hat{y}$ is the predicted values, and $\bar{y}$ is the mean of the true values.

4.4 Prediction Performance

In this section, we provide both quantitative and qualitative evaluation of the proposed predictive model. The quantitative reports the experimental results using unimodal and multi-modal fMRI data performed both with different representation learning models as well as graph representation learning models while the qualitative evaluation discusses the visual interpretation of our predictive model.

Quantitative Evaluation. As mentioned previously, the standard methods used by neuroscientists are based on single fMRI modality studied independently, i.e., task-, or rest-fMRI which results in a univariate correlation analysis. Hence, we address firstly the prediction performances performed with different representation learning models using both unimodal and multi-modal fMRI data and evaluate them according to the best average MSE obtained across 10-fold cross-validation. Therefore, the same procedure will be carried out using different graph representation learning models in which we emphasize the effectiveness and the added value of fusing activation- and connectivity based information.

1. Unimodal Representation Learning: the noisy nature of brain MRI data poses critical challenges to accurate analysis, mitigate the high dimensionality problem of the raw data, and apply different reduction methods to enhance data interpretability. These approaches are typically based on traditional PCA, and ICA, whereas, it has been now a growing interest in applying advanced deep learning techniques such as AE to improve comprehensibility and computation costs. Therefore, we compared these three techniques to explain the usefulness of the AE model for better-compressed representation learning data. The AE was trained using different pairs of activation functions for the hidden layers and output layer: *(linear, linear), (linear, sigmoid), (relu, linear)* and *(relu, sigmoid)*. Therefore, Fig. 5, and 6 report the average MSE across encoding dimensions learned on task- and rest-fMRI data respectively. Hence, we can deduce that with few dimensions, all AE models display compromising results for both data, in which the best MSE value learned on task-fMRI data is reached using AE(*relu, linear*) on 10 encoding dimensions equal to 0.08, while the best MSE value on the rest-fMRI data goes for the AE (*linear, linear*) across 20 encoding dimensions equal to 0.34.

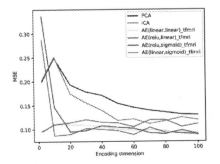 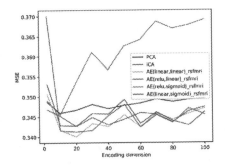

Fig. 5. Average MSE using representation learning methods on task-fMRI.

Fig. 6. Average MSE using representation learning methods on rest-fMRI.

2. Multi-modal Representation Learning: to ensure completeness, we also compared the performances of the models obtained using multi-modal fMRI data with two different architectures: concatenated inputs and concatenated latent representation. Hence, we report in Fig. 7, the best average MSE versus encoding dimensions across 10-fold cross validation learned on fused fMRI data per model using concatenated inputs and in Table 1, the best average MSE and R^2 using concatenated latent representation. Therefore, we can deduce that, for the first architecture, the best results are obtained using the MDAE(*relu, linear*) with an MSE value equal to 0.08 learned on 10 features that are hardly better than those obtained from the unimodal model using task-fMRI. Moreover, all MDAE models exceeds the unimodal ones which really emphasizes the completeness of information from two modalities and that the predictive model provides better efficiency by multi-modal data.

In addition, we can also interpret that, with our multi-modal architecture, the best performances applies to all MDAE models and, in particular, the MDAE(*relu, linear*) model is most suitable for compressing the data and learning them a better representation with an MSE value equal to 0.062 and $R^2 = 0.282$. As a result, we may deduce that an efficient representation learning scheme for the interpretation of human behavior is a multi-modal autoencoder that operates a concatenation of the latent representation compared to performances obtained with the first architecture.

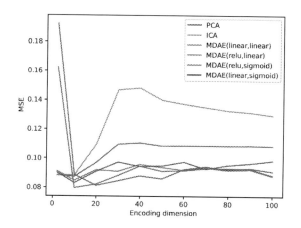

Fig. 7. Average MSE using representation learning methods on multi-modal fMRI data.

Table 1. Best average MSE, and R^2 ($\pm$ standard deviation) using concatenated latent representation estimated on trace regression model based on PCA, ICA, and different MDAE models.

	$Z_t + Z_r$	
Model	MSE	R^2
PCA	N/A	N/A
ICA	N/A	N/A
MDAE (*linear, linear*)	0.065 ($\pm$ 0.0058)	0.273 ($\pm$ 0.0033)
MDAE (*linear, sigmoid*)	0.079 ($\pm$ 0.0124)	0.249 ($\pm$ 0.0204)
MDAE(*relu, linear*)	**0.062 ($\pm$ 0.0095)**	**0.282 ($\pm$ 0.0044)**
MDAE (*relu, sigmoid*)	0.073 ($\pm$ 0.0086)	0.254 ($\pm$ 0.0051)

3. Unimodal Graph Representation Learning: in this section, our model SCGATE is compared to various graph representation learning models including Node2vec, Graph-Sage, DeepWalk, Metapath2vec, and our previous approach GATE [8] based on the reconstruction error MSE which computes the prediction error between the true behavioral score and the estimated one. Therefore, Figs. 8, and 9 report the obtained results where the MSE value varies according to different encoding dimensions using task-, and rest-fMRI based on the constructed BSCG respectively. Thus, we can deduce that when the cerebral similarities are added to the process of GAE, our proposed SCGATE remains the appropriate one for learning representation from both fMRI data which was to be expected as it makes full use of both spatial connectivity, and cerebral features between voxels to learn new latent feature space. Moreover, the obtained MSE is equal to **0.052** learned on 10 dimensions for task-fMRI and **0.1** for encoding dimension $= 30$ for rest-fMRI compared to our previous approach with $= 0.07$, and 0.12 on 10 and 30 features respectively. Furthermore, we can observe that all of the models using task-fMRI perform slightly better than those using rest-fMRI because it fits the task completed with the behavioral GVMT test compared to rest-fMRI with less information about the total brain functional connectivity. Consequently, the Graphsage model appears to have an MSE value of 0.085 on 50 features better than others, i.e., Node2vec, Metapath2vec and Deepwalk with 0.1, 0.11, and 0.12 on 20, 50, and 60 features respectively.

4. Multi-modal Graph Representation Learning: to enrich our experiments and assess the effectiveness of our proposed MSCGATE, another architecture was introduced which is based on the concatenation of inputs (X_t, X_r) to be compared then with the performances obtained in the case of mid-level fusion with different operators such as *AVG(), Max(), Product() and Concat()* using three evaluation metrics MSE, MAE and R^2. Hence, we report in Table 2 and 3 the best average values versus encoding dimension using concatenated inputs and concatenated latent representation for each method respectively. Compared to our previous work, it can be seen that for the first architecture, an important gain of performances is achieved with our proposed MSCGATE for

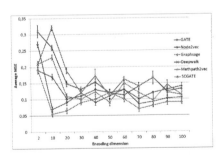

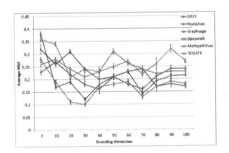

Fig. 8. Average MSE versus encoding dimension across 10-fold cross validation using task-fMRI.

Fig. 9. Average MSE versus encoding dimension across 10-fold cross validation using rest-fMRI.

which the MSE, MAE, and R^2 values climb from 0.057 to 0.055, 0.057 to 0.052, and 0.281 to 0.288, respectively. Besides that, we obtain also, with our second architecture, significant performance improvements with our MSCGATE with all fusion operators, where in particular the inner-product operator reached the best MSE, MAE, and R^2 values equal to 0.047, 0.045, and 0.297, respectively out of 20 features of which 10 were extracted from task,- and 10 of rest-fMRI. Here, we can justify the effectiveness of the complementarity of the information offered by the two modalities based on BSCG constructed compared to the unimodal modality ($MSE_{Z_t+Z_r} < MSE_{task-fMRI}$) and ($MSE_{X_t+X_r} < MSE_{rest-fMRI}$) and that the mid-level fusion is more appropriate for achieving our contribution objective in predicting the behavioral score. In addition, and compared to the performances obtained from multi-modal fMRI data using the MDAE model in Table 1, the added importance of the integration of spatial and cerebral informations in the analysis of human behavior has been clearly demonstrated.

Table 2. Best average MSE, MAE, and R^2 ($\pm$ standard deviation) using concatenated inputs estimated on trace regression model based on Node2vec, Graphsage, Deepwalk, Metapath2vec, MGATE, and MSCGATE models.

Model	$X_t + X_r$		
	MSE	MAE	R^2
Node2vec	0.114 ($\pm$ 0.026)	0.112 ($\pm$ 0.019)	0.120 ($\pm$ 0.014)
Graphsage	0.099 ($\pm$ 0.010)	0.097 ($\pm$ 0.021)	0.141 ($\pm$ 0.017)
Deepwalk	0.122 ($\pm$ 0.013)	0.119 ($\pm$ 0.010)	0.117 ($\pm$ 0.025)
Metapath2vec	0.103 ($\pm$ 0.012)	0.099 ($\pm$ 0.020)	0.142 ($\pm$ 0.016)
MGATE	0.057 ($\pm$ 0.009)	0.057 ($\pm$ 0.010)	0.281 ($\pm$ 0.010)
MSCGATE	**0.055 ($\pm$ 0.013)**	**0.052 ($\pm$ 0.021)**	**0.288 ($\pm$ 0.032)**

Qualitative Evaluation. The aim here is to project estimated beta maps $\hat{beta}$ on the white cortical mesh in order to get a visual interpretation. Therefore, Fig. 10 reports the obtained average beta maps estimated using MSCGATE and trace regression model. Actually, in order to extract significant regions, we use statistical tests including $t-test$ and $p-value$ where $t = 1.985$ and $p < 0.005$. The goal is to assess the evidence presented by the data against a statistical hypothesis, presenting two complementary hypothesis called the *null hypothesis* which defines no significant region. It will be rejected if it appears to be incompatible with the sample data, and the *alternative hypothesis* denoted by H_0, and H_1 respectively. The $t-test$ is a set of parametric statistical tests where the calculated test statistic follows a Student t distribution under the null hypothesis. It is used to assume if the mean of a population varies from the hypothesized value. For instance, giving a sample data $\{Z_1, ..., Z_n\}$, the hypothesis

Table 3. Best average MSE, MAE, and R^2 ($\pm$ standard deviation) using concatenated latent representation estimated on trace regression model based on Node2vec, Graphsage, Deepwalk, Metapath2vec, MGATE (*Avg()*), MGATE (*Max()*), MGATE (*Concat()*), MGATE (*Product()*), MSCGATE (*Avg()*), MSCGATE (*Max()*), MSCGATE (*Concat()*), and MSCGATE (*Product()*) models.

Model	$Z_t + Z_r$		
	MSE	MAE	R^2
Node2vec	0.103 ($\pm$ 0.032)	0.09 ($\pm$ 0.081)	0.122 ($\pm$ 0.014)
Graphsage	0.098 ($\pm$ 0.042)	0.091($\pm$ 0.073)	0.145 ($\pm$ 0.009)
Deepwalk	0.119 ($\pm$ 0.023)	0.104 ($\pm$ 0.154)	0.102 ($\pm$ 0.013)
Metapath2vec	0.098 ($\pm$ 0.010)	0.092($\pm$ 0.123)	0.136 ($\pm$ 0.016)
MGATE (*Avg()*)	0.056 ($\pm$ 0.015)	0.052 ($\pm$ 0.093)	0.284 ($\pm$ 0.019)
MGATE (*Product()*)	0.051 ($\pm$ 0.009)	0.049 ($\pm$ 0.008)	0.296 ($\pm$ 0.008)
MGATE (*Concat()*)	0.054 ($\pm$ 0.009)	0.052 ($\pm$ 0.010)	0.289 ($\pm$ 0.009)
MGATE (*Max()*)	0.061 ($\pm$ 0.025)	0.058 ($\pm$ 0.012)	0.274 ($\pm$ 0.019)
MSCGATE (*Avg()*)	**0.055 ($\pm$ 0.043)**	**0.051 ($\pm$ 0.021)**	**0.290 ($\pm$ 0.067)**
MSCGATE (*Product()*)	**0.047 ($\pm$ 0.029)**	**0.045 ($\pm$ 0.009)**	**0.297 ($\pm$ 0.039)**
MSCGATE (*Concat()*)	**0.053 ($\pm$ 0.012)**	**0.052 ($\pm$ 0.066)**	**0.286 ($\pm$ 0.041)**
MSCGATE (*Max()*)	**0.058 ($\pm$ 0.064)**	**0.056 ($\pm$ 0.114)**	**0.284 ($\pm$ 0.079)**

$$H_0 : \mu = \mu_0 \quad compared \quad to \quad H_1 : \mu \neq \mu_0 \tag{29}$$

can be computed using the test statistic t:

$$t = \frac{\bar{Z} - \mu_0}{s\sqrt{n}} \tag{30}$$

where $\bar{Z}$ is the sample mean, n the sample size and s refers to the sample standard deviation. Once the t statistic is computed, a $p-value$ can be determined from the values of a Student t distribution. It indicates the probability of obtaining a test statistic as extreme as the results actually reported if the *null hypothesis* is true, quantifying the power of the proof against it. Therefore, the statistical significance is deduced only when $p-value$ is typically ≤ 0.05. By admitting this, we obtained then a satisfactory results, which confirm the performance of the proposed method. The maps in Fig. 10 describe brain activation through voxels whose t-values surpass a certain statistical threshold for significance. The assumption that the experimental task stimulates these voxels. Moreover, we can see that the MSCGATE model can provide several significant regions responsible for a substantially higher response to vocal than non-vocal sounds, distributed in both the temporal and frontal lobes. This could be induced by improved robustness of the information present in the latent representation of the fused task- and rest-fMRI data.

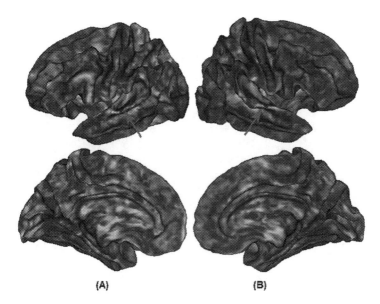

Fig. 10. Average weight maps $\hat{\beta}$ estimated using best MSCGATE model, thresholded after a test for statistical significance ($t > 1.985$, $p < 0.005$). Significant regions appear in yellow color. (A) left hemisphere mesh (B) right hemisphere mesh.

5   Conclusion

This work proposes a new multi-modal graph deep learning approach that leads to a better interpretation of human behavior from the integration of both fMRI modalities using the BSCG built on both spatial (sMRI) and cerebral fMRI features. Three major phases were defined, including our proposed MSCGATE model, which seeks to learn a fused representation estimated at the cortical location level, which is then used as input to our trace regression predictive model to quantify each subject's behavioral score in the voice recognition and identification task. Aside from being innovative, this method was able to manage the irregular structure provided by neuroimaging data while retaining both the cerebral features and the connectivity information. Our experimental findings demonstrate that our model outperforms previous state-of-the-art deep, and graph representation learning techniques in terms of effectiveness and performance operating on both regular and irregular data.

References

1. Demirci, O., Clark, V.P., Magnotta, V.A., et al.: A review of challenges in the use of fMRI for disease classification/characterization and a projection pursuit application from a multi-site fMRI schizophrenia study. Brain Imaging Behav. **2**(3), 207–226 (2008)
2. Mihalik, A., Ferreira, F.S., Rosa, M.J., et al.: Brain-behaviour modes of covariation in healthy and clinically depressed young people. Sci. Rep. **9**, 1–11 (2019)

3. Sui, J., Adali, T., Yu, Q., et al.: A review of multivariate methods for multimodal fusion of brain imaging data. J. Neurosci. Methods **204**(1), 68–81 (2012)
4. Sui, J., Pearlson, G.D., et al.: In search of multimodal neuroimaging biomarkers of cognitive deficits in schizophrenia. Biol. Psychiat. **78**(11), 794–804 (2015)
5. Blackmon, K., Barr, W.B., Kuzniecky, R., et al.: Phonetically irregular word pronunciation and cortical thickness in the adult brain. Neuroimage **51**(4), 1453–1458 (2010)
6. Saygin, Z.M., Osher, D.E., et al.: Anatomical connectivity patterns predict face selectivity in the fusiform gyrus. Nat. Neurosci. **15**(2), 321–327 (2012)
7. Du, W., Calhoun, V.D., et al.: High classification accuracy for schizophrenia with rest and task FMRI data. Front. Hum. Neurosci. **6**(145) (2012)
8. Hanachi, R., Sellami, A., Farah, I.: Interpretation of human behavior from multi-modal brain mri images based on graph deep neural networks and attention mechanism. In: Proceedings of the 16th International Joint Conference on Computer Vision, Imaging and Computer Graphics Theory and Applications 4: VISAPP, pp. 56–66 (2021)
9. Jiang, J., Ma, J., Chen, C., et al.: SuperPCA: A superpixelwise pca approach for unsupervised feature extraction of hyperspectral imagery. IEEE Trans. Geosci. Remote Sens. **56**(8), 4581–4593 (2018)
10. He, X., Cai, D., Yan, S., Zhang, H.-J.: Neighborhood preserving embedding. In: Tenth IEEE International Conference on Computer Vision (ICCV 2005), pp. 1208–1213 (2005)
11. Ma, L., Crawford, M.M., Tian, J.: Anomaly detection for hyperspectral images based on robust locally linear embedding. J. Infrared Milli Terahz Waves **31**, 753–762 (2010)
12. Belkin, M., Niyogi, P.: Laplacian eigenmaps for dimensionality reduction and data representation. Neural Comput. **15**(6), 1373–1396 (2003)
13. Perozzi, B., Al-Rfou, R., Skiena, S.: Deepwalk. In: Proceedings of the 20th ACM SIGKDD International Conference On Knowledge Discovery and Data Mining - KDD 2014 (2014)
14. Dong, Y., Chawla, N.V., Swami, A.: Metapath2vec: Scalable representation learning for heterogeneous networks. In: Proceedings of the 23rd ACM SIGKDD International Conference on Knowledge Discovery and Data Mining (KDD 2017), pp. 135–144. Association for Computing Machinery, New York (2017)
15. Grover, A., Leskovec, J.: Node2vec: scalable feature learning for networks. In: Proceedings of the 22nd ACM SIGKDD International Conference on Knowledge Discovery and Data Mining, pp, 855–864. Association for Computing Machinery (2016)
16. Wu, Z., Pan, S., Chen, F., Long, G., et al.: A comprehensive survey on graph neural networks. IEEE Trans. Neural Netw. Learn. Syst. **32**(1), 1–21 (2020)
17. Hamilton, W., Ying, Z., Leskovec, J.: Inductive representation learning on large graphs. In: Proceedings of the 31st International Conference on Neural Information Processing Systems (NIPS 2017), pp. 1025–1035. Curran Associates Inc., Red Hook (2017)
18. Ngiam, J., Khosla, A., Kim, M., Nam, J., Lee, H., Ng, A.Y.: Multimodal deep learning. In: ICML, pp. 689–696 (2011)
19. Alam, M.T., Kumar, V., Kumar, A.: A Multi-view convolutional neural network approach for image data classification. In: 2021 International Conference on Communication information and Computing Technology (ICCICT), pp. 1–6 (2021)
20. Sun, C., Yuan, Y.-H., Li, Y., Qiang, J., Zhu, Y., Shen, X.: Multi-view fractional deep canonical correlation analysis for subspace clustering. In: Mantoro, T., Lee, M., Ayu, M.A., Wong, K.W., Hidayanto, A.N. (eds.) ICONIP 2021. LNCS, vol. 13109, pp. 206–215. Springer, Cham (2021). https://doi.org/10.1007/978-3-030-92270-2_18
21. Bhatt, G., Jha, P., Raman, B.: Representation learning using step-based deep multi-modal autoencoders. Pattern Recogn. **95**, 12–23 (2019)
22. Khosla, M., Setty, V., Anand, A.: A comparative study for unsupervised network representation learning. IEEE Trans. Knowl. Data Eng. (2020)

23. Mikolov, T., Chen, K.: Greg Corrado. Efficient Estimation of Word Representations in Vector Space, Jeffrey Dean (2013)
24. Zhang, Z., Cui, P., Zhu, W.: Deep learning on graphs: A survey. CoRR (2018)
25. Kadri, H., Ayache, S., Huusari, R., Rakotomamonjy, A., Ralaivola, L.: Partial trace regression and low-rank kraus decomposition. In: International Conference on Machine Learning (2020)
26. Koltchinskii, V., Lounici, K., Tsybakov, A.B.: Nuclear-norm penalization and optimal rates for noisy low-rank matrix completion. Ann. Stat. **39**(5), 2302–2329 (2011)
27. Fan, J., Gong, W., Zhu, Z.: Generalized high dimensional trace regression via nuclear norm regularization. J. Econom. **212**(1), 177–202 (2019)

Enhancing Backlight and Spotlight Images by the Retinex-Inspired Bilateral Filter SuPeR-B

Michela Lecca$^{(\boxtimes)}$ (iD)

Fondazione Bruno Kessler, Digital Industry Center, 38123 Trento, Italy
lecca@fbk.eu
https://tev.fbk.eu/people/profile/lecca

Abstract. Backlight and spotlight images are pictures where the light sources generate very bright and very dark regions. The enhancement of such images has been poorly investigated and is particularly hard because it has to brighten the dark regions without over-enhance the bright ones. The solutions proposed till now generally perform multiple enhancements or segment the input image in dark and bright regions and enhance these latter with different functions. In both the cases, results are merged in a new image, that often must be smoothed to remove artifacts along the edges. This work describes SuPeR-B, a novel Retinex inspired image enhancer improving the quality of backligt and spotlight images without needing for multi-scale analysis, segmentation and smoothing. According to Retinex theory, SuPeR-B re-works the image channels separately and rescales the intensity of each pixel by a weighted average of intensities sampled from regular sub-windows. Since the rescaling factor depends both on spatial and intensity features, SuPeR-B acts like a bilateral filter. The experiments, carried out on public challenging data, demonstrate that SuPeR-B effectively improves the quality of backlight and spotlight images and also outperforms other state-of-the-art algorithms.

Keywords: Image enhancement · Retinex theory · Bilateral filter

1 Introduction

Despite the modern cameras enable the acquisition of images of increasing quality, algorithms for image enhancement are still necessary to remove undesired effects mainly due to wrong camera settings and to illumination issues. In fact, low exposure times, low-light, back-light, flashes, colored lights, multiple lights may strongly alter the image quality, producing noise, color distortion, strong shadows and hampering the visibility and readability of the details and content of the observed scene. The many enhancers proposed in the literature rely on a set of assumptions about the illumination of the scene, the reflectance of the materials composing the scene and some spectral properties of the acquisition device [1, 17, 35]. For instance, some methods assume that the light is uniform or varies slightly across the scene, that the objects in the scene are matte and/or that the gamut of the camera is known. While these hypotheses lead to fair mathematical models and solutions of the enhancement problem, they also circumscribe the applicability of the enhancer to specific contexts. In general, image enhancement is still an open problem and in particular, the improvement of *backlight* and *spotlight* images has been scarcely investigated. Backlight images are pictures where the

© Springer Nature Switzerland AG 2023
A. A. de Sousa et al. (Eds.): VISIGRAPP 2021, CCIS 1691, pp. 328–347, 2023.
https://doi.org/10.1007/978-3-031-25477-2_15

light source is located behind the objects to be acquired so that these latter appear very dark while the background is very brilliant. Spotlight images are pictures of dark environments with very brilliant but not diffuse light sources. In both these images, there are dark regions with illegible content. High dynamic range (HDR) cameras attempt to improve the visibility of the dark region content by acquiring multiple shots of the scene at different exposure times and merging them in an unique image by tone mapping. Nevertheless, this hardware solution suffers of two main problems: first, tone mapping often introduces color distortions and thus is a topic under research, and second, HDR imaging cannot solve the problem of improving the quality of an existing image captured with standard devices. Different software solutions have been proposed. Multi-resolution Retinex algorithms attempt to simulate the HDR imaging mechanism by processing the input image at multiple scales and averaging together the results [9]. These algorithms effectively brighten the dark regions but have long execution times and often generate halos and artifacts. Multiple enhancement is implemented also in [33], where logarithmic stretching and gamma correction are applied to the image brightness to over-enhance dark regions while contrast is adjusted separately. This method avoids artifacts and is computational inexpensive, but experiments presented in [19] show some cases with an unsatisfactory enhancement of the dark regions. Other solutions are proposed in [2, 21–23, 25, 30, 31, 34]. All these works partition the input image in dark and bright regions and process them differently in order to enhance the first ones without over-enhance the second ones. Borders between dark and bright regions are reworked separately to avoid artifacts on the image edges. The use of different enhancing functions on dark and bright regions generally provide good results, but these latter strongly depend on the accuracy of the segmentation. The work in [27] processes separately edges and flat regions and merges together the enhancement results. It performs well on images with slight illumination changes, while performs poorly on images with near-black portions. In general, smoothing operations are applied to remove noise and color distortions, as e.g. guided filters in [21] and Laplacian operators in [27].

This work describes SuPeR-B, a novel Retinex inspired bilateral filter which enhances color images without needing for segmentation and smoothing. SuPeR-B is a variant of the algorithm SuPeR [20], that enhances real-world color images based on a pixelwise local spatial processing of the channel intensities in accordance with some principles of the Retinex theory [11]. Both SuPeR and SuPeR-B partition the support of the input image by regular, non overlapping tiles, extract from each tile the maximum values of its red, green and blue components, and use them to rescale the red, green and blue intensities of each pixel. SuPeR and SuPeR-B differ to each other in the way the rescaling factor - which varies from pixel to pixel - is computed. While in SuPeR this factor depends on the spatial distance of the tiles from the pixel to be enhanced, in SuPeR-B it also depends on the difference between the intensities of the pixel and the intensities extracted from the tiles. Thanks to this modification, SuPeR-B can tune the contributions from the tiles accounting both for spatial and intensity features. In this sense, SuPeR-B works as a bilateral filter. In particular, given a pixel x in a dark region, SuPeR-B improves it by weighting more the contributions from tiles close to x both in terms of intensity and spatial distance. Moreover, if the contribution of the intensity differences is switched off, SuPeR-B implements SuPeR.

SuPeR-B was firstly introduced in the conference paper [19], where a set of preliminary experiments show that it effectively enhances backlight and spotlight images also in comparison with other state-of-the-art methods. This paper extends [19] by providing a more detailed description of SuPeR-B and a more comprehensive analysis, including both an objective and a subjective assessment of a set of visual features of the enhanced pictures. In particular, tests and comparisons are here performed on the large dataset TM-DIED [32] and on another dataset collected by this author and made available for free along with the enhancement results [18].

2   Background

As mentioned in Sect. 1, SuPeR-B is derived from the algorithm SuPeR [20]. This latter is a real-world color image enhancer implementing some principles of the Retinex theory, which was developed by Land and McCann to understand how humans see colors [11,12]. Specifically, Retinex is grounded on some experiments which demonstrated that, when looking at a same point, humans and cameras may report different colors [14]. This is because humans process the color of any observed point p based not only on the photometric properties of that point but also on the local spatial distribution of the colors surrounding that point. In particular, colors closer to p influence more the human color sensation of p than colors located farther. Moreover, the Retinex experiments reported that humans acquire and re-work the red, green and blue components of the light independently and implement the so-called *color constancy*, which is the capability to smooth or even remove eventual chromatic dominants of the light sources illuminating the scene. The Retinex algorithm proposes a computational routine to simulate this mechanism and to infer from any input digital color image the corresponding human color sensation. When used on a digital color image without implementing color space transformations related to the human vision system, the Retinex algorithm works as an image enhancer, i.e. it increases the brightness, the contrast and the dynamic range of the input image while decreases possible color casts due to the light. Due to the importance of image enhancement in many computer vision fields, the local spatial color processing proposed by Retinex has been widely investigated and many variants have been developed, including also multi-resolution implementations that - as mentioned in Sect. 1 - were used for backlight image enhancement, [5,7,8,10,24,26,29,36,37].

SuPeR is one of these variants. It belongs to the Milano Retinex family [16,29], that is a set of algorithms widely used as enhancers and grounded on the Retinex evidences described above. These algorithms propose different models for the local spatial color distribution, reaching different levels of enhancement. The interest for SuPeR is justified by the good results it achieves both in terms of image enhancement and execution time.

SuPeR enhances any input color image J by four steps:

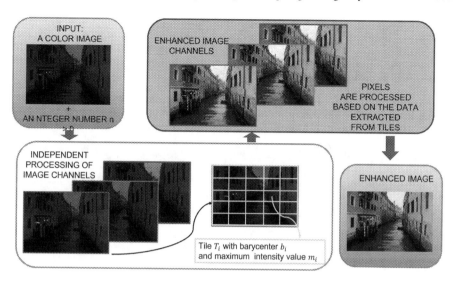

Fig. 1. Workflow of SuPeR.

1. *Global Image Processing*: The spatial support of J, i.e. the rectangle of pixels defining the image, is partitioned by N regular, rectangular, non overlapping tiles $T_1, \ldots, T_N$;
2. *Channelwise Pre-processing*: For each color channel I of J, the values of I are rescaled over $[0,1]$. Moreover, the null values of I are set to a small value close to zero. This operation is needed to enable the computation of the intensity ratios described in the next. In this phase, SuPeR computes the set $T_I = \{(b_i, m_i) : i = 1, \ldots, N\}$, where for each i, b_i is the barycenter of T_i and m_i is the maximum value of I over T_i;
3. *Pixelwise Processing*: For each channel I and for each pixel x, SuPeR computes the subset $T_I(x) \subseteq T_I$ defined as:

$$T_I(x) = \{(b, m) \in T_I : m \geq I(x)\}, \tag{1}$$

i.e. $T_I(x)$ contains the pairs (b, m) such that m exceeds $I(x)$. Then, SuPeR maps the intensity $I(x)$ onto a new value $L_I(x)$ defined as:

$$L_I(x) = \begin{cases} \dfrac{\sum_{(b,m) \in T_I(x)} (1-d(x,b))\frac{I(x)}{m}}{\sum_{(b,m) \in T_I(x)} (1-d(x,b))} & \text{if } T_I(x) \neq \emptyset \\ 1 & \text{otherwise} \end{cases} \tag{2}$$

where d is the squared Euclidean distance between x and b, normalized by the square of the length D of the diagonal of the image support so that d ranges over $[0, 1]$:

$$d(x, b) = \frac{\| x - b \|^2}{D^2}. \tag{3}$$

4. *Merging operation*: For each channel I, the values of L_I are rescaled over $\{0, \ldots, 255\}$ and the obtained images L_Is (one for each channel) are packed together into a new color image L, which is the enhanced version of J.

Fig. 2. Examples of image enhancement by SuPeR.

Equation (2) implements a spatial color processing in line with the Retinex principles. In fact, Equation (2) is applied channel by channel, in agreement with the fact that human vision system processes the long, medium and short wavelengths separately. Moreover, the computation of intensity ratios allows to smooth possible chromatic dominant of the light, since for the most devices, the change of the RGB triplet of any pixel due to a light variation is well approximated by a linear diagonal transform of that triplet [6,13]. Dividing $I(x)$ by greater values and remapping the values of L_I over $\{0, \ldots, 255\}$ enable to increase the brightness and the contrast of the image and to stretch the distribution of the channel intensity. Finally, the maximum intensities of the tiles involved in Equation (2) are weighted by a function of the spatial distance of the tile barycenters from x so that the contributions of farther tiles are less important than the contributions of closer tiles. In this way, as Retinex, SuPeR processes the image colors based on their spatial position and so implements a Retinex inspired local spatial analysis of the colors.

The name SuPeR summarizes the main characteristics of this algorithms, i.e. the use of tiles as *Su*per *Pi*xels and the implementation of some principles of the *R*etinex theory.

Fig. 1 schematizes the workflow of SuPeR, while Fig. 2 displays some examples of image enhancement by SuPeR. In general, SuPeR provides good performance on real-world low-light color images and some examples are shown in Fig. 2. Nevertheless, the performance of SuPeR decreases when the images are captured under extreme light conditions. An example is given in Fig. 3 and discussed in the next Section.

3   SuPeR-B

Figure 3 shows an example of an image with backlight, where the foreground object, a statue located close to a tree, is displayed against a brilliant background, i.e. the blue sky, and appears very dark. The enhancement provided by SuPeR, showed in the middle of Fig. 3, is quite unsatisfactory: while the bluish color of the light is removed and the overall image brightness is higher, the statue is still dark and most of its details are not

INPUT   SuPeR   SuPeR-B
$\alpha = -1, a = 0, b = -1$

Fig. 3. An example of enhancement of a backlight image by SuPeR and SuPeR-B.

visible. The reason of this result is that the intensities of the dark pixels of the statue are divided by the much greater intensities values sampled from the sky. Despite penalized by the spatial distance weights, the sky intensities influence heavily the values of L on the statue region. As already mentioned in Sect. 1, to solve this issue, multiscale Retinex approaches, like for instance the original Retinex algorithm [12] or its variants in [29] applied at multiple scales, tune the spatial locality of the color processing as follows. The enhancement of any pixel x is performed by accounting for the spatial color distribution over neighborhoods of x with decreasing size. For the smallest size, the spatial color distribution around x is computed on a set of pixels very close to x and thus generally having intensities similar to x. In this case, the intensities of x are rescaled by similar values sampled from the computed spatial color distribution. These intensities are thus mapped on values close to 1, so that the enhanced region becomes very bright. This operation improves the dark regions, but tends to over-enhance already bright images. On the contrary, the enhancement computed over large neighborhoods of x does not improve the visibility of the dark regions, as observed for Fig. 3, while preserves the appearance of the bright regions. The final enhanced image is obtained by averaging the different enhancement results and this avoids over- and under-enhancement. Nevertheless, multi-scale approaches often present two main issues: they generate noise and artifacts along the edges and have a long execution time.

The algorithm SuPeR-B proposes an alternative solution exploiting Retinex principles. As the multi-resolution approaches described above, SuPeR-B observes that any pixel x in a dark region can be better improved by weighting more the contribution of pixels close to x and with similar intensity. Based on this fact, SuPeR-B inherits from SuPeR the general computational workflow: it implements the global and the channel-wise processing and the merging operation of SuPeR, while modifies the pixel-wise processing by replacing the spatial weighting function in Eq. (2) with a new one, indicated by f and accounting both for spatial and intensity features. Equation (2) is thus substituted by the following one:

$$
L_B(x) = \begin{cases} \dfrac{\sum_{(b,m)\in T_I(x)} f(\delta I(x,b), d(x,b)) \frac{I(x)}{m}}{\sum_{(b,m)\in T_I(x)} f(\delta I(x,b), d(x,b))} & \text{if } T_I(x) \neq \emptyset \\ 1 & \text{otherwise} \end{cases} \tag{4}
$$

where $\delta I(x,b) = I(b) - I(x)$ and f is designed to weight more the intensities of $T_I(x)$ that are closer to x both in terms of spatial and intensity distance. In this way, SuPeR-B acts like a bilateral filter, working both on the spatial and intensity domains. The letter 'B' in the name SuPeR-B has three meanings: it indicates that SuPeR-B is a second version of SuPeR, that it has been developed to enhance *backlight* images and that it is a *bilateral* filter.

There is not an unique expression for f. The current implementation of SuPeR-B models f by a Coon patch, which is a compact surface whose boundaries are described by four paths $c_0, c_1, d_0, d_1 : [0,1] \rightarrow \mathbf{R}^2$ intersecting two by two at four corners, i.e. $c_0(0) = d_0(0)$, $c_0(1) = d_1(0)$, $c_1(0) = d_0(1)$ and $c_1(1) = d_1(1)$. The equation of the Coon patch C limited by c_0, c_1, d_0, d_1 is:

$$C(s,t) = S(s,t) + T(s,t) - U(s,t) \tag{5}$$

where

$$
\begin{aligned}
S(s,t) &= (1-t)c_0(s) + tc_1(s) \\
T(s,t) &= (1-s)d_0(t) + sd_1(t) \\
U(s,t) &= c_0(0)(1-s)(1-t) + c_0(1)s(1-t) + \\
&\quad c_1(0)(1-s)t + c_1(1)st.
\end{aligned}
$$

Pictorially, the surface described by Eq. (5) can be imagined to be formed by moving the endpoints of c_0 along the paths d_0 and d_1 modifying the shape of c_0 accordingly until c_0 reaches (and coincides with) c_1. The same surface can be obtained by moving the endpoints of d_0 along the paths c_0 and c_1 modifying the shape of d_0 until d_0 reaches (and coincides with) d_1. Changing the position of the corners and/or the equations of the paths enable to model many different Coon patches.

The Coon surface used in the current implementation of SuPeR-B has a parametric expression and is bounded by four lines defined as follows:

$$c_0(s) = s(\alpha - 1) + 1 \tag{6}$$
$$c_1(s) = s(b - a) + a \tag{7}$$
$$d_0(t) = t(a - 1) + 1 \tag{8}$$
$$d_1(t) = t(b - \alpha) + \alpha \tag{9}$$

where α, b, a are real-world user parameters and $s, t \in [0,1]$.

Function f is thus defined as:

$$f(s,t) = \max(C(s,t), \varepsilon), \tag{10}$$

where ε is a strictly positive, real number close to zero introduced to guarantee that f is positive for any choice of the paths and to prevent division by zero in Eq. (4). In Eq. (10), the parameters s and t represent respectively the variation of intensity δI and the value of d between two image pixels. Moreover, the variability range of the parameters α, a and b must be chosen so that f satisfies two important requirements, i.e. for any x

1. f guarantees the respect of the Retinex principle stating that the pixels of $T_I(x)$ whose barycenters are spatially closer to x influence more the enhancement than the other pixels of $T_I(x)$;

2. f guarantees that the the pixels of $T_I(x)$ with barycenters closer to x and with intensity closer to $I(x)$ are weighted more than the other pixels of $T_I(x)$.

These requirements are satisfied when

$$\alpha \le 1, a < 1, b \le \min\{a, \alpha\}. \tag{11}$$

In fact, if $a \ge 1$, the intensities of the pixels in $T_I(x)$ far from x become more relevant than those close to x, violating the requirement 1. Similarly, if $\alpha > 1$, the pixels in $T_I(x)$ with intensity values much greater than $I(x)$ contribute more to the value $L_B(x)$, leading to unsatisfactory results, as shown by the case displayed in Fig. 3. Finally, the value of b must be smaller than α and b to avoid that f increases when (s, t) approaches to 1, violating in this way one or both the requirements 1 and 2. Some examples of function f are shown in Fig. 4.

The parameter a controls the spatial locality of the image processing. Decreasing a makes the higher the contribution of the pixels of $T_I(x)$ close to x to $L_B(x)$. The parameter α controls the contribution of the intensity differences δI and the lower α, the higher is the weight given to the intensities of $T_I(x)$ close to $I(x)$. In particuar, when $\alpha = 1$ the intensity variations are weighted equally, regardless of their amount. The parameter b controls the value of f when d and δI grow up: the lower b, the less important the effects of high values of d and δI on $L_B(x)$ are. Finally, it is to note that for $\alpha = 1$, $a = 0$, $b = 0$, SuPeR-B exactly implements SuPeR. Therefore, SuPeR-B can be also considered as a generalized version of SuPeR.

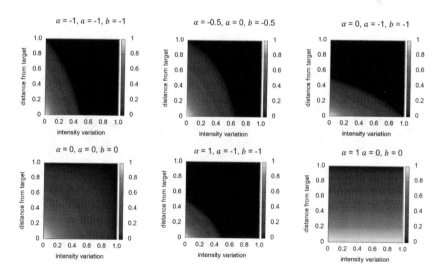

Fig. 4. Examples of function f for different values of the parameters α, a, b.

4   Evaluation

Evaluating the performance of an image enhancer is in general a hard task and there is not an agreed measure for this [3]. Therefore, the evaluation proposed by this work considers a set of objective measures that capture different features of image quality, i.e. the brightness, the contrast, and the color distribution, that are usually improved by enhancing. In addition, a subjective evaluation is performed: a set of volunteers observed the images enhanced by SuPeR-B with different parameters and chose the image that they consider to have the best quality in terms of visibility of content and details. This analysis enables to establish when humans consider SuPeR-B outperforming SuPeR, i.e. when tuning the spatial and /or intensity features through the parameters of SuPeR-B provides better results than the spatial tuning of SuPeR.

Objective and subjective evaluations are carried out on a dataset of 55 real-world images extracted from a personal collection of pictures of the author and for this reason called Personal-DB. The images depict both indoor and outdoor environments captured under natural or artificial illuminations, including backlight, spotlight, low-light and/or colored lights. Personal-DB and all the enhancement results obtained by SuPeR-B and discussed here are freely available [18].

In addition, the objective evaluation has been carried out on the larger, publicly available dataset TM-DIED (The Most Difficult Image Enhancement Dataset) [32], which contains 222 real-world pictures considered highly challenging for the enhancement task and including low-light and backlight images as well. On TM-DIED, the enhancement by SuPeR-B has been performed by using the parameter triplets (α, a, b) which have been mostly selected in the subjective analysis performed on Personal-DB. Some examples of images from Personal-DB and TM-DIED are given in Fig. 5.

The results obtained on both the datasets have been finally compared with the enhancement achieved by four algorithms used to improve the quality of backlight images, i.e. [21,24,27,33].

Fig. 5. Some examples of images from Personal-DB (first row) and TM-DIED (second row).

4.1 Objective Evaluation

Given a color image J, the objective evaluation is performed by considering three features that are usually modified by enhancement and by comparing them on input and enhanced images. Precisely, these features are the brightness, the contrast, the color distribution of an image. These features are computed on the gray-level image BJ obtained from J by averaging pixel by pixels its color intensities, i.e. for any pixel x of J,

$$BJ(x) = \frac{1}{3} \sum_{j=1}^{3} I_j(x) \tag{12}$$

where I_j is the jth color channel of J. According to this notation, the features used for the objective evaluation are:

1. Mean brightness (m_0): This is the mean value of the intensity values of BJ.
2. Mean multi-resolution contrast (m_1): This is a measure of the local intensity variations, computed at different scales and averaged to get a measure of the image contrast. Proposed in [28], m_1 is computed by considering k half-scaled versions $BJ_1, \ldots BJ_k$ of BJ; for each $j = 1, \ldots, k$, a pixel-wise and a global contrasts are computed. Specifically, the pixel-wise contrast is computed at the pixel x of BJ_j and is defined as the average of the absolute differences between $BJ_j(x)$ and the intensities of its 8 neighboring pixels. The global contrast of BJ_j is obtained by averaging its pixel-wise contrasts. Finally, the value of m_1 is the mean value of the global contrasts of the BJ_js.
3. Deviance from color distribution flatness (m_2): this is a measure of the entropy of the distribution of the values of BJ and is defined as the L^1 distance between the probability density function of the values of BJ and the uniform probability density function.

The objective evaluation is performed by comparing the features m_is before and after enhancing. Precisely, the brightness and the contrast are expected to be increased by enhancing, while the color distribution flatness is expected to decrease. It is to note that the exact amount of the values m_is varies from image to image. In particular, images with an already clear content, i.e. images that do not need for enhancement, are expected to report slight variations of the m_is. On the contrary, images with an unreadable content are expected to be heavily modified by the enhancer and thus the variations of their m_is are expected to be noticeable. For a fair assessment, the measures m_is must be evaluated together. In fact, for instance, a high value of m_0 may correspond to a saturated image, where the details are completely lost; in this case, checking the values m_1 and m_2 can provide additional information about edges and saturated colors. For the backlight images, the assessment of m_1 must be treated with particular attention, since brightening the dark regions may decrease the global contrast of the image, especially along the edges with the brighter regions. To provide a more accurate evaluation, the measures m_is have been computed on the whole image as well as separately on the dark and on the bright regions. To this purpose, the image to be evaluated is segmented in two regions P_B and P_D by a threshold procedure such that:

$$P_B = \{x \in S : BJ(x) > \tau\} \tag{13}$$
$$P_D = \{x \in S : BJ(x) \leq \tau\} \tag{14}$$

where

$$\tau = \frac{\max_{x \in S} BJ(x) - \min_{x \in S} BJ(x)}{2}. \tag{15}$$

P_B and P_D correspond respectively to bright and dark regions. The values of the measures m_is computed on P_B and P_D are indicated respectively with m_i^Bs and m_i^Ds. Some examples of such an image segmentation are shown in Fig. 6.

On Personal-DB the evaluation of the m_is is performed on the original images as well as on the images enhanced by SuPeR-B for different values of the parameters α, a and b, listed in Table 1. As already observed, the triplet (α=1, a=0, b=0) corresponds to SuPeR. On the images of TM-DIED the objective evaluation has been performed by considering the parameters of SuPeR-B mostly selected in the subjective analysis described in the next.

Table 1. Parameters of SuPeR-B used for the objective and subjective evaluations on Personal-DB. Each column reports a triplet of parameters.

α	-0.5	-0.5	-1	-1	0	0	0.5	1	1	1
a	-0.5	0	-1	0	-1	0	0	-1	0	0
b	-0.5	-0.5	-1	-1	-1	0	0	-1	-1	0

Fig. 6. Some examples of image segmentation in dark and bright regions from Personal-DB. See text for more explanation.

4.2   Subjective Evaluation

In the subjective evaluation, 55 panels, each displaying an image J from Personal-DB and 11 versions of J enhanced by SuPeR-B with the parameters (α, a,b) listed in Table 1, were shown to a set of 10 volunteers (see Fig. 7 for an example). Each volunteer was independently asked to indicate the image that she/he considered having the higher quality in terms of visibility of content and details. This analysis aims at measuring the performance of SuPeR-B in a qualitative way, also in comparison with SuPeR, as well as at detecting whose parameters of SuPeR-B provide the best performance from human perspective. These parameters have been then used to enhance the images of TM-DIED.

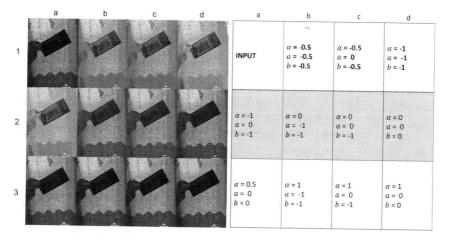

Fig. 7. On left, an example of panel used for the subjective evaluation. The first image on top is the input image with a strong backlight, the last image on bottom is obtained by SuPeR. On right, a graphical legend specifying the parameters used by SuPeR-B for each enhancement. For example, the image at the position (2, b) has been enhanced by setting $(\alpha, a, b) = (0, -1, -1)$.

4.3   Comparison

The performance of SuPeR-B has been compared with those of SuPeR and of other three algorithms specifically designed to improve the quality of backlight images. Precisely, these algorithms are the multi-scale version of the Retinex algorithm [24] (here MSR for short), the content-aware dark image enhancer based on channel division [27] (here CHANNEL-DIVISION for short), the fusion-based method for single backlight image enhancement [33] (here FUSION for short) and the learning-based restoration method for backlit images [21] (here L-RESTORATION for short).

As already mentioned in Sect. 1, MSR implements the Retinex algorithms at multiple resolutions, i.e. it processes the channel intensities of each pixel by considering neighborhoods with decreasing size and averages the results. At the smallest resolution, i.e. when the size of the pixel neighborhood is the 3×3 window centered at the pixel, the image enhanced by MSR looks like a color gradient, where only the strongest edges are highly visible and colors of flat regions tend to the white color so that any possible chromatic dominant of the light is removed. Enlarging the size of the neighborhood leads to images with different levels of removal of the light effects. In principle, averaging these results enables to brighten the dark regions without over-enhancing the bright ones, but in practice MSR often produces artifacts along the strongest image edges, while chromatic dominants of the light are still visible. It is also to note that the MSR method considered here is based on the work [10], which models the spatial locality of Retinex by considering Gaussian functions. Precisely, at each scale, MSR divides the channel intensity $I(x)$ of each pixel x (or the V component of the image at x, depending on the implementation) by $(I \star G)(x)$ where G is a Gaussian function and $\star$ denotes the convolution. The support of G varies with the scale allowing to consider different neighborhoods of x.

To avoid artifacts along edges, CHANNEL-DIVISION represents the input image in the HVS color space and partitions its V component (i.e. the image intensity) in edges and textured regions based on local contrast. CHANNEL-DIVISION enhances these latter separately with ad-hoc functions and merges together the results boosting the details in dark areas while preserving the smoothness of the flat portions of the image. The enhanced version of V is then packed with the original H and S channels in a new image, which is converted back to the RGB color space. Since CHANNEL-DIVISION acts on the intensity only, possible chromatic dominants of the light are not removed. Generally, this algorithm provides good results for a wide range of images, but it poorly performs in extreme conditions, as for example when the image contains near-zero areas where the signal is very noisy and the contrast computation is less accurate.

FUSION also represents the input image in the HSV color space. It computes from the channel V three new images, where the first one is a logarithmic stretch of V, the second one is a gamma-corrected version of V, and the third one is obtained by an unsharp masking algorithm applied on V. These operations aim at improving the detail visibility in dark areas while avoiding the over-enhancement of the bright portions. The three images obtained from V are combined into a new image W, which is an enhanced version of V. In this fusion process, the contributions of the three images are weighted by Gaussian functions computed pixel by pixel and then smoothed to reduce halos. The components H, S and W are then mapped back to the RGB color space to yield the final enhancement of the input color image. As CHANNEL-DIVISION, FUSION does not remove possible color casts due to the illumination.

L-RESTORATION segments the input image in bright and dark regions and enhances them differently. Segmentation is based on the analysis of the peaks in the illumination spatial distribution and of some statistic differences between bright and dark regions (i.e. luminance values, skewness of the luminance distribution, luminance saturation). L-RESTORATION re-works each segmented region by a tone mapping function which stretches the Weber contrast of the region while controls possible tone distortions. Boundaries between bright and dark regions are enhanced by a mixture of the tone mapping functions applied to the dark and bright regions. L-RESTORATION provides good results, but these latter heavily depend on the segmentation accuracy. Moreover, since L-RESTORATION mainly works on the luminance channel, it neither smooths nor removes possible color casts due to the illumination.

All these methods have been compared against SuPeR-B on Personal-DB because the smaller number of images and their smaller size with respect to TM-DIED enable a simpler qualitative analysis of the results and guarantee faster execution times of the codes of MSR, CHANNEL-DIVISION, FUSION and L-RESTORATION.

5   Results

The code of SuPeR-B used in these experiments has been derived from the repository of SuPeR available on GiThub[1] by replacing the SuPeR spatial weights with the new function f. For all the datasets, the number of tiles have been set to 100. For FUSION the

---

[1] SuPeR-B code: https://github.com/StefanoMesselodi?tab=repositories,.

code used here is a version provided by the authors some years ago at a link specified in [33], while for L-RESTORATION the code is available online[2] For CHANNEL-DIVISION an implementation provided by the authors has been employed. For the contrast computation, the number of rescaled images varies from image to image, precisely each image is rescaled kth times, until the area of the kth images is smaller than 256 pixels.

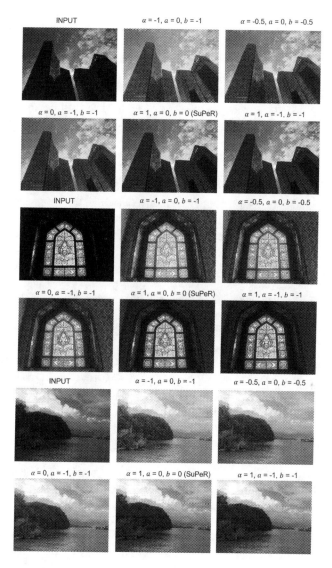

Fig. 8. Comparison among SuPeR-B with different parameters on three images from TM-DIED.

---

[2] L-RESTORATION code: https://github.com/7thChord/backlit.

Table 2 reports the mean values of the objective measures m_is computed on the dataset Personal-DB. For any choice of the triplets (α, a, b) in Table 1, SuPeR-B improves the brightness, the contrast and the entropy of the color distribution on the whole image. In particular, the comparison between the m_i^Bs and the m_i^Ds reveals that dark regions are remarkably improved by SuPeR-B: in fact, the values of m_0^D and m_1^D (m_2^D, resp.) after enhancing are higher (lower, resp.) than those measured on the images without enhancement. In general, the lower α, a and b, the higher the locality of the spatial and intensity processing is and the better the values of m_i^Ds are. On the contrary, the enhancement of the bright regions makes them even brighter but decreases their contrast and worses their deviance from the histogram flatness. This is because, as SuPeR, SuPeR-B tends to remove slight edges that, according to Retinex theory, are considered to be irrelevant for understanding the main content of the image. As a consequence, the histogram of the image brightness becomes more peaked and the contrast decreases. Therefore, for low values of α, a and b, the details of dark regions become much more visible, but the risk here is to over-enhance the brightest ones, creating artifacts or removing important edges. The selection of the triplet (α, a, b) granting the best result is not trivial, since it depends on the image content as well as on the application for which the enhancement is performed. In this framework, the subjective assessment of the panels built up from the images of Personal-DB and their enhanced versions leads to some important outcomes. First, in general, given a panel, the volunteers express different preferences, meaning that the process of image quality assessment by humans is hard to be modeled. Second, on average, people consider the enhancement by SuPeR satisfactory for the 23.63% of the images, they prefer SuPeR-B for the 72.0% of the images, while for the remaining 0.04% of the images they judge the enhancement useless or pejorative. On average, humans consider SuPeR-B necessary and outperforming SuPeR when the input image has a strong backlight (see e.g. Figure 7), while SuPeR is judged to provide a similar or better result on images with spotlights (see e.g. panels 50 and 51), on low light images (see e.g. panels 10 and 41), and on images where illumination differences between dark and bright regions are moderate (see e.g. panels 9 and 17). Finally, the subjective evaluation reports that the parameters triplets of the most preferred enhanced versions are (α=-1, a=0, b=-1), (α=1, a=-1, b=-1), (α=0, a=-1, b=-1), (α=-0.5, a=0, b=-0.5) and (α=1, a=0, b=0). These parameter triplets have been employed in the experiments on the larger dataset TM-DIED and the results, shown in Table 3, have a trend similar to that reported on Personal-DB. Some examples of enhancement of TM-DIED pictures are shown in Fig. 8: on these cases, SuPeR-B with $(\alpha, a, b = 0) \neq (1, 0, 0)$ outperforms SuPeR.

The comparison of SuPeR-B with SuPeR, MSR, CHANNEL-DIVISION, FUSION and L-RESTORATION has been performed on Personal-DB. Some examples of images processed by these algorithms are displayed in Fig. 9. From Table 1, MSR provides the best results in terms of brightness, contrast and deviance from color histograms both on the whole images and on its dark and bright regions. Nevertheless, a qualitative inspection of the results shows that the images enhanced by MSR look like cartoons, with very evident dark edges and not natural colors. Moreover, in some cases, the brightest regions are under-enhanced due to the Gaussian smoothing proposed in [10] (see for instance the sky in the third and fourth images of Fig. 9).

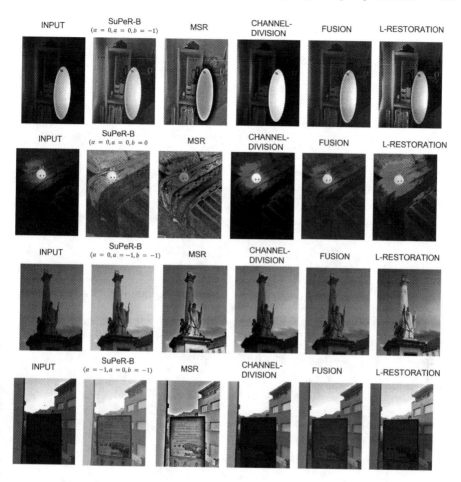

Fig. 9. Comparison among SuPeR-B and other enhancers on some images from Personal-DB. See text for more details.

In general, on the whole images as well as on their dark regions, CHANNEL-DIVISION, FUSION and L-RESTORATION perform similarly to SuPeR-B in terms of contrast, while they report worse values of brightness and - except for L-RESTORATION - of deviance from color distribution flatness. Qualitatively, this means that in backlight and spotlight images, CHANNEL-DIVISION, FUSION and L-RESTORATION still preserve a remarkable difference between the dark and the bright regions, so that the details of the first ones appear less readable than in the images enhanced by SuPeR-B. On the contrary, On the bright regions CHANNEL-DIVISION, FUSION and L-RESTORATION provide a higher contrast and a lower deviance from color distribution flatness. This in general indicates that SuPeR-B over-enhances the bright regions slightly more than the other algorithms. Among the algorithms compared with SuPeR-B, L-RESTORATION is that providing more similar results to SuPeR-B, especially on low-light images and on images with a moderate difference between dark and bright regions.

Table 2. Objective evaluation on personal-DB.

Algorithm	m_0	m_1	m_2	m_0^B	m_1^B	m_2^B	m_0^D	m_1^D	m_2^D
None	58.78	5.88	4.47	189.89	14.74	4.95	31.61	5.08	5.22
SuPeR-B (α=−1, a=−1, b=−1)	136.13	9.54	2.84	219.89	7.77	5.86	118.83	10.32	3.12
SuPeR-B (α=−1, a=0, b=−1)	135.01	9.33	2.94	219.58	7.74	5.89	117.48	10.06	3.26
SuPeR-B (α=−0.5, a=−0.5, b=−0.5)	127.75	9.27	2.91	215.95	8.86	5.65	108.74	9.73	3.36
SuPeR-B (α=−0.5, a=0, b=−0.5)	127.13	9.16	2.99	215.88	8.83	5.66	107.93	9.59	3.45
SuPeR-B (α=0.5, a=0, b=0)	105.37	8.48	3.28	212.04	11.21	5.42	80.96	8.43	3.91
SuPeR-B (α=0, a=−1, b=−1)	118.54	9.16	2.99	213.73	10.36	5.48	97.11	9.34	3.56
SuPeR-B (α=0, a=0, b=−1)	118.65	8.97	3.06	213.83	10.10	5.52	97.19	9.15	3.62
SuPeR-B (α=0, a=0, b=0)	114.84	8.78	3.18	213.46	10.33	5.50	92.36	8.89	3.76
SuPeR-B (α=1, a=−1, b=−1)	100.32	8.43	3.31	210.93	11.94	5.34	75.18	8.29	3.94
SuPeR-B (α=1, a=0, b=−1)	101.88	8.37	3.32	211.20	11.65	5.38	76.94	8.26	3.95
SuPeR-B (α=1, a=0, b=0)	99.98	8.24	3.39	211.00	11.71	5.37	74.66	8.10	4.03
MSR	121.35	20.21	2.48	191.20	16.26	4.84	107.82	21.82	2.59
FUSION	84.85	9.41	3.59	199.63	14.81	4.92	61.77	9.14	4.30
CHANNEL-DIVISION	75.54	7.58	4.15	229.94	13.42	6.02	43.25	7.54	4.45
L-RESTORATION	101.51	8.60	2.50	200.09	9.52	4.75	83.03	9.15	2.80

Table 3. Objective evaluation on TM-DIED.

Algorithm	m_0	m_1	m_2	m_0^B	m_1^B	m_2^B	m_0^D	m_1^D	m_2^D
None	80.40	8.81	3.58	187.64	14.65	4.50	35.59	8.22	5.04
SuPeR-B (α = −1, a=0, b=−1)	139.22	12.02	2.67	213.14	8.21	5.70	107.21	14.60	3.09
SuPeR-B (α=−0.5, a=0, b=−0.5)	130.46	11.72	2.61	208.55	9.55	5.38	96.01	13.73	3.35
SuPeR-B (α=0, a=−1, b=−1)	120.60	11.43	2.66	206.05	11.48	5.20	82.73	12.74	3.59
SuPeR-B (α=1, a=−1, b=−1)	104.21	10.50	3.03	202.71	13.12	5.05	61.41	11.06	4.12
SuPeR-B (α=1, a=0, b=0)	104.04	10.40	3.06	202.70	12.98	5.07	61.06	10.94	4.16

6   Conclusions

This work presented the Retinex inspired bilateral filter SuPeR-B, which modified the image enhancer SuPeR for better improving backlight and spotlight images. The experiments reported in the previous Section show that SuPeR-B effectively increases the visibility of content and details of such images, also outperforming other methods proposed in the literature for this task. The bilateral processing of spatial and intensity information, which is the core of SuPeR-B, is modeled by a Coon patch, whose parameters can be tuned by the users. In the current implementation, the Coon patch is basically a piece-wise planar patch whose slope depends on the parameters α, a and b and defines the weights of the spatial and intensity features involved in the input image enhancement. The choice of the values of α, a and b providing the best enhancement of a given image is a crucial point for SuPeR-B, because different parameters' value lead to different enhancement results. By this way, the objective and subjective evaluations performed in this study draw general guidelines to set these parameters according to the input image. Precisely, for backlight and spotlight images, low values of α, a and b are recommended, while higher values are suitable for images with global low light or with moderate difference between bright and dark regions. These outcomes suggest to automatize the parameter settings based on the shape of the channel distribution: in case of bi-modal distribution, α, a and b must be low, while in case of more uniform distributions higher values may be used. This general suggestion should be further investigated in future work, taking also into account the context in which image processing is done and the final application, like human inspection, e.g. for entertainment [4], or computer vision tasks, e.g. for image description and matching, where robustness to light and high quality of details are crucial [15]. Moreover, the experimental data made available for free would like to promote future comparison and analysis.

References

1. Ackar, H., Abd Almisreb, A., Saleh, M.A.: A review on image enhancement techniques. Southeast Europe J. Soft Comput. **8**(1) (2019)
2. Akai, M., Ueda, Y., Koga, T., Suetake, N.: A single backlit image enhancement method for improvement of visibility of dark part. In: 2021 IEEE International Conference on Image Processing (ICIP), pp. 1659–1663 (2021). https://doi.org/10.1109/ICIP42928.2021.9506526
3. Barricelli, B.R., Casiraghi, E., Lecca, M., Plutino, A., Rizzi, A.: A cockpit of multiple measures for assessing film restoration quality. Patt. Recogn. Lett. **131**, 178–184 (2020). https://doi.org/10.1016/j.patrec.2020.01.009, https://linkinghub.elsevier.com/retrieve/pii/S0167865520300076
4. Bellotti, S., Bottaro, G., Plutino, A., Valsesia, M.: Mathematically based algorithms for film digital Restoration. In: Imagine Math 7, pp. 89–104. Springer, Cham (2020). https://doi.org/10.1007/978-3-030-42653-8_6
5. Chang, H., Ng, M.K., Wang, W., Zeng, T.: Retinex image enhancement via a learned dictionary. Opt. Eng. **54**(1), 013107 (2015)
6. Finlayson, G.D., Drew, M.S., Funt, B.V.: Color constancy: generalized diagonal transforms suffice. JOSA A **11**(11), 3011–3019 (1994)
7. Fu, X., Sun, Y., LiWang, M., Huang, Y., Zhang, X.P., Ding, X.: A novel retinex based approach for image enhancement with illumination adjustment. In: 2014 IEEE International Conference on Acoustics, Speech and Signal Processing (ICASSP), pp. 1190–1194. IEEE (2014)
8. Jiang, Z., Li, H., Liu, L., Men, A., Wang, H.: A switched view of retinex: Deep self-regularized low-light image enhancement. Neurocomputing **454**, 361–372 (2021)
9. Jobson, D.J., Rahman, Z., Woodell, G.A.: Properties and performance of a center/surround retinex. IEEE Trans. Image Process. **6**(3), 451–462 (1997)
10. Jobson, D.J., Rahman, Z.u., Woodell, G.A.: A multiscale retinex for bridging the gap between color images and the human observation of scenes. IEEE Trans. Image Process. **6**(7), 965–976 (1997)
11. Land, E.: The Retinex. Am. Sci. **52**(2), 247–264 (1964)
12. Land, E.H., John, McCann. J.: Lightness and Retinex theory. Optical Soc. Am. **1**, 1–11 (1971)

13. Lecca, M.: On the von Kries model: estimation, dependence on light and device, and applications. In: Celebi, M.E., Smolka, B. (eds.) Advances in Low-Level Color Image Processing. LNCVB, vol. 11, pp. 95–135. Springer, Dordrecht (2014). https://doi.org/10.1007/978-94-007-7584-8_4

14. Lecca, M.: Color vision is a spatial process: the retinex theory. In: Bianco, S., Schettini, R., Trémeau, A., Tominaga, S. (eds.) Computational Color Imaging, pp. 26–39. Springer International Publishing, Cham (2017)

15. Lecca, M.: Comprehensive evaluation of image enhancement for unsupervised image description and matching. IET Image Processing 14(10), 4329–4339 (December 2020). https://digital-library.theiet.org/content/journals/10.1049/iet-ipr.2020.1129

16. Lecca, M.: Generalized equation for real-world image enhancement by milano retinex family. J. Opt. Soc. Am. A 37(5), 849–858 (2020). https://doi.org/10.1364/JOSAA.384197. http://www.osapublishing.org/josaa/abstract.cfm?URI=josaa-37-5-849

17. Lecca, M.: Machine colour constancy: a work in progress. Color. Technol. 137(1), 72–77 (2021)

18. Lecca, M.: Personal-DB (Dec 2021). https://tev.fbk.eu/resources/imageenhancement

19. Lecca, M.: A retinex inspired bilateral filter for enhancing images under difficult light conditions. In: VISIGRAPP (4: VISAPP), pp. 76–86 (2021)

20. Lecca, M., Messelodi, S.: SuPeR: Milano Retinex implementation exploiting a regular image grid. J. Opt. Soc. Am. A 36(8), 1423–1432 (Aug 2019). https://doi.org/10.1364/JOSAA.36.001423, http://josaa.osa.org/abstract.cfm?URI=josaa-36-8-1423

21. Li, Z., Wu, X.: Learning-based restoration of backlit images. IEEE Trans. Image Process. 27(2), 976–986 (2018)

22. Li, Z., Cheng, K., Wu, X.: Soft binary segmentation-based backlit image enhancement. In: 2015 IEEE 17th International Workshop on Multimedia Signal Processing (MMSP), pp. 1–5 (2015). https://doi.org/10.1109/MMSP.2015.7340808

23. Ma, C., Zeng, S., Li, D.: A new algorithm for backlight image enhancement. In: 2020 International Conference on Intelligent Transportation, Big Data & Smart City (ICITBS), pp. 840–844. IEEE (2020)

24. Morel, J.M., Petro, A.B., Sbert, C.: A PDE formalization of Retinex theory. IEEE Trans. Image Process. 19(11), 2825–2837 (2010)

25. Peicheng, Z., Bo, L.: Backlit image enhancement based on illumination-reflection imaging model. In: 2021 6th International Conference on Automation, Control and Robotics Engineering (CACRE), pp. 438–443 (2021). https://doi.org/10.1109/CACRE52464.2021.9501394

26. Petro, A.B., Sbert, C., Morel, J.M.: Multiscale retinex. Image Processing On Line pp. 71–88 (2014)

27. Ramirez Rivera, A., Byungyong Ryu, Chae, O.: Content-aware dark image enhancement through channel division. IEEE Trans. Image Process. 21(9), 3967–3980 (2012)

28. Rizzi, A., Algeri, T., Medeghini, G., Marini, D.: A proposal for contrast measure in digital images. In: CGIV 2004–2nd European Conference on Color in Graphics, Imaging, and Vision and 6th Int. Symposium on Multispectral Color Science, pp. 187–192. Aachen (2004)

29. Rizzi, A., Bonanomi, C.: Milano Retinex family. J. Electron. Imag. 26(3), 031207–031207 (2017)

30. Tsai, C.M., Yeh, Z.M.: Contrast compensation by fuzzy classification and image illumination analysis for back-lit and front-lit color face images. IEEE Trans. Consum. Electron. 56(3), 1570–1578 (2010)

31. Ueda, Y., Moriyama, D., Koga, T., Suetake, N.: Histogram specification-based image enhancement for backlit image. In: 2020 IEEE International Conference on Image Processing (ICIP), pp. 958–962. IEEE (2020)

32. Vonikakis, V.: Tm-died: The most difficult image enhancement dataset (Dec 2021). https:// sites.google.com/site/vonikakis/datasets
33. Wang, Q., Fu, X., Zhang, X., Ding, X.: A fusion-based method for single backlit image enhancement. In: 2016 IEEE International Conference on Image Processing (ICIP), pp. 4077–4081 (2016)
34. Wang, S., Zheng, J., Hu, H.M., Li, B.: Naturalness preserved enhancement algorithm for non-uniform illumination images. IEEE Trans. Image Process. 22(9), 3538–3548 (2013)
35. Wang, W., Wu, X., Yuan, X., Gao, Z.: An experiment-based review of low-light image enhancement methods. IEEE Access 8, 87884–87917 (2020)
36. Wei, C., Wang, W., Yang, W., Liu, J.: Deep retinex decomposition for low-light enhancement. arXiv preprint arXiv:1808.04560 (2018)
37. Yang, W., Wang, W., Huang, H., Wang, S., Liu, J.: Sparse gradient regularized deep retinex network for robust low-light image enhancement. IEEE Trans. Image Process. 30, 2072–2086 (2021)

Rethinking RNN-Based Video Object Segmentation

Fatemeh Azimi[1,2(✉)], Federico Raue[2], Jörn Hees[2], and Andreas Dengel[1,2]

[1] TU Kaiserslautern, Kaiserslautern, Germany
[2] German Research Center for Artificial Intelligence (DFKI), Kaiserslautern, Germany
{fatemeh.azimi,federico.raue,jorn.hees,andreas.dengel}@dfki.de

Abstract. Video Object Segmentation is a fundamental task in computer vision that aims at pixel-wise tracking of one or multiple foreground objects within a video sequence. This task is challenging due to real-world requirements such as handling unconstrained object and camera motion, occlusion, fast motion, and motion blur. Recently, methods utilizing RNNs have been successful in accurately and efficiently segmenting the target objects as RNNs can effectively memorize the object of interest and compute the spatiotemporal features which are useful in processing the visual sequential data. However, they have limitations such as lower segmentation accuracy in longer sequences. In this paper, we expand our previous work to develop a hybrid architecture that successfully eliminates some of these challenges by employing additional correspondence matching information, followed by extensively exploring the impact of various architectural designs. Our experiment results on YouTubeVOS dataset confirm the efficacy of our proposed architecture by obtaining an improvement of about 12pp on Yout-TubeVOS compared to RNN-based baselines without a considerable increase in the computational costs.

Keywords: Video Object Segmentation · Recurrent neural networks · Correspondence matching

1 Introduction

nOe-shot Video Object Segmentation (VOS) is the task of densely tracking the intended foreground objects in a video, given the first mask of the object's appearance. VOS plays an important role in various applications such as video editing, autonomous driving, and robotics.

During the last years, a wide variety of learning-based solutions have been proposed for VOS trying to maximize the segmentation accuracy via addressing different challenging scenarios such as tracking smaller objects, handling occlusion, fast motion, crowded scenes with similar object instances, etc. [1,4,45,47,49]. The suggested approaches in the literature can be roughly categorized to three main groups.

The first category naively tries to extend an image segmentation model to video domain [9,29]. During inference, these models try to adapt the trained network to the specific scene and foreground object. This is usually done via further finetuning the network using the single object mask provided for the first frame (this process is known

© Springer Nature Switzerland AG 2023
A. A. de Sousa et al. (Eds.): VISIGRAPP 2021, CCIS 1691, pp. 348–365, 2023.
https://doi.org/10.1007/978-3-031-25477-2_16

as online training). Therefore, these models are relatively slow and their performance is sub-optimal as training on a single image can result in overfitting behavior.

The second class deploys a memory component for memorizing the object of interest and processing the motion information [1,40,47]. Although using memory is a natural choice for processing the sequential data and these methods can achieve a good performance without requiring online training, their accuracy is limited by the functioning of the memory module. For example, their performance considerably drops for longer sequences due to the limited memory capacity and error propagation.

The third group is based on template matching [41,45,49]. These methods capture the target in each frame through finding the correspondences between the frame at hand and a reference frame (e.g. the given mask at $t = 0$). These approaches can also obtain a good performance with a fast run-time; however, their performance degrades in scenes with multiple similar object instances or when the object appearance changes drastically with respect to the reference frames. As it is expected, the model struggles to find the similarities in these scenario, resulting in low segmentation accuracy.

In this paper, we extend our previous work [2] that builds on top of a sequence-to-sequence (S2S) [47] baseline for VOS, due to its good performance and straightforward design and training procedure. The S2S architecture is an encoder-decoder network with an RNN module in the bottleneck which is responsible for processing the spatiotemporal features and tracking the target object. To improve the performance of this method in segmenting the longer sequences, we take inspiration from the matching-based algorithms [45]. We hypothesize that the matching-based methods complement S2S model by providing additional training signals that can enhance the segmentation accuracy and reduce the adverse effect of error propagation. Utilizing the reliable information in the reference frame can be especially useful in handling occluded scenes where the RNN may struggle to lose the target object after several time steps. To this end, we employ both RNN and matching branches and develop a fusion block to merge the RNN spatiotemporal features with the template matching and refer to our model as hybrid S2S (HS2S).

Additional to [2], we experiment with two architecture variants of our model. In the first form, we explore the effectiveness of bidirectional design [33] where in addition to utilizing the information from the past time steps, we integrate the future frames via a bidirectional RNN network. In the second variation, we explore a multi-task training setup by joint training the VOS model together with the unsupervised optical flow objective. Our intuition is that since optical flow and VOS are well-aligned tasks (in both cases the model has to learn pixel motion between the consecutive frames), training the model with both objectives might bring additional benefits via utilizing the optical flow-related constraints. We perform extensive experiments and ablations on YouTubeVOS dataset [47] to study the role of different components in our HS2S model. Our experimental results confirm the effectiveness of our hybrid design by obtaining an increase of about 12pp in the overall segmentation accuracy compared to the RNN-based baseline.

2   Related Work

In this section, we provide a summary of the traditional variational methods based on energy minimization as well as more recent learning-based approaches proposed for solving the VOS task.

In [7, 16, 39], the authors attempt to solve foreground object estimation using super-voxels to capture similar regions across space and time. These methods cluster similar pixels across spatial dimensions into superpixel nodes and find the edges between these nodes across time and space by employing motion and appearance similarities to form the supervoxels. Accordingly, the object masks are obtained via processing and merging the connected supervoxels. In [8], Brox *et al.* develop a bottom-up approach for segmenting the foreground objects and utilize the optical flow motion information to enforce temporal consistency across a video shot. The main idea here is that pixels with similar motion patterns should belong to the same object. Similarly, Papazoglou *et al.* [25] propose a two-stage segmentation algorithm where in the first stage, the initial segmentation masks are obtained through processing the optical flow and motion boundaries. In the next stage, the masks are refined by applying two smoothness constraints. The first constraint enforces spatio-temporal consistency across video frames while the second implies that the foreground objects should only change smoothly over time. In [12], the authors suggest that optical flow only provides local information across neighboring frames which is not optimal. To address this limitation, they develop a model that integrates non-local information across space and time.

With [11, 14, 20] and the release of specialized and large-scale VOS datasets [29, 30, 47], the learning-based solutions for VOS have replaced more traditional models during the last few years. In [9], the authors present a training strategy to extend a network designed for medical image segmentation [22] for VOS. Starting from VGG16 [34] weights pretrained on ImageNet [11], they further train the network with segmentation objective on a VOS-specific dataset. During the inference, they perform online training and additionally fine-tune the network to be specialized for capturing the object of interest within the test scene. Perazzi *et al.* [28] also only rely on static images; to track the target object, they guide the network by inputting the object mask from the previous time step to the network. This method also needs online training for achieving acceptable performance. To address this limitation, [48] employs a modulator network that generates the normalization values of the main segmentation network, specific to each video.

Another line of work suggests utilizing RNNs for computing the spatio-temporal features, integrating the motion information, and memorizing the target object [1, 38, 47], [40]. These methods achieve good performance without online training, however, their segmentation accuracy worsens for longer sequences due to limited RNN memory and error propagation. This limitation is improved by incorporation of an external memory in [23]; however, this causes additional hardware memory constraints to the system. As a result, in practice, only a fraction of the frames can be stored in the memory which can be sub-optimal.

Differently, Wug *et al.* suggest detecting the foreground object via finding the correspondences between each frame and reference frames using a Siamese architecture [45]. In [50], the authors propose a transductive approach that instead of only relying on a limited number of reference frames, additionally integrate the information from the past segmented frames while [6, 17], develop a system that learns the appearance model of the object of interest and using this model, it captures the target throughout the rest of the video. These methods are efficient with a good performance, but their accuracy degrades in the presence of multiple similar objects as the model is confused by finding multiple correspondences. To improve this challenge, [49] additionally incorporates background correspondence matching. They demonstrate this design helps the model to better handle ambiguities in the correspondence search.

3   Method

In this part, we describe our proposed architecture based on a hybrid propagation policy, referred to as HS2S. Our model builds on top of S2S [47], a sequence-to-sequence model for video object segmentation. Following a detailed study on the performance of the S2S model, we address multiple shortcomings of the S2S design by inserting additional information obtained from correspondence matching.

The S2S model consists of an encoder-decoder network similar to U-Net [31] that learns the mapping between the RGB color space and the object segmentation mask. S2S uses a ConvLSTM [46] module between the encoder and the decoder, intended for processing the spatiotemporal features and tracking the target object. This memory component is accountable for maintaining the temporal coherency between the predicted segmentation masks across several video frames. To this end, S2S utilizes an *initializer* network that generates the initial ConvLSTM hidden states through processing the first RGB frame and foreground object mask. The S2S model can be summarized as follows [47]:

$$h_0, c_0 = \text{Initializer}(x_0, y_0) \tag{1}$$

$$\tilde{x}_t = \text{Encoder}(x_t) \tag{2}$$

$$h_t, c_t = \text{RNN}(\tilde{x}_t, h_{t-1}, c_{t-1}) \tag{3}$$

$$\tilde{y}_t = \text{Decoder}(h_t) \tag{4}$$

where h and c are the hidden and cell states for the ConvLSTM, t is the time step, x is the RGB input, y is the ground-truth mask and $\tilde{y}$ is the predicted output.

Having a closer look at the failure cases in the S2S model, we observed the model's performance degrades for longer videos. There are multiple factors that can potentially contribute to this limitation. First, the limited memory of RNNs is an inherent challenge for RNN-based architectures. Due to this issue, the model struggles to fully capture the essential information in the scene as well as the evolution of the object's appearance. Moreover, as the video sequences become longer, they tend to lose access to the information from the earlier time steps. This is particularly problematic for the occluded scenes; as, if the model forgets the occluded object, it will not be able to re-capture the object once it re-appears in the scene. Finally, due to the feedback connection in the RNN module, the erroneous predictions will flow to the future time steps. These results in drift and error propagation in the final results, exacerbating the model's accuracy for segmenting the frames further in time.

3.1 Hybrid Sequence-to-Sequence VOS

We propose to supplement RNN module with *correspondence matching* for tracking the object of interest in a video. The benefits of matching-based solutions [45] for one-shot VOS gives the opportunity to solve some problems inherent in RNNs. For example, Oh *et al.* design a siamese architecture that obtains a good segmentation accuracy through matching with reference frames at $t = 0$ and the guidance information from the previous mask [45]. However, these models struggle in scenes with similar objects or when the object's appearance changes drastically over time as the model cannot detect the object via matching to the reference frames anymore.

We hypothesize that the pros and cons of the RNN-based and matching-based VOS solutions complement each other. The informative signals computed from template matching are crucial for better handling the occluded videos; no matter how long the occlusion duration, the model would still have the chance to re-capture the object through matching it with the reference frames at $t = 0$. Moreover, these additional training signals reduce the adverse effect of error propagation thus improving the overall segmentation quality. On the other hand, integrating the motion features and the spatiotemporal model learned by RNNs can serve as prior for the approximate object location at time step t. This combination helps the model to disambiguate the situations with similar objects by employing the location prior.

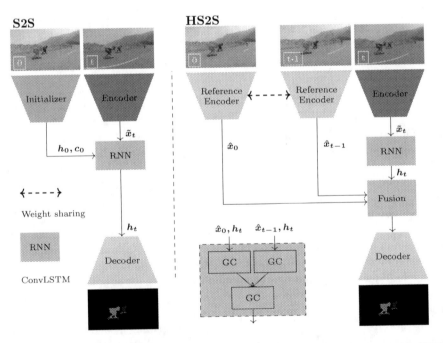

Fig. 1. The HS2S architecture combining the RNN-based and matching based features for VOS. We utilize a fusion block consisting of multiple Global Convolution (GC) [26] layers that merges the spatiotemporal features from RNN with the reference frames from the first and the previous time steps.

Our proposed architecture is shown in Fig. 1. We utilize one encoder for the input frames and another encoder for the reference frames and masks. As suggested by previous works [28,45], we utilize the time steps 0 and $t-1$ as our reference frames. Time step 0 is specifically important since the ground-truth segmentation mask for this frame is available at inference; therefore, the information from this step is highly reliable for the model. Moreover, integrating the information from $t-1$ serves as an additional signal about the approximate object location.

To reduce the model complexity, we replace the initializer network with a teacher-forcing training strategy [28]. Having the initializer network removed, we simply initialize the memory hidden states with zero vectors. Next, we feed the segmentation mask from the previous time step as an additional input to the encoder [28]. By receiving the previous segmentation mask as input, the model is informed about the approximate location of the target object.

In the next step, we merge the reference and the spatiotemporal RNN features through a nonlinear fusion function. To properly combine the information from these to branches, this module requires both local and global connections across the spatial feature dimensions. Accordingly, one could design this module using convolution layers with very big kernel sizes [26], or utilize attention mechanisms to span the height and width dimensions and incorporate all the features [43,44]. Ablation on the impact of various designs for merge block architecture is provided in subsection 4.5.

Finally, the output of the merge block is then passed through a decoder network and transformed into the segmentation masks through a stack of upsampling and convolution layers. With the same notation as in eqs. (1) to (2) amd (4), the overall steps can be summarized into the formulation below [2]:

$$h_0, c_0 = \mathbf{0} \tag{5}$$

$$\hat{x}_0 = \text{Reference\_Encoder}(x_0, y_0) \tag{6}$$

$$\hat{x}_{t-1} = \text{Reference\_Encoder}(x_{t-1}, y_{t-1}) \tag{7}$$

$$\tilde{x}_t = \text{Encoder}(x_t, y_{t-1}) \tag{8}$$

$$h_t, c_t = \text{RNN}(\tilde{x}_t, h_{t-1}, c_{t-1}) \tag{9}$$

$$\tilde{y} = \text{Decoder}(\tilde{x}_0, \tilde{x}_{t-1}, h) \tag{10}$$

As the architectures for encoder and reference encoder in Fig. 1 are identical, we experimented with weight-sharing between the two encoders; however, this architecture resulted in lower segmentation accuracy. This behavior can be due to two reasons: First, reduction in model's expressive power, and second, the misalignment between the reference features and the teacher-forcing training strategy. As we can see in Fig. 1, the RGB frame and mask fed to the ref-encoder are from the same time step while the input to the encoder differs by 1 ($t-1$ and t). Therefore, the functions learned by these two encoders are not the same and that weight sharing would not be applicable to this scenario.

Training Loss. We train our model with a combination of Balanced BCE loss and an additional auxiliary term of border classification [2]:

$$L_{\text{total}} = \lambda \, L_{\text{seg}} + (1 - \lambda) \, L_{\text{aux}} \tag{11}$$

The BCE term assigns either foreground or background label to each pixel in the image. As in the image, the portion of background pixels usually outweighs the foreground, the training will be biased towards paying higher attention to the background. This issue is addressed by multiplying the loss terms with a balancing factor [9]:

$$L_{\text{seg}}(\mathbf{W}) = \sum_{t=1}^{T} (-\alpha \sum_{j \in Y_+} \log P(y_j = 1 | X; \mathbf{W}) - (1 - \alpha) \sum_{j \in Y_-} \log P(y_j = 0 | X; \mathbf{W})) \tag{12}$$

with α being the ratio of background to foreground pixels. The Border classification objective additionally classifies each pixel based on their relative distance to the object border. As a result, this term provides finer information about the pixel location and improves the quality of detected object edges. Further explanation and an in-depth analysis of this loss-term's effects can be found in [1].

3.2 Bidirectional Architecture

In HS2S architecture, the video frames are processed sequentially passing the information from the past to the future. Bidirectional sequence-to-sequence architectures enable the model to integrate information from the past as well as the future; they have been effective in improving the performance of sequential processing tasks such as Machine Translation [13,33,36,38]. Therefore, it is natural to conjecture that integrating the information from the future frames might benefit the HS2S model. However, based on the task definition in VOS, we need the object mask in the last frame ($t = T$) to process the video backward in time. Otherwise, the model will not recognize which object to track. To address this challenge, we design the bidirectional HS2S (Bi-HS2S) architecture shown in Fig. 2.

As explained earlier, there are two different ways to inform the network about the object of interest. One is through using an initializer network that processes the first RGB and the mask frames and initializes the memory hidden states. The second way is by simply feeding the segmentation mask from the previous time step to the encoder network as a guidance signal. The second option does not fit the bidirectional design as in the backward processing of the video sequence, we do not have access to the initial object mask. As a result, we resort to the first alternative.

As illustrated in Fig. 2, we initialize the memory hidden states with the initializer network in the forward path. For the backward processing, we simply initialize the backward memory with the last hidden state h_t obtained from the forward path. Our intuition is that h_t contains information about the target object at $t = T$ and can serve as a reasonable initialization. Finally, we combine the information from the forward and backward paths together with the reference features via the fusion block and pass it to the decoder to predict the segmentation masks.

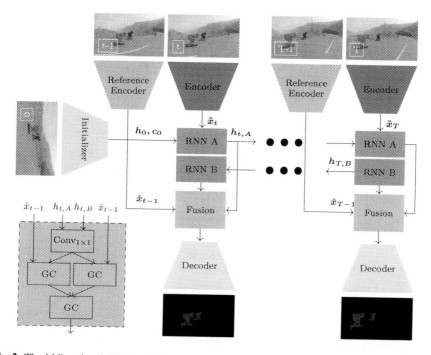

Fig. 2. The bidirectional HS2S architecture. The hidden states from the forward and backward RNNs are combined using a convolution layer and then merged with the reference features and passed to the decoder.

3.3   Multi-task Training with Optical Flow Prediction

In multi-task learning, several tasks are combined within a single problem formulation and network architecture. This approach has been shown to be a successful training technique when the combined tasks are aligned in the objective and can provide supplemental information to each other [32]. In this section, we take inspiration from RAFT [37], a recent state-of-the-art optical flow architecture and design an architecture that combines video object segmentation with optical flow prediction, referred to as RAFT-HS2S. Our intuition is that VOS and optical flow objectives are similar as they both tend to learn the pixel movement from one frame to the next. Accordingly, we explore whether combining these two learning objectives brings additional information to the model and enhances the segmentation accuracy.

RAFT model [37] receives two consecutive images (I_t and I_{t-1}) as input and generates the flow field capturing the pixel motion between the consecutive frames. It consists of two encoders with the same architecture but separate weights; The first encoder extracts the features f_t and f_{t-1} while the second encoder only processes I_{t-1} to provide additional context to the network. Inspired by traditional optical methods, RAFT iteratively refines the estimated flow utilizing a ConvGRU [35] that produces the flow delta at each time step.

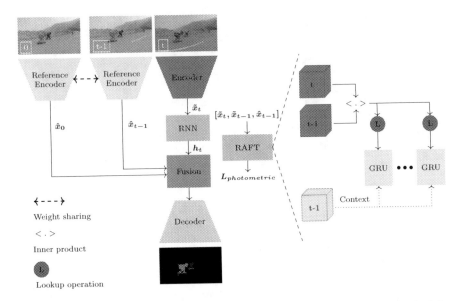

Fig. 3. The multi-task training setup in RAFT-HS2S, combining HS2S with an optical flow method named RAFT. RAFT module computes the correlation between frames at t and $t-1$ using the inner product between the respective feature vectors and generates an initial estimate of the optical flow between these consecutive frames. Then, it iteratively refines the approximated flow using a ConvGRU module that performs lookup operations based on the correlation volume and a context feature vector computed from the frame at $t-1$.

Motivated by the commonality in VOS and optical flow training objectives, we adapt HS2S to accommodate the RAFT components as depicted in Fig. 3. As can be seen in this plot, the reference encoder additionally takes the role of context encoding for the RAFT model, and the Encoder is employed for processing I_t and I_{t-1}. For the optical flow loss which is added to the objective in Eq. 11, we use an unsupervised objective, namely photometric loss [18]:

$$L_{photometric} = \sum |I^{(1)} - w(I^{(2)})| \tag{13}$$

Here $L_{photometric}$ is the photometric loss over all the pixels and w is the warping operation that warps $I^{(2)}$ to $I^{(1)}$ using the optical flow between these two frames. This term implies that having the precise motion, the pixel colors resulting from warping one image to the other should match.

4   Experiments

4.1   Implementation Details

In this section, we explain the implementation and the training details of our HS2S model explained in Subsect. 3.1. We use the same experimental setup and hyperparameters for the other architecture variants unless mentioned otherwise. Additional ablations are provided in Sects. 4.3 to 4.5.

The encoder backbone in Fig. 1 is based on ResNet50 [14] architecture pretrained on ImageNet [11], with the following modifications. We remove the final fully connected layer which generates the image classification output and add $conv_{1\times1}$ to reduce the number of channels in the bottleneck from 2048 to 1024. In the first layer, we add a convolution layer to process the segmentation mask and combine it with the RGB features.

For the memory module, we use a ConvLSTM layer [46] with 3×3 filters as suggested in [47]. The merge module consists of a stack of two Global Convolution layers [26] with a kernel size of 7×7, following the setup in [45].

The decoder consists of 5 upsampling layers followed by convolution layers with 5×5 kernel sizes and $1024, 512, 256, 128, 64$ number of channels respectively. The last layer activation function is a sigmoid nonlinearity that outputs the probability of each pixel belonging to the foreground or background. Moreover, we utilize skip connections [31] and skip-memory connections [1] for obtaining refined segmentation masks and better tracking the smaller objects.

As mentioned in Subsect. 3.1, we use a teacher-forcing training strategy, feeding the ground-truth segmentation masks from time step $t-1$ as input in time t. Since we do not have access to the ground-truth labels during the inference, the masks predicted by the model are used instead. As pointed out by [3,5], this training approach is problematic since the model predictions are often erroneous, and the accumulation of errors result in a gap between the training and testing phases. Following the recipe suggested in [5], we deploy a curriculum learning policy to address this issue. At the beginning of the training when the model does not generate high-quality masks, we use the ground-truth labels; once the training loss is stable, we follow a probabilistic scheme to decide whether to choose from the ground-truth or use the model prediction as input. The probability of selecting the model predictions is gradually increased from 0 to 0.5.

We use a batch size of 16 and Adam [19] optimizer with a starting learning rate of $1e-4$. Once the training loss is stabilized, the learning rate is reduced every 5 epochs by a factor of 0.9.

4.2 Experimental Results

We assess our method on YouTubeVOS [47], the largest dataset for VOS consisting of $3,471$ and 474 videos in training and validation sets respectively. We report F and J scores, the standard metric for evaluating VOS models [27]. YouTubeVOS evaluation additionally reports *seen* and *unseen* scores to separately measure the model's accuracy for the objects that have been present or absent during the training. The *unseen* scores quantify the model generalization to new object types.

In Table 1, we present the results obtained from HS2S model (plus its variants as explained in Sects. 3.1 to 3.2) as well as our baseline S2S, and the other state-of-the-art models. The results provided in the upper half of the table are for the methods with additional online training. Using the first object mask, these approaches further train the network at test time; as a result, they often achieve a better accuracy but they are considerably slower. As can be seen from the results in Table 1, our HS2S method reaches a significant improvement in comparison with the S2S baseline and outperforms this approach even when it is fine-tuned by additional online training (S2S(OL)). Moreover, we observe that utilizing the Bi-HS2S leads to further improvement of about 1pp while RAFT-HS2S achieves similar performance as HS2S. This implies that the information provided from the optical flow loss is already included in the VOS objective and combining these additional terms does not bring additional benefits to the model.

Table 1. Comparison of the experimental results from the HS2S model [2] with state-of-the-art methods on YouTubeVOS dataset. OL refers to methods with additional Online Training.

Method	OL	J_{seen}	J_{unseen}	F_{seen}	F_{unseen}	Overall
OSVOS [21]	✓	59.8	54.2	60.5	60.7	58.8
MaskTrack [28]	✓	59.9	45.0	59.5	47.9	50.6
OnAVOS [42]	✓	60.1	46.6	62.7	51.4	55.2
S2S(OL) [47]	✓	**71.0**	**55.5**	**70.0**	**61.2**	**64.4**
OSMN [48]	✗	60.0	40.6	60.1	44.0	51.2
RGMP [45]	✗	59.5	45.2	–	–	53.8
RVOS [40]	✗	63.6	45.5	67.2	51.0	56.8
A-GAME [17]	✗	66.9	61.2	–	–	66.1
S2S(no-OL) [47]	✗	66.7	48.2	65.5	50.3	57.7
S2S++ [1]	✗	68.7	48.9	72.0	54.4	61.0
STM- [23]	✗	67.1	63	69.4	71.6	68.2
TVOS [50]	✗	–	–	–	–	67.2
HS2S [2]	✗	73.6	58.5	77.4	66.0	68.9
Bi-HS2S	✗	74.9	59.6	78.0	66.7	69.8
RAFT-HS2S	✗	73.2	58.7	77.3	66.1	68.8

In Fig. 4, we provide a qualitative comparison between the segmentation results from S2S [47] baseline and our HS2S model. As can be seen, our model can successfully maintain the segmentation accuracy for later time steps. Moreover, our method can handle scenes with multiple similar objects, which is challenging for matching-based algorithms.

To quantify the impact of our hybrid architecture on the accuracy of longer videos, we select a subset of sequences from YouTubeVOS training set that consist of more than 20 frames for evaluation and use the rest for training. We resort to using this subset since the ground-truth masks for the YoutubeVOS validation set are not provided. Then, we calculate the segmentation accuracy for earlier frames ($t < 10$) and later frames ($t > 10$) independently. As can be seen in Table 2a, These two models have similar performance for earlier frames, while HS2S significantly outperforms the S2S model for frames in the further time steps. Additionally, we experiment with our HS2S model when using either 0th or $(t-1)$th frame as a reference in order to assess the role of each one in the final performance. The results for this experiment are provided in Table 2b.

4.3   Ablation on the Impact of Encoder Architecture

The encoder networks in Fig. 1 are responsible for extracting descriptive features which will be then processed through the memory and decoded into a segmentation mask via

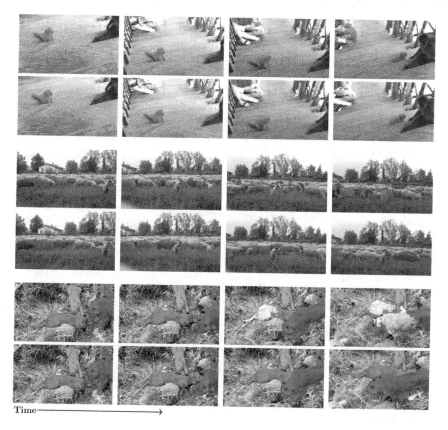

Fig. 4. Visual comparison between the S2S and HS2S results in the upper and lower rows, respectively. We observe that our hybrid method can successfully maintain the segmentation accuracy at the later time steps.

the decoder network. Thus, improving the quality of the encoder network is expected to directly reflect on the segmentation quality. In this section, we study the behavior of HS2S model when employing various encoder architectures including VGG [34], ResNet50 [14], DeepLab [10], and Axial-DeepLab [43].

The DeepLab backbone is a modified ResNet50 with less pooling operations resulting in increased spatial feature dimension at the output (Higher spatial dimensions are presumably beneficial for dense prediction methods due to preserving fine local information). Furthermore, it consists of an Atrous Spatial Pyramid Pooling (ASPP) module composed of a stack of convolution layers with various dilation rates. We experiment with a DeepLab backbone pretrained on image segmentation, with and without the ASPP module. Different than CNN-based backbones, Axial-DeepLab [43] consists of fully-attentional blocks. In this model, the authors propose to break the attention into horizontal and vertical attentions to reduce the computational cost of the attention-based backbone (from quadratic to linear). However, this model still requires significantly

Table 2. (a) Comparison of our model with S2S baseline for shorter and longer sequences (S2S* is our implementation of this model with ResNet50 backbone which achieves about 1pp higher accuracy compared to [47]). We observe that our method significantly improves the performance for frames in later time steps. **(b)** The performance of HS2S model when either the first frame is used as reference (HS2S$_{0,t-1}$ shows the accuracy of our model when either 0_{th} or the $t - 1_{th}$ frames are used as reference). We observe that both frames contribute to boosting the segmentation accuracy and the best results are obtained when using both reference frames.

(a) Performance comparison considering shorter ($t < 10$) and longer ($t > 10$) sequences [2].

Method	$F_{l<10}$	$J_{l<10}$	$F_{l>20}$	$J_{l>20}$
S2S*	74.4	73.7	54.5	54.6
HS2S (ours)	77.1	76.3	65.5	64.2

(b) Performance of HS2S model when either the first or previous frame is used as reference [2].

Method	J_{seen}	J_{unseen}	F_{seen}	F_{unseen}
HS2S$_0$	72.6	55.4	76.7	61.2
HS2S$_{t-1}$	72.2	55.1	76.1	61.3

higher memory compared to the CNN-based backbones. Due to memory limitation, we experimented with *small* Axial-DeepLab architecture as elaborated in [43]

Table 3. An ablation on the impact of backbone network.

Backbone	J_{seen}	J_{unseen}	F_{seen}	F_{unseen}	*overall*
VGG16 [34]	71.4	56.0	74.9	64.8	66.8
ResNet-50 [14]	73.6	58.5	77.4	66.0	68.9
ResNet-101 [14]	73.9	58.5	77.3	66.2	69.0
ResNet-50-DeepLab (without ASPP) [10]	73.3	59.1	77.2	66.0	68.9
ResNet-50-DeepLab (w/ ASPP) [10]	72.3	56.9	76.5	64.2	67.4
Axial [43]	70.5	55.0	73.1	61.8	65.1

As can be seen in Table 3, we obtained the best results when applying the ResNet-based encoder. Surprisingly, integrating the additional ASPP module from the DeepLab architecture resulted in lower performance. This behavior can be due to the added complexity from combining the spatiotemporal RNN features with multi-scale processing in the ASPP module resulting in a more challenging optimization problem and suboptimal performance.

4.4   Ablation on the Impact of RNN Architecture

One of the main blocks in the HS2S architecture is the RNN block, accountable for memorizing the target object. In this section, we provide an ablation studying the HS2S performance when deploying three different RNN-based memories. The first variant is ConvLSTM [46]. This module is developed for processing sequential visual data by replacing the fully connected layers in LSTM with convolution layers, adjusting the LSTM layer for visual pattern recognition.

As the second model, we study DeepRNN [24]. In this model, the authors address the challenges in training deep RNN models. Although deeper networks are expected to learn better representations compared to their shallow counterparts in the case of CNNs, deep RNN architectures designed by simply stacking the RNN layers does not lead to considerable improvement in the model accuracy. In [24], Pang *et al.* suggest this behavior roots in the complex optimization operation when dealing with RNNs. Processing the entangled spatial and temporal information in sequential visual data leads to the optimization process becoming overly complex. This condition could become even more extreme for deeper RNNs, resulting in sub-optimal performance. To this end, they propose to disentangle the information related to the spatial flow from the temporal flow. They design a *Context bridge module (CBM)* which is composed of two computing blocks for processing the representation and the temporal flows. By enforcing these sources of information to flow independently, the optimization process could potentially be simplified. In our experiments, we deployed a stack of 5 RNN layers following the setup proposed in [24].

In the third variant, TensorLSTM [35], the authors attempt to improve the learning of long-term spatiotemporal correspondences for processing longer videos. They design a higher-order convolutional LSTM architecture named TensorLSTM that can better capture extended correlations. TensorLSTM consists of a preprocessing and a convolutional tensor-train module. The preprocessing module computes feature vectors from multiple overlapping sliding windows from the previous hidden states. These embeddings are then further processed through the convolutional tensor-train module and passed to the LSTM. Consequently, they are able to efficiently integrate the information from the previous hidden states and improve the capturing of long-term correlations.

Table 4. An ablation on the choice of RNN module.

Method	J_{seen}	J_{unseen}	F_{seen}	F_{unseen}	*overall*
ConvLSTM [46]	73.6	58.5	77.4	66.0	68.9
DeepRNN [24]	72.4	57.3	75.8	64.9	67.6
Tensor-TrainLSTM [35]	**74.7**	**60.2**	**78.5**	**66.4**	**70.0**

As it can be seen from the results in Table 4, TensorLSTM achieves a better segmentation accuracy compared to the other variants. This implies that in HS2S architecture, we do not require deeper RNNs to carry the information about the object of interest. However, accessing the information from multiple frames over an extended time period is beneficial for the model. In a way, TensorLSTM applies attention to a limited past context via the sliding-window mechanism in the preprocessing module. This observation is in line with employing the dual propagation strategy in Subsect. 3.1 where simply merging the information from the time-step $t - 1$ improves the segmentation results.

4.5   Ablation on Various Designs for the Fusion Block

In this section, we study the model's performance when working with three different fusion block architectures in Table 5. Intuitively, the fusion block needs to provide global connections across the spatial dimensions as the object might be displaced to a further location compared to the reference frames. Additionally, it has to assign higher attention to the locations that belong to the foreground. In HS2S$_{sim}$, the spatiotemporal RNN features are merged with the reference features based on cosine similarity. HS2S$_{GC}$ merges these two branches using global convolution layers as suggested in [26] while HS2S$_{attn}$ replaces this operation with an attention layer [15]. We obtained similar performance for different fusion architecture options, but the design using attention attained the highest accuracy.

Table 5. An ablation on the impact of backbone network.

Method	J_{seen}	J_{unseen}	F_{seen}	F_{unseen}	*overall*
HS2S$_{GC}$	73.6	58.5	77.4	66	68.9
HS2S$_{sim}$	72.3	56.4	76.2	62.5	66.9
HS2S$_{attn}$	**73.9**	**58.7**	**77.5**	**66.3**	**69.1**

5   Conclusion

In this paper, we expanded our previous HS2S approach [2] to generate a hybrid architecture for VOS that combines the merits of RNN-based and matching-based methods. As before, we find that all of our hybrid approaches are especially beneficial for the segmentation of objects that are occluded and re-appearing, as well as in cases where many similar objects need to be tracked and segmented. In this paper, we have investigated two derived architectures: a bi-directional and a multi-task (optical flow) extension of our previous approach. Further, we expanded our previous ablation study by investigating further segmentation backbones, RNN, and fusion blocks of the underlying architectures. Resulting from these investigations, we found that our bi-directional extension (Bi-HS2S) improves over our previous architectures by nearly 1 pp and more than 12pp when compared to other state-of-the-art RNN-based baselines (such as S2S(no-OL) [47]). To our surprise, our multi-task extension also taking optical flow into account (RAFT-HS2S) failed to improve over HS2S. In the expanded ablation study, we found that the ResNet-101 based backbone network, Tensor-TrainLSTM RNN architecture, and attention fusion blocks seemed to be the most beneficial design choices.

For future work, we aim to investigate the potential benefit of utilizing the depth information either as input or as an unsupervised learning objective integrated into our HS2S model.

Acknowledgement. This work was supported by the TU Kaiserslautern CS PhD scholarship program, the BMBF project ExplAINN (01IS19074), and the NVIDIA AI Lab (NVAIL) program. Further, we thank Christiano Gava, Stanislav Frolov, Tewodros Habtegebrial and Mohammad

Reza Yousefi for the many interesting discussions and proofreading of this paper. Finally, we thank all members of the Deep Learning Competence Center at the DFKI for their feedback and support.

References

1. Azimi, F., Bischke, B., Palacio, S., Raue, F., Hees, J., Dengel, A.: Revisiting sequence-to-sequence video object segmentation with multi-task loss and skip-memory. In: 2020 25th International Conference on Pattern Recognition (ICPR), pp. 5376–5383. IEEE (2021). arXiv:2004.12170

2. Azimi, F., Frolov, S., Raue, F., Hees, J., Dengel, A.: Hybrid-s2s: Video object segmentation with recurrent networks and correspondence matching. In: VISAPP, pp. 182–192 (2021). arXiv:2010.05069

3. Azimi, F., Nies, J.F.J.N., Palacio, S., Raue, F., Hees, J., Dengel, A.: Spatial transformer networks for curriculum learning. arXiv preprint arXiv:2108.09696 (2021)

4. Azimi, F., Palacio, S., Raue, F., Hees, J., Bertinetto, L., Dengel, A.: Self-supervised test-time adaptation on video data. In: Proceedings of the IEEE/CVF Winter Conference on Applications of Computer Vision, pp. 3439–3448 (2022)

5. Bengio, S., Vinyals, O., Jaitly, N., Shazeer, N.: Scheduled sampling for sequence prediction with recurrent neural networks. In: Advances in Neural Information Processing Systems, pp. 1171–1179 (2015)

6. Bhat, G., et al.: Learning what to learn for video object segmentation. In: Vedaldi, A., Bischof, H., Brox, T., Frahm, J.-M. (eds.) ECCV 2020. LNCS, vol. 12347, pp. 777–794. Springer, Cham (2020). https://doi.org/10.1007/978-3-030-58536-5_46

7. Brendel, W., Amer, M., Todorovic, S.: Multiobject tracking as maximum weight independent set. In: CVPR 2011, pp. 1273–1280. IEEE (2011)

8. Brox, T., Malik, J.: Object segmentation by long term analysis of point trajectories. In: Daniilidis, K., Maragos, P., Paragios, N. (eds.) ECCV 2010. LNCS, vol. 6315, pp. 282–295. Springer, Heidelberg (2010). https://doi.org/10.1007/978-3-642-15555-0_21

9. Caelles, S., Maninis, K.K., Pont-Tuset, J., Leal-Taixé, L., Cremers, D., Van Gool, L.: One-shot video object segmentation. In: Proceedings of the IEEE Conference on Computer Vision and Pattern Recognition, pp. 221–230 (2017)

10. Chen, L.C., Papandreou, G., Schroff, F., Adam, H.: Rethinking atrous convolution for semantic image segmentation. arXiv preprint arXiv:1706.05587 (2017)

11. Deng, J., Dong, W., Socher, R., Li, L.J., Li, K., Fei-Fei, L.: Imagenet: A large-scale hierarchical image database. In: 2009 IEEE conference on computer vision and pattern recognition, pp. 248–255. IEEE (2009)

12. Faktor, A., Irani, M.: Video segmentation by non-local consensus voting. In: BMVC, p. 8 (2014)

13. Graves, A., Fernández, S., Schmidhuber, J.: Bidirectional LSTM networks for improved phoneme classification and recognition. In: Duch, W., Kacprzyk, J., Oja, E., Zadrożny, S. (eds.) ICANN 2005. LNCS, vol. 3697, pp. 799–804. Springer, Heidelberg (2005). https://doi.org/10.1007/11550907_126

14. He, K., Zhang, X., Ren, S., Sun, J.: Deep residual learning for image recognition. In: Proceedings of the IEEE Conference on Computer Vision and Pattern Recognition, pp. 770–778 (2016)

15. Ho, J., Kalchbrenner, N., Weissenborn, D., Salimans, T.: Axial attention in multidimensional transformers. arXiv preprint arXiv:1912.12180 (2019)

16. Jain, S.D., Grauman, K.: Supervoxel-consistent foreground propagation in video. In: Fleet, D., Pajdla, T., Schiele, B., Tuytelaars, T. (eds.) ECCV 2014. LNCS, vol. 8692, pp. 656–671. Springer, Cham (2014). https://doi.org/10.1007/978-3-319-10593-2_43

17. Johnander, J., Danelljan, M., Brissman, E., Khan, F.S., Felsberg, M.: A generative appearance model for end-to-end video object segmentation. In: Proceedings of the IEEE Conference on Computer Vision and Pattern Recognition, pp. 8953–8962 (2019)

18. Jonschkowski, R., Stone, A., Barron, J.T., Gordon, A., Konolige, K., Angelova, A.: What matters in unsupervised optical flow. In: Vedaldi, A., Bischof, H., Brox, T., Frahm, J.-M. (eds.) ECCV 2020. LNCS, vol. 12347, pp. 557–572. Springer, Cham (2020). https://doi.org/10.1007/978-3-030-58536-5_33

19. Kingma, D.P., Ba, J.: Adam: A method for stochastic optimization. arXiv preprint arXiv:1412.6980 (2014)

20. Krizhevsky, A., Sutskever, I., Hinton, G.E.: Imagenet classification with deep convolutional neural networks. In: Advances in Neural Information Processing Systems, pp. 1097–1105 (2012)

21. Maninis, K.K., Caelles, S., Chen, Y., Pont-Tuset, J., Leal-Taixé, L., Cremers, D., Van Gool, L.: Video object segmentation without temporal information. IEEE Trans. Patt. Anal. Mach. Intell. (TPAMI) **41**(6), 1515–1530 (2018)

22. Maninis, K.-K., Pont-Tuset, J., Arbeláez, P., Van Gool, L.: Deep retinal image understanding. In: Ourselin, S., Joskowicz, L., Sabuncu, M.R., Unal, G., Wells, W. (eds.) MICCAI 2016. LNCS, vol. 9901, pp. 140–148. Springer, Cham (2016). https://doi.org/10.1007/978-3-319-46723-8_17

23. Oh, S.W., Lee, J.Y., Xu, N., Kim, S.J.: Video object segmentation using space-time memory networks. In: Proceedings of the IEEE International Conference on Computer Vision, pp. 9226–9235 (2019)

24. Pang, B., Zha, K., Cao, H., Shi, C., Lu, C.: Deep rnn framework for visual sequential applications. In: Proceedings of the IEEE/CVF Conference on Computer Vision and Pattern Recognition, pp. 423–432 (2019)

25. Papazoglou, A., Ferrari, V.: Fast object segmentation in unconstrained video. In: Proceedings of the IEEE International Conference on Computer Vision, pp. 1777–1784 (2013)

26. Peng, C., Zhang, X., Yu, G., Luo, G., Sun, J.: Large kernel matters-improve semantic segmentation by global convolutional network. In: Proceedings of the IEEE Conference on Computer Vision and Pattern Recognition, pp. 4353–4361 (2017)

27. Perazzi, F., Pont-Tuset, J., McWilliams, B., Van Gool, L., Gross, M., Sorkine-Hornung, A.: A benchmark dataset and evaluation methodology for video object segmentation. In: Computer Vision and Pattern Recognition (2016)

28. Perazzi, F., Khoreva, A., Benenson, R., Schiele, B., Sorkine-Hornung, A.: Learning video object segmentation from static images. In: Proceedings of the IEEE Conference on Computer Vision and Pattern Recognition, pp. 2663–2672 (2017)

29. Perazzi, F., Pont-Tuset, J., McWilliams, B., Van Gool, L., Gross, M., Sorkine-Hornung, A.: A benchmark dataset and evaluation methodology for video object segmentation. In: Proceedings of the IEEE Conference on Computer Vision and Pattern Recognition, pp. 724–732 (2016)

30. Pont-Tuset, J., Perazzi, F., Caelles, S., Arbeláez, P., Sorkine-Hornung, A., Van Gool, L.: The 2017 davis challenge on video object segmentation. arXiv preprint arXiv:1704.00675 (2017)

31. Ronneberger, O., Fischer, P., Brox, T.: U-Net: convolutional networks for biomedical image segmentation. In: Navab, N., Hornegger, J., Wells, W.M., Frangi, A.F. (eds.) MICCAI 2015. LNCS, vol. 9351, pp. 234–241. Springer, Cham (2015). https://doi.org/10.1007/978-3-319-24574-4_28

32. Ruder, S.: An overview of multi-task learning in deep neural networks. arXiv preprint arXiv:1706.05098 (2017)

33. Schuster, M., Paliwal, K.K.: Bidirectional recurrent neural networks. IEEE Trans. Signal Process. **45**(11), 2673–2681 (1997)
34. Simonyan, K., Zisserman, A.: Very deep convolutional networks for large-scale image recognition. arXiv preprint arXiv:1409.1556 (2014)
35. Su, J., Byeon, W., Kossaifi, J., Huang, F., Kautz, J., Anandkumar, A.: Convolutional tensortrain lstm for spatio-temporal learning. arXiv preprint arXiv:2002.09131 (2020)
36. Sundermeyer, M., Alkhouli, T., Wuebker, J., Ney, H.: Translation modeling with bidirectional recurrent neural networks. In: Proceedings of the 2014 Conference on Empirical Methods in Natural Language Processing (EMNLP), pp. 14–25 (2014)
37. Teed, Z., Deng, J.: RAFT: recurrent all-pairs field transforms for optical flow. In: Vedaldi, A., Bischof, H., Brox, T., Frahm, J.-M. (eds.) ECCV 2020. LNCS, vol. 12347, pp. 402–419. Springer, Cham (2020). https://doi.org/10.1007/978-3-030-58536-5_24
38. Tokmakov, P., Alahari, K., Schmid, C.: Learning video object segmentation with visual memory. In: Proceedings of the IEEE International Conference on Computer Vision, pp. 4481–4490 (2017)
39. Vazquez-Reina, A., Avidan, S., Pfister, H., Miller, E.: Multiple hypothesis video segmentation from superpixel flows. In: Daniilidis, K., Maragos, P., Paragios, N. (eds.) ECCV 2010. LNCS, vol. 6315, pp. 268–281. Springer, Heidelberg (2010). https://doi.org/10.1007/978-3-642-15555-0_20
40. Ventura, C., Bellver, M., Girbau, A., Salvador, A., Marques, F., Giro-i Nieto, X.: Rvos: End-to-end recurrent network for video object segmentation. In: Proceedings of the IEEE Conference on Computer Vision and Pattern Recognition, pp. 5277–5286 (2019)
41. Voigtlaender, P., Chai, Y., Schroff, F., Adam, H., Leibe, B., Chen, L.C.: Feelvos: Fast end-to-end embedding learning for video object segmentation. In: Proceedings of the IEEE/CVF Conference on Computer Vision and Pattern Recognition, pp. 9481–9490 (2019)
42. Voigtlaender, P., Leibe, B.: Online adaptation of convolutional neural networks for video object segmentation. arXiv preprint arXiv:1706.09364 (2017)
43. Wang, H., Zhu, Y., Green, B., Adam, H., Yuille, A., Chen, L.-C.: Axial-DeepLab: stand-alone axial-attention for panoptic segmentation. In: Vedaldi, A., Bischof, H., Brox, T., Frahm, J.-M. (eds.) ECCV 2020. LNCS, vol. 12349, pp. 108–126. Springer, Cham (2020). https://doi.org/10.1007/978-3-030-58548-8_7
44. Wang, X., Girshick, R., Gupta, A., He, K.: Non-local neural networks. In: Proceedings of the IEEE Conference on Computer Vision and Pattern Recognition, pp. 7794–7803 (2018)
45. Wug Oh, S., Lee, J.Y., Sunkavalli, K., Joo Kim, S.: Fast video object segmentation by reference-guided mask propagation. In: Proceedings of the IEEE Conference on Computer Vision and Pattern Recognition, pp. 7376–7385 (2018)
46. Xingjian, S., Chen, Z., Wang, H., Yeung, D.Y., Wong, W.K., Woo, W.c.: Convolutional lstm network: A machine learning approach for precipitation nowcasting. In: Advances in Neural Information Processing Systems, pp. 802–810 (2015)
47. Xu, N., Yang, L., Fan, Y., Yue, D., Liang, Y., Yang, J., Huang, T.: Youtube-vos: A large-scale video object segmentation benchmark. arXiv preprint arXiv:1809.03327 (2018)
48. Yang, L., Wang, Y., Xiong, X., Yang, J., Katsaggelos, A.K.: Efficient video object segmentation via network modulation. In: Proceedings of the IEEE Conference on Computer Vision and Pattern Recognition, pp. 6499–6507 (2018)
49. Yang, Z., Wei, Y., Yang, Y.: Collaborative video object segmentation by foreground-background integration. In: Vedaldi, A., Bischof, H., Brox, T., Frahm, J.-M. (eds.) ECCV 2020. LNCS, vol. 12350, pp. 332–348. Springer, Cham (2020). https://doi.org/10.1007/978-3-030-58558-7_20
50. Zhang, Y., Wu, Z., Peng, H., Lin, S.: A transductive approach for video object segmentation. In: Proceedings of the IEEE/CVF Conference on Computer Vision and Pattern Recognition, pp. 6949–6958 (2020)

Author Index

Printed in the United States
by Baker & Taylor Publisher Services